T0330562

Financial Crimes
A Threat to
Global Security

Advances in Police Theory and Practice Series

Series Editor: Dilip K. Das

Financial Crimes: A Global Threat
Maximillian Edelbacher, Peter Kratcoski, and Michael Theil

Police Integrity Management in Australia:
Global Lessons for Combating Police Misconduct
Louise Porter and Tim Prenzler

The Crime Numbers Game: Management by Manipulation
John A. Eterno and Eli B. Silverman

The International Trafficking of Human Organs: A Multidisciplinary Perspective
Leonard Territo and Rande Matteson

Police Reform in China
Kam C. Wong

Mission-Based Policing
John P. Crank, Dawn M. Irlbeck, Rebecca K. Murray, and Mark Sundermeier

The New Khaki: The Evolving Nature of Policing in India
Arvind Verma

Cold Cases: An Evaluation Model with Follow-up Strategies for Investigators
James M. Adcock and Sarah L. Stein

Policing Organized Crime: Intelligence Strategy Implementation
Petter Gottschalk

Security in Post-Conflict Africa: The Role of Nonstate Policing
Bruce Baker

Community Policing and Peacekeeping
Peter Grabosky

Community Policing: International Patterns and Comparative Perspectives
Dominique Wisler and Ihekwoaba D. Onwudiwe

Police Corruption: Preventing Misconduct and Maintaining Integrity
Tim Prenzler

Financial Crimes
A Threat to
Global Security

Edited by
Maximillian Edelbacher
Peter Kratcoski
Michael Theil

CRC Press
Taylor & Francis Group
Boca Raton London New York

CRC Press is an imprint of the
Taylor & Francis Group, an **informa** business

CRC Press
Taylor & Francis Group
6000 Broken Sound Parkway NW, Suite 300
Boca Raton, FL 33487-2742

First issued in paperback 2019

© 2012 by Taylor & Francis Group, LLC
CRC Press is an imprint of Taylor & Francis Group, an Informa business

No claim to original U.S. Government works

ISBN-13: 978-1-4398-6922-2 (hbk)
ISBN-13: 978-0-367-86652-5 (pbk)

Visit the Taylor & Francis Web site at
http://www.taylorandfrancis.com

and the CRC Press Web site at
http://www.crcpress.com

This book is dedicated to all of the organizations and agencies, both public and private, that are diligently working to assist those who were victimized by financial criminal activity and to develop national and personal strategies for financial security.

Contents

Section I

NEW SECURITY CONCEPTS

PETER C. KRATCOSKI

Section II

FINANCIAL CRIMES: A GLOBAL THREAT

MAXIMILLIAN EDELBACHER AND MICHAEL THEIL

Section III

PREVENTING ANOTHER FINANCIAL CRISIS: ROLES OF CONTROL MECHANISMS

MAXIMILLIAN EDELBACHER AND MICHAEL THEIL

Series Editor's Preface

While the literature on police and allied subjects is growing exponentially, its impact upon day-to-day policing remains small. The two worlds of research and practice of policing remain disconnected even though cooperation between the two is growing. A major reason is that the two groups speak different languages. The research work is published in hard-to-access journals and presented in a manner that is difficult for a lay person to comprehend. On the other hand, police practitioners tend not to mix with researchers and remain secretive about their work. Consequently, the two groups exchange little dialogue and rarely attempt to learn from one another. Dialogues across the globe among researchers and practitioners on different continents are, of course, even more limited.

I attempted to address this problem by starting the International Police Executive Symposium (IPES) where a common platform has brought the two together. IPES (www.ipes.info) is now in its seventeenth year. The annual meetings that constitute most major annual events of the organization have been hosted in all parts of the world. Several publications have resulted from these deliberations, and a new collaborative community of scholars and police officers has been created whose membership runs into several hundreds.

Another attempt was to begin a new journal, aptly called *Police Practice and Research: An International Journal* (PPR) that opened the gate to practitioners to share their work and experiences. The journal attempts to focus upon issues that help bring the two to a single platform. PPR completed its first ten years in 2009 and continues to evidence the growing collaboration between police research and practice. PPR began with four issues a year, expanded to five in its fourth year, and is now issued six times a year.

Clearly, these attempts, despite their success, remain limited. Conferences and journal publications do help create a body of knowledge and an association of police activists but cannot address substantial issues in depth. The limitations of time and space preclude larger discussions and more authoritative expositions that can provide stronger and broader linkages between the two worlds.

It is this realization of the increasing dialogue between police research and practice that encouraged many of us connected closely with IPES and PPR across the world to conceive and implement a new attempt in this direction. I am now embarking on a book series titled Advances in Police Theory and

Practice that seeks to attract writers from all parts of the world. The need is for practitioner contributors. The objective is to make the series a serious contribution to our knowledge of the police and improve police practices. The focus is not only on work that describes the best and successful police practices but also work that challenges current paradigms and breaks new ground to prepare a police for the twenty-first century. The series seeks a comparative view that highlights achievements in distant parts of the world and encourages an in-depth examination of specific problems confronting police forces.

Financial Crimes: A Threat to Global Security examines the effects of these types of crimes on financial infrastructures throughout the world and the mechanisms various countries are using to counteract these threats to national security. The white collar crimes of fraud, corruption, and illegal business transactions are rampant. The role of organized crime in financing terrorism and preying on the vulnerabilities of persons caught up in the financial crises is described. Government officials contributed to the financial crises by failing to control the corrupt practices of financial institutions, even though they were aware of them.

It is hoped that through this series it will be possible to accelerate the process of building knowledge about policing and help bridge the gap between the two worlds of police research and police practice. This is an invitation to police scholars and practitioners across the world to come and join in this venture.

Dilip K. Das

Founding President, International Police Executive Symposium (IPES)
www.ipes.info

Founding Editor-in-Chief, Police Practice and Research: An International

Journal (PPR) www.tandf.co.uk/journals

Financial Crimes Preface

A Global Threat?

The world financial crisis started in 2007, was expected to have ended in 2009, and continues to the present. It opened the eyes of government leaders to how vulnerable nations are in times of crisis. From the beginning of the crisis, it seemed very clear that the enormous threat to the security of the countries affected by the crisis was created by the leaders of a small number of financial institutions who behaved like gamblers and had no concern for carrying out their responsibilities to the people, the governments, or the nations where they resided. Their only goals were to satisfy their greed and make as much money as possible in as short a time as possible. Taking risks that exceeded those generally considered responsible practices in banking and business were condoned as long as the result was profit.

Many of the leaders of finance engaged in risky—and illegal—practices that often led to financial ruin. In my former occupation as a police chief in Vienna, Austria, I was involved with many white collar crime cases relating to fraud, corruption, and illegal business transactions. The three elements of fraud cases are that criminals cheat their victims by hiding their identities, act with malicious intentions, and are motivated by greed. On viewing the performances of leaders during the financial crisis, it was ironic to see how their behaviors and actions were very similar to the actions of fraudsters who cheat their victims with promises they never keep, act with malicious intentions, and are driven by greed. The only difference was they did not hide their identities; they cheated their victims openly.

My first reaction to the financial crisis was that it could have been prevented if more investigative knowledge had been used. As a consequence, I resolved to promote the idea that remembering experiences gathered by solving white collar crime cases could serve as a tool to prevent and warn potential victims of future financial crises.

In June 2010, the Academic Council on the United Nations System (ACUNS) held its twenty-third Annual Meeting in Vienna. The theme of "new security challenges" was the starting point to gather national and international experts on three issues which fit together as a so-called "red line" in understanding the topics. I organized three roundtables on topics pertinent to the meeting theme.

The first roundtable dealt with "Changing Concepts of Security" and was chaired by Pierre Lapaque, chief of the Law Enforcement, Organized Crime, and Anti-Money Laundering Unit of the United Nations Office on Drugs and Crime (UNODC). Contributors were Docent Günter Stummvoll, Keele University; Professor Gilbert Norden, Vienna University Department of Sociology; and Maximillian Edelbacher. The participants discussed changes in Europe, especially in the European Union, as a result of events that were challenges to security. For example, in Austria, the tragedy of avalanches in Tyrol, Galtür, in Winter 2003 that destroyed houses, killed people, and threatened the villagers and tourists served as the starting point to discuss and implement a new security philosophy.

Security forces like fire brigades, the military, and police tried to find and implement new early warning systems to protect people living in dangerous areas in a much better way. Austria decided to create an "Austrian Security Promotion Agency" and concentrated all research activities in our country in this agency to improve our professional techniques. In 2003, Austria chose "Comprehensive Security" as its working model. This model is now followed by the European Union and Austria took the lead in implementing it. During the roundtable, different models of preventing security threats were discussed and led to the idea of publishing these diverse models. The roundtable theme of "Changing Concepts of Security" is the focus of Section I of this book.

A second roundtable dealt with "White Collar Crime and Corruption." Experiences in fighting financial fraud, white collar crime, counterfeiting, economic crime, and corruption and the methods used to identify special types of behaviors and criminals were reported. Participants were Katharina Noussi, researcher, who spoke about learning institutions; Professor Arije Antinori, sociologist, geopolitics analyst, and criminologist at University of Rome La Sapienza who also works for the Italian police; Martin Kreutner, board chairman of the International Anti-Corruption Academy in Austria (IACA); Walter Bödenauer, former international vice president of the International Financial Crime Investigators Organization and an executive of Eurolife, the Austrian branch of MasterCard, one of the largest credit card systems in the world; and I who specialized in insurance and banking fraud. The knowledge gathered by experts who fight fraud activities can help prevent future fraud cases.

The third roundtable theme was "Preventing Another Financial Crisis: The Roles of Control Mechanisms" and it is the foundation for Section III of this book. I chaired the roundtable on preventing another financial crisis. Contributors were Professor Michael Theil, Vienna University of Economics and Business Administration, Financial Department; Professor Tatyana Bikova, Riga International School of Economics and Business Administration, a macro-economist; and Clemens Fath of General Motors Corporation's financial operation in Austria. The members of the roundtable discussed which model could be most helpful for preventing another financial crisis.

The experiences of the ACUNS roundtables expanded when UNODC sponsored a conference in October 2010 to recognize the tenth anniversary of the United Nations Convention against Transnational Organized Crime. The conference on "Working Together to Combat Transnational Organized Crime" included many auxiliary events. One was a roundtable on "Organized Crime, White Collar Crime, and Corruption in Europe and Globally." It was an honor for me to chair this roundtable, and the participants brought new perspectives of understanding, repressing, and preventing these kinds of crimes. Two important discussion questions were

- Can we select methods of fighting new financial crises by learning from repression of organized crime, white collar crime, and corruption?
- How can we prevent a new financial crisis?
- Is there a model that provides better strategies to avoid these enormous losses caused by wild speculation, especially in the U.S.?

Two answers provide hope. One deals with human nature. It tries to analyze the weaknesses and strengths of human beings in dealing with the economy, crisis, greed, and society. The other answer can be found in comparing models of reinsurers. American reinsurers failed dramatically, and European reinsurers did not lose as much.

This book will not offer the golden keys of answers to the problems of financial crisis, but the authors hope that the information and insights offered by the contributors will alert those in authority to the patterns of activity that led to the current difficulties.

Maximillian Edelbacher

Foreword

This book, which focuses on the ways organized crime, white collar crime, and corruption affect the financial stability of nations throughout the world, is timely written, since the worldwide financial crisis has been dominating the political debate since 2008. It is well known that financial stability is essential for a nation's overall economic stability and growth. There is a broad consensus that, without comprehensive financial market reform, future crises cannot be prevented. To date, financial market reform has predominantly focused on the threats to stability that arise from legal activities in the financial industry characterized by excessive risk-taking, distortive incentives, and the lack of controls in the overall regulatory financial framework. These problems need to be addressed, but the threats to the economic security and financial security of a nation brought about by illegal activities relating to organized crime, white collar crime, and corruption should not be ignored. In fact, these types of crimes are sometimes facilitated by the lack of regulation and weak supervision of the activities of the financial sector. Thus, any comprehensive plan for reforming the financial sector must take into account the effects of criminal activities on the financial security of the country.

Financial Crimes: A Threat to Global Security deals with the effects of these activities on the financial sector and the threats they pose to the wider financial and economic security of a nation. These threats are considerable. In globalized financial markets, organized crime, white collar crime, and corruption are also globalized. Effective strategies to safeguard the financial infrastructure, such as ensuring transparency, economic security, and respect for the rule of law, must be coordinated globally.

Against the background of the current financial crisis, this collection of articles written by outstanding experts in their respective fields of study is an important and timely contribution to the debate on how to prevent financial crises in the future. I am confident that this book will be a valuable contribution to informing both experts and policy makers on this issue.

Andreas Schieder
State Secretary at the Federal Ministry of Finance

Acknowledgments

Many of the contributors to this book presented papers at the annual meeting of the Academic Council on the United Nations System. The idea that these papers could serve as the core for a book on financial crime was developed by Maximillian Edelbacher during this meeting. Peter C. Kratcoski and Michael Theil were asked to serve as co-editors when it became evident that integrating the papers into a cohesive whole would be a tremendous task. The authors approached the topics from very different perspectives and decided to solicit materials from other experts in the field so that the themes of the book could be addressed successfully.

The book would not have become a reality without the significant assistance of Dilip K. Das. His endorsement of the proposed book and his confidence in the editors were instrumental in convincing the publisher that this book would make a significant contribution to the International Police Executive Symposium Co-Publications Series published by CRC Press.

Many individuals contributed in some way to the development of this book. The co-editors, Michael Theil, Peter C. Kratcoski, and Maximillian Edelbacher, wrote selected chapters and section introductions. Peter C. Kratcoski, with the assistance of Lucille Kratcoski, worked to edit and standardize the writing styles in accordance with the publisher's specifications. Denise Kerr assisted with technical computer-related matters involved in preparing the manuscript for delivery to the publisher.

Of course, major gratitude should be reserved for contributors who were not mentioned above: Gerald Schöpfer, Günter Stummvoll, Gilbert Norden, Walther Lichem Alexander Seger, Wolfgang Hetzer, Anthony Mills, Bojan Dobovšek, Roman Tomasic, Matija Mastnak, Christian Felsenreich, Katharina Noussi, and Clemens Fath.

Finally, we wish to express our thanks to the partners of CRC Press/Taylor & Francis Group, especially Carolyn Spence and Jennifer Ahringer, for their support and guidance.

Maximillian Edelbacher, Peter C. Kratcoski, and Michael Theil

Editors

Maximillian Edelbacher was born in 1944 in Vienna, Austria. He graduated from Vienna University (Mag. Jur.) and the Hofrat of the Federal Police of Austria. He served as the chief of the Major Crime Bureau, an international expert for the Council of Europe, OSCE, and UNO. He also chaired the Austrian Antifraud Insurance Bureau and lectured at several universities including the Vienna University of Economics and Business Administration, Danube University in Krems, and the Vienna University Department of Sociology. Edelbacher was appointed a special investigator of the AVUS Group on White Collar Crime Cases, a board member of the Austrian Criminal Investigators Association, a member of the Academic Senior Advisory Council to the United Nations (ACUNS), and is the author of a number of books and journal articles.

Peter C. Kratcoski was born in Pennsylvania. He earned a PhD in sociology from the Pennsylvania State University, an MA in sociology from the University of Notre Dame, and a BA in sociology from Kings College. He was selected for several post-doctoral study grants by the National Science Foundation. He taught at the College of St. Thomas, St. Paul, Minnesota and The Pennsylvania State University before assuming the position of assistant professor of sociology at Kent State University in 1969. He retired as a professor of sociology and justice studies in 1998. During his career, he served as chair of the Department of Criminal Justice Studies until his retirement. Dr. Kratcoski also held positions as an instructor of sociology at the University of Akron, temporary instructor at the College of Wooster and at John Carroll University, and guest lecturer at Eastern Illinois University. He is currently a professor emeritus at Kent State University and director of the Justice Volunteer Center at the university. His interests are juvenile justice, corrections, crime prevention, and international crime prevention. He currently serves as official recorder of the International Police Executive Symposium and is a member of IPES, the Society for Police and Criminal Psychology, and the Academy of Criminal Justice Sciences. He has written many books, book chapters, and journal articles.

Michael Theil was born in Vienna, Austria. He earned an MBA with a major in transport, logistics, management, and insurance in 1991. He was awarded a PhD in risk management, insurance, and information management in

1994. Dr. Theil earned honors. In 2001, he finished habilitation and became a university docent at the Vienna University of Economics and Business Administration. He is a member of the Board of Governors of the Association of University Professors, a member of the Senate and Works Council of the University professors, and a cooperation delegate for partnerships with different universities. Currently, he is an associate professor at the Institute of Risk Management and Insurance at the Vienna University. He has published numerous articles, reviews, and book chapters and is the author of *Crimes against Insurances*. His specialty areas include accounting, general management, insurance, marketing, and quality management. He cooperates with the Institute of Finance and Management Science, the Norwegian School of Economics at Bergen, and Bradley University, Peoria, Illinois.

Contributors

Arije Antinori was born in Rome. He earned a PhD in criminology from the University of Bologna in consortium with University of Rome La Sapienza. Dr. Antinori has worked as a sociologist, criminologist, and geopolitics analyst. He also earned a master's in theories and methods of criminal investigation. He is currently a research area coordinator at the Criminology, Crisis Communication, and Media Laboratory at La Sapienza. He is a member of the Italian Society of Criminology, the Italian Society of Victimology, the Academic Council on the United Nations System (ACUNS), the Italian National Security Watch, and the International Police Executive Symposium (IPES). He is a qualified researcher at the Centre for Military and Strategic Studies (CEMISS) and an election observer for the European Union. Dr. Antinori researches and teaches several master's level subjects including "Terrorism and Media," "Crisis Management and Communication," "Counter-Terrorism," "Communication and Crime," and "Islam and Terrorism."

Bojan Dobovšek was born in Slovenia. After earning a PhD in social science from the University of Ljubljana, he became an associate professor of criminal investigation and is a vice dean of the faculty of Criminal Justice and Security of the University of Maribor, Slovenia. He served on the Commission for the Prevention of Corruption and is on the board of trustees of the Association for Research into Crimes Against Art. He is the author of a book about organized crime and editor of several publications on corruption and organized crime. Ongoing research projects focus on corruption in state institutions; corruption networks; organized crime and terrorism; methodological obstacles in measuring corruption; analyses of conventions on corruption; and art crime investigations. He is the author of draft recommendations for a number of OECD projects: Anti-Corruption Networks for Transition Economies, Anti-Corruption Action Plan for Armenia, Azerbaijan, Georgia, Kazakhstan, the Kyrgyz Republic, the Russian Federation, Tajikistan and Ukraine; and Ecologic Crime.

Clemens Fath was born in Austria. He earned a PhD from the Vienna University of Economics and Business Administration and an MBA from the Executive Academy of the same university. He received the Rudolf Sallinger Award for his doctoral thesis. He is the controller of General

Motors Powertrain Austria GmbH, and he teaches entrepreneurship and business planning at Europäische Wirtschafts- und Unternehmensführung Fachhochschule (European Economics- Management Academy).

Christian Felsenreich was born in Austria. He studied engineering and earned a BA and a MSc from the Technical Engineering School for Mechanics and Production Engineering. He also studied psychotherapy science at the Sigmund Freud Private University in Vienna and earned another BA. He earned a second MSc in human factors and system safety from the Lund University School of Aviation in Sweden. He is a trainer in the fields of human factors and system safety and teaches a course in high-risk environments, lectures at Sigmund Freud University, and is an active member of Plattform – Menschen in komplexen Arbeitswelten (www.plattform-ev. de) and also maintains a private counseling practice and has written several books and articles.

Wolfgang Hetzer passed A-level examinations (1970) and became a volunteer in the First Airborne Division of the German Army for two years. He then studied law at the University of Göttingen and successfully completed the First Judicial State Examination in 1977. He then worked as a junior barrister in Germany and Brazil. In June 1979, Dr. Hetzer passed the Second Judicial State Examination. He became a lawyer and research associate at the University of Saarbrücken where he completed his PhD in 1982. In 1983, he joined the Federal Tax Administration of Germany and held a number of senior positions. After the reunification of Germany, Dr. Hetzer was appointed deputy head of the Tax Division in the Ministry of Finance in Potsdam. Between 1992 and 1997 he worked as a legal adviser to the Federal Parliament of Germany on issues such as organized crime, tax evasion, money laundering, police operations, secret services, and other security matters. Before joining the European Anti-Fraud Office (OLAF), Dr. Hetzer was responsible for supervising the intelligence services in the Federal Chancellery in Berlin. He is now an advisor to the Director General of OLAF.

Walther Lichem studied law and Oriental archeology at the University of Graz and was awarded a J.D. He also earned an MA in political science and international relations at the University of North Carolina and received a diploma from the Ford Foundation's Institute for Advanced Studies in Vienna. Dr. Lichem started his professional career at the United Nations Secretariat in New York (1966–1974). His assignment to the Centre for Natural Resources, Energy, and Transport led to participation in UN missions in Ethiopia (1971), Argentina (1971–1974), and Senegal (1980). After joining the Austrian Foreign Service in 1974, he assumed responsibilities in the Department of International Organisations and in the Cabinet of the

Foreign Minister. He was named Consul General to Slovenia (1976–1980), Ambassador to Chile (1980–1984), and Ambassador to Canada (1993–2000). His academic engagements included teaching at the Vienna Diplomatic Academy, the International Peace Academy, and the University of Alberta. He was president of the European Space Agencies (EURISY) from 2003 to 2006) and Interpress Service from 1997 to 2003, and is a member of the board of PDHRE. Dr. Lichem has published numerous articles and books dealing with human security, international development cooperation, outer space, UN reform, human rights, and East–West relations.

Matija Mastnak was born in Slovenia. He earned a BA in criminal justice and security science, worked as a sociologist, and also as an editor of a daily information program on Television Slovenia, a public television network. He is currently conducting PhD research on investigative reporting at the Faculty of Criminal Justice and Security, University of Maribor, Slovenia.

Anthony Mills was born in the United Kingdom. He spent almost ten years in Beirut as a freelance correspondent for CNN, Deutsche Welle, and other news outlets before joining IPI as its press and communications manager. He is responsible for IPI's press freedom monitoring and campaigning, external communications, and media relations. Mills covered the 2005 assassination of former Lebanese Prime Minister Rafiq Hariri, the 2006 Israel–Hezbollah war, and the brief takeover by Hezbollah-led gunmen of West Beirut in 2008. A political and media specialist on Lebanon, Syria, and the broader Middle East, as well as on the media's role in combating corruption, he earned a bachelor's degree in international relations, with a focus on the Middle East, from Brown University in the U.S. and a master's degree in international journalism from City University, London. He also undertook graduate studies in criminology at Cambridge University, where he focused on organized crime. He speaks English, German, French, Arabic, and Luxembourgish.

Gilbert Norden was born in Vienna and studied sociology and economics at the University of Vienna. He has worked at the Institute of Sociology at the University of Vienna since 1981; since 1995 he has worked as an assistant professor and before that as a scientific assistant. He has written a number of publications about the sociology of police, lectured on sociology at the Academy for Security Affairs in Mödling and Traiskirchen in Lower Austria, and conducted seminars for Gendarmerie post commanders. He currently conducts a seminar in policing at the Vienna University with Maximillian Edelbacher, Professor Josef Hörl, and Simone Jungwirth.

Katharina Noussi was born in Linz, Austria. She holds a BA (Hons.) in international development from the University of East Anglia in the United

Kingdom with overseas study at the Université de Dschang in Cameroon (1999). She earned an MAS (Hons.) in arts management from the University of Music and Performing Arts of Vienna. During her work for the Light for the World consortium, she became interested in investigating the political economy of institutional development and reforms in developing countries. Since 2007 she has been writing her doctoral thesis in political science at the University of Vienna on "Why do reforms to strengthen public finance accountability succeed in some countries and fail in others?" Noussi has been awarded a University of Vienna doctoral research grant and completed research visits to the London School of Economics and Political Science, the Institute of Development Studies, and the Overseas Development Institute in England, and participated in the Stanford University Graduate Student Exchange Program.

Gerald Schöpfer is a full professor of economic and social history and chairman of the Department of Social and Economic History at the SOWI Fakultät (Faculty for Social and Economic Sciences), a guest professor at the Technical University in Graz lecturing on economics and international economic relations, and director of the University Program for the Management of Social and Health Facilities. He has written several publications on Austrian economic history and other social and business history topics. He served as research director of the 1989 and 1993 Styrian Exhibitions, an advisor for the 1995 Carinthian Exhibition, and director of research for the 1996 special exhibition on the Liechtenstein Dynasty. In 2004, Schöpfer was elected a member of the Styrian government; from 2005 to 2010, he served as a representative of the Styrian Parliament, and since 2009, has served as president of the Landesverband Steiermark Red Cross.

Alexander Seger was born in Germany. He earned a PhD in political science, law, and social anthropology after studies in Heidelberg, Bordeaux, and Bonn. He heads the Economic Crime Division at the Council of Europe. He has served with the Council of Europe in Strasbourg, France since 1999. He is responsible for the council's cooperative programs against cyber crime, corruption, money laundering, trafficking in human beings, and measures in support of the information society. From 1989 to 1998, he was with the United Nations Office on Drugs and Crime in Austria, Laos, and Pakistan, and served as a consultant for German Technical Cooperation (GTZ) in drug control matters.

Alexander Siedschlag was born in West Berlin, Germany. He studied political science, sociology, history, and psychology at the Ludwig Maximilian University in Munich and earned an MA in 1994 and a PhD in 1996. He was named a postdoctoral fellow in security studies at the Free University and at

Humboldt University in Berlin. In February 2000 he received his habilitation (venia legendi) from Humboldt. His research covers theory and method in international politics, European security and defense policy, use of new media in politics, and several areas of security research. He has partnered in several research studies and is coordinating a security research project in the Seventh Framework Program of the European Union. Siedschlag held the Endowed Chair of the Republic of Austria for European Security Policy at the University of Innsbruck. Since June 2009, he has been a professor and founding chair of the Institute of Security Research at Sigmund Freud Private University in Vienna.

Günter Stummvoll was born in Austria. He studied architecture in Vienna and sociology in Vienna and Melbourne, Australia. He earned a PhD from the Faculty of Humanities and Social Science of the University of Vienna. He pursued post-graduate training in sociology at the Institute for Advanced Studies (IHS) in Vienna and in criminology at Keele University in England. He worked as a research assistant at the Institute for Traffic Psychology (KfV), at the Institute for Advanced Studies, and at the Institut für Rechts und Kriminalsoziologie (Institute for Sociology of Law and Criminology), all in Vienna. He also was a European Research Fellow at the Centre for Criminological Research at Keele University in England. He completed professional training at the International Security Management and Crime Prevention Institute (ISMCPI) in Canada and a program for "Crime Prevention Design Advisors" at the National Policing Improvement Agency (NPIA) in the UK. He published articles and book chapters on juvenile delinquency, juvenile justice, and urban criminology. In October 2010, he joined Danube University in Krems as a social scientist and lecturer at the Department for Building and Environment.

Roman Tomasic was born in Linz, Austria. He is a professor of and holds the chair in company law at Durham University and has doctorates from the University of New South Wales (PhD) and the University of Wisconsin-Madison (SJD). Before moving to Durham, he worked in Australia at Victoria University and the University of Canberra. Dr. Tomasic was a founding editor of the *Australian Journal of Corporate* Law and has written widely about corporate law reform and theory, comparative insolvency law, and comparative corporate governance. His recent work reviewed corporate governance of leading Chinese companies. His current interests focus on the limits of corporate law, corporate sanctions and regulation, and the wider implications of their failures.

New Security Concepts

I

PETER C. KRATCOSKI

Introduction: The Concept of Security

The term security can take on various meanings, depending on the context in which it is used. For example, in *Webster's New Collegiate Dictionary* (1973, 1045), security is defined as "being free from danger; freedom from fear or anxiety; freedom from want or deprivation." Having total security in the sense of not having to be afraid of being physically harmed, and having sufficient food, clothing, and housing is a state of existence sought after throughout the centuries.[1]

Although the concept of security has acquired new meanings in recent years, the basic needs of people for security have not changed. Humans still desire to be free from want, free from harm (internally or externally created), free from fear of the future, and free to express their feelings and emotions. Although human needs for security have not changed, the question arises as to who is responsible for providing the security. Is it the individual, the family, the group, or the state?

In this book we will show how the responsibility for providing security has gradually moved from the individual to the family, extended group, state, and eventually, at least in part to a global responsibility. Maslow (1954), a behavioral psychologist, developed a Hierarchy of Needs schema to illustrate how human motivation pertains to the understanding of the way a person is motivated and responds to basic needs for security.[2] The first and most basic need obviously is satisfying basic physical requirements such as food and water. Throughout most of the history of mankind, human activities were directed toward the security of knowing that these basic biological needs would be fulfilled.

The second level of needs cited by Maslow related to security and safety. Again, the interpretation of "need" differs based on the period of time in the development of civilization considered. For example, early in human development security needs were defined predominantly as protection against the elements and wild animals. As society became more structured and the powers of leaders and governments increased, protection against major threats to physical security was taken over by the state. Edelbacher and Kratcoski, (2010, 78) note that:

Throughout history, all political entities, whether they were cities, city-states, or nations, have had to be concerned with protecting their borders from external threats.[3] These threats might take the form of military invasions, the entrance of criminal elements, or migration of poverty-stricken people seeking a better standard of living. The leaders built massive walls, constructed fortifications in strategic locations and maintained standing armies for the sole purpose of providing security from external threats.

We have long known that such methods of safeguarding against threats to the security of a country are obsolete, particularly in relation to the types of security threats that will be discussed in this book, However, the recent attempt of the U.S. government to build a wall across its border with Mexico to protect it from threats from Mexico shows that this mentality among leaders still exists. Maslow also noted that most people are not satisfied with merely having their basic needs of freedom from want and freedom from harm met. They also develop psychological needs, for example a social need to belong to, interact with, and be accepted by others. The most basic way of having this need filled is through family.

Ironically, for a child, his or her family also provides the physiological and safety needs. Many people also strive to fill other needs (recognition or self-esteem) and the highest level of security that is seldom achieved: self-actualization in which a person is totally free from want or fear.

For an individual, the need for sociability can be achieved through intimate interactions with a single person, family, or group. For example, knowing that one is loved and recognized as a good parent is all the recognition, self-esteem, and security a person requires to fulfill the security need for sociability, recognition, and self-esteem. Others, however may find the recognition security they need through the accumulation of great amounts of money or status as a famous leader, entertainer, scholar, or athlete.

An individual's quest for self-actualization is manifested in constantly trying to be a better leader, accumulating more money, or perfecting his or talents even beyond the high quality of perfection already achieved. As noted, self-actualization is rarely achieved because those who seek it are seeking perfection. The leaders of a nation, at a minimum, are expected to "protect and serve" the people who reside in the countries they lead. This, of course, is a very difficult task, and the resources of some countries are inadequate to even assist people in times of natural disasters, as witnessed in Haiti, or protect them from external invasions.

Unfortunately, major threats against people may come from the leaders who are supposed to provide their security, for example, during Khadaffi's rule in Libya. In short the amount of physical, financial, and psychology security provided by governments throughout the world varies greatly. Generally, the citizens of most nations feel confident enough about their security to conduct their daily lives and plan for their futures without fear of a major catastrophe. However, in no country is security so perfect that self-actualization is common. The state of self-actualization is unachievable.

This book focuses on financial security. However, it is necessary to show how closely the financial security of people is related to other forms of security needs—physical and psychological. Tomasic (2011, 22) states, "The dominance of self-interest and a culture of greed have undermined trust in market institutions such as banks, securities advisors, regulators, and the capacities of the legal system."[4] Thus, it is unlikely that the legal systems will be capable of convincing the public that they can make financial institutions accountable for their actions. This lack of confidence in the government's abilities to fix the faults of financial institutions spills over to other security related areas.

The chapters presented in this section of the book were selected because they add some insight or a new dimension to the concept of security. In Chapter 1, on the changing concepts of security, Günter Stummvoll discusses how changes in the defensive design of a country are grounded in changes in its security and public safety needs. Historically, security measures that protected empires, kingdoms, cities, and aristocratic properties involved building walls, fortresses, and border checkpoints gradually shifted to protecting individuals—creating a transformation from national security to human security. This change also stimulated the growth of the security industry with an influx of industrial products for protecting private property holders. At present, defenses employed to provide physical, social, or financial security consist of a combination of government activities (laws and regulations) and private activities (gated communities, urban design for crime prevention, electronic devices, and community crime prevention measures).

In Chapter 2, on the history of crisis and the quest for security, Gerald Schöpfer notes that every nation is in a permanent state of change, and thus the challenges to security will also change constantly. He notes that even in ancient civilizations, the state assumed some responsibility for individual financial security; for example, the Roman Empire gave grants to veterans and widows of soldiers. In looking for current major threats to the financial security of a nation, we must consider both internal and external sources. Modern threats can arise from poor management of resources, invasions and wars, natural disasters, global warming, depletion of natural resources, criminal activities, and corruption. Schöpfer further concludes that all these factors can threaten the financial security of a nation and the entire universe if they are not curtailed or properly regulated.

Chapter 3 discusses the development of a security society in Austria. Maximillian Edelbacher and Gilbert Norden introduce the security society concept and illustrate how various concepts have attempted to capture the ethos or essence of a society at different stages of history. The "Me Society," the "Service Society," the "Leisure Society," and other phrases attempted to capture the essence of the values and the behavior of certain groups. Using Austria as an example, the authors make a case for labeling the modern world the "Security Society" by showing that security has become the major focus of both governments and people. They also show how the police and military have decreased their security efforts and explain how public and private concerns have joined to provide security in some nations. This is accomplished by reducing or eliminating the risks from man-made hazards and natural disasters, joining with public agencies to prevent crime, abolishing the so-called "borders" between internal and external security, developing international security protection programs, professionalizing the security sciences, and outsourcing security services to private entrepreneurs.[4]

Chapter 4 details the concept of security in the European Union. Alexander Siedschlag uses the results of his research on changing perceptions of security and intervention employed by European countries to develop security strategies. He found that member countries of the European Union tended to develop their security strategies based on the needs of individual nations rather than meeting the needs of the entire union. For example, the critical security risks of Austria may relate to critical infrastructure protection. The Netherlands may focus on climate change, and the United Kingdom may seek permanent cooperation with European Union members and other countries in dealing with crime prevention, violent crime issues, and terrorist attacks.[6] He concludes that standardizing and enhancing the security technologies across the member nations will lead to reduction of the security risks; improving the distribution of responsibilities and labor among the different actors in government and society is needed instead of increased investments.

In Chapter 5, Walter Lichem discusses the gradual expansion of the role of the Security Council of the United Nations. He noted that although the council's past role was determining whether the United Nations should act in cases in which a country's security was in jeopardy from invasion by outside aggressors, the council now becomes involved in protecting people from government leaders who oppress them. He notes that the "principle of the responsibility to protect was adopted by consensus of the 2005 Summit Meeting of the General Assembly," and thus the protection of human security and human sovereignty has more priority than state sovereignty in terms of the United Nations Security Council's role.

References

1. *Webster's New Collegiate Dictionary.* (1973). New York: Merriam Webster: 1045.
2. Maslow, A. (1954). *Motivation and Personality.* New York: Harper and Row.
3. Edelbacher, M. & Kratcoski, P. (2010). Protecting the borders in a global society: an Austrian and American perspective. In *Border Security in the Al-Qaeda Era*, Winterdyk, J.A. & Sundberg, K.W., Eds. Boca Raton, FL: CRC Press.
4. Tomasic, R. (2011). The financial crisis and the haphazard pursuit of financial crime. *Journal of Financial Crime* 18: 7–31.

Changing Concepts of Security
The Preventive Turn in Defensive Design

1

GÜNTER STUMMVOLL

Contents

Introduction

Criminology—the "specific genre of discourse and inquiry about crime" (Garland, 2002, p. 7)—covers a variety of topics, scientific approaches, and different disciplines, according to prevalent institutional, political, and cultural contexts. In a strict legal sense, criminology focuses on the making and breaking of laws and society's reaction to the breaking of laws (Sutherland and Cressey, 1960/1924). In a broader sense, criminology is associated with the study of deviance and social control in societies along with policing, order maintenance, and the adherence to and perpetuity of norms and values of a society. Again, another thread of criminological endeavor is interested in the consequences of crime such as feelings of insecurity and fear of crime.

Theoretical discourse in criminology often takes a historical view to identify current features in the perception and production of security and developments over time. This is particularly true about the work of David Garland, who planned to write a "history of the present" to identify historical and social conditions that would provide a better understanding of present-day practices in crime control (Garland, 2001). In his influential book, *The Culture of Control: Crime and Social Order in Contemporary Society*, Garland identifies a number of indices of change that describe a paradigm shift in the culture of control observed at least in the U.S. and Great Britain during the twentieth century.

Most significant, he says, is the decline of "penal welfarism" and the shift from rehabilitative to punitive ideals in criminal justice politics. Garland proclaims the end of a system of rehabilitation and social reintegration as the ultimate reason for punishment. The old system has given way to the recurrence of arguments for retribution and "just deserts." The traditional welfarist picture of the delinquent as a disadvantaged, needy person who acts from necessity has disappeared in the public view. Instead the new crime control has been supported by stereotypes of professional criminals as members of organized crime networks and terrorist cells.

This shift from a welfarist to a punitive form of criminal justice has been supported by a collective popular demand for general protection in the name of potential victims. Criminal justice politics shifted toward issues of risk management and crime prevention, thus entailing a shift in criminological thinking from topics like anomie, relative deprivation, subcultural theory, and labelling to a more pragmatic approach of crime control. Crime was formerly thought to be committed by individuals who lacked education, employment, and intelligence. The picture has changed to seeing criminals as rational actors who lack social, situational, and self-control—a picture that reminds us of Thomas Hobbes' dark concept of natural characters as evil wolves that tend to exhibit anti-social, selfish, and criminal behavior as soon as they are left alone.

It seems today that security can be guaranteed only through a complex system of institutional and formal control. To borrow Garland's terms, the "Lombrosian project" based on the premise that criminals can somehow be scientifically differentiated from non-criminals, has terminated in favor of a "governmental project" that seeks to enhance the efficiency and effectiveness of criminal justice institutions and promote a tight system of surveillance by police or private security guards. Security shall be achieved by a number of new surveillance techniques and technical devices of control developed at the end of the twentieth century.

Strategies of crime control now focus on "criminogenic situations" that offer crime opportunities for crime to anyone who can be tempted. For almost a century, criminal dispositions of individuals were at the heart of preventive action, whereas in recent years the study of criminality as a personal trait lost the race against research studying crime events. Furthermore, crime prevention has been extended from an exclusive task for criminal justice institutions (police, courts, prisons, and probation services) to a multitude of civil institutions including private security guards and a range of inspectors who manage public order.

Securitization

In his book about risk society, Ulrich Beck (1986) discussed the idea that modern industrial societies create many new risks that were unknown earlier. New threats including nuclear war and industrial pollution emerged as secondary and unintended consequences of modernity. Other than natural risks like floods, earthquakes, and floods in earlier times, Beck argues that modern risks are manufactured by humans. The extensive discourse in theory that followed Beck's theses on risk society (e.g.: Beck and Lau, 2004; Giddens 1990) yielded at least two consequences. First, it broadened the security agenda and second, it led to large volumes of research and development in the field of security management.

Today, the security agenda has reached beyond national military threats, and we recognize that economic, societal, environmental, and health problems pose significant security burdens. Zedner (2009, 40) observes: "Whereas the traditional focus of security was upon the nation state and the protection of territory, human security makes the protection of individuals its primary referent." According to the United Nations Development Programme, human security shall be addressed by political, social, environmental, economic, and cultural agendas designed collectively to furnish the building blocks of survival, livelihood, and dignity (UNDP, 1994).

Critical security scholars raised concerns about this stretch of security issues to a definition that views economic, social, health and educational problems through the lens of security. Zedner (2009, 45) observed that, "Making social or economic policy in the name of security may be a way of enhancing its priority and attracting more resources but potentially has a distorting effect, captured by the term 'securitization.'" Societies that experience considerable levels of crime and fear of crime, have already adapted to this development, whereas societies subjected to low crime rates and moderate fears have managed to keep crime prevention issues separate from policy programs covering youth welfare, migration, housing, and urban and environmental redevelopment.

The globalization of risks and fears that emerge with massive migrations, financial crises, and religious fundamentalism nurture these developments of securitization in all Western societies. As a consequence, security has become a holistic concept now tackled by governments and also by the industrial and service sectors in a variety of economic fields. Security has become a major commodity and subject for research and development within its own industry. This trend caused a paradigm shift in the field of crime prevention from *social prevention* and social support for law abiding behavior to *situational prevention* and the reduction of opportunities for offending.

Critical criminologists, who explain crime mainly in terms of social inequality and structural root causes (lack of education or unemployment) pointed out that the so-called administrative paradigm must be underpinned by a scientific agenda that uses experimental methods and empirical investigation to identify "what works" in crime prevention. In a "whole of government" approach (Sutton et al., 2008), the criminal justice system receives support from a range of other agencies (education, housing, urban planning, gender mainstreaming, surveillance technology) within governmental institutions and the private sector of the economy. In traditional socialist countries, the state as a central service provider has a prominent position vis-à-vis the people as consumers of welfare and protection. In contrast, the U.S., Great Britain, and the Netherlands are examples of the neo-liberal thrust in security governance during the 1980s that emphasized a "nodal" form of governance in an increasingly "hollowed-out" state that cedes policing responsibilities to the private sector (Johnston and Shearing, 2003).

In the following section, I will demonstrate this preventive turn on the basis of an example: Defensive design has gone through a dramatic transformation in form and function over the centuries. I will argue that defensive design is perhaps the oldest form of crime prevention and was deployed long before the establishment of a modern criminal justice system during the second half of the eighteenth century. However, with the rise of nation-states, defensive design has lost influence. Only with increasing demands for crime prevention in the late twentieth century, has defensive design re-emerged as *crime prevention through environmental design* (CPTED). I must add some thoughts about future developments of defensive design and possible pathways to re-integrate social and situational approaches to crime prevention for a comprehensive understanding of community safety.

Defensive Design

A brief look at history quickly reveals that defensive design has been employed from prehistoric times to the modern era (Crowe, 2000; Schneider and Kitchen, 2002). The possibility of accumulating the first food surplus in the course of the agricultural revolution of the Neolithic era (around 9000 BC) had extraordinary implications for human development. The transformation from nomadic life to settlements required people to develop ways to protect surplus production and property from weather, insects, and predatory humans. Since then, defensive designs can be found in many forms and shapes, beginning with the fortification of Jericho around 7000 BC.

Defensive structures such as the Great Wall of China, Hadrian's Wall, the walls surrounding Constantinople, and finally modern defensive measures such as the Maginot Line, the Iron Curtain, and the Berlin Wall reveal the close link between architecture and some form of physical protection against predatory attacks. In addition, the construction of city walls, citadels, and castles in the Middle Ages protected residences and also were linked strongly to community organization and land economics. Walls and edges marked boundaries and determined inclusion and exclusion of residents—important considerations for taxing systems and the general concept of citizenship. The geopolitical landscape in the Middle Ages was characterized by scattered centers of governance. Princedoms, aristocracies, and churches were separated by stretches of "no man's land." The gradual formation of nation-states caused a transition from fairly isolated centers of power to territories that shared borders.

The political transformation from empires to democratic nation-states in Europe in the nineteenth and twentieth centuries caused defensive design to lose popularity as security became an administrative concept involving diplomacy and state politics. Peace and stability in Europe became functions of democratic states. Sovereignty of democratic states in connection with international alliances such as the European Union superseded the fragile balance of power maintained during the Cold War. National security in earlier times was limited to border checkpoints on the ground and radar systems monitored at military installations. Defensive design as a means of protection has been outmoded by the development of professional armed forces entrusted with the responsibility of protecting borders to prevent intrusion.

By the end of the twentieth century, the strict national order of security in Europe started to crumble. As a result of economic globalization and worldwide migration, the standard model of the nation-state deteriorated. The old "matryoshka metaphor"—every state contains counties, every county contains cities, every city contains districts, every district contains blocks of houses, which again contain single houses and dwellings—is being undermined by regional development across borders, city partnerships in Europe, and the establishment of cities as worldwide financial hubs. The modern geographic landscape became fluid as border controls were removed with the rise of the European Union as a single European market. This development produced two consequences.

First, the decline of international threats exerted more pressure on governments to develop security concepts within the states and understand security in terms of individual needs and public safety. Second, conventional defensive design became obsolete, and the need for defensive measures such as armed borders and city fortifications disappeared.

The crime–design nexus has taken a new shape under contemporary conditions of security threats. Defensive design lost its international scope and was relegated to reducing opportunities for property crimes, vandalism, and social disorder. In a critical review of environmental criminology, David Garland (2000) points out that considerations of environmental design have only recently re-emerged in crime prevention politics, after an absence from the mainstream common sense of criminology for most of the discipline's history.

This, he says, is remarkable since the concept of rationality was prominent as a general ideology and, in particular, in policing at the end of the eighteenth century, when Patrick Colquhoun, the founder of the first preventive police force in England, claimed that crime was a matter of temptation and opportunity, not a matter of individual disposition. Thus, efforts to control crime should focus on reducing the occasions and opportunities for crime events rather than trying to change criminal dispositions (Colquhoun, 1795, quoted in Garland, 2000, 3).

However, during the twentieth century crime control was seen as the primary task of a specialized criminal justice system that focused on sanctioning individual offenders and trusted in achieving prevention through deterrence. Under the influence of the natural human sciences, mainly biology, medicine, and psychology, crime was conceptualized as "criminality"—a characteristic of individuals rather than an event. Hence, we can speak of a re-emergence of defensive design in a new shape: a set of recipes for steering and channelling behavior in ways to manipulate opportunity structures for motivated offenders.

The special field of environmental criminology has developed in two directions. The first focus is on crime science and methods for studying the geography of crime using geographic information systems (GIS). Crime mapping has been established as a highly specialized field of research employing spatial statistics to study artificial neural networks, space syntax, and other applications for analysis.* This strand within criminology developed as an academic support system for policing. The second focus is on industrial production and the design of urban environments, architecture, and products against crime (Wortley and Mazerolle 2008). "Design against crime" and "designing out crime" are the buzz phrases of strategies for target hardening and natural control.

Crime Prevention through Environmental Design

Environmental criminology has set out not simply to improve technology for target hardening, but to modify the environment by reducing opportunity structures, deflecting offenders, and reducing fear of crime. The overall concept can be summarized in two quotes aimed to promote the concept of *crime prevention through environmental design* (CPTED):

---

* For an overview on applications of spatial statistics for crime analysis see Chainey and Ratcliffe (2005).

The goal of CPTED is to reduce opportunities for crime that may be inherent in the design of structures or in the design of neighborhoods (Wortley and Mazerolle, 2008). The proper design and effective use of the built environment can lead to a reduction in the fear and incidence of crime and to an improvement in the quality of life (Crowe, 2000).

The rationale for this approach in crime prevention is found in two theoretical concepts that regained value in the past three decades. Rational choice and routine activity theory emerged as leading concepts in crime prevention politics. Instead of conceiving crime in terms of sociopathologies of offenders, the rational choice perspective takes the view that crimes are purposive and deliberate acts committed with the intention of benefiting an offender, who balances costs and benefits in a rational decision process before an offense (Newman et al., 1997). The perspective assumes that offenders are rational utility maximizers who consider the effort, reward, risk of detection, and risk of punishment when searching for crime opportunities. This opens the door to myriad techniques for responding to burglaries, shop lifting, bank robberies, and assaults.

The routine activity perspective first articulated by Lawrence Cohen and Marcus Felson in the "American Sociological Review" (1979) explained the increase in crime rates by substantial changes in social and technological patterns and accordingly by change in "recurrent and prevalent activities" that people pursue to meet their needs (Chamard, 2010). The wider social explanations of the approach, particularly the broad changes in society, their effects on community life, and their potential to create new opportunities for crime have often been neglected in academic appraisals. Instead, criminological interpretations focus on the microlevel of the theory and the assumption that crime occurs when three elements (likely offender, suitable target, absence of capable guardian) converge in time and space. Thus, a situational perspective in crime prevention includes assumptions about (1) a rational offender, (2) an attractive target or product: concealable, removable, available, valuable, enjoyable, disposable—the CRAVED model of a "hot product" (Clarke, 1999), and (3) the specific characteristics of a place.

The CPTED concept includes a variety of measures to change opportunities for crime and deflect offenders and is also concerned with urban design to increase feelings of security. This makes it a psychological concept that looks beyond the latest electronic or mechanical security tools (alarm systems, CCTV, security doors, body scanners, and other devices). Crime opportunities require more complex measures.

Target hardening is considered a creative and clever job for landscape designers, urban planners, architects, interior designers, and product designers. Bank robbery, for example, can be prevented when this kind of psychology of space is taken into account: An offender wants to explore a situation in anonymity before committing an offense. He is less obvious when standing at a bus stop in front of a bank. He wants to see who is inside the bank (usually robbers avoid contact with children). He wants to enter and leave the bank quickly (more difficult when he has to walk through a foyer separated from the main room by electronic sliding doors). He wants to escape quickly (difficult if the cash counters are at the far end of the room) and leave the area as fast as possible. Designing parking areas in front of a bank or on a side street may help him or hamper his flight. CPTED takes the psychology of the situation into account and makes crime prevention an important issue for the building industry.

The prevention of property crimes in public or private spaces becomes more complex when other factors such as infrastructures as social magnets, demographic composition, social conflicts, more or less reliable social control mechanisms through neighbors or strangers at a scene, anonymity, and non-involvement are added. In these cases, CPTED counts on the principle of informal surveillance in the form of community policing and civil courage to take responsibility for more formal mechanisms. Thus, CPTED becomes a normative and moral concept for solidarity and social interaction in favor of crime prevention. Even more important, and this is where we leave the strict disciplinary boundary of criminology, crime prevention interferes in public order management and general "quality of life" aspects in that environmental design should:

- Be aesthetically pleasing.
- Promote desirable (and legal) behavior.
- Support territoriality (feeling of belonging).
- Encourage residents to peacefully share public space.

The original concept of defensive design for crime prevention (protection of territory) has turned into a concept to promote public safety (protection of individuals). This demonstrates clearly the transformation discussed above from national to human security. Furthermore, it shows the practice of securitization and indicates a paradigm shift in the governance of security from state to nodal governance (Wood and Shearing, 2007). Nodal governance involves a blurring of the functional specialization of former times, particularly between public and private nodes of crime control as noted on page 29:

> In schematic terms, it has been argued that state authorities operate according to a 'punishment mentality' which denotes a backward-looking orientation focused on redeeming the past through the righting of wrongs. In contrast, corporations are said to operate through risk, denoting a more forward-looking orientation focused on shaping the future by manipulating present flows of

events. A nodal governance perspective, however, serves to confound this rather neat distinction between ways of thinking across 'public' and 'private' nodes.

In the remaining sections of this chapter, I will consider how defensive design can position itself in this modern era for governance of crime control and try to anticipate the development of CPTED thinking in the future. Two situations are conceivable. First, CPTED remains a managerialist concept that merely looks at quick-fix solutions to block crime in practical and simple ways. Without aspiring to deeper understanding of the causes of crime, crime prevention managers "design out" opportunities for crime in spatial situations based on the microlevel of routine activity theory (convergence of motivated offender, suitable target, and absence of capable guardians). The situational perspective on crime prevention is considered a direct, immediate, and systematic response to criminal events.

More distant explanations for crime in a society (subcultural, social disorganization, demographic and socioeconomic change, and social strains) are ignored because the solutions to the causes of crime seem unachievable to security managers. Therefore, practitioners who follow this stream of policies also walk on thin ice between "designing out" crime and "crowding out" troublesome people. Practitioners in environmental criminology who follow this path seem to resist the scrutiny from deeper grounds of society, cultural conflicts, social capital, and urban development.

Secondly and alternatively, concepts in design-led crime prevention may develop in a different way by considering social dynamics and sociospatial structures in urban development that respond to crime and insecurity in compliance with a sociological analysis of spatial situations. A re-merger with social and communal strategies in crime prevention may offer an opportunity to destigmatize environmental criminology and untangle it from its reputation as a pragmatic, theoretical, and purely administrative approach to crime prevention.

From the Psychology of Situations to the Sociology of Space

The psychology of public space captures a range of attributes such as the deliberate consideration of shape, color, material, lighting, smell, and sound in architecture, public order management, good maintenance, and conflict resolution as factors that contribute to keeping peace and public order. Design-led crime prevention has responded well to the microlevel approach to routine activity theory, that is, as the basis for the "chemistry of crime" (Felson and Boba 2010). If the psychology of space is taken seriously, designers can manipulate all three elements of crime in very specific settings: (1) deflect an offender, (2) protect a victim or target, and (3) provide capable guardians for natural surveillance. However, this powerful and optimistic approach in security management overlooks the macrolevel of the routine activity approach and the wider trends in modern societies. A holistic analysis of causes of crime with regard to prevention that goes beyond target hardening offers opportunities to see unintended consequences for security resulting from decisions in a number of political fields.

Societal trends have consequences for urban structures that again may affect opportunities for crime. These side effects often remain unnoticed in both the theory and practice of environmental criminology. Three of the many social areas where developments are significant for opportunity structures of crime are:

Consumerism—The historical development of commerce and shopping habits, from medieval central market places to inner city shopping malls after World War II, to late-modern shopping centers on the peripheries of cities created new opportunities for property crimes, new targets, and new control cultures. Commercial centers have been isolated from other uses of public space in cities such as housing, trade, arts and crafts, businesses, and transportation. This geographic transformation demands new forms of control. For example, security control in shopping centers has turned into a frenzy of rule setting by private owners or operators, private policing, and preventive social exclusion of trouble-makers (Shearing and Stenning, 1987; Jones and Newburn, 1998; Wakefield, 2003).

Education—Small schools formerly scattered in cities have been merged to establish education centers on university campuses. These areas often remain isolated during long vacation times. Schools and universities are increasingly equipped with high-technology systems (computer servers, laptops, video beamers, software licenses, and other expensive items). This makes educational establishments more attractive for criminals, thus raising the demands for further securitization of such facilities. Therefore, the location and environmental setting may be essential components of future crime prevention measures. The demographic side effect of the campus trend is also considerable because university campuses pull students away from the social fabrics of cities and leave behind social structures without student cultures.* University campuses lack social interactions with families, elderly people, pets, and tradespeople and foster social segregation. This unintended effect of social exclusion through urban planning represents new demands for security management to correct some of the past mistakes in security planning.

---

* Tübingen, Cracow, Ljubljana, and Utrecht are examples of European towns with major proportions of students.

Women in the labor market—Increasing participation of women in the labor market during the twentieth century changed family lifestyles. Parents drive their children to school, go to work, do errands, pick up their children on the way home, and enter their houses through garages. More and more middle-class women are involved in this daily routine that leaves housing areas deserted during working hours. This lifestyle combined with the design of wide streets and monofunctional housing estates leaves very little opportunity for or interest in socializing with neighbors. This effect was described by Baumgartner (1988) on page 3 of her study titled *The Moral Order of a Suburb*:

> A kind of moral minimalism pervades the suburbs, in which people prefer the least extreme reactions to offences and are reluctant to exercise any social control against one another at all. A result is the widespread tranquillity so often noted in suburbia.

This structural change of routine activities has consequences for opportunity structures for burglaries in anonymous suburban neighborhoods where neighbors do not know each other, people who walk down the street are considered suspicious, and residences are unattended during most of the day.

There may be other social developments in the employment sector that point to a revision of this trend. For example, changes in work regulations that allow work to be completed from home may give employees more flexibility, and this may disturb the regularity and rearrange the social construction of routine activities. In other words: The concept of defensive design has been modified to capture the *psychology of situations* and the *sociology of space*.

Dialectics of Crime and Place

The history of defensive design may be a striking example for the social transformation of security concepts. Physical protection and target hardening, psychological features of crime opportunities, and a sociological analysis of deeper structural transformations represent different stages in the development, although the last stage is not yet molded. In particular, it is not clear whether criminology can resist the temptation to fall for a kind of *environmental determinism* that makes crime and deviance contingent upon design features in public space.

A rejection of environmental determinism, however, calls for an alternative concept that may be found easily in traditional writings of urban sociologists who take a *dialectic view* of the social construction of space. The following examples argue that social situations must be regarded under a dual aspect of influence, that is, environment shapes behavior and behavior shapes environment.

The sociological roots of the environmental perspective can be traced back to a human ecological movement known as the Chicago School that was prominent in the United States in the early part of the twentieth century. At the time of extensive migration and city growth, a group of researchers including Robert Park, Ernest Burgess, Clifford Shaw, and Henry McKay, studied the social dynamics in the city of Chicago and found a clear association between poor quarters of the city and what they called "social disorganization." The "zone in transition" was characterized by run-down houses, high unemployment among immigrants, and high rates of poverty and disease. Communal ties were lost and impersonal relationships prevailed. What made this tradition of research important for criminology was the empirical evidence of the connection between geographically patterned socio-economic standards and crime and delinquency.

Explanations for crime and deviance were found in migration, segregation, and social disruption. The Chicago School (Park et al., 1925) contended that delinquency is not a pathological factor of the individual, but a consequence of spatially patterned social circumstances that construct the environment. Urban space is a social construction and subject to influence from a number of institutions, cultural traditions, structures, habits, and social interactions.

One of the first sociologists on the European continent who considered the relationship of space and society was Georg Simmel. His essay on the "Sociology of Space" (1903) is regarded as one of the most crucial contributions to urban sociology up to the present. One of the most important insights for our discussion of crime prevention through environmental design is Simmel's understanding of space as a product of social interaction. Urban environments shape both social phenomena and the quality of social interaction.

The concept of *Raumqualitäten* shapes the figures in space (*Raumgebilde*). In simpler terms, physical space shapes social interaction and social interaction also shapes the physical structures in a city. Space is not considered a pre-social entity; it is a social phenomenon that becomes manifest in spatial realities that reflect onto society. Space should be analyzed as a construct of social activities and the effects of spatial configurations on social activities. For example, a church is both a religious structure and a place that guides social behavior. A church is a symbol and a cultural product on the one hand and a place of silence on the other. The same dialectic principle applies to schools, transportation facilities, sports centers, and public places in cities.

Many years later, Pierre Bourdieu elaborated on the same topic in his writings on the relationship of social and spatial structures and the mechanisms of their reproduction. Bourdieu argued that urban space functions as a mechanism for stability of social order, whereas social mobility in urban space is rather inert. The social composition and distribution of social groups in urban space is stable and is a result of *self-structuration* according to the distribution of economic, cultural, and social capital. Bourdieu contends that "the habitus makes the habitat" (2000). Thus the choice of urban settlement and housing style follows the endowment with capital. Therefore he considers spatial segregation a natural phenomenon and urban space the visualisation of the social world like a screen on which social segregation is projected.

The reverse is also true, as the "habitat makes the habitus," for example, the effects of experiences in a low income, high unemployment, poor housing estate on social status. Bourdieu contends that spatial patterns and elements in public space tell us something about power relationships of the social world. Social structures reinforce spatial structures and vice versa. This is illustrated in the conceptual distinction of the *club effect* and the *ghetto effect*: The club effect is represented in exclusive spaces such as gated communities, reserved for people with sufficient capital who gain additional social status as members of the club. In contrast, the ghetto effect stigmatizes inhabitants of poor areas due to their permanent residence in run-down, low-quality urban neighborhoods (Bourdieu, 1991, quoted in Schroer, 2006, p. 99). In this respect, Bourdieu exerted a major influence on research of social inequalities in urban sociology.

The particular dialectic concept of space was supported and further developed by Henri Lefebvre. In "La Production de l'Espace" (2000), he links his conception of space with a critique of capitalism. One of his major arguments is that the production and control of space represent the principal means of power in capitalism, and the state ensures its power by managing and planning space. Lefebvre calls this activity *"representations of space"* and he means the cognitive conception and development of space by architects, urban planners, and designers. On the other hand, the triviality of everyday life points at the alienation of the passive individual who uses public space and is subject to structural constraints. This second aspect of space Lefebvre calls *"spatial practice,"* and it reflects spatial forms of conduct that produce and reproduce daily routines of experiencing public spaces. Lefebvre complements these concepts of structure and action by a third aspect known as *"spaces of representation"* that describes the symbolic expression of images inherent in certain neighborhoods. Images also refer to myths, rituals, symbols, traditions, and historical knowledge about conceptions of space. Together the three elements for the production of space (urban imagination for planning, everyday practice, and myths and images of space) shape Lefebvre's dynamic model of the social production of space.

The list of theorists who support relational and constructivist concepts of space may be extended by drawing on Durkheim, Marx, Giddens, Luhmann, Harvey, and Foucault (Schroer, 2006). More importantly, however, is the particular insight that connects them and the potential for the future conceptualization of urban security. A dialectic concept of space that replaces the assumption of environmental determinism inherent in so many prevailing models of crime control offers a more fundamental understanding of criminogenic situations. An etiological approach to crime prevention that re-introduces theoretical models of crime causation may help clarify the complexities of opportunity structures where crime happens.

Conclusion

The historical development of defensive design is indicative for a transformation in security concepts. Simultaneously, the particular techniques in defensive design employed at different stages in history traces the shift in perceptions of risk and threat. The construction of walls, citadels, and defensive edges was meant to protect the territories of empires, kingdoms, city–states, and aristocratic private properties. Border checkpoints in the nineteenth and twentieth century were meant to protect territories of states.

The shift to protect individuals within countries was a consequence of a transfer of security from national level to individual level that caused a dispersion of accountability for public safety including a variety of bodies in the public and private sectors. Public safety has turned into a multi-disciplinary effort that triggered an influx of industrial production for target hardening for private properties. At the end of the twentieth century, architects discovered indirect effects of informal surveillance through design-solutions in urban planning and building design. Most recently, defensive design took another turn to be based on socio-structural analyses of criminal situations in urban space.

This view may be fundamental for future solutions in crime prevention that consider crime as a consequence of social conflicts in society. Considerations of social disorganization and relative deprivation in urban areas, natural spatial segregation, and the social construction of images in cities can help in a macro-structural analysis of crime. We may not return to a system of penal welfarism, but perhaps the stakeholders in multi-agency management of crime control will consider the potential consequences of urban development for security and public safety.

References

Baumgartner MP. (1988). *The Moral Order of a Suburb*. Oxford University Press, New York.
Beck U. (1986): *Risikogesellschaft*. Suhrkamp, Frankfurt am Main.

Beck U. and Lau C. (Eds.) (2004). *Entgrenzung und Entscheidung.* Edition Zweite Moderne. Suhrkamp, Frankfurt am Main.

Bourdieu P. (1991). Physischer, sozialer und angeeigneter physischer Raum. In Wentz M. (Ed.). Stadt-Räume. Frankfurt am Main.

Bourdieu P. (2000). *Sozialer Raum und Klassen. Lecon sur la lecon.* Zwei Vorlesungen. Suhrkamp, Frankfurt am Main.

Chainey S. and Ratcliffe J. (2005). *GIS and Crime Mapping.* Wiley-Blackwell. West Sussex.

Chamard S. (2010). Routine activities. In McLaughlin E. and Newburn T. (Eds.). *The Sage Handbook of Criminological Theory.* Sage, London.

Clarke R.V. (1999). *Hot Products: Understanding, Anticipating and Reducing Demand for Stolen Goods.* Police Research Series Paper 112. Home Office, London.

Cohen L.E. and Felson M. (1979). Social change and crime rate trends: a routine activity approach. *American Sociological Review,* 44, 588–608.

Crowe T. (2000). *Crime Prevention through Environmental Design: Applications of Architectural Design and Space Management Concepts.* 2nd ed. Butterworth-Heinemann, Boston.

Felson M. and Boba R. (2010). *Crime and Everyday Life.* 4th edition. Sage. Thousand Oaks.

Garland D. (2000). Ideas, institutions and situational crime prevention. In Von Hirsch, A., Garland D. and Wakefield A. (Eds.). *Ethical and Social Perspectives on Situational Crime Prevention.* Hart Publishing, Portland, OR.

Garland D. (2001). *The Culture of Control: Crime and Social Order in Contemporary Society.* University of Chicago Press, Chicago.

Garland D. (2002). Of crime and criminals: the development of criminology in Britain. In Maguire M., Morgan R. and Reiner R. (Eds.), *Oxford Handbook of Criminology,* 3rd ed. Oxford University Press, Oxford.

Giddens A. (1990). *Consequences of Modernity.* Polity Press, Oxford.

Hobbes Th. (1990/1651). *Leviathan.* Ed. Richard Tuck. Cambridge. Cambridge University Press.

Johnston L. and Shearing C. (2003). *Governing Security: Explorations in Policing and Justice.* Routledge, London.

Jones T. and Newburn T. (1998). *Private Security and Public Policing.* Oxford University Press, Oxford.

Lefebvre H. (2000). *La Production de l'Espace.* Editions Anthropos/Economica.

Newman G., Clarke R.V., and Shoham S.G. (Eds.) (1997). *Rational Choice and Situational Crime Prevention: Theoretical Foundations.* Darthmouth-Ashgate, Aldershot.

Park R.E., Burgess E.W., and McKenzie R.D. (1925). *The City.* University of Chicago Press, Chicago.

Shearing C. and Stenning P. (1987). *Private Policing.* Sage, London.

Schneider R.H. and Kitchen T. (2002). *Planning for Crime Prevention: A Transatlantic Perspective.* Routledge, London.

Schroer M. (2006). *Räume, Orte, Grenzen — auf dem Weg zu einer Soziologie des Raumes.* Suhrkamp, Frankfurt am Main.

Simmel G. (1903). The sociology of space. In Frisby D. and Featherstone M., *Simmel on Culture*). Sage, London.

Sutherland E.H. and Cressey D.R. (1960). *Principles of Criminology* (6th edition). Chicago Lippcott. (1st edition: 1924).

Sutton A., Cherney A., and White R. (2008). *Crime Prevention: Principles, Perspectives and Practices*. Cambridge University Press, New York.

United Nations Development Programme. (1994). *New Dimensions of Human Security*. Oxford University Press, New York.

Wakefield A. (2003). *Selling Security*. Willan Publishing, Portland, OR.

Wood J. and Shearing C. (2007). *Imagining Security*. Willan Publishing, Portland, OR.

Wortley R. and Mazerolle L. (Eds.) (2008*). Environmental Criminology and Crime Analysis*. Willan Publishing, Portland, OR.

Zedner L. (2009). *Security. Key Ideas in Criminology Series*. Routledge, Abingdon.

History of Crisis and the Quest for Security

2

GERALD SCHÖPFER

Contents

Security in the ancient world was an undreamed of and unachievable utopia. The nascence of religions and legislation was a fundamental step to improve co-existence within a more peaceful society and to ensure security. We can assume that even in prehistoric times a quest for security against physical violence, extreme weather conditions, and famine was pursued.[1] However, technical skills were minimal, production of goods was not very effective, and rural economies depended on the unpredictable upturns and downturns of the annual harvest cycles. Therefore ancient societies were unable to afford important surpluses they could use to fund a framework of social security.[2]

To a certain extent, the family, the clan, and the neighborhood were able to help when serious threats arose. People commonly had the conviction that fate affected eveyone's life, no one could escape fate, and everyone had to come to terms with his fate.[4] However, until the nineteenth century, living conditions in central Europe were generally very poor for the mainstream of society. Because of the unpredictable fluctuations in agricultural output, society was not immune to collective famine.[3]

Governments attempted to establish some security benefits for the *disadvantaged* people in societies thousands of years ago. The ancient world's public authorities tried to establish social benefits for those who needed them. For example, veterans and the surviving dependents of soldiers killed in action received grants from the Roman state, and the government granted cereal allowances to poor people. At the end of the first century, there were supposedly 320,000 beneficiaries ("plebs frumentaria") of this benefit.[4]

From the Middle Ages until the end of the system of feudal tenure and the establishment of governments, the lord of the manor had the duty to protect his subjects. The system of feudal tenure implied not only the exploitation of subordinated peasants, but also commitments to mutual loyalty and mutual respect. Early forerunners of institutions that supported social security were the extended family, the neighborhood (that led to establishment of rural insurances in Austria), the guild system, and a number of special guilds, for example, that protected against the consequences of bone fractures or fires.

Over the centuries of conducting businesses, producing crafts and artisan products, and participating in trade, the guild system guaranteed members minimum standards of security. For instance, the guilds fixed the wages of workers and the prices of the goods, the numbers of employees, working times, and technology applied in production. They offered subsidiaries to families when members died or fell seriously ill. The union of journeymen ("Gesellenbruderschaften") granted social benefits to members when specific types of damages or losses occurred.

For centuries in the German speaking world, the only support that victims of fires had was provided by public authorities. Security consisted of a certificate attesting to the fire damage. The certificate allowed a family to beg for money, and they had better chances of recouping their losses. Handicapped persons had only the hope that the kindness of their fellow men would help them. For example, Anastasius Sincerus, an exponent of cameralism (the German variety of mercantilism that dominated economic thought in Europe from the fifteenth to eighteenth centuries) demanded that every businessman do his best to avoid damages and to take the measures necessary to guard against future risks.[5] Even in ancient times, the concept of modern insurance existed. A very important example was the "foenus nauticum,"—a special kind of marine insurance (bottomry bond) used in the Roman Empire.

Capitalism and Rational Risk Management

For the development of the modern capitalist market economy, it was necessary to create effective instruments for rational risk assessments. Capitalism owes some of its growth to the willingness of underwriters to bear risks. People have very different ways of dealing with risks and this fundamental psychological fact was the motive for the creation of new instruments on the financial markets.

Two new occupations were critical to the development of the modern economy: the entrepreneur and the bookkeeper. In the old agrarian economy, few people were able to read, write, and calculate. However, a rational economic activity required improvement of existing methods of calculating. It was crucial for Arabic numerals to replace Roman numerals. The Roman use of multiples of I, V, X, L, C, D, and M to represent numbers made it impossible to perform complicated computations such as actuarial calculations.

The influences of the Hindu and Arabic numeral systems led to progress in the areas of navigation, astronomy, and commerce. The core piece of the Hindu–Arabian system was the invention of the cipher null ("cifr" in Arabic). This revolutionized the old Roman system of numerals, because it became every thinkable number of any size simply with ten numerals (0 to 9). In 825 AD, al-Charismi published the first scientific paper on Arabic arithmetic. He was the eponym for calculation rules (algorithms).

In 1202, Leonardo Pisano ("Fibonacci") wrote a book titled *Liber Abaci* in which he demonstrated practical applications for administrative accounting, for the calculation of profit margins and exchanges of money and interest. In 1494, Fra Luca Bartolomeo de Paccioli wrote *Summa de Arithmetica, Geometria, Proportioni et Proportionalitá* and explained double-entry accounting. He also published a preparatory work concerning the quantification of risks.[6]

Gerolamio Cardano wrote a book titled *Liber de Ludi Aleae* in 1585. He wrote about his attempts to devise statistic rules concerning mathematical probability. This was another important milestone in the development of modern risk management.[7] Additional important steps to improving insurance mathematics were achieved by Blaise Pascal who invented efficient calculating machines that were the ancestors of modern computers and by Pierre de Fermat's mathematical research. Both verged on using the theory of probability for economic purposes and for the prediction of losses.[8]

Another important factor was the change of the intellectual environment through the influence of the Age of Enlightenment and the Reformation that brought more maturity and individual responsibility. Protestant ethics pointed out the power of choice and of decision options of individuals. Thriftiness and economic activity gained new significance as factors influencing the futures of individuals. Affluence became an indication of a blessing from God. In Max Weber's important work, *Die Protestantische Ethik und der Geist des Kapitalismus* (1920) it is pointed out that capitalism was implemented earlier in the Protestant countries than in the Catholic-dominated territories, and the spirit of individualism that grew out of the Protestant Revolution explains the reasons for the differences in economic development in the Catholic and Protestant countries.

The Origins of Assurances

For a long time the Catholic faith and superstition were serious obstacles for the implementation of insurance, because events of damage or loss were interpreted as divine punishments. A proposal for fire damage insurance failed because of the fear that such an invention would anger divine predetermination.[9] Thus, the development of insurance was for a long time prevented by religious objections.

In the history of modern insurance the famous coffeehouse of Edward Lloyd (1687) in Tower Street in the center of London played a major role and made it possible to insure against various risks. There were different types of life assurance, ocean marine insurance, assault insurance, assurances against casualties of horses, burglary, and drug consumption (too much rum). It was also possible to purchase insurance to protect feminine virginity. The emerging insurance industry endeavored to improve its own security. For this purpose the development of counter-insurance (insurance purchased by an insurance company from another insurance company as a way of risk management) was very important. The first reinsurance companies arose to protect ocean transport in Italy in the fourteenth century. Sometime after that, Amsterdam and London became the centers of counter-insurance.

In Germany 1846 the first professional reinsurance company, the Kölnische Rückversicherungs-Gesellschaft, was founded. It was followed in 1853 by Aachen Re, in 1857 by Frankfurt Re, in 1863 by Schweizer Rückversicherungsgesellschaft (Swiss Re) and in 1880 by Münchener Rückversicherung (Munich Re). In today's society, counter-insurance is very important for providing security after natural disasters like earthquakes and hurricanes. For example, Hurricane Katrina in the U.S. caused losses exceeding $80 billion.

Development of Modern Social Security

Starting in the Middle Ages, some forms of social security were created for miners because their occupation was extremely dangerous. The German cameralists recognized the importance of social security and developed a lot of new ideas for social facilities.[10]

In the ensuing years in Germany, the Historische Schule and its leader Gustav Friedrich von Schmoller promoted the idea of social assurance. He was one of the most important founders of the Verein für Socialpolitik (1873) that demanded the implementation of social assurances led the German Imperial Chancellor, Fürst Otto von Bismarck, to establish health insurance coverage in 1883. In 1884, casualty insurance followed, and in 1889 old age and disabled persons insurances were established despite a great deal of opposition to establishing these insurances for the old and disabled.

In the following years, the German prototypes of social assurances were cloned in other European countries, particularly by the Austrian–Hungarian monarchy under Prime Minister Eduard Graf Taaffé.

Poverty in an Affluent Society

In comparison with the past, modern society demonstrates considerable improvements in the working environments and implemented safety provisions for workers. Child labor and night work by women were abolished. Pregnant women were assured of special legal protection. Company medical officers and special public surveyors were hired to supervise these new provisions for the benefit of employees. We now enjoy better living conditions than the privileged classes of yesteryear. We can state that in most countries social security is far better than in centuries past, and the average modern citizen is in a comparatively better living situation. However, although we generally live in affluent societies,[11] this does not exclude the existence of poverty even in rich and high-developed countries. Most countries today provide more efficient social safety nets than existed centuries ago.

In summary, we live in better conditions than ever and have more security. However, a general feeling of uncertainty continues to grow. It can be expressed in new expressions such as Weltrisikogesellschaft (global risk society).[12] Also noteworthy is the fact that the general satisfaction of most people has not increased and the naïve belief in progress has vanished despite genuine improvements stemming from the industrial revolution.

In today's world, the average life expectancy in the industrial nations is higher than ever. We live in healthier conditions and have access to more nutritional food than ever. Most countries have very sophisticated food legislations. For example, The Codex Alimentarius Commission* was created in 1963 by the Food and Agriculture Organization (FAO) and the World Health Organization (WHO) of the United Nations to develop food standards to protect consumers. Austria implemented the Codex Alimentarius Austriacus† in 1891 and efforts to enforce it continue.

In spite of the large advances and expansions of transportation activities, road safety has increased and in most countries traffic deaths diminish every

---

* *Codex Alimentarius* in Latin means "food book." It contains a collection of internationally recognized standards, codes of practice, guidelines, and additional recommendations in regard to foods, food production, and food safety.
† Austrian collection of standards and production descriptions for a wide variety of foods.

year. Automobiles are safer and easier to operate. Regular car inspections, traffic and speed monitoring, safer tunnels, improved warning systems, and efficient rescue services have made road conditions safer.

Although we face increasing catastrophic weather and climate risks, we now have better methods of forecasting and are thus better prepared to make provisions for such unpleasant events. In Austria, we know that flood waters normally cause yearly damage of €159 million and can rise as high as €135 billion. Forecasting methods continue to improve, and it is now possible to obtain specific site-related data.[13]

In summary, highly developed technology is generally available today. We have very efficient production systems and prosperity in the developed countries is impressive, but this progress has also brought disadvantages such as the problems of elderly people and regional overpopulation. We face dangers from holocaust through nuclear and biologic weapons or natural disasters. We are confronted with unemployment, inhumane working conditions, and the growing gap between wealthy and poor nations.[14]

Progress and Speculation Provoke Radical Changes and Uncertainties

Since the beginning of time, every economy has always been in a permanent state of change. Joseph A. Schumpeter, a famous economist and political scientist, described the capitalist market economy as a system of "creative destruction."[15] Creative entrepreneurs and innovations took center stage in his economic theory. He highly valued their impacts as promoters of economic progress. The competition in capitalistic markets is also a competition of economic creativity.

An entrepreneur must be both a "homo economicus" and a "homo creativus." He must act according the rules of business administration and also have the creativity to develop new goods or services. According to Schumpeter's innovation theory (1912), which is similar to the idea of Nikolai Kondratiev, a Russian economist, major economic cycles arise from the impetus of basic innovations that provoke technological revolutions that in turn create leading industrial or commercial sectors.[16]

Economic progress, however, does not generate only winners. Throughout economic history, a lot of losers were unable to keep up with change. For instance Colin Clark[17] and Walt Whitman Rostow[18] tried to describe the different economic stages of developing economies. Numerous theories attempt to explain business cycles and periodic economic crises.[19]

The basis of technical innovation and forward-looking large-scale enterprises was the growth of modern equity markets. The facility of risk diversification raised the willingness to take risks, thus releasing energies and activating a market economy. Joint-stock companies created a broadly based financial foundation. One of their antecedents was the so-called Commune (founded 1415)[20] and the Innerberger Hauptgewerkschaft (an alpine mining company located in the Styria region of Austria) in 1625. Ore mining and iron processing were very expensive. The financial bases of the Austrian company[21] were the Kuxe (mine share certificates whose values varied) bought by merchants, noblemen, and monasteries.

The first modern joint-stock company was the Dutch East India Company (Vereenigde Oost-Indische Compagnie or VOC) founded in 1602.[22] The States-General of the Netherlands granted VOC a monopoly for colonial trading in Asia and thus created one of the first multinational corporations. The newly developing companies strengthened capitalism, but some uncertainties remained within the capitalist market economy because of the striving for high profit margins that also entailed high risk.

Short Remarks about the Very Long History of Speculation

During past centuries, a lot of serious crises arose from similar processes provoked by gigantic speculation. During the so-called Kipper und Wipperzeit (tipper and see-saw time) related to a financial crisis during the Thirty Years' War, some city–states in the Holy Roman Empire debased their currency by manipulating coins in circulation. The first stock exchange crash happened during the Dutch Golden Age. During "tulip mania," the prices of tulip bulbs reached unimaginable levels, and asset prices deviated far from real intrinsic values.[23] At the peak of this economic bubble, special tulip bulbs sold for more than 10 times the average annual wage of a qualified skilled worker. In 1637, the speculative bubble collapsed and a lot of adventurers lost their money.

The Darién scheme was a venturesome project developed by the Kingdom of Scotland around 1700. The aim of the venture was to found a colony on the Isthmus of Panama. The catastrophic failure of company meant it was unable to honor its shares and Scotland was almost ruined. The result was weakened Scottish political resistance to the Act of Union.[24]

Twenty years later, the Scottish economist and gambler, Johan Law (1671–1729) shocked the contemporary financial world. Under King Louis XV, he was appointed France's Controller General of Finances. In 1716, he founded the Banque Générale that initiated the use of paper money. The main assets of this bank consisted of government bills and government-accepted notes. In 1717, Law bought the Mississippi Company and established a joint-stock trading company called the Compagnie d'Occident.[25]

Law was named the company's director and the French government granted the company a trade monopoly in the West Indies and North

America. The company absorbed rival trading companies. and the bank continued to issue more notes. This led to widespread speculation in the shares of the company. In 1720, the French had to admit that the issued paper notes were not covered by coinage. The Mississippi bubble burst at the end of 1720 and Law was forced to flee France.[26]

In the nineteenth century, the first worldwide economic crisis occurred. The Panic of 1857 in the U.S. was caused by extensive speculation in the sector of railway construction. The Ohio Life Insurance Company became bankrupt, and the ensuing financial panic spread over the whole world. The global economic crisis of 1873 that erupted in Austria with the crash of the Vienna Stock Exchange was triggered by speculation. It spread through most of Europe and North America, and was followed by the Gründerkrise (long depression) that continued until 1896.

The most famous—and most severe—worldwide economic crisis started with the crash of the stock market in New York on Black Tuesday, October 29, 1929. From there, it spread throughout the world and lasted until the late 1930s. Some striking economic crises also occurred in recent history. In 1990, the Japanese asset price bubble collapsed. A decade later, in April 2000, the speculative dot-com bubble* burst when the technology-heavy NASDAQ Composite Index fell.

Currently we are witnessing a global financial and economic crisis that started in the U.S. in 2007 as a sub-prime mortgage crisis. Recognized as the worst financial slump since the Great Depression of 1929, this economic crisis was caused by a liquidity shortfall in the American banking system.[27] The financial crisis quickly influenced the entire economy and resulted in declines in economic production and widespread bankruptcies. Large financial institutions collapsed, and the bailouts of banks by national governments became necessary. Downturns in stock markets around the world followed and unemployment rose.

A special problem of the modern world economy is that the different markets are closely connected, but a disconnectedness of financial markets and commodity markets creates new types of risks. The uncertainties and the volatilities in currency exchange rates have led to the creation of new instruments in the finance markets, for example, forward exchange transactions. To hedge simple risk in international trading, many different derivatives have been developed. One irony of the modern global economy is that some speculators abuse these instruments that were developed to provide more stability in the international market. As a result, dealings in the futures segments of financial markets are even more unstable.[28]

---

* The "dot-com bubble" (also IT bubble or TMT bubble) was a speculative trend marked by the founding and often spectacular failures of Internet-based companies commonly called "dot-coms."

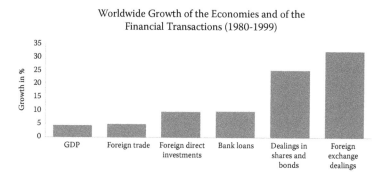

Figure 2.1 Annual statistics of Bank for International Settlements and International Monetary Fund.

Across the board, the volume of international trade has seen greater increases than the volume of the global production. This means that the connection between national economies is growing faster than their gross domestic products. Even faster growth has occurred in foreign investments, bank loans, and equity and bond transactions, but foreign exchange dealings have shown the most impressive growth. This is a very disturbing fact because it indicates exuberant growth of speculation (see Figure 2.1). In general, modern financial markets have much larger extensions and are far more important than markets that produce goods.[29]

Today we have efficient risk management against general business risks, credit risks, the risks of fixed assets, underwriting risks, and others, but uncertainty still exists in our global economy. Most representatives of classical economics, like Adam Smith, David Ricardo, Thomas Malthus, and John Stuart Mill, did not worry much about economic crises because they were convinced that free markets could regulate themselves. We can cite many examples showing that crises can also have positive impacts via regeneration and strengthening of the economy through new initiatives.

Additional Reasons for Economic Crises

Besides the economic crises caused by speculation, other dangers threaten the world economy. Headlines about global warming and pollution from dusts, emissions, and other sources are indicators of environmental crisis. We are also faced with possible shortages of nonrenewable resources, and we already reached the peak in oil demand that indicates we may not be able to meet future needs for oil. Another significant danger for the economy is the increase in numbers of white collar crimes.

Crime comes in all forms. Murders, burglaries, muggings, and drug dealings are considered important kinds of crime that can affect our security, but in reality white-collar crime is responsible for the greatest damages.[30]

In 1960, the German Minister for economic affairs stated: "Konjunktur ist nicht unser Schicksal, Konjunktur ist unser Wille" (Economic cycles are not our fate, economic cycles are our will).[31] Today we are more realistic and optimism has vanished. We now realize that most problems of disadvantageous business cycles cannot be solved through the instruments of a Keynesian economic policy. The current anxiety related to the future of the European system of social security has made security a crucial theme for election campaigns.

The social structures in Europe (families, working environments, and population age structures) have changed fundamentally. Modern populations include increasing numbers of unmarried people, single parents, unemployed workers, and aged residents.[32] As an aging society, Europe is confronted with serious challenges to its global economy. Its former status as the world's factory and its long-lasting historical supremacy in science, economy, and engineering are continually questioned.

Another reason for more global insecurity is the growing gap between the rich and the poor countries. The gap constitutes a breeding ground for international terrorism.

The quest for more security is understandable, but too much security can generate a nightmare. There is always a tradeoff between security and liberty. Security research led to development of devices that allow debriefing of electronic data, the evaluation of biometric distinguishing marks, and surveillance at workplaces and public places. But we must acknowledge that these instruments can be abused if they fall into the wrong hands.[33]

Types of Risks

In any discussion of economic risks and crisis, we must differentiate endogenous and exogenous onsets. An example of the former is when a risk or crisis starts within a company, for example, because of poor management. An exogenous cause comes from outside, for example, a war or natural disaster. Another distinction is related to the potential insurability or lack of insurability of a specific risk.

We can also differentiate the different types of risks, for example, natural, technical, environmental, and other types. These characteristics distinguish local limited or ubiquitous crises, short-term or long-term crises, slowly developing or suddenly arising crises (ad hoc crunch), and reversible or irreversible crises.

What are the symptoms for possible business risks? In various departments of an enterprise, possible risks are often obvious. For example, in the area of human resources, we can see problems such as personnel turnover and increasing amounts of sick time as indicators of problems within an organization and take action to correct the problems.

In the financial area of a business, stagnant business volume, decreasing returns on investments, increased long-term debt levels, and decreasing net assets are disconcerting symptoms of a "sick" business and should create concern. In the management of materials, we can note sinking rates of inventory turnover or increasing delivery delays as indicators of a business at risk for failure. If an organization structure is characterized by vague responsibility assignments, unclear allocations of rights and duties, and a lack of project planning and control, the business enterprise is at risk for failure. In a production area, issues such as diminishing production, decreasing percentage utilization, escalating error probability, increasing average fixed cost, management has cause for alarm. In the distributive trades, a decreasing market share, decreasing volumes of orders, reduced price elasticity, diminishing rates of inventory turnover, and increasing customer complaints indicate that an enterprise is in poor health.

Generally we can state that in modern business management, enterprise management knowledge is very important because know-how is the most important production factor in determining success in the world of business in this society.[34] Companies must counter the risk of fluctuation and the loss of knowledge to prevent competitors from gaining advantages. As an example, in the areas of securities management and loans, Deutsche Bank AG lost within a very short time about $60 billion worth of invested capital because the New York City Employee Retirement System (NYCERS) drifted to other investment companies. The reason was the migration of former top managers of Deutsche Bank to other investment groups.

Conclusions

Today, a number of legal and other types of precautions are available to help avoid business crises. However, based on the experiences of recent years, we must accept the fact that many boards of directors and external credit assessment institutions failed in their functions as controlling bodies. We must also understand that an entrepreneur is not a perfect working engine, but rather a human being with faults who is subject to making mistakes. A successful entrepreneur requires professional competence, intellectual capacity, creativity, resourcefulness (e.g., finding market niches), ability to handle complexity, originality, and flexibility, along with the powers of imagination and vision.

In reality, in today's world, we are confronted with management mistakes, mismanagement, waste, fraud, corruption, and other illegal behaviors, along with insufficient equity bases and other problems that are hard to control. As a result, we face increased risks to our personal security and the overall security of our global society.[35] In addition, the blending of practices that fall between legal and criminal behavior is generally a very smooth transition process.[36]

We must realize that a dynamic economy without risk is not possible. The Soviets tried to eliminate the economic uncertainties, but their planned economy destroyed the hope of any economic and social progress. Even sophisticated methods of market research cannot prevent errors. Entrepreneurs always face uncertainty. An entrepreneur who tries to avoid every risk will have to take the highest risk as noted in a Chinese proverb: "High risk, high profit." Finally let us quote Carl Amery (1922–2005): "Risk is the bow wave of success".[37]

References

1. Rosenzweig, R. (1998). *Das Streben nach Sicherheit*, Marburg: Metropolis.
2. Metz, K.H. (2008). *Die Geschichte der sozialen Sicherheit*, Stuttgart: Kohlhammer, p. 17.
3. Abel, W. (1978). *Agrarkrisen und Agrarkonjunktur in Mitteleuropa*, vom 13. bis zum 19. Hamburg: Parey.
4. Metz, K.H. (2008). *Die Geschichte der sozialen Sicherheit*, Stuttgart: Kohlhammer, p. 14.
5. Sincerus, A. (1717). *Projekt der Oeconomie in Form einer Wissenschaft*. Ein sorgfältiger Ökonom stehet auf seiner Hut /und hat überall ein wachsames Auge/ damit er beyzeiten allen sich hervorthuenden Schäden und Unglücks-Fällen/so viel immer möglich/vorbeugen möge. Frankfurt: Renger, p. 5.
6. Schöpfer, G. (1989). Zu den Commercien erziehen. In Schöpfer, G. (Ed.), *Menschen & Münzen & Märkte, Katalog der Steirischen Landesausstellung*. Judenburg: Podmenik, p. 113–121.
7. Hoffmann, T.S. (2007). *Philosophie in Italien. Eine Einführung in 20 Porträts*. Wiesbaden: Marixverlag; Krischer, T. (1994). Interpretationen zum Liber de ludo aleae. In Eckhard Keßler (Ed.). *Girolamo Cardano: Philosoph–Naturforscher–Arzt*. Wiesbaden: Harrassowitz, pp. 207–217.
8. Schmidt-Biggemann, W. (1999). *Blaise Pascal*. München: Beck.
9. Schöpfer, G. (1976). *Sozialer Schutz im 16–18 Jahrhundert*, Graz: Leykam, p. 82.
10. Small, A.W. (1909). *The Cameralists: The Pioneers of German Social Policy*, Chicago: University Press.
11. Galbraith, J.K. (1958). *The Affluent Society*, Boston: Houghton Mifflin.
12. Cf. Holzinger, M., May, S., and Wiebke, P. (2010). *Weltrisikogesellschaft als Ausnahmezustand*, Weilerswist: Velbrück.

13. Cf. Steininger, K.W., Steinreiber, C., and Ritz, C. (Eds.). (2005). *Extreme Wetterereignisse und ihre wirtschaftlichen Folgen. Anpassung, Auswege und politische Forderungen betroffener Wirtschaftsbranchen.* Berlin: Springer.
14. Cf. Münkler, H., Bohlender, M., and Meurer, S. (Eds.). (2010). *Sicherheit und Risiko. Über den Umgang mit Gefahr im 21. Jahrhundert.* Bielefeld: Transcript.
15. McCraw, T.K. (2007). *Prophet of Innovation: Joseph Schumpeter and Creative Destruction,* Cambridge: Harvard University Press.
16. Schumpeter, J.A. (1912). *Theorie der wirtschaftlichen Entwicklung,* Leipzig,: Duncker & Humblot.
17. Clark, C. (1940). *Conditions of Economic Progress,* London : Macmillan.
18. Rostow, W.W. (1960). *The Stages of Economic Growth: A Non-Communist Manifesto,* Cambridge: Cambridge University Press.
19. Schumpeter, J.A. (1961). *Konjunkturzyklen,* Göttingen: Vandenhoeck & Ruprecht.
20. Tremel, F. (1954). *Der Frühkapitalismus in Innerösterreich,* Graz: Leykam, p. 101.
21. Tremel, F. (1969). *Wirtschafts und Sozialgeschichte Österreichs.* Wien: Franz Deuticke, pp. 256–257.
22. Kindleberger, C.P. (1984). *A Financial History of Western Europe.* London: George Allen & Unwin, p. 48; Israel, J.I. (1991). *The Anglo-Dutch Moment.* New York: Cambridge University Press, pp. 407–438.
23. Kindleberger, C.P. (1978). *Manias, Panics and Crashes. A History of Financial Crises,* New York: Basic Books.
24. Furber, H. (1976). *Rival Empires of Trade in the Orient 1600–1800.* Minneapolis: Oxford University Press, p. 217.
25. Devine, T.M. (2003). *Scotland´s Empire 1600-1815,* London: Allan Lane, p. 44.
26. Fry, Michael (2001). *The Scottish Empire,* Edinburgh: Tuckwell Press., pp. 19–30.
27. Buchanan, J. (1997). *Frozen Desire. An Inquiry into the Meaning of Money,* London: Picador, pp. 127–151.
28. Galbraith, J.K. (2010). *Eine kurze Geschichte der Spekulation,* Frankfurt am Main: Eichborn, pp. 48–55.
29. Thurow, L. (2004). *Die Zukunft der Weltwirtschaft,* Frankfurt am Main: Campus Verlag.
30. Coleman, J.W. (2002). *The Criminal Elite. Understanding White-Collar Crime.* 5th ed. New York: St. Martin's Press.
31. Deutsche Bundesbank. (1998). *Fünfzig Jahre Deutsche Mark, Notenbank und Währung in Deutschland seit 1948,* München: Beck.
32. Carigiet, E. (1998). *Gesellschaftliche Solidarität. Prinzipien, Perspektiven und Weiterentwicklung der sozialen Sicherheit,* Basel: Helbing & Lichtenhahn, p. 1.
33. Cf. Siebert, H. (Ed.). (1998). *Redesigning Social Security,* Tübingen: Mohr Siebeck, p.vii.
34. Cf. Eberhard, H., et al. (Eds.). (2009). *Constitutional Limits to Security. Proceedings of 4th International Constitutional Law,* Baden-Baden: Nomos.
35. Goold, B.J. and Lazarus, L (Eds.). (2007). *Security and Human Rights,* Portland, OR: Hart Publishing.
36. Cf. Schmid, N. (1980). *Banken zwischen Legalität und Kriminalität. Zur Wirtschaftskriminalität im Bankwesen.* Heidelberg: Kriminalistik Verlag.
37. Schmidt, K. *Der IT Security Manager,* München: Hauser, p. 12.

Development toward a "Security Society" The Case of Austria

3

MAXIMILLIAN EDELBACHER
GILBERT NORDEN

Contents

Introduction: Different Views of Societies

Modern societies try to describe themselves and their characteristics by using impressive titles (Prisching 2003, 13). Some choose terms that define economic structure (Service Society); terms that express the end of an epoch (Post-Industrial Society, Post-Growth Society); and terms that attempt to cover up the nature of a complex society. Among the many examples are the Working Society, Achieving Society, Performance Society, Education Society, Life-Style Society, Consumer Society, Leisure Society, Thrill-Seeking Society, Fun Society, Hedonistic Society, Mass-Culture Society, Immigration Society, Multi-Cultural Society, Pluralistic Society, Secularised Society, Creative Society, Communication Society, Media Society, Film Society, E-Society, Knowledge Society, Scientific Society, Progress Society, Organization Society, Therapy Society, Demanding Society, Multi-Optional Society, 24-Hour

Society, Mc-Society, One-Child-Society, Egocentric Society, Individualistic Society, Autistic Society, Elbow Society, Risk-Society, Prevention Society, and, finally, as noted in the title of this chapter, Security Society.

What does *Security Society* really mean? Which social changes, which changes of the system of internal security justify the name? Starting with these questions, we will explain the concept of a Security Society and illustrate it on the basis of developments in Austria, but first we define *security*.

Definition of *Security*

The word originated from the Latin *securus*, meaning *sine cura*, or free from all sorrows. It can be understood only from a negative view, that is, the absence of danger or fear of danger (Magenheimer, 2001, 10). Thus already in 1765 an Austrian scholar named Joseph Freiherr von Sonnenfels remarked, "Security is a state we have nothing to fear" (Die Sicherheit ist ein Zustand, worin man nichts zu fürchten hat) (Sonnenfels, 1819, § 12, 14). A more accurate definition describes security as "the absence or avoidance of insecurity. That means the absence or avoidance of threats, danger, and of fear of insecurities" (Sicherheit ist die Abwesenheit bzw. Vermeidung von Unsicherheit, das heißt von Bedrohung, Gefährdung sowie Furcht vor diesen Unsicherheiten) (Nohlen & Schultze, 2005, 837). Of course, an enormous variety of possible dangers and threats exist. Therefore, as Spreen (2010, 192, following Kaufmann, 1970) formulates, the word is a kind of "container term" (Behälterbegriff) in which different political and societal order ideas and understandings of security find their places.

These different understandings will not be discussed in this chapter; they will be mentioned only as examples of a broader understanding of security that serves as the basis of human security (concentration on the individual as the object of security policy instead of the earlier concentration on the state).

What exactly does human security represent? The 1994 *Human Development Report* of the United Nations Development Programme describes it very bluntly: "Human security is a child who did not die, a disease that did not spread, a job that was not cut, an ethnic tension that did not explode, a dissident who was not silenced. Human security is not a concern with weapons. It is a concern with human life and dignity" (UNDP, 1994, 22). As a result *human security* became a common catch phrase in the field of political science in the late 1990s. At about the same time, *Security Society* was introduced in scientific discussions.

Security Society Concept

Aldo Legnaro created the *Security Society* term in 1997, shortly after Lyon (1994) and Lindenberg & Schmid-Semisch (1995) created *Surveillance Society* and *Controlling Society*, respectively. Legnaro's *Security Society* term closely followed Beck's *Risk Society* concept, which can be briefly characterized: Human beings have always been exposed to risks such as natural disasters; these risks have been perceived as produced by non-human forces. Modern Societies, however, are exposed to risks that are the result of the modernization process itself, e.g., industrial pollution, newly discovered illnesses, change of climate, nuclear catastrophes (Beck 1986). These man-made risks do not stop at the borders of national states.

Beck (2007) speaks about a World Risk Society in which, as a result of globalization, risks are no longer controlled by borders because national borders have disappeared. However, national states try to implement international strategies to protect inner security. The consequence is that new structures of control mechanisms are emerging. The concept of a Security Society starts at this point, but also underlines an important characteristic of a so-named society: the development of new forms of state control mechanisms and also new forms of social control in everyday life. Hence the particularity of a Security Society is that state actors and private actors are involved steadily and increasingly in the production of security. Surveillance is intended to protect the state in a narrow sense, but also controls activities of all citizens. Citizens in turn want to minimize their risks. As a result, security is not only the task of the state, but a permanent societal effort pursued in everyday life. This notion is expressed in German in the following way:

> ...dass nicht nur staatliche, sondern allmählich und in stetig zunehmendem Ausmaß auch private Akteure an der Produktion von Sicherheit teilnehmen, dass die Überwachung nicht nur dem Staatsschutz im engeren Sinne gilt, sondern Aktivitätskontrollen von allen Bürgern – tendenziell durch alle Bürger – mit dem Ziel der Risikominimierung für alle angestrebt werden und dass schließlich die Produktion von Sicherheit nicht nur eine staatliche Aufgabe ist, sondern eine permanente gesellschaftliche Anstrengung, ein Règime des täglichen sozialen Lebens. (Legnaro, 1997, 271)

These considerations were continued by Singelnstein & Stolle (2006, 15) to the point that in a Security Society the striving for comprehensive security represents a value by itself. Attempts to realize this value seem to be economically profitable, because enormous amounts of money are invested into research and development of security technologies and security-relevant education and training. Security businesses and industries continue to grow.

When we speak of Security Society today, in addition to the growth of commercial security efforts and the development of international strategies, the following developments are thought to justify speaking about a fundamental change in the field of inner security (Cf. Groenemeyer, 2010, 13):

Omnipresence of dangers to security
Changes of logic of political and state security production
New configurations of public spaces especially by technization of social control

The application of these changes and developments will be illustrated more specifically by explaining activities in Austria.

Growth of Security Business, Establishment of Academic Training Courses in Security Management, and Institutionalization of Research in the Field of Security

The fall of the Iron Curtain in Europe in 1989 opened the borders to legal and illegal immigrants and thus led to a wave of imported crime. This crime wave and the start of cutbacks in police services a few years after the fall of the Iron Curtain were a turning point for the security industry in Austria.

The history of private security goes back to 1904 when the first private firm in Austria was founded, but it played only a marginal role. After the fall of the Iron Curtain, private security became an important partner of the police and expanded steadily. The expansion increased after 2000 due to cutbacks in police personnel and further cutbacks in police services. Since then, the sales figures and the number of employees in security businesses and industries have doubled (Löff, 2010, 84). The percentage of these employees among all persons working in the public and private security sectors has increased from 16% in 2000 to about 38% today.

The total investment of funds in security activities in 2009 was about €847 million. Of this sum, €220 million was spent for security engineering mechanisms, (locks, secure doors, safes, strong rooms), €280 million for security technology mechanics (electronic locks, secure electronic alarm systems, closed circuit television, access control devices, fire alarm systems), and €347 million for security services.[*] The services include patrols (for example of shopping areas and ski runs), observing customers in shops, doorkeepers, elevator security, factory protection, transport of money and of valuables, transport of hazardous or heavy goods, maintaining order at public events

---

[*] Data from SecureLINE SicherheitsGmbH, Vienna.

such as soccer matches and fairs, house protection when owners are on holidays, personal guards, searches for missing persons, private investigations, gathering of evidence, surveillance, controlling activities of employees who are away sick, defense against wiretapping, copying, and destruction of electronic data, alarm monitoring centers, risk analysis, and security advisory and special training programs. In addition, services are offered which have been outsourced by the public sector because of economic considerations.

This outsourcing started in the early 1990s, when the then Austrian Federal Minister of the Interior declared that all security issues could not be covered any longer by the police. In 1994, the security checks at the Vienna International Airport were privatized (Stückler, 2010). Thus, according to the then Federal Minister of the Interior, forty police officers have been axed because the security checks by private firms are financed through a passenger fee. Since 1998 security checks at the airports at Linz (Upper Austria), Graz (Styria), Klagenfurt (Carinthia), Innsbruck (Tyrol), and Salzburg have been outsourced to private companies. In addition, the security checks at justice courts and at the conferences of the Organization for Security and Cooperation in Europe (OSCE) in Vienna have been privatized since the middle of the 1990s. Not only these security checks have been outsourced. The air emergency was conferred on the Austrian Automobile, Motorcycle and Touring Club (*Osterreicher Automobil, Motoraa und Touring Club* or OAMTC). Other public services are now offered by private security firms, for example, surveillance of public spaces ordered by communities in Tulln, Krems, and Perchtoldsdorf (Lower Austria); administration of asylum-seekers' hostels; protection of embassies; car registration; regulation of traffic in road construction areas; surveillance of private parking; control of toll roads; and ticket control on public transportation (Löff, 2010, 84).

As a result of this expansion and diversification of activities of private security firms in recent years, academic training in security management has been established. At the Danube University in Krems, two master courses were started. One deals with general security issues, the other with fire safety. At the University of Applied Science in Wiener Neustadt (Lower Austria) and at the University of Applied Science Campus Vienna (Vienna), bachelor and master courses in security management were established. Another master course in security management is planned at the Sigmund Freud Private University in Vienna in cooperation with Hungarian private universities. This course may be held in Kittsee (Burgenland).

The Sigmund Freud Private University established an Institute for Security Research which is completing a feasibility study on the "Development of an Austrian Center for Comprehensive Security Research."* This study is

* http://www.sfi-sfu/eu (March 3, 2011).

conducted within the framework of the KIRAS research program. *KIRAS is* derived from two Greek words (*kirkos* = circle and *asphaleia* = security) and is the name of a national security research program established in Austria in 2005 (see Chapter 4 by Alexander Siedschlag). The program became a model for national security research programs of other member states of the European Union (Weinandy, 2009, 54).

Implementation of International
Strategies for Inner Security

Austria tried to counter the increase of border crossing crime very early after the fall of the Iron Curtain by creating a security belt around the country. Security partnerships were built with neighboring countries. In 2000, Austria as an EU member country joined with non-EU member countries, namely, Czech Republic, Hungary, Slovenia, Slovakia, and Poland to create the Middle European Security Partnership (or Salzburg Group named for the city where it was founded). The goal was to achieve with these countries the same cooperation standards already in place with Germany (Bavaria).

Later Bulgaria and Romania became member countries of the Salzburg-Group and Croatia became a member with observatory status. After these countries became EU member countries, with the exception of Croatia, the intensity of cooperation in security matters increased further. The increase was absolutely necessary because of the intensified economic cooperation and the four great freedoms in the EU: freedom of traffic of (1) persons, (2) goods, (3) services, and (4) money transfers. The intensified cooperation in security issues in the EU was accompanied by the foundation and strengthening of other different European institutions such as:

Frontex—The name is a contraction of the French phrase, Frontières extèrieures. The agency coordinates cooperation among member states in the field of border security. It is also charged with ensuring that the external borders of the so-called Schengen zone remain permeable and efficient for bona fide travellers while also serving as effective barriers to cross-border crime. With 42,672 km of external sea borders and 8,826 km of land borders, the Schengen free-movement area covers twenty-five countries (including a number of non-EU member states) enabling free internal travel for nearly half a billion people across the continent.

Europol—This European police organization coordinates police activities to combat transnational organized crime, terrorism, illegal trafficking of weapons, drugs, child pornography, and other criminal activities.

OLAF—This is the European anti-fraud office (OLAF is an acronym for Office de Lutte Anti-Fraude). It was created to fight fraud affecting the EU budget, corruption, and other irregular activities including misconduct within the European institutions.

Eurojust—This European unit focuses on cooperation in justice matters by coordinating transnational legal cooperation related to penal procedures.

Austria is represented in all these institutions and the Austrian strategy of building security partnerships with non-EU member countries in the area to fight crime is applied by the EU, which tries to build or extend a security belt around its territory.

Omnipresence of Security Dangers and Participation in Implementation of Security

From a population view, the increase of crime in recent decades is a very important development based on a survey conducted in Austria. The survey contained the following question.

Even if you have not experienced by yourself a period of time you have an imagination about this period of time just by feeling. If you compare the time 40 years ago, the time of around 1970, with the time today, in your opinion, what is different today? (Auch wenn man eine Zeit selbst noch nicht erlebt hat, besitzt man von ihr ja eine gefühlsmäßige Vorstellung. Wenn Sie einmal die heutige Zeit mit den Verhältnissen vor rund 40 Jahren, also ungefähr 1970, vergleichen: Was ist Ihrer Meinung nach heute anders als damals?)

In response to the question, both elderly persons who remembered 1970 and younger people most frequently answered that crime increased greatly (Die Kriminalität hat stark zugenommen) (IMAS, 2009). Along with this perception, the level of social fear of crime is relatively high compared with the actual level of victimization in Austria (social fear of crime is related to the perception of crime as a problem in society, regardless of personal impact, see Chapter 4 by Alexander Siedschlag). Significantly contributing to this high level of social fear of crime is the political and media indignation about the development of crime especially by non-Austrians.

The resulting indignation of citizens resulted in the creation of a neighborhood watch organization called proNEIGHBOR (proNACHBAR). Viennese citizens founded this association and adopted a slogan: Crime concerns everybody, not only victims (Kriminalität geht uns alle an und nicht erst als

Betroffene). The goal of the association is to increase sensitivity of citizens against burglaries and other crimes in the neighborhood and prevent them. The association cooperates with the police. Police itself—may not be as intensive as in some other EU-countries (Czapska/Stangl 2007, 53)—tries to get citizens and representatives of firms in the boat of their own crime prevention projects (e.g., area-patrol officers, contacting-officers). Firms try to motivate their employees to participate in security education and act as "security-employees".

Changes of Logic Surrounding Political and State Security Production

The criminological literature discusses the change of paradigm in the field of crime control in countries of the Western World. The paradigm of resocialization and reintegration of offenders (the penal welfare state) has dominated security thinking for three decades. However, according to Garland (2001 and 2008), this model was replaced by the idea of protecting society by avoiding situations leading to crimes and by implementing a law-and-order strategy.

This new security philosophy no longer follows the principle of fighting social causes of crime and responding to the personalities of offenders. Instead, it proposes situational prevention of crime and the exclusion of criminals from society by imposing stricter punishments including imprisonment. In this connection Garland (2008, 142) speaks of a "strategy of punitive segregation" or "punitive turn." This change in philosophy and practice was observed for the first time in the U.S., then in Great Britain and other European countries including Germany (Sack, 2010).

Austria too adopted a tendency toward increased punishment although somewhat later than other countries did so. This tendency became clearly visible as a consequence of the political turn that took place in Austria in 2000. Although the conservative People's Party (Österreichische Volkspartei or ÖVP) lost the elections in 1999, a deal between the leader of this party, Wolfgang Schüssel, and the leader of the right-wing populist Freedom Party (Freiheitliche Partei Österreichs or FPÖ), Jörg Haider, allowed a government to be formed by both parties in 2000 and immediately the security policy was changed.

Whereas as late as in 1999, diversion measures for adults had been introduced into the penal code, in 2000, a "Law and Order" policy was initiated. The number of arrested persons per 100,000 inhabitants in Austria increased from 85 on September 1, 2001, to 106 on February 1, 2005. A group of experts commented on this increase of the rate of arrests as a development never before witnessed in the history of democratic Austria. The increase was a consequence of a policy reducing the possibilities for (premature) prison release, increasing trial custody requirements, and imposing (longer) imprisonments. These practices were supported by corresponding law changes.

For example, the quantities of hard drugs that distinguished drug dealing from drug use were reduced, and the principle of therapy instead of punishment was applied less frequently. Life imprisonment was introduced for special drug offenses and penalties for drug-related offenses were increased. Provisions of the penal code (Strafgesetzbuch or StGB) concerning terrorism (especially after 9/11), organized criminal activities, and sexual crimes were strengthened. Furthermore, the upper age limit of the juvenile penal law that includes special treatment of juvenile offenders and measures of diversion was lowered from nineteen to eighteen years and the Juvenile Court of Vienna was closed. This court (existing since 1928 and abolished only during the rule of the Nazis between 1938 and 1945) had been for the conservatives and right-wing populists a symbol of a progressive law. Since the closure of the court, juvenile justice policy functions only within the system of ordinary justice and all its disadvantages apply to juvenile offenders.

Besides abolishing the separate juvenile justice system and reforming the penal code and drug laws, the criminal procedural law (Strafprozessordnung or StPO) was reformed by changing the roles of judges, prosecutors, and police. The former investigative judge system was eliminated, and the prosecutor's service took the leading roles in investigations. The next target of reform was the police organization. As a proposed plan to combine the Federal Ministry of the Interior and the Federal Ministry of Defence into the Federal Ministry of Security did not succeed, in 2002, the Ministry was reorganized otherwise.

A lot of public servants in the Ministry lost their managerial functions and they appealed to the independent Senate at the Federal Chancellery that ruled that the reformers violated laws in forty of the seventy-five cases. Although the public servants lost their management jobs, they had to be paid the same salaries they earned earlier. These decisions did not stop the reform of police functions, and the reorganization continued in Vienna. Each of Vienna's twenty-three districts had an individual police organization of uniformed and criminal police. Uniformed police districts were reduced from twenty-three to fourteen and criminal districts from twenty-three to only five.

A so-called "Century Reform Plan" was implemented in 2005 and involved unification of the police and the gendarmerie. Since the time of the Austrian–Hungarian monarchy, the gendarmerie operated in rural areas and the police worked in the cities. Both groups were combined into a single police organization. New uniforms (European dark blue) and a new design for police cars were created to give the new organization a new image. Along with these cosmetic measures was a strong move to centralize, hierarchize, and militarize the police system.

In addition to the organizational changes, the technical capacities and enforcement powers of the police were expanded. For example, in 2006, undercover investigations and video and audio recording were permitted even in the absence of concrete suspicion. Finally, in 2011, under a social democratic and conservative coalition government and according to the guidelines of the EU, the preservation of data (Vorratsdatenspeicherung) from mobile and fixed-line telephones, emails, and Internet activity was allowed to increase the effectiveness of criminal investigations.

Furthermore, the possibilities for situational prevention of crime were improved. One example was the creation of safe areas (Schutzzonen) around schools and public areas—like the Karlsplatz in Vienna and Rapoldi Park in Innsbruck—from which the police can order the removal of suspected drug addicts and dealers.

New Configurations of Public Spaces by Technization of Social Control

For the reasons cited above, situational crime prevention measures are used more frequently. One example of a technical measure is videotaping using closed circuit television (CCTV). Great Britain led the way, and the rest of Europe followed in the mid 1980s. In Austria, CCTV is commonly used by both private and public institutions. The Austrian police started using it in 2005, long after city officials and private persons and firms started to use the technique.

The first police cameras were installed in the parking area of Shopping City South (Shopping City Süd or SCS) in Vösendorf (Lower Austria) and in the area of Schwedenplatz (a hot spot of drug crime) in Vienna. It followed the installation of police CCTV in the underground Kärntnertorpassage near Karlsplatz where drug addicts and dealers were common, at the Westbahnhof (rail station) where drunks, beggars, and prostitutes appeared regularly, both in Vienna. Other criminal hotspots throughout Austria were also equipped with police cameras, e.g., in Klagenfurt, Villach, Linz, Graz, Innsbruck, Salzburg, Wiener Neustadt, and Schwechat/Vienna International Airport.

Private installations of CCTV are now common in public transportation facilities, parking garages, churches, museums, shopping centers, shopping malls, stores, banks, post offices, casinos, and other commercial properties. CCTV is also in use at the entrances of twenty-two communal residential buildings in Vienna. In these buildings, altogether 2,800 cameras have been installed. The total number of cameras installed in the whole of Austria is not known. However, the Society for Data Protection (Gesellschaft für

Datenschutz) estimates the number at about a million (that would be one surveillance camera per eight citizens).

The increasing number of CCTVs in use in Austria has been documented, but the extent of their success in preventing crime remains unanswered. In Great Britain, a number of studies have examined this question. A meta-analysis of twenty-two CCTV projects showed that in half of the cases crime was reduced, in a quarter of the cases crime increased, and in the remainder no effects could be registered (Welsh & Farrington, 2002). In another meta-analysis, Gill and Spriggs (2005) found that of the fourteen projects they examined, only one showed a decrease in crime that was statistically significant and might plausibly be related to CCTV. Many of the other projects showed increases in crime.

Likewise, the result of a study in Austria revealed that the number of bank robberies increased between 2001 and 2006, although banks were covered 100% by CCTVs (Trojanow & Zeh, 2010, 61, 155, footnote 61). Conversely, data published by the police and other non-bank CCTV-users showed a clear decrease of crime due to the use of CCTVs. For example. the Wiener Linien (Vienna Traffic Enterprise) reported a decrease of about 90% in cases of vandalism in metro trains and trams. The Wiener Wohnen (Vienna Municipal Housing Organization) reported a reduction of vandalism of about 52%. The Industrial Center of Lower Austria South (Industriezentrum Niederösterreich Süd) reported a decrease of burglary of 88%, and the police reported a decrease of burglaries into cars of 75% in the parking area of the Shopping Centre South in Vösendorf since the installation of CCTVs.[*]

At the Vienna Schwedenplatz a reduction of drug dealing and drug-related crimes (robberies, brawls) has been attributed to CCTV (Heger, 2010, 346). However, the drug problem has not been solved; it simply moved to places where it is less disturbing. The shift of problems to other places may be viewed as success, especially from the standpoint of a criminal policy which is no longer focused on reducing the causes of the problems. The interest now is in assuring that these problems do not occur on certain places. The consequence of such a policy is a new configuration of public space.

Conclusions

The new configuration of public space, the blending of inner and outer security, the institutionalization of security science, and the outsourcing of security services to private entrepreneurs are undeniably new developments in the field. What remains from earlier history is the tendency to increase

---

[*] Öffentliche Sicherheit 9-10/05, 34; 9-10/06, 71. Der Standard, January 22., 2010; January 15/16, 2011, 16.

punishment and control—a tendency that finds its expression in Austria today in expansions of agencies controlling administrative offenses.

For example, in Vienna "waste watchers" are responsible for registering and punishing cleanliness offences. Naturwächter (representatives of the Nature Conservation Authority) monitor compliance with conservation laws. Ordnungsberater (order advisors) watch for violations of house rules in communal residential buildings. Employees of the Linienaufsicht (line surveillance) ensure that no-smoking and other regulations are followed by public transport users. These and other activities discussed in this chapter shape Austrian society at least not less than developments which are stressed to justify the usage of some of the other names of society mentioned in the enumeration of such names at the beginning of the chapter. At least insofar it seems justified to speak of "Security Societies" and to qualify the Austrian society as such a society.

References

Beck, U. 1986. *Risikogesellschaft. Auf dem Weg in eine andere Moderne.* Suhrkamp, Frankfurt/M. English: 1992. *Risk society: Toward a new modernity.* Sage Publ., London.

Beck, U. 2007. *Weltrisikogesellschaft. Die globalen Gefährdungen – vom Terror bis zum Klimawandel.* RM-Buch und Medien-Vertrieb, Rheda-Wiedenbrück.

Czapska, J. & Stangl, W. 2007. Wenn Wissen reist: Kriminalprävention als Teil europäisierter Kriminalpolitik. Sessar, K./Stangl, W. & Swaaningen, R. van (Hg.), *Großstadtängste. Untersuchungen zu Unsicherheitsgefühlen und Sicherheitspolitiken in europäischen Kommunen.* Lit Verlag, Wien, 45–68.

Garland, D. 2001. *The Culture of Control. Crime and Social Order in Contemporary Society.* Oxford University Press, Oxford. German: 2008. Kultur der Kontrolle. Verbrechensbekämpfung und soziale Ordnung in der Gegenwart. Campus Verlag, Frankfurt/M.

Gill, M. & Spriggs, A. 2005. *Assessing the Impact of CCTV* (Home Office. Research Development and Statistics Directorate), London. (http://www.homeoffice.gov.uk/rds/pdfs05/hors292.pdf, March 21, 2011).

Groenemeyer, A. 2010. Wege der Sicherheitsgesellschaft – Transformationen der Konstruktion und Regulierung innerer Unsicherheiten. Groenemeyer, A. (Hg.), *Wege der Sicherheitsgesellschaft.* VS Verlag für Sozialwissenschaften, Wiesbaden, 9–22.

Heger, N. 2010. Die Entwicklung der Sicherheitsgesellschaft am Beispiel der Videoüberwachung am Wiener Schwedenplatz. Groenemeyer, A. (Hg.), *Wege der Sicherheitsgesellschaft.* VS Verlag für Sozialwissenschaften, Wiesbaden, 343–357.

IMAS 2009. Umfrage. Antworten zum Tempora Mutantur. *IMAS-Report* Nr. 10, August 2009 (http:www.imas.at, February 4., 2011).

Kaufmann, F.-X. 1970. *Sicherheit als soziologisches und sozialpolitisches Problem.* Enke, Stuttgart.

Kreissl, R. 2008. Das Selbstverständnis der Polizei zwischen neuen Sicherheitsbedürfnissen, kommunaler Orientierung und bürokratischer Organisationsform. Kreissl, R./Barthel, C. & Ostermeier, L. (eds.), *Policing in Context*. Lit Verlag, Berlin, 31–52.

Legnaro, A. 1997. Konturen der Sicherheitsgesellschaft. Eine polemisch-futurologische Skizze. *Leviathan* 25, 271–284.

Lindenberg, M. & Schmidt-Semisch, H. 1995. Sanktionsverzicht statt Herrschaftsverlust.

Herrschaftsverlust. Vom Übergang in die Kontrollgesellschaft. *Kriminologisches Journal* 27, 2–17.

Löff, M. 2010. Privates Sicherheitsgewerbe. *Öffentliche Sicherheit* 3-4/10, 84–85.

Lyon, D. 1994. *The Electronic Eye: The Rise of Surveillance Society*. Oxford University Press, Oxford.

Magenheimer, H. 2001. *Comprehensive Security*. [Schriftenreihe der Landesverteidigungsakademie 2001, 2], Wien.

Nohlen, D. & Schultze, R.-O. (Hg.) 2005. *Lexikon der Politikwissenschaft*. Band 2 N – Z. Beck, München.

Prisching, M. 2003. Die Etikettengesellschaft. Prisching, M. (Hg.): *Modelle der Gegenwartsgesellschaft*. Passagen-Verlag, Wien, 13–32.

Sack, F. 2010. Der weltweite „punitive Turn" – Ist die Bundesrepublik dagegen gefeit? Groenemeyer, A. (Hg.), *Wege der Sicherheitsgesellschaft*. VS Verlag für Sozialwissenschaften,. Wiesbaden, 165–191.

Singelnstein, T. & Stolle, P. 2006. *Die Sicherheitsgesellschaft. Soziale Kontrolle im 21. Jahrhundert*. VS Verlag für Sozialwissenschaften, Wiesbaden.

Sonnenfels, J. v. 1819. *Grundsätze der Polizey, Handlung, und Finanzwissenschaft*. Teil I, 8. Auflage, erstmals erschienen 1765, Wien.

Spreen, D. 2010. Die Sicherheit der Weltgesellschaft. Groenemeyer, A. (Hg.), *Wege der Sicherheitsgesellschaft*. VS Verlag für Sozialwissenschaften,. Wiesbaden, 192–229.

Stückler, H.-P. 2010. *Privatisierung der Sicherheit unter besonderer Berücksichtigung der Erfahrungen des BM.I mit der Besorgung der Sicherheitsaufgaben durch private Rechtsträger*. Dissertation, Universität Wien.

Trojanow, I. & Zeh, J. 2010. *Angriff auf die Freiheit. Sicherheitswahn, Überwachungsstaat und der Abbau bürgerlicher Rechte*. RM-Buch und Medien-Vertrieb, München.

UNDP. 1994. *Human Development Report: New Dimensions of Human Security*. United Nations Development Programme, New York.

Weinandy, K. 2009. Sicherheitsforschungsprogramme. *Öffentliche Sicherheit* 7-8/09 52–54.

Welsh, B.C. & Farrington, D.P. 2002. *Crime Prevention Effects of Closed Circuit Television. A Systematic Review*. Home Office. Research, Development and Statistics Directorate, London (http.//www.chs.ubc.ca/archives/files/Crime, 18.3.2011).

The Concept of Security in the European Union

4

ALEXANDER SIEDSCHLAG

Contents

Introduction: The New Security of the European Union

By extrapolating the member states' prerogatives over security on a national scale,[*] the Lisbon Treaty introduced the concept of the security of the European Union (EU). Based on its new legal personality,[†] it aims "to promote peace, its values and the well-being of its peoples."[‡] To ensure the security of the Union and its citizens, the Union "shall define and pursue common policies and actions, and shall work for a high degree of cooperation."[§] The EU's concept of security is based on a comprehensive approach that underscores "transversal" issues[¶] that include:

- Linkages between external and internal threats to the security of the Union as a whole and its citizens
- Interrelations between terrorism and crime
- Interconnections of different sectors of (in)security, e.g., political, financial, and societal security

---

[*] Article 4 of the Treaty on the Functioning of the European Union in the version of Lisbon (2007).
[†] Article 47 of the Treaty on the Functioning of the European Union in the version of Lisbon (2007).
[‡] Article 3 of the Treaty on the Functioning of the European Union in the version of Lisbon (2007).
[§] Article 21, paragraph 4 of the Treaty on European Union in the version of Lisbon (2007).
[¶] European Security Research and Innovation Forum (ESRIF): *Final Report*, Part 1 (December 2009) <http://www .esrif.eu>, p. 208–212.

In addition, the *Treaty on the Functioning of the European Union* executed in Lisbon explicitly lists certain forms of severe criminality that shall be fought on the Union level: terrorism, trafficking in human beings, sexual exploitation of women and children, illicit drug trafficking, illicit arms trafficking, money laundering, corruption, counterfeiting, computer crime, and organized crime.[*]

Nevertheless, the concept of security on the EU level is not as progressive in every respect. While some member states have started to count the financial sector among critical infrastructures, the process of identifying and designating European critical infrastructures (ECIs) is not as advanced. The relevant Directive 2008/114/EC concentrates on the energy and transport sectors and does not particularly envisage financial ECIs, just as it says nothing about information, communication, and technology-related infrastructure and related risks such as cyber crime.

However, the new EU internal security strategy, based on both the new Lisbon Treaty regulations and the Stockholm Programme[†] builds on the assumption that "the concept of internal security must be understood as a wide and comprehensive concept which straddles multiple sectors in order to address these major threats and others which have a direct impact on the lives, safety, and well-being of citizens."[‡]

The Stockholm Programme listing of common threats and challenges includes terrorism in any form, serious and organized crime, cyber crime, cross-border crime, violence, and natural and man-made disasters. While financial risks are not explicitly addressed, they are clearly covered. A couple of the components of the European security model advocated by the strategy appear directly relevant for the financial sector and for tackling the security risks posed by financial crises. This includes addressing the causes of insecurity (not only the effects); prioritizing prevention and anticipation, and involving all sectors with roles to play in public protection (political, economic, social, etc.).

Moreover, in the Stockholm Programme based on the assumption that the EU "must reduce the number of opportunities available to organized crime as a result of a globalised economy, in particular during a crisis that is exacerbating the vulnerability of the financial system, and allocate appropriate resources to meet these challenges effectively," the European Council (head of state and government of member states) invited the European

[*] Article 83, paragraph 1 of the Treaty on the Functioning of the European Union.
[†] European Council: Stockholm Programme. (2010). An Open and Secure Europe Serving and Protecting Citizens. 2010/C115/01. Brussels http://eur-lex. europa.eu/LexUr iServ/ LexUriServ .do?uri=OJ:C:2010:115:00 01:0038:EN:PDF.
[‡] Council of the European Union. (2010). Draft Internal Security Strategy for the European Union: Towards a European Security Model. 5842/2/10 Rev 2. Brussels, p. 2.

Commission to reflect on the prevention of financial crime and consider all-European measures to facilitate that prevention.*

The financial crisis and the concern about financial crime as a political and societal security issue sparked by it may be seen as instances of the so-called "Titanic effect" developed from risk research.[†] The new ability to control leads to a rollback in cultural achievements of risk management. For the concept of security, this means that new technology-based capabilities must not let us forget human and cultural factors underlying both threats to security and the effectiveness of security-enhancing measures.

In contrast, the cyber crime problem has been found by research to be typically perceived as a problem of weak law or poor technological control but not as a societal security problem.[‡] Regardless of this, a tendency of Europeanization is also evident in the financial sector and the area of financial crime, where the European Commission is soon to present a proposal to support and monitor member state activities to fight corruption. Public opinion in EU member states has always strongly (by more than a two-thirds majority) supported the Europeanization of the external security and defense of the Union, and it now is also in favor of the Europeanization of civil security.

It is ironic that European citizens are generally concerned about criminality in their respective countries and wish for more European-level decision making and activities in fighting crime, while, at the same time, most citizens perceive the Union as an amplifier of criminality.[§] However, *Eurobarometer,* the all-EU opinion survey, does not address security items on a regular basis.

The latest referable data are those of *Special Eurobarometer* 266 on "The role of the European Union in justice, freedom and security policy areas," based on field work done in the summer of 2006.[¶] According to its results, fighting organized crime and trafficking are on the same level as the fight against terrorism—the area for which most Europeans (86%) believed decision making should occur on a European rather than national level. Moreover, almost four out of five EU citizens (78%) believe the Union should

* Stockholm Programme, op. cit. (fn 8), p. 23.
† Cf. Kenneth, E. & Watt, F. (1974). *The Titanic Effect: Planning for the Unthinkable.* New York: Dutton.
‡ Wall, D.S. & Williams, M. (2007). Policing diversity in the digital age: maintaining order in virtual communities. *Criminology and Criminal Justice,* 7, 391–415 (p. 410).
§ See opinion survey analysis presented in the course of the CPSI project. Siedschlag, A. & Jerkovic, A. (2008). Primary interpretation of survey findings to identify national citizen security cultures. Center for European Security Studies (CEUSS). *Analytical Standpoint,* 12. http://www.european-security.info/aspl2.pdf
¶ European Commission. The role of the European Union in justice, freedom and security policy areas. *Special Eurobarometer,* 266. http://ec.europa.eu/public_opinion/archives/ebs/ebs_266_en.pdf

make more decisions with regard to the exchange of police and judicial information among member states. For more than half (56%) of the EU people, the fight against organized crime and trafficking should be the top priority, even slightly ahead of the fight against terrorism (55%).

This chapter will contrast the legal scope for Europeanization in civil security affairs and first-sight supporting public opinion with EU member states' policy initiatives and national security cultures. It will then explore the consideration of finance-related issues in national security strategies. A main conclusion will be that while member states agreed on introducing the concept of the security of the Union as a whole into the Lisbon Treaty, both the political and private sectors vary considerably across countries in their perceptions and concepts of security. The concept of security in the EU therefore is not one of its own but the result of a group of Union-level initiatives and member state-level actions.

Member States' Policy Initiatives

In contrast to Union-level developments and trends of Europeanization, the countries of Europe continue to rest on distinguished symbols of what they value and need to safeguard. They show different public and citizen security cultures, and both the political and private sectors of all the member states have different perceptions of the locus of responsibility for citizen and public security. This is also evident in the field of national security strategies and related research programs. In a study performed as part of the EU-funded research project titled "Changing Perceptions of Security and Interventions" (CPSI), we analyzed the following security-related national strategic documents devised by EU member states:[*]

Austria: National Security Research Programme (KIRAS)[†]
France: Appels à projets 2008: Concepts Systèmes et Outils pour la
   Sécurité Globale[‡]

---

[*] Siedschlag, A. (2008). European countries' national security research policy compared in the light of FP 7. Center for European Security Studies (CEUSS). *Analytical Standpoint,* 10. http://www.e uropean-s ecurity.info/asp10.pdf; also published in *ESRIF Final Report,* op. cit. (fn 6), part 2, ch. 10.

[†] http://www.kiras.at; also *Security Research. Austria Innovative Special Edition,* 3a/2008 http://www.kiras.at/ cms/fileadmin/datei en/allgemein/S ecurity_Research_2.pdf.

[‡] Agence Nationale de la Recherche: *Appels à projets 2008: Concepts Systèmes et Outils pour la Sécurité Globale.* http://www.agenc e-nationale-re cherche.fr/?NodId=17&lngAAPId=188.

Germany: Research for Civil Security. Programme of German
  Federal Government[*]
Italy: Italian Civil Protection National Service[†]
Netherlands: National Security. Strategy and Work Programme
  2007–2008[‡]
Spain: Spanish National Plan for Scientific Research, Development, and
  Technological Innovation 2008–2011[§]
Sweden: Knowledge to Safeguard Security: Proposals for a National
  Strategy for Security Research[¶]
United Kingdom: United Kingdom Security & Counter-Terrorism
  Science & Innovation Strategy[**]

We found these countries tend to set clear, nationally informed priorities.
In the case of *Austria*, this is critical infrastructure protection (with the
inclusion of social and cultural aspects). In the *Netherlands*, the issue is climate change; *Spain* is concerned with climate change and nanoscience. In
Germany's program, civil security research (research on civil protection) is
the leading theme. This is also the case in *Italy*, where the focus is on a specific combination of strategic natural disaster reduction, enhancement of
preparedness, and rapid response civil protection based on comprehensive
risk assessment by real-time early warning capabilities and collections of
national and international technical and scientific expertise.

---

[*] Federal Ministry of Education and Research: *Research for Civil Security. Programme of the German Federal Government. Bonn/Berlin 2007* http://www.bmbf.de/pub/research_for_civil_security_.pdf.

[†] Presidenza del Consiglio dei Ministri, Dipartimento de la Protezione Civile: *The Italian Civil Protection National Service* http://www.p rotezionecivile.it/cm s/attach/bro-churedpc_eng2.pdf [This is not a security research programme document, but it contains relevant information on how civil protection is based on technically scientific insight and seeks to engage with scientific research.]

[‡] Ministry of the Interior and Kingdom Relations: *National Security. Strategy and Work programme 2007-2008.* The Hague, May 2007 http://www.minbz k.nl/aspx/download.a spx?file=/contents/pag es/88474/natv eiligh.bwdef.pdf.

[§] Comisión Interministerial de Ciencia y Tecnología: *The Spanish National Plan for Scientific Research, Development and Technological Innovation 2008-2011* http://www.plann acionalidi.es/documento s/Plan_ingles_web.pdf.

[¶] VINNOVA: Swedish Agency for Innovation Systems, Swedish Emergency Management Agency, Swedish Armed Forces, Swedish Defence Materiel Administration, Swedish Defence Research Agency, Swedish National Defence College, and Confederation of Swedish Enterprise. *Knowledge to safeguard security: proposals for a national strategy for security research.* June 2005. http:// www.vinnova .se/upload/EPiStore PDF/vp-05-03.pdf.

[**] Home Office, Office for Security & Counter-Terrorism, The Counter-Terrorism Science Unit. *United Kingdom Security & Counter-Terrorism Science & Innovation Strategy.* London 2007 http://security.hom eoffice.gov.uk/news-publications/publ ication -search/general/science-inn ovation-strate gy1?view=Binary.

Network-based solutions in security affairs (with respect for ethics, integrity, and human rights) are the main themes in *Sweden*. The *United Kingdom* focuses on permanent cooperation with EU and non-EU partners in the fields of conventional crime, violence prevention, and protection against terrorist attacks. *France* addresses, in addition to critical infrastructure protection, conventional crime and violence as well as broad management of crises (independent of their origins).

Member States' Security Cultures

In addition to national policy initiatives, the concept of the security in the EU is also clearly marked by national security cultures. Risk research produced valuable assumptions about cultural determinants of perceived risk and (in) security. Dake's (1991) cognitive concept of culture is a set of "orienting dispositions" guiding perception of and cognitive response to complex situations.* Another pertinent concept, the "cultural theory of risk," developed by Douglas and Wildavsky (1982),† assumes that different perceptions and disputes about risk and security can be linked to competing worldviews, that is, different conceptions of risk, security, and solutions to security problems vary according to the organization of political and social relations.

Risks and security threats are selected as important because they reinforce established interpretations and relations within a culture, thus reproducing the symbolic foundations of a community. The fit between security strategies and related research programs as addressed above and broader cultural conditions of EU member states becomes clear by investigating nations' public security cultures.

Our analysis of citizen security cultures performed in the EU project CPSI aimed to comparatively identify types of citizen security cultures based on a secondary analysis of social and victimological survey data that were not analyzed comprehensively in the past. The results are reported in detail in separate papers.‡ We used two main descriptors for citizen security cultures:§

---

* Dake, K. (1991). Orienting dispositions in the perception of risk: an analysis of contemporary worldviews and cultural biases. *Journal of Cross-Cultural Psychology*, 22, 61–82.
† Douglas, M. & Wildavsky, A. (1982). *Risk and Culture*. Berkeley, CA: University of California Press.
‡ Siedschlag & Jerkovic. Primary interpretation of survey findings to identify national citizen security cultures, op. cit. (fn 12). Siedschlag, A. & Jerkovic, A. (2010). Summary of CPSI Country Case Studies. Austria – Bulgaria – France – Germany – Italy – Netherlands – Sweden – United Kingdom. Center for European Security Studies (CEUSS). *Analytical Standpoint*, 13. http://www.european-se curity.info/asp13.pdf.
§ These indicators described in detail in Siedschlag & Jerkovic. Summary of CPSI Country Case Studies, op. cit. (fn 25).

- Personal fear of crime (crime perceived as an individual or individualized problem) versus social fear of crime (crime perceived as a problem "out there" in society regardless of personal impact)
- Realistic, underfear or overfear of crime based on the relations between personal fear of crime and victimization, social fear of crime and victimization, and crime rate and perception of crime as prior problems

We now describe citizens' concepts of security blended with more structural factors in describing the security cultures of the EU member states under consideration.

Austria has a low victimization and personal fear of crime level, but the social fear of crime level is relatively high compared to the actual level of victimization. Reflecting this social overfear of crime, public debates tend to center on perceived rather than actual security. The country's tradition and structure of consocialism and consensus democracy limit the potential for developing a shared European understanding of security problems and agreeing on a common interpretation of related challenges and acceptable interventions. It seems that citizens have a less Europeanized feeling of security. This fact can be expected to limit the social acceptability of international solutions for security problems, including measures to fight financial crime, if they are not specifically designed to national needs.

France has a citizen security culture of overfear. This may partly be due to the split preferences of French citizens for EU-based as opposed to national decision making and action in crime fighting. The EU is a locus of fear of crime for some citizens in France, and this is matched by the noted reluctance of the political sector to making reference to EU in crime-related security issues beyond reasons of symbolic legitimacy.

Germany's history as a "front state" in the Cold War and key driver of the international change that ended the Cold War led to a preponderant perception of security problems as transnational and international and security as a symbol of preserving the values acquired by the state and society as a whole. In consequence, security has become a symbol of preparedness and ability to defend the nation against threats from without and within, resting on higher ranking international values such as democracy, rule of law, and European integration. With an average level of victimization and low levels of personal and social fear of crime, Germany has an underfear citizen security culture. Public debates and policy interventions tend to center more on perceived than on actual security, reflecting the symbolic character of security. The political approach to internal security centers on prevention and is also informing German policy in the EU, which is directed to solving questions related to big crimes on a European level. German citizens have even exhibited a preference for the EU as opposed to national decision making and action in fighting crime although they tend to perceive the EU as a cause of crime, particularly in the financial realm.

Italy's citizens perceive internal security and public safety as national tasks, including the centralization of policing and criminal justice structures. At the same time, political culture is open to the Europeanization of the security sector due to long experience with international organized crime. However, the problem remains of implementing European practices into the action repertoires of national agencies—a difficult task because of the problems that surround attempts to coordinate the actions of the agencies. In sum, Italian public security culture can be described as network-centered, closely related to the normative foundations of statehood, reflecting threats to the idea of the state as a collective security provider with a focus on fighting organized crime.

In the perception of *Netherlands'* citizens, security has become a fuzzy concept and, in public opinion, associated with or even equated to failures of both state and society to confront recent problems of crime. Over-average victimization along with personal underfear and social overfear make the Netherlands a country that has a balanced citizen fear of crime culture, but the social fear character of the security culture remains important. The Dutch, much more than average EU citizens, perceive the Union as a bringer of more insecurity and thus more crime. In particular, probably due to media influence, public perception is that security is becoming more important than other values like privacy and freedom of opinion. The emerging high public demands on policy and politics produced a kind of permanent feeling of a security crisis, where security is interpreted as a task that must be completed at the level of the state organization as a whole, including societal stakeholders. This limits the scope for Europeanization and results in a policy guided by the interpretation of security as a sector that requires an alignment of the national approach with those of other states and organizations. While perceiving the EU as bringing more crime, Dutch citizens show a clear preference for the decisions of the EU as opposed to national decision making and action in fighting crime.

In *Sweden,* security awareness and vulnerability are significant issues in the public economy and in the political sectors. Social overfear is mirrored by above average public acceptance of technological solutions to security problems. Technology, including the Internet, is generally seen as a part of the solution of security problems, and not as a security problem or critical infrastructure. Citizen preference for EU or national decision making and action in crime fighting is indecisive, but the balance has recently been in favor of the EU. In Sweden, questions of public opinion framed as security questions are very closely related to the normative foundations of statehood, reflecting threats to the idea of the state as a collective security provider. Network-based solutions in security affairs (with respect for ethics, integrity, and human rights) are momentous themes in Sweden. Public discussions consequently focus on whether it is more difficult to protect security in modern information and communication systems that also give rise to legal problems. Nevertheless, there is agreement that a coherent information security policy is required and the Swedish government's overall goal is to maintain a high level of information security throughout society. Sweden is developing an information security strategy capable of serving as a basis for both private and public efforts.

The *United Kingdom* is a multi-cultural country. Public security and the role of the state as security provider are framed above average in terms of readily available information and knowledge. In public perception, crime levels have generally increased a lot over the past few years. At local level, citizens' perceptions of crime levels and confidence in security interventions have reduced. However, the level of trust in the police has increased. Various government agencies aim to examine new or emerging types of crime such as fraud and technology-related activities. Experts claim that the fraud and technology-related crime statistics recorded by the police do not provide reliable information about the extents and trends in that many of these types of offenses go unreported. The common view is that victimization surveys can provide information about these crimes, although sometimes victims are not aware of certain offenses such as the cyber crime of identity theft. This helps explain the underfear security culture with regard to financial crimes committed via information and communication technology. However, other critical interpretations apply to the UK culture of underfear. For example, critics argue that information technology-based solutions to security problems (including the use of video surveillance) are not suited to confront threats but only to reassure the public that something is being done. This facilitates the rise of a security culture of moral panic as illustrated by the London bombings in 2005. In fact, as David Garland argues, a new type of intervention emerged, not directed at actual crime levels, but at levels of public fear of crime.[*]

In summary, security referents (objects perceived or interpreted as representing security issues) can change within the scope of a few years, but the parameters for societal and political definitions of security referents appear very stable, that is, the process by which something becomes a security issue and starts changing citizens' fear of crime and perception of (in)security can be expected to be more predictable than which issue will be framed as

---

[*] Garland, D. (2001). *The Culture of Control: Crime and Social Order in Contemporary Society.* Chicago: University of Chicago Press, p. 122.

security-related. This means that we cannot reliably predict the concept(s) of security that the citizens of the EU will demand, accept, or reject. Also, we cannot predict the specific security value that citizens will agree to financially support and the extent to which they will perceive financial crime as a particular type of security challenge. Nevertheless, we can assess the current level of the so-called securitization of financial crime using national security strategies as indicators.

Finance-Related Issues in National Security Strategies

While the economics of security have been components of security studies for some time (beginning with defense expenditure analysis in the Cold War and extending to the cost–benefit relations of security technologies), financial security is a relatively new concept.[*] It builds on the securitization of what was formerly perceived as financial risk and now concerns the financial security related to the daily lives of the people. This marks a tremendous concept shift because finance was traditionally considered an allocation of resources to secure "a fickle future, tame uncertainty, and insure against disaster."[†]

Today, securitized financial instruments are described in public discourse by "the ability to engender business security, or alternatively, to cause spectacular societal insecurity."[‡] Against this background, it is interesting to analyze to what extent finance as a security concept is addressed in European security research programs. On the European level, the thematic area of security in the *Seventh European Union Framework Program* addressed finances in the contexts of prevention (control of financial infrastructures), mitigation (anticipation of terrorist attacks by analysis of financing), and expansion of the concept of critical infrastructure.[§] The national security strategies described yield a differentiated picture of EU member states' approaches to finance as a security theme as shown below:

---

[*] See de Goede, M. (2011). Financial security. In Burgess, J.P. (Ed.), *Routledge Handbook of Security Studies*. London: Routledge, pp. 100–109.

[†] Op. cit., p. 103.

[‡] Op. cit., p. 109. For an up-to-date account of the concept of securitization, see Balzacq, T. (Ed.). (2011). *Securitization Theory: How Security Problems Emerge and Dissolve*. London: Routledge.

[§] Cf. European Commission Work Programme 2011. Cooperation. Theme 10. Security. C(2010)4900. Brussels, 19 July 2010). ftp://ftp.cordis.europa. eu/pub/fp7/docs/ wp/cooperation/securit y/k-wp-201101_en.pdf.

- *Austria's* national security research program explicitly refers to the financial sector (banking and finance, insurance, reinsurance, investments, and others) as critical infrastructures particularly worthy of protection, but gives the matter no further consideration.
- *France's* security research program, following what could be called a holistic approach to civil security (*securité globale*), defines its objectives as the prevention of and protection against all kinds of threats and malicious impacts that may disrupt development, life, and individual as well as collective activities. Criminality and fraud are explicitly listed as malicious impacts. To realize its objective, the program calls for a systematic approach in considering the vulnerabilities and interdependencies of the vital infrastructures, where financial flows are expressly listed. In addition, programmatic activities include taking part in the work of United Nations bodies, the Council of Europe, and the OECD to combat corruption and address issues of good governance in the public sector.
- *Germany's* civil security research program notes the financial system as a vital infrastructure at risk of terrorist attack, but the civil security research program of Germany does not cite sources of insecurity within the financial system.
- In *Italy,* long-standing practical concern with organized crime has promoted electronic surveillance and a concentration on technological solutions to security problems and a culture of information sharing that, however, is challenged by intranational coordination among different levels of government. Comprehensive risk assessment and management are guiding political norms. Comprehensive risk assessment also covers the financial sector, even though related risks are not specifically addressed in the country's approach to security research, which thematically focuses on disaster management and civil protection.
- The *Netherlands'* national security strategy addresses the finance sector only by referring to the need to prioritize scarce resources.
- The *Spanish* plan for research, development, and technological innovation, which also covers several other security issues, calls for the development of technologies of security and trust to improve data security, protect intellectual property, and prevent fraud.
- *Sweden* does not address financial security in its national security research strategy proposal.
- The *United Kingdom's* strategy does not refer to finance.

As a comparative study covering sixteen European countries has shown, corruption at the governmental level explains the public distrust of security authorities.* Keeping this fact in mind, it is easy to see why financial crime strongly impacts the implementation of security in Europe, both at national and Union levels. However, a common awareness of finances as an integral part of European critical infrastructure has yet to be developed for security policies or related research initiatives.

Conclusion

European countries continue to rest on distinguished concepts and symbols of what they value and need to safeguard. They show different public and citizen security cultures, and both the political sector and the public vary across countries in their perceptions and concepts of security. Most citizens of EU countries still perceive national approaches to be most suitable to enhance the security of the countries in which they live, in particular security against crime.

Although public support for EU decision making and action against crime has increased recently, the EU generally is not perceived as a locus of successful intervention to enhance citizen security against crime. Thus, the security of the EU as a whole remains an important policy initiative and the Lisbon treaty provision, but it must be supplanted by supportive adaptation of policies and culture on national levels.

While research programs in the EU have standardized technological building capacities (e.g., intelligent surveillance), European citizens do not believe that enhanced security technologies alone can eliminate insecurity. Improved distribution of responsibility and division of labor among the various actors in government and society are needed more than increased investments: more than technical matters must be considered. A mixture of legislation, best practices, processes, technology, culture, and behavior must be integrated correctly into a security system. Common symbols and values representing the concept of security on a European level should be preceded by a process of convergence of national practices and security cultures.

Acknowledgments

This chapter in part reports results from a research project titled "Changing Perceptions of Security and Interventions" (CPSI) funded by the European Commission under the Seventh Framework Programme (Theme: Security),

---

* Kääriäinen, J.T. (2007). Trust in the police in 16 European countries: a multilevel analysis. *European Journal of Criminology,* 4, 409–435 (p. 410).

Call FP7-SEC-2007-1, Project/Grant Agreement 217881. The project ran from April 2008 to March 2010.

   I am grateful to Andrea Jerkovic for valuable comments on the final version of the text.

Human Security and the United Nations Security Council

5

WALTHER LICHEM

Contents

Introduction

The Security Council is to be understood as the organ of the international community with the highest responsibility, with supra-national power of decision-making and as an organ mastering an ever broader spectrum of our Global Agenda. It is the example of the definition of the United Nations as reflecting both "continuity and change".

The founders of the United Nations conferred on the Security Council the primary (though not exclusive) responsibility for the maintenance of international peace and security in accordance with the purposes and principles of the Charter of the United Nations. Its supra-national power is defined both in Article 24 which asserts the fundamental agreement of the UN members that the Security Council acts on their behalf and in Article 25 according to which "the Members of the United Nations agree to accept and carry out the decisions of the Security Council". Decisions of the Security Council bind to some extent even non-members.

The powers and responsibilities of the Security Council were a first step in the process of *relativisation* of national sovereignty. Only five countries, the permanent members of the Security Council (Republic of China/now People's Republic of China, France, USSR/now Russian Federation, United Kingdom and the United States), still can claim absolute sovereignty as no political decision, legal or institutional change will include them unless these countries form part of the agreement.

The responsibilities of the Security Council are laid down in Chapters V (institutional framework), Chapter VI (Pacific Settlement of Disputes), Chapter VII (Action with Respect to Threats to the Peace, Breaches of the Peace, and Acts of Aggression) and in Chapter VIII (Regional Arrangements) of the Charter.

The Evolution of Security Council Agenda

The Security Council's history of achievements are reflected in the respective global political developments. The decades of the Cold War were not only determined by repeated veto-based paralysis of the Security Council's decision-making capacity[i] but also by the traditional concept of threats to peace and security through conflicts between sovereign states. This situation of the post-war era led to a rather limited agenda of the Security Council. It focused almost exclusively on inter-state issues related to post-war situations, decolonisation and issues of state sovereignty assertions. Although certain innovations, for example, the creation of truce supervision missions developing into peacekeeping did occur in the security agenda, the institutional expansion of the United Nations during the first three decades of the organisation occurred primarily in the non-security agenda areas such as matters regarding the development of cooperation[ii], natural resources[iii], human environment[iv], urbanisation[v], industrial development[vi] and others. These matters were not with regard to the United Nations' capacity of addressing issues of peace and security.

The noteworthy first innovations after the Second World War, the creation of truce supervisory missions and then of peace-keeping operations were not the result of the Security Council's deliberations but of a Western majority led General Assembly[vii] and the various operations like UNTSO[viii], UNEF[ix] and UNFICYP[x], reflecting the still predominant concept of an inter-state peace and security agenda. For decades the UN did not recognize a responsibility to address the societal dimension of conflicts. Article 2.7 of the Charter was not put in question[xi].

The end of the Cold War and the profound reorientation of Soviet and then Russian global engagement has led to a situation where the Security Council more than other UN organs, has agenda areas or programmes that benefits from the new capacity of the UN for consensus and commitment. At the same time the Security Council's agenda broadened from inter-state to internal wars and conflict situations, from state security to human security issues and in its response from single-dimensional to complex multi-dimensional policies for the attainment of peace and security.

The original focus on conflicts, threats to peace and security and acts of aggression has now been complemented by an agenda that increasingly includes general "thematic issues" which were addressed by soft-law general appeals to the international community or even, if adopted under Chapter VII, with obligatory hard-law obligations, with respective reporting and monitoring processes, recognizing the Security Council as a law-maker. A new shared vision of peace and security emerged, shaping a new and constantly broadening agenda of the Security Council. This new agenda reflected three main issue areas:

Intrastate conflicts, civil wars and terrorism with a growing focus on human security and the affectedness of human beings by these acts of violence;

Conflict prevention and post-conflict peace building, including the societal and development dimension of these operations; and

Weapons of mass destruction potentially at the disposal of state and non-state actors with uncertain relations to the basic principles of the international community.

The Evolving Human Security Agenda

The new patterns of victimisation of intrastate conflicts and wars[xii] made it necessary for the Security Council to address the issues of civilians, children and women in war. This implied a move in the Security Council's agenda from *state security* to the concept of *human security* which in turn required new inputs of knowledge, vision and operational capabilities.

In 1999, The Canadian Chairmanship of the Security Council provided an important opportunity for addressing the thematic issue of civilians in armed conflicts. In addition, the Chairman also brought the issue of human security to the Council's agenda. Children in armed conflicts, the issue of child soldiers became long-term conceptual and policy preoccupations of the Security Council, thus moving it from crisis management to the formulation of general policies for the international community. Several presidencies of the Security Council started a longer-term approach to the policy-making and norm-setting agenda. Over the past ten years more than twenty resolutions and numerous Statements by the President of the Security Council were adopted on issues of civilians, women and children in armed conflict[xiii].

Conflict Prevention and Internal Conflicts

The threats to peace emerging in the process of the disintegration of the former Socialist Federal Republic of Yugoslavia led to the deployment of a first *United Nations Preventive Deployment Force (UNPREDEP)*[xiv] to Macedonia to protect it against possible aggression from the Serbian Republic. The Council then addressed the issue of conflict prevention in a series of resolutions affirming that prevention had to be seen as an integral part of the Security Council's primary responsibility for the maintenance of international peace and security[xv]. Conflict prevention was seen as an operation in accordance with Chapter VI of the Charter. Conflict prevention missions were increasingly implemented in cooperation with regional organisations in Africa and in Europe under Chapter VIII of the Charter.

At the same time it is interesting to note that the number of internal conflicts and wars expanded during the 1990s, often in association with the consequences of traditional inter-state wars.

Terrorism

Terrorism was another case area of internal violence given increased significance and attention by the Security Council. Terrorism was first dealt with by the Security Council in 1989 when at the initiative of the ICAO Council it unanimously adopted a resolution urging ICAO and states to devise an international regime regulating the marking of plastic or sheet explosives for the purposes of detection.[xvi] Resolution 638 of 31 July 1989 addressed the issue of terrorist hostage taking. Terrorism became a new priority focus of the Security Council with Resolution 1269 (1999),[xvii] which condemned all acts, methods and priorities of terrorism, the terrorist organizations used in their attacks of 11-09-2001in New York, Washington and Pennsylvania.

The urgency of the challenges of terrorism led to a position where the Security Council expressed "its readiness to take all necessary steps to … combat all forms of terrorism in accordance with its responsibilities in the Charter"[xviii].

Resolution 1373 on threats to international peace and security by terrorist acts[xix] was the first "thematic" resolution adopted under Chapter VII of the Charter imposing a series of legal and political obligations on the member countries including "to implement fully the international anti-terrorism conventions".

New Human Security Oriented Peace Operations

The new multi-dimensionality of peace and security led to a broadening of the Security Council's perception of peace operations. Peace operations were now becoming increasingly complex, with the military dimensions being integrated with non-military human security-oriented operations, including humanitarian assistance, economic and social development, human rights education, democratisation and electoral observation. As some of these policy issues were new on the Council's agenda there was a definite need to address them in sessions dedicated not to concrete conflicts, threats to security and peace, but in sessions in which they were dealt with as "thematic issues". As civil wars began to move on the agenda of the Security Council, the issue of small arms and light weapons was not only dealt with in the General Assembly but was also addressed by the Security Council[xx].

In 1992, after the first Iraq war, the General Assembly created the first United Nations Peacekeeping operation which was exclusively dedicated to the assurance of human security through the effective humanitarian assistance operations[xxi].

Peacebuilding

As conflicts tend to have a fifty per cent probability of erupting again within a period of six years, the Security Council had to address the interrelated issues of conflict prevention and of post-conflict peace-building. Both approaches are marked by internal programmes of development, including state-building, economic and social development and societal capacity-building. The UN peacekeeping operations mandated by the Security Council in Cambodia[xxii] and in Haiti[xxiii] included for the first time programmes of human rights education and learning and provided very important inputs to the processes of transition to legitimate governments and to democracy. It became increasingly visible that (human) (human) security would be based on development and on an effective culture of human rights.

Peacebuilding was first addressed by the Security Council in 1998[xxiv] and became a focused objective of the 2005 Summit Meeting of the General Assembly, the Summit Meeting that[xxv] led to the creation of a Peace Building Commission with the essential substantive and institutional inputs coming from the Security Council, the General Assembly and from the Economic and Social Council. The transition from peacekeeping to peace building required a multi-functional, human security and human development focused programme of action, that included disarmament, demobilisation, and reintegration of the members of armed entities. The non-military dimensions of peace building required a new composition of peace-operations, that contained enhanced police elements, civilian personnel, a coordination of peacekeeping and peace building, and new strategies of cooperation with the private sector, financial institutions and with civil society organisations.[xxvii]

The peace building programme in Liberia is an example of a dramatic human security-focused peace-building success story. It was based on leadership, the creation of employment opportunities and the development of a culture of self-responsibility in Liberia. Even with the successes, the situation in the country still reveals a broad agenda spectrum to be addressed, including the societal dimension of different tribal and historical identities living together in a country charged with the burdens of a long-term violence potential.

Climate Change and Human Security

Another interesting and for some UN member countries a controversial example of this new broader understanding of the Security Council's role in addressing longer term policy challenges related to human security, is the issue of the impact of climate change on human security. In April of 2007, under the presidency of the United Kingdom, the Security Council held its first ever debate on the impact of climate on security. The day-long meeting focused on examining the relationship between energy, security and climate. More than 50 delegations intervened, many of them representing imperilled island nations as well as greenhouse gas emitters. Several delegations, however, also raised doubts about the Security Council's responsibility on this agenda.

The Human Security Dimensions of Sanctions

The political dimension of conflict management entered the Security Council's new capacity for containing conflicts and reducing conflict capacity by imposing sanctions[xxviii] on state and non-state actors who were perceived as a threat to international peace and security. The practical application of sanctions led in April 2000 to a re-examination of sanctions as a principle for maintaining peace and security. The record of the 1990s turned out to be rather mixed, in that the harmful impact of sanctions on the human security of innocent civilians was revealed. This revelation led to the questioning of the legitimacy and credibility of imposing sanctions on state and non-state actors who were perceived as a threat to international peace and security.

The Security Council moved to a more refined and specified approach to this measure, integrating sanctions into a broader strategy of conflict prevention and resolution. It was to aim rather at changing the behaviour of wrongdoers including war criminals, warlords and rebel movements than being addressed to a "nation", its government and its citizens.[xxix] Sanctions that specifically named individuals have created a more specific controversy. Names of individuals in some cases have unfairly or hastily been placed on the Security Council's lists with these persons having little or no recourse for "de-listing".

New Patterns of Participation in the Security Council's Deliberations

The broadening of the concepts of peace and security, the express inclusion of human security and the related interdependence of issues and of peace and human security strategies required a new inter-institutional cooperation that had not been envisaged originally in the design of the organs of the United Nations. Security was not any more achievable without addressing the economic, social, cultural, societal dimensions of internal and interstate relations. It required new modes of deliberation which would broaden the knowledge input and also the participatory basis of the decision making process. In addition to the inclusion of parties to a conflict and states affected by a threat to peace and security, this approach of inclusion, was particularly indicated with regard to general thematic issues which aimed at the definition of general norms and standards without concrete reference to a crisis situation.

One basic problem for the development of policy discourse in the Security Council was that only delegations, high government officials and UN officials could speak at regular Council meetings and consultations. The issue of refugees and internally displaced persons required the input of the competent UN entities as well as of nongovernmental international organisations. It was also somehow logical to invite Sadako Ogata, UN High Commissioner for Refugees and Sergio Vieira de Mello, Special Representative of the Secretary-General, to the Security Council to open its respective deliberations with introductory statements. During the 1990s, a practice evolved that initiated "thematic" discourses with public meetings. This also provided an opportunity for non-member countries to take the floor and to participate in the general debate.

In 1993 Ambassador Diego Arria, representing Venezuela in the Security Council, searched for ways which would give the Council members a broader basis of understanding of the real conflict situation in Bosnia and Herzegovina. Ambassador Arria invited Council members to gather over coffee in the Delegates' Lounge. This meeting was considered to have been a great success and as a result, today *Arria formula* meetings take place continuously.

Attendance at these meetings is usually at a high level and only rarely do Security Council members fail to attend. The meetings are announced by the Council president at the beginning of each month or whenever organized, as part of the regular Council schedule. They are informal meetings, held outside the Council chamber and chaired by the inviting member. The meetings give opportunities for briefings by one or more persons considered to be especially knowledgeable on a matter of concern of the Council.

The issue of women in armed conflicts is normally related to the agenda of the Economic and Social Council's Commission on the Status of Women shaped by the conclusions of the World Conference on Human Rights, by the Beijing Platform of Action and by the Special Session of the General Assembly in March 2000 on "Women 2000: Gender Equality, Development and Peace for the Twenty-First Century". The issue of women and armed conflict has been pursued with rising insistence by human rights and women's rights institutions. The Arria Formula provided NGOs with the appropriate informal access to the Security Council which then adopted Resolution 1325 (2000), which served as the basis for longer term policy and operational adjustments in peace operations, taking into account the human security dimension of women in armed conflict.

Security Council members usually undertake consultations in a variety of ad hoc groups established for specific purposes. "Groups of Friends" are being established to generate support for a specific draft resolution. They consult with other Council members on amendments necessary to achieve a consensus on the text[xxx]. A special case are the *Friends of Women, Peace and Security*, now titled *Friends of 1325*, a group of 31 countries chaired by the Canadian delegation, engaged in sustaining the basic policy concepts regarding the issue of women in armed conflicts. Meetings of Contact Groups and of Groups of Friends are private and informal.

The human security dimension is not only defined by state authorities, military operations, and humanitarian assistance by non-governmental organisations, but also by action taken by the private sector. In 2004, the Security Council wanted to explore ways in which business plays good and bad roles in conflicts and how the UN system and the wider international community should respond if corporations breach accepted norms and standards. At the meeting the Council not only listened to the President of the World Bank and the President of the UN Economic and Social Council but also to the President and Chief Executive Officer of a private company, the Siemens AG, Germany, who underlined the importance of people living in conflict-affected countries to see the positive impact the private sector could have on their lives.

The Arria Formula evolved in yet another important way when in 2000 the Security Council permitted other UN member states to attend Arria Fomula meetings thus giving countries who were not members of the Security Council important access to information.

Security Council Interacting with Other UN Organs and Institutions

Human security has also institutional implications requiring the visions, values and operational know-how of other UN organs. From this perspective the Chilean Ambassador Juan Somavia as President of the Security Council launched the initiative to open the Council to the development related capacities and visions of the bureaux of the Economic and Social Council and of the Second Committee (economic issues) and Third Committee (social issues and human rights) of the General Assembly. The meeting which provided for a briefing on the situation in the Great Lakes region (with more than 100.000 civilian victims) by three humanitarian Non Government Organizations(NGOs), OXFAM, Medecins sans frontières and CARE, was chaired, not by the President of the Security Council, but by the Undersecretary-General for Humanitarian Affairs. While this move certainly has to be seen as a very positive response to the growing agenda interdependence between these organs of the United Nations, member countries who were not on one of three bureaux objected to being excluded. The Somavia Formula has not been repeated.

The developed openness and interaction with other UN organs, International Financial Institutions and NGOs is also being practiced in some of the subsidiary bodies of the Security Council. An example is the briefing on 26 October 2009 provided to the Security Council's Counter Terrorism Committee by the President of the Financial Action Task Force[xxxi]

The Peacebuilding Commission established by joint resolutions of the Security Council and the General Assembly has been mandated "to marshal resources and to advise on and propose integrated strategies for post-conflict peacebuilding and recovery". The complexity of the issues to be addressed and programmes and operations to be developed led to a similar approach by the initiative of Ambassador Somavia. It is reflected in the innovative composition of the Peacebuilding Commission which includes seven members (including the five permanent) of the Security Council, seven members of the Economic and Social Council, five of the top ten contributors to UN budgets, five of the top ten providers of personnel to UN peace missions, and seven additional members elected by the General Assembly.

Subsidiary Organs of the General Assembly Dealing with Aspects of Human Security

The development of the Council's Agenda both in terms of quantity and complexity required also a certain institutional development within the setting of the Security Council as well as in its relations with the other organs of the United Nations. The Charter provided only for the establishment of a Military Staff Committee[xxxii] authorized the Security Council, however, to "establish such subsidiary organs as it deems necessary for the performance of its functions"[xxxiii]. The different security concepts are well reflected in the various subsidiary organs of the Security Council dealing with a broad range of different responsibilities, both concrete conflict related or dealing with general issues of norm-setting and compliance monitoring.

Related to the agenda spectrum of human security the following subsidiary organs of the Security Council should be mentioned:

> ad hoc working groups dealing with such issues of conflict prevention in Africa, with practical measures imposed on individuals designated by the Al-Qaida/Taliban Sanctions Committee, and on children and armed conflict;
>
> the Counter Terrorism Committee; and
>
> the various sanctions committees dealing with sanctions imposed on Somalia, Sierra Leone, Al-Qaida and the Taliban, Iraq, Liberia, DRCongo, Côte d'Ivoire, Sudan, Lebanon, DRKorea, and with sanctions regimes related to the non-proliferation of weapons of mass destruction.

The Security Council Creating International Criminal Tribunals

The issue of war crimes, crimes against humanity and genocide required a response by the international community especially regarding the genocide in Rwanda and in Bosnia-Herzegovina, in Burundi, Sierra Leone and in Liberia. The Security Council, acting under Chapter VII, moved towards the establishment of new types of institutions. The Council established, with simple resolution, International Criminal Tribunals for the prosecution of people responsible for serious violations of international humanitarian law committed in the former Yugoslavia and in Rwanda and contributed to the special courts established in Sierra Leone, Cambodia and in Lebanon.

The UN also contributes to the work and staffing of the Extraordinary Chambers in the Courts of Cambodia (ECCC) created to try serious crimes committed during the Khmer Rouge regime. An agreement of the UN with the Government of Sierra Leone led to the creation of the Special Court for Sierra Leone. It is mandated to try those who bear the greatest responsibility for serious violations of international humanitarian law committed since 1996 in the context of civil war.

The "Responsibility to Protect"

The principle of the "responsibility to protect" adopted by consensus by the 2005 Summit Meeting of the General Assembly[xxxiv] can be understood as putting human security and human sovereignty even above state sovereignty, in that the responsibility of state governments to assure the human rights and human security to their citizens can be assumed by the international community in subsidiarity if states fail to do so.

Conclusions

The new security challenges and the related agenda items have led to new patterns of participation of non-member countries in the deliberations as well as to interactions with non-state partners in global affairs such as civil society, the private sector and representatives of other United Nations organs and institutions. The Security Council's deliberations and the decisions made on human security issues reflect the Council's evolving capacity for responding to these profound changes in our global security agenda.

The primary concerns for security and sovereignty of states as a key field of responsibility of the Security Council has been increasingly replaced by issues of human security such as civilians, including especially women and children in armed conflict, issues of the rule of law, of state building, governance building and human rights.

This also has had implications for the knowledge required for the Council's deliberations and also for the inter-institutional cooperation between the different organs of the United Nations, as well as between the institutions of the international system of organisations. The joint establishment of the Peacebuilding Commission by the General Assembly and the Security Council with the Economic and Social Council mandated to provide important inputs, is just one example of the institutional implications of the new security agenda. The new dimensions of our peace and security issues focus on the citizen, the human being, and are inherently multi-dimensional and complex, with implications for different actors, interveners and potential victims. The Security Council has responded to these developments. More changes are, however, to be expected.

Notes and References

[i] The Soviet Union cast 106 vetoes on SC resolutions between 1946 and 1965
[ii] The creation of the Expanded Programme for Technical Assistance, the Special Fund and then of UNDP

[iii] The staff capacities of the United Nations Centre for Natural Resources, Energy and Transport at the UN Secretariat in New York had the same size as the Department of Political Affairs

[iv] United Nations Conference on Human Environment, Stockholm, 1972, leading to the creation by the UN General Assembly of the UN Environment Programme (UNEP)

[v] The Vancouver UN Conference on Human Settlements in 1976 led to the Creation of the UN Habitat as a programme of the UN General Assembly headquartered in Nairobi

[vi] the UN-General Assembly created the United Nations Industrial Development Organisation in 1966 first as a programme of the General Assembly which in 1985 was transformed into a UN specialized agency

[vii] In 1956 when the Security Council was paralysed because of British and French vetoes, the General Assembly in a Emergency Special Session (according to Res. 377 (V) created an "emergency international United Nations Force to secure and supervise the cessation of hostilities" between Egypt, France, Israel and the United Kingdom with the first peace-keeping troops positioned between two conflict partners .

[viii] United Nations Truce Supervision Organization, established by SC Resolution 50 (1948 of 29 May 1948; see *The Blue Helmets – A Review of United Nations Peacekeeping*, United Nations, DPI, New York, 1996

[ix] United Nations Emergency Force, established by SC Resolution 998 (ES-I) of 4 November 1956

[x] United Nations Peace-keeping Force in Cyprus, established by SC Resolution 186 (1964) of 4 March 1964

[xi] Art. 2.7 proviedes that nothing contained in the Charter shall authorize the United Nations to intervene in matters which are esentially within the domestic jurisdiction of any state or shall require the Members to submit such matters to settlement und er the present Charter.

[xii] With between 85 and 95 % of victims being civilians, primarily women and children

[xiii] Only between August and November 2009 two resolutions on Women and Peace were adopted by the Security Council, Resolution 1888(2009) of 30 September 2009 and Resolution 1889(2009) of 5 October 2009, one on the Protection of Civilians in Armed Conflict, Resolution 1894(2009) of 11 November 2009, and one on Children and Armed Conflict, Resolution 1882 (2009) of 4 August 2009.

[xiv] Security Council Resolution 983 of 31 March 1995

[xv] Security Council Resolution 1366 (2001) of 30 August 2001 on the role of the Security Council in the prevention of armed conflict

[xvi] Security council Resolution 615 (1989) of 14 June 1989

[xvii] Security Council Resolution 1269 (1999) of 19 October 1999

[xviii] Security Council Resolution 1368 of 12 September 2001

[xix] Security Council Resolution 1373 of 12 November 2001

[xx] Statement of the President of the Security Council S/PRST/99/28

[xxi] United Nations Guards Contingent in Iraq composed of police contingents in UN uniforms

xxii United Nations Transitional Authority in Cambodia (UNTAC), Security Council resolution 745(1992) of 28 February 1992

xxiii United Nations Mission in Haiti (UNMIH), Security Council resolution 867(1993) of 23 September 1993

xxiv Statement of the President of the Security Council on "Maintenance of peace and security and post-conflict peacebuilding" (PRST/1998/38) of 29 December 1998

xxv A/RES/60/1, par. 97-105

xxvi General Assembly resolution A/60/180 and Security Council Resolution 1645 (2005)

xxvii See Report of the Secretary General on the role of UN peacekeeping in disarmament, demobilisation and reintegration (S/2000/101)

xxviii Articles 41 and 42 of the Charter

xxix See David Cortright, George A. Lopez and Linda Gerber-Stellingwerf, "Sanctions", pp 349-369, Thomas G. Weiss and Sam Daws, *The Oxford Handbook on The United Nations*, Oxford University Press, New York, 2007

xxx Such 'Groups of friends' were created on issues related to Haiti, Gergia, El Salvador and Guatemala.

xxxi FATF was established in 1989 by the G-7 Summit in Paris in response to large amounts of drug money being laundered. The FATF is an intergovernmental body that develops and promotes policies and concrete standards to combat money laundering and terrorist financing.

xxxii Article 47 of the Charter

xxxiii Article 29 of the Charter

xxxiv UN Doc. A//RES/60/1 par. 138-139 based on the Report *Responsibility to Protect*, containing the conclusions of the International Commission on Intervention and State Sovereignty, Ottawa 2001

Financial Crimes: A Global Threat

MAXIMILLIAN EDELBACHER AND MICHAEL THEIL

Introduction to Financial Structure and Crime

Section I demonstrated that peoples' needs for security have not changed over the centuries, but the concept of security has changed and some of the major threats to security have also changed. Even after we determine which individuals, organizations, and agencies are primarily responsible for providing security (from physical harm or from deprivation of basic physical needs such as food, clothing, and shelter), we still must analyze the factors that threaten these needs for security and ways to avoid them. In addition, as societies change, their potential security threats also change. Thus, it is necessary for those who provide security to be able to predict when new threats will appear and make recommendations for responding to these security threats effectively.

Changes in threat potentials always require the adaption of countermeasures. What adjustments must be made and how can these countermeasures be used effectively? These questions are not easily answered. Thus, the second part of this book is devoted to learning about some of the more promising potential responses to financial threats to the security of nations as well as global society.

It is always fruitful to predict what will likely happen in the future by studying the past and the present. Lessons learned from the past and present are many. First and foremost, it is necessary to first have a clear analysis of the status quo and how it is developed. Abstract analyses of the types of threats that may arise and what forms they will take should be made, even though these threats are not yet obvious. Otherwise new threat situations may be neglected.

This section of the book will present an analysis of the present state and models and plans for preventing financial crises on a more abstract level. The chapters selected for this section address the problem of responding to financial security threats.

In Chapter 6 titled "White Collar Crime," Edelbacher and Theil start with an explanation of the many facets of this type of crime. Many manifestations of financial crime fall within this spectrum—various forms of fraud, for instance those linked with bankruptcy, insider trading, and pyramid schemes. Some white collar criminal events attracted significant public attention as in the case of Bernard Madoff.

Very often, white collar crime produces huge financial losses. Because this type of crime is often cleverly concealed, it creates manifold problems for the public. It is also worth noting, that people are unable or unwilling to see the criminal aspects of many types of white collar crime, for example, insurance fraud. And many are eager to participate in fraudulent activities such as Madoff's schemes purely because of greed.

Seger notes in Chapter 7 on cyber and economic crime, that because electronic data processing used for communications and financial transactions is a key element in everyone's daily life, it presents potential for everyone to become a victim of some form of cyber crime. In today's economy, it would be impossible to conduct large-scale financial transactions without using computers. Seger concludes that cyber criminals can find unprecedented opportunities to organize and operate in a global context at relatively low risk and low cost. He predicts that criminals will continue to use new technologies for purposes of enhancing personal and public communications and transactions to exploit the vulnerabilities of individuals and public and private organizations including financial agencies that rely on computers as necessary tools for daily use.

In terms of combating cyber criminal activity, the most promising strategy is developing the technology and expertise required to combat cyber crime and trace the money earned through illegal practices. In Chapter 8, "Organized Crime, the Mafia, White Collar Crime, and Corruption," Antinori, first distinguishes organized crime, white collar crime, and the Mafia and briefly traces the development of several of the more prominent criminal organizations operating in Italy and internationally. He notes that all these criminal organizations pose major threats to the global society. Through various forms of corruption, then can make huge profits by using illegal mechanisms, then connect with legal economic enterprises and eventually blend into legitimate business. He notes that considerable political will is a requirement for reducing and eventually eliminating the great influence of organized crime on the political and economic systems of the nations in the global society of today.

Clearly, financial crime can pose a considerable threat to a democratic society. Chapter 9 is titled "Rule of Law versus Financial Crime," and Dobovšek explains how violations of the rule of law can threaten the very foundations of a democratic society and destroy its economic base. He notes that financial crime distorts the economic system and also harms the political structure when members of informal networks choose to ignore rules and legislation and perform actions that benefit only themselves and fellow members. Corruption and financial crime appear to have increased in Eastern Europe—a development many blame on the transition to democracy.

Is the financial crisis a turning point in financial regulation? In Chapter 10 relating the crisis to the pursuit of financial crime, Tomasic analyzes the effectiveness of new regulations in curtailing financial crises brought about by criminal financial activities. He notes that a period of minimal regulation of financial markets led to a number of unintended but certainly undesirable consequences such as insider trading, corrupt practices, tax avoidance, money laundering, and other frauds. Criminals were able to avoid detection and prosecution. Therefore, Tomasic sees the need for more effective control mechanisms and institutions.

Chapter 11 is titled "Global View on Organized Crime, White Collar Crime, and Corruption." Mills discusses the dangers of reporting corruption. In fact, journalists face risks of death, assault, torture, intimidation, harassment, and wrongful imprisonment in many parts of the world for investigating and delivering information about corruption. It may surprise many people that covering corruption stories is more dangerous than reporting about war. Mills provides several examples to illustrate the hazards of investigative reporting, particularly when an investigation involves the alleged corruption of high level, powerful government officials. He also notes that corruption may be found in every country, not just certain countries we normally associate with high levels of political corruption.

Finally, in Chapter 12, Wolfgang Hetzer complains that the "financial crisis" term suggests that serious economic woes result from natural disasters—acts of God—and no one is to be blamed or held guilty for them. This is, of course, a misconception because human decision making is behind all financial crises. Hetzer, however, feels that penal law is not helpful for preventing such events or punishing those responsible. He sees a close network of bankers and politicians who are interested in business, not in trials. Therefore, those responsible for illegal practices in the financial area are in positions to influence legislation and jurisdiction.

White Collar Crime

6

MAXIMILLIAN EDELBACHER
MICHAEL THEIL

Contents

Conditions of Economic Life

Growing up in the Western World, living in today's rather wealthy states of Europe, you are used to the philosophy of free markets. You can afford nearly everything and can buy what you want. Supermarkets, financial institutions, insurance, industry, and food production are thriving. Europe has experienced sixty years of peace.

Younger generations did not experience conditions at the ends of the First and Second World Wars when money systems broke down, it was impossible to purchase goods with money, and unemployment rates were enormous. Especially after the end of the Second World War, countries like Germany and Austria that started the war were supported by the Marshall Plan and their economies recovered quickly after the end of the war. At first, people were supported by food and basic goods, then industrial production was financed by loans and a free economy following western market models was developed. In the 1950s and 1960s, Europeans spoke of their "economic wonder."

Economic Life in a Secure Environment

In Western Europe, economic progress was possible because of peace and stability. Eastern Europe, dominated by the Communist regimes from 1945 to 1989 experienced a much different development. A regulated market is far less prosperous. Priorities in Eastern Europe were far different from those of Western Europe and therefore living standards improved very slowly. The Western Europe model compared to the Eastern Europe model was much more efficient in the view of the average citizen.

Western Economic Model of Free Market

The economies in democratic societies function through market mechanisms and also on deeper principles of a democratic society. Financial institutions and insurance companies exist on the principle of *pacta sunt servanda.*[1] It is an important principle that we talk to each other, make contracts and deals, and are presuming our partners will act correctly and fulfil their parts of spoken and written agreements. Members of societies can and will trust each other that treaties will be followed. This principle is called *uberimae fidei,*[2]

If the number of criminal attacks escalates, the market balance will be lost because the arithmetical system of check and balances will run out of control and financial and insurance institutions will become vulnerable to these attacks. Organized criminals are capable of destroying democracies. For example, it was estimated that the Italian Mafia owns 15% of the world's securities. If the Mafia challenges the security market by manipulating this volume, the market immediately will change so dramatically that it may collapse. Boutros-Boutros-Ghali, a former secretary general of the United Nations (UN), stated in a meeting of high ranking officials, ministers, and representatives of governments in Naples that criminal organizations, like the South American drug cartels were financially more powerful than small countries. Antonio Maria Costa, a former head of the UN Office on Drugs and Crime (UNODC) in Vienna argued throughout his tenure that organized crime and white collar crime could destabilize democratic systems.[3]

Factors Influencing Economy

A number of factors serve as frame conditions for the development of economies throughout the world. They exert enormous influence on the future and cannot be controlled and predicted. For example, the UN predicts that by 2050, the world population will be 9 to 12 billion people and fears that two-thirds of them will live in poor circumstances. Only a third will live in conditions customary in the Western Hemisphere.[4]

Exogenous Factors

Exogenous factors create tremendous challenges. Warming of the earth, climate changes, dangers of earthquakes, flooding, and drought may lead to struggles and even wars resulting from shortages of resources. Exogenous factors endanger our hopes for a peaceful and stable future. Despite the widespread activities of the UN, we have little chance to change production practices and living conditions for all people. One military expert noted in a speech in October 2009 that in the near future 300 million people would have to leave their home countries because of infertile soil and lack of water. This migration by poor and hungry people who want to improve their living conditions will create tremendous pressure on all world economies.

Movements of Populations

If the UN and other organizations are correct, we must expect an increasing tendency of people to move. We are already experiencing strong movements from East to West and South to North. The richer countries are faced with integrating economic refugees into their wealthy societies. A 1990s study showed that 4% of the European Union population (12.8 million people among 327 million) came from non-European backgrounds. The result was fear of a clash caused by cultural and religious diversity. Many immigrants came from Muslim countries, and they wanted to live as they did in their native lands where they worshiped at mosques with minarets and their women wore special clothing. Their wishes are not always respected by the people of their chosen countries. Immigrant issues are very controversial and political discussions and elections bring out a lot of emotions.

Causes of Movements

The collapse of the Communist regime in 1989 became a tragedy for the European Continent. The dreams of freedom and unification became realities, but many people feared the new freedoms and were unhappy with their new situations. A stream of people, especially economic refugees, flowed over Central, Southern, and Western Europe and became threats to the societies in these richer countries. Both ordinary crime and organized crime increased. Law enforcement agencies and justice systems became unable to handle the load and citizens felt insecure and helpless. Why did this happen? These refugees left their home countries because of:[5]

- Hopes for a better economic situation
- Strong desires to improve living conditions
- Political instability at home and fear of the future
- Increasing violence, unrest, and civil war at home
- Violations of human rights
- Poor living conditions

In summary, these people wanted to improve their lives. Young people, informed by modern information technology (television, radio, Internet), learned better lives might be possible if they left their home countries, and they moved.

Various factors support legal and illegal immigration. Modern technologies allow people to move easily. Information is available worldwide and in real time, and this allows refugees to find places where they can live better. Development of transport facilities opened travel to most people, even if the travellers faced dangers. Recall the "boat people" who left intolerable living conditions for perilous journeys with uncertain endings. The high commissioner of the UNHCR noted that the world is shrinking, geographical distances are of no importance, and the boat people have been replaced by the "jet people." Among the consequences of these global changes[6] are:

- Crime is increasing because of mobility
- Non-citizen crime is increasing
- Terrorism and organized crime are increasing
- Violent tendencies are increasing

Immigration from Africa and Asia is very common, and the difference between rich and poor people remains enormous. The European Union is called Fortress Europe because Spain, France, Italy, and Greece try to protect their borders. A special organization called Frontex was created to protect European borders against illegal immigration.

Increases in Crime Rates

The result of the huge gap between poor people and rich people is increased crime. Criminal organizations that specialize in trafficking of humans cheat their victims. They tell their victims about excellent working possibilities in destination countries. People from the poorest villages pay great amounts of money for transportation and counterfeit passports. They arrive in Europe or the U.S. full of hope. When they see the realities in their new countries, their only alternative for staying alive is often criminal activity.

Tendencies toward Violence and Terrorism

Similar explanations help explain the tendency for increasing violence and sympathy for terrorism. Inhabitants of poorer countries, often Muslim countries, hate capitalism and the rich West. Teaching religious fundamentalism is an easy way to motivate and militarize these poor people. Many of them become guest workers in western societies. They observe all the conditions in capitalistic countries, then return to their home countries where they are confronted with poor living conditions, no water, no fertile land, no hope, and no future. They understand how much oil and other resources of their countries are "stolen" by capitalistic regimes. Very often the reactions are violence and terrorism. These examples of exogenous factors cannot be influenced to a great extent. Most small countries lack the power and the importance to be heard by international companies and big, powerful states, and they do not care. Money is the only concern international companies like BP, Shell, and others that have no intention of changing these conditions.

Endogenous Factors

Compare the current shrinking consciousness of law and order with conditions in society when you were a child. Michael Sika, Austria's former general director for security, gave an excellent speech on "Society and Crime" in the late 1990s and said that our society is much more vulnerable to international and transnational crime because the will to defend is disappearing.

Changes of Ethical Values

Ethical values have certainly changed. Materialism, nepotism, and egoism are more important than solidarity and common values. We live in a materialistic world in which most people want to be wealthy. Community is far less important. Michael Sika said, "Family and school are the cornerstones of our societies." What happened? Two-thirds of violent crimes, murders, and physical injuries occur at home. Parents neglect their children, schools cannot educate students, and the general impression is that civil society is out of control and rules and laws are no longer followed. We live in a society that no longer values law and order and discipline. Moral concepts have changed because of:

- Damaged family structures
- Damaged educational structures

- Problems caused by selfishness
- Hidden economies
- Fiscal, tax, and insurance frauds
- Assaults

Changing Views of Rule of Law

One observation after more than thirty-five years of police work is a change in attitudes about crime. Young people in particular care very little about non-violent crimes. During the 1950s and1960s, shoplifting and insurance fraud crimes were serious but now are considered "nothing."

Shoplifting—Because of changes in selling strategies, more supermarkets are stocked with more varieties of goods and stealing from them is not considered a crime in many segments of society. The Austrian Chamber of Commerce reported that merchandise worth more than €50 million is stolen from supermarkets annually.

Insurance Fraud—Many insurance frauds are not recognized as crimes. Studies performed in America and Europe show that people do not consider cheating an insurance company as a criminal action.

Definition of White Collar Crime

Edwin H. Sutherland defined white collar crime in 1939 in the *American Sociological Review*[7] as "crime committed by a person of respectability and high social status in the course of his occupation." By this definition, white collar criminals wear suits and dresses; they look good and convey the impression that you can trust them. The basic elements of fraud are (1) hiding behind a trusted identity, (2) being driven by greed (money is the ruling factor), and (3) cheating is the basic action.

Jay S. Albanese, a famous criminology professor, wrote in *White Collar Crime in America*[8] that, "Attempts to explain the deviant and criminal acts of individuals have a long history that crosses boundaries of biology, psychology, sociology, and many other disciplines." Unlike the criminology of individuals, the criminology of organizations (and the individual members of those organizations) has gained the attention of researchers and policy makers only recently. One reason for this delayed study of organizational, economic, professional, and white collar crime is the complexity of organizational behavior. Unlike crimes committed by individuals, it is more difficult to isolate and ascribe meaningful motives, qualities, and distinguishing characteristics to corporate entities and those working within them. As a result, many fundamental questions remain about white collar crime including an exact definition.

Much of the confusion about precisely what constitutes white collar crime can be attributed to Sutherland's introduction of the original definition to criminologists in 1939. He refers to crimes by "persons of high social status" committed "in the course of" occupations. Clearly, he includes the acts of individuals in this definition. The second part of the definition, however, appears to exempt individual crimes such as income tax evasion and credit card fraud that are normally not functions of occupations. Likewise, occupational thefts (embezzlement, bribery) committed by working class individuals also appear to fall outside Sutherland's definition.

Sociologist Edwin Lemert claims to have asked Sutherland whether he meant a specific type of crime or a crime committed by specific type of person in the definition of white collar crime. Sutherland said he was not sure and probably had reasons not to be specific. Little specific information about crime was available to Sutherland in the 1940s. As Gilbert Gels notes,[9] Sutherland's belief that all criminal behavior could be explained by his theory of different associations made definitional precision inconsequential. Modern definitions go further than Sutherland's although some of the practices remain the same. Some modern definitions refer back to Sutherland's because the high ranking employee committing crime in his firm is still the typical fraudster. Fraud perpetrators come from all social classes but the more dangerous ones are those who have access to "big money."

Development of White Collar Crime

As we will see, white collar crime is far more widespread than it was in the 1940s. The intent of a white collar criminal[10] is to "defraud someone with the intention to enrich himself or a third person unlawfully."

In business activities and individual transactions, victims are cheated by many different types of actions and non-actions. When does fraud start and when does white collar crime start? A study in Austria investigated starting points of criminal actions. One starting point is tax fraud. In Europe, "shadow economies" form, especially in countries with high taxes. A number of studies showed that the tendency to invest in shadow economies increases where taxes are higher. Another tendency is to transfer money to offshore "tax havens." About one-third of the BNP flows to shadow economy activities in Austria. This represents a huge budget loss because Austria is the fourth richest country of the European Union.

Shadow Economies

Where does economic crime start? In 1991 a study in Austria focused on when and where deviant behavior starts. Friedrich Schneider, a professor at the

Johann Kepler University in Linz, is famous for publishing an annual report about the economic dimensions of shadow economies in Austria.[11] Clearly shadow economies increase in economically difficult times. In Austria, the shadow economy was estimated at about €22 billion in 2009.[12] The literature distinguishes shadow economies from black markets.

Financial Crimes

White collar crimes are based on deviant and criminal acts committed by individual persons of high social status based on Sutherland's definition. Financial crimes are offenses against financial institutions, and they are on the increase. The Internet and cyber crime expanded opportunities to "hit" financial institutions. Typical methods such as disguising identity and theft of identity are used to cheat financial institutions directly or indirectly. Organized criminals have created specialized "think tanks" to find new ways of launching virtual attacks against financial institutions and train criminals on new types of cyber attacks.

Spectrum of White Collar Crimes

Bankruptcy Fraud

A bankrupt or insolvent person is not capable of paying his or her debts. Bankruptcy is a legal declaration of inability or impairment of ability of an individual or organization to pay creditors. Creditors may file a bankruptcy petition against a business or corporate debtor (involuntary bankruptcy) in an effort to recoup what they are owed or initiate a restructuring. In most cases, however, bankruptcy is voluntary—initiated by an insolvent individual or organization debtor.[12]

The debtor in a voluntary bankruptcy or the creditor in an involuntary proceeding petitions the court for an order of bankruptcy. A bankrupt is a person or organization declared by a court to be incapable of meeting financial obligation. The bankrupt's affairs are put into the hands of a trustee. Bankruptcy fraud is crime.[13]

While it is difficult to generalize across jurisdictions, common criminal acts under bankruptcy laws typically involve concealment of assets, concealment or destruction of documents, conflicts of interest, fraudulent claims, false statements or declarations, and fee fixing or redistributing arrangements. Falsifications on bankruptcy forms often constitute perjury. Multiple filings are not criminal unless they violate provisions of relevant bankruptcy laws. In the U.S., bankruptcy fraud statutes consider the mental conditions of parties. Bankruptcy fraud should be distinguished from strategic bankruptcy, which is not a criminal act, but may work against a filer. All assets must be disclosed on bankruptcy schedules even if a debtor believes they have no net value. After a bankruptcy petition is filed, only the creditors may decide whether a particular asset has value.

The ramifications of omitting assets from schedules can be very serious for an offending debtor. A closed bankruptcy may be reopened by the discovery of an "unscheduled asset" after all debts are discharged. The trustee may then seize the discovered asset and liquidate it for the benefit of the formerly discharged creditors. Whether the concealment of such an asset should also be considered for criminal prosecution as fraud and/or perjury is at the discretion of the judge and/or trustee.[14]

Insider Trading

Insider trading[15] is the trading of a corporation's stocks or other securities (bonds or stock options) by individuals who have access to non-public information about the company. In most countries, trading is conducted without taking advantage of non-public information. However, insider trading often describes a practice by which an insider or a related party trades securities based on material non-public information obtained during the performance of his or her duties at the corporation, in breach of a fiduciary or other relationship of trust and confidence, or through misappropriation of non-public information from the company.

In the U.S. and several other jurisdictions, trading conducted by corporate officers, key employees, directors, and significant shareholders (defined as beneficial owners of 10% or more of a firm's equity securities) must be reported to regulators or publicly disclosed, usually within a few business days of a trade. Many investors follow the summaries of these insider trades in the hope that mimicking them will be profitable.

While "legal" insider trading cannot be based on material non-public information, some investors believe corporate insiders nonetheless may have better insights into the health of a corporation and that their trades may convey important information (e.g., pending retirement and sales of shares by an important officer, greater commitment to the corporation evidenced by officer share purchases). Illegal insider trading is believed to raise the cost of capital for securities issuers, thus affecting overall economic growth.

Bank Robbery

Bank robbery[16] is not a classic fraud scheme, but it affects security levels wherever it occurs. The number of bank robberies every year in a country and the clearance rate tells us much about the security standards of a country. The phenomenon of bank robbery impacts the public trust of the financial sector on the one side and also reveals the level of trust in police and private security standards. A top priority of security strategy in Austria is to keep the numbers of bank robberies low and invest a lot of resources in doing so. For example, the federal bank in Austria organizes regular meetings of the banking sector to discuss what can be done to prevent bank robberies.

Investment Capital Fraud

Investment capital fraud[17] (also known as securities fraud and stock fraud) induces investors to make purchase or sale decisions based on false information that frequently leads to losses and violates securities laws. Generally speaking, securities fraud consists of deceptive practices in the stock and commodity markets and occurs when investors are enticed to part with their money based on untrue statements. Security fraud includes outright theft from investors and misstatements on a public company's financial reports. The term also encompasses other actions, including insider trading, front running, and other illegal acts on the trading floor of a stock or commodity exchange. According to the FBI, securities fraud includes false statements on financial statements and Securities and Exchange Commission (SEC) filings, lying to corporate auditors, insider trading, stock manipulation schemes, and broker embezzlement. The nine types of securities frauds are:

Corporate fraud
Internet fraud
Insider trading
Microcap fraud
Accounting fraud
Boiler room operation
Mutual fund fraud
Short selling abuses
Ponzi schemes

Pyramid Schemes

A pyramid scheme[18] is a non-sustainable business model that promises participants payments primarily for enrolling other people into the scheme; profits do not come from genuine investments or sales of products or services. Pyramid schemes constitute fraud and are illegal in many countries including Albania, Australia, Brazil, Canada, China, Colombia, Denmark, France, Germany, Hungary, Iceland, Iran, Italy, Japan, Malaysia, Mexico, Nepal, Netherlands, New Zealand, Norway, the Philippines, Poland, Portugal, Romania, South Africa, Sri Lanka, Switzerland, Taiwan, Thailand, United Kingdom, and United States.

These types of schemes have existed for at least a century. Variations were developed to hide their true nature, and many people still contend that multilevel marketing (which is legal) is nothing more than a pyramid scheme. Victims of pyramid schemes are primarily members of weak social classes. A successful pyramid scheme combines a fake but seemingly credible business with a simple-to-understand money-making formula that sounds sophisticated and appears to have potential for profit.

The essential idea is that a con artist we will call X makes only one payment. To start earning, X must recruit others who will also make one payment each. X is paid from receipts from new recruits who then go on to recruit others. As each new recruit makes a payment, X gets a cut. He is thus promised exponential benefits as the "business" expands, even though it probably does not involve sales of real products or services that represent monetary value. A payment may even be a non-cash valuable.

To enhance credibility, most such scams are well equipped with fake referrals, testimonials, and information. The flaw is that most participants receive no end benefit. The money simply travels up the pyramid. Only the originator (sometimes called the "pharaoh") and a very few at the top levels make significant amounts of money. The amounts dwindle steeply down the pyramid slopes. The many individuals at the bottom (who subscribed to the plan but were unable to recruit followers) end up with deficits. A very simple mathematic model is behind the pyramid scheme. Assume level 1 represents the pharaoh who enlists four recruits, each of whom then adds four recruits and so on. By the time level 11 is reached, the pyramid has grown to more than 4 million participants who gain no profits.

Pyramid Level	Number of Participants
1	4
2	16
3	64
4	256
5	1024
6	4096
7	16,384
8	65,536
9	262,144
10	1,048,576
11	4,194,304

Similar schemes like the "Eight Ball" model and matrix plans use the same fraudulent, non-sustainable systems as the pyramid. Participating in a matrix scheme means joining a waiting list for desirable products.

Figure 6.1 Photograph of Bernard Madoff.

How much did Bernard Madoff's scheme cost? Madoff's claim[19] to have defrauded investors out of $50 billion may have been exaggerated, attorneys say, and it may take years to unravel the true cost. According to CNN and various newspaper accounts, the Madoff scandal (Figure 6.1) will be the most expensive Ponzi scheme in U.S. history, but the $50 billion price tag claimed by Madoff may be as fictitious as the returns he promised investors. Madoff was charged with defrauding investors and may have calculated the $50 billion based on double-digit returns he promised but never delivered. Subscribe to Companies feed://rss.cnn.com/rss/money_news_companies.rss. See all CNNMoney.com RSS FEEDS. "Taking Bernard Madoff's word for the total number is probably not an accurate way of accounting for the losses," said Jonathan Levitt, an attorney representing individuals who lost money in the scandal. "I don't think there's any way to know the total amount yet," said Greg Blue, an attorney with Morgenstern, Jacobs & Blue. "Everything we've heard is that his books and records are in disarray. There's no official tally yet."

The task for investigators poring over Madoff's muddled books is to determine the scope of the losses. A Ponzi or pyramid scheme is an investment fraud in which high profits from fictitious sources are promised to investors. Early investors and those who take early returns are paid with funds raised from later investors. If an investor invested $100,000 with Madoff in 1990 and saw that figure rise on paper to $1 million in 2010, did he or she lose the $100,000 principal or the principal plus a large profit that never existed? Yeshiva University recently announced that of its $110 million in Madoff investment losses, only $14 million represented principal.

These questions are complicated by the distributions taken by many investors on their investments over the years. For example, if an investor withdrew 10% per year in returns and achieved return of his principal, could he be accused of profiting from Madoff's system of repaying old money with new? Could he also be subject to lawsuits from other defrauded investors?

Some questions relate to "opportunity cost." An investment placed with Madoff could have been made elsewhere and realized actual returns. Irving Picard of the law firm of Baker & Hostetler and a court-appointed trustee is currently analyzing Madoff's investments for eventual distributions to defrauded investors. Madoff complied with a court order to supply a list of his assets to the SEC by December 31, 2008. Levitt, who represents investors, said that untangling Madoff's web of financial dealings could take years and a team of 500 accountants, lawyers, and researchers. "I think the accounting will cost hundreds of millions of dollars," Levitt said, "and the taxpayer is going to foot the bill."

Madoff was sentenced to a jail term of 150 years. In December 2010, his son committed suicide. Also in December 2010, a lawsuit filed in the U.S. by Irving Kohn, a manager of the Medici Bank in Austria, claimed $19.6 billion or €14.8 billion.

Fraud in Opening Bank Accounts

A very dangerous and expensive international financial fraud results from opening bank accounts under false identities.[20] In most cases, foreigners who present false identity papers when they open accounts are not known to bank officials and visit bank premises only twice: to open an account and to withdraw funds. Stolen or fake checks are often presented to open accounts. A similar technique is used for fraudulent transfers by fax orders because banks cannot verify such transfer orders quickly.

Counterfeiting is often detected only after withdrawals of large amounts. Very often, fraudulent bank customers use well known company names. These companies are known by the banks to transfer large amounts, so that a transfer order does not seem suspicious, and it is not always possible to use security codes. In a similar way, fake invoices are used for bank transfers. With these fake guarantees, the bank issues checks which unknown fraudsters immediately change into cash. Only later are the irregularities detected.

Transaction Fraud, Fraud through Mediation, and Ghost Money Operations

Another plague is fraud through mediation.[21] The victims are usually individuals who need to borrow money and cannot do so because they are no longer credit worthy. They fall prey to dubious money-lenders who act as mediators and refer them to fraudsters who attempt to sell guarantees that can be used as securities for credit at a bank. The guarantees are worthless; they were issued by a letter box company or are counterfeit.

A similar scheme is advanced fee fraud. The victim participates in a collateral funding exchange, which means raising money against bank guarantees. It is common to all these forms of mediation fraud that the victim must make an initial payment in the form of a commission, fee deposit or other charge. Another scheme involves trading in gold or foreign currencies (Kuwaiti dinars, Russian rubles, etc.).

A self liquidating loan is paid off through interest generated and can even result in a profit. The role of a bank in these transactions is secondary. Its role is to provide evidence of legitimacy and an air of respectability, while money is laundered on its premises. Other defrauders regularly use banks for their fraudulent activities. They build a chain of correspondence with a bank and try to persuade the bank to act as a trustee for very large financial transactions. In 99% of such cases, the crime is not money laundering. It is fraud against business and is called a ghost money operation.

Counterfeit and Stolen Securities and Gem Frauds

It is said that fraudulent bonds thought to be valued at billions of euros are lying like bombs in bank vaults. Since the fall of the Iron Curtain, many "joint ventures" were started with false or stolen securities certificates.[22] Two groups of criminals are connected with these frauds. The first group deals in artificial diamonds and issues false certificates of authenticity. The artificial stones are presented as genuine diamonds to be sold for large sums of money. The second group deals in uncut gems such as rubies from the Ural Mountains. This group also issues false certificates that inflate the values of the gems. In reality, they are not worth refining and cutting. The original certificates referred to "stones" rather than describing the items in question.

Check and Card Fraud

One form of crime that has not been sufficiently addressed at the international level is fraudulent use of payment cards (credit, debit, ATM, check guarantees, prepaid cards) and checks (individual and organization checks, Eurocheques, and travelers' checks).[23] This type of fraud has grown rapidly in line with the increase in numbers of transactions paid by these methods. The wide use and acceptance of these cards and instruments encouraged criminal groups to engage in falsification and counterfeiting.

In 1968, the Eurocheque system was introduced. European banks agreed to redeem checks of other banks according to standardized conditions. In 1972, standardized forms of checks and check cards were issued. The standardized Eurocheque-system depends on fraud-proof checks and cards. Today, the checks can be redeemed in 210,000 banks in Europe for about 40 million bank clients. Forms of crime related to checks and check cards are theft, falsification, fraudulent use, counterfeiting, check issue without sufficient funds, and theft or falsification of identity documents. In an effort to combat fraud, advanced technology and fraud-prevention measures have been introduced:

- Use of holograms and lithographic printing to protect against card counterfeiting
- Increased transaction authorization requirements to prevent use of lost or stolen cards
- Increasingly sophisticated monitoring systems
- Measures ensuring that cards reach legitimate cardholders and are not intercepted
- Use of technology to protect magnetically encoded account data on magnetic stripes
- Transition to integrated circuit (chip) cards

These security measures provide effective deterrents to fraud carried out by individuals, but organized criminal groups have been able to overcome many of the current security measures to produce very high quality counterfeit cards.

Debit Card Fraud: Bankomat

Since 1984, payments can be made using a card and personal identification number (PIN) code.[24] Every Bankomat card has a four-digit PIN code on a magnetic strip that can be read by a machine. By 1987, 20 million Bankomat cards were in use in Germany; 1.5 million were issued in Austria. It is possible to withdraw money fraudulently from an account using a Bankomat card based on the principle that "it is better to hack than crack."

Credit Card Fraud

In 2010, more than 600 million credit cards were used in the U.S. More than 2 million credit cards are currently in use in Austria. A credit card entitles a holder to obtain money, goods, or services. All well known credit cards, such as Eurocard, Visa, MasterCard, American Express, and others follow this pattern. About 70% of credit cards are lost and 30% are falsified or stolen.[25] Card forgery is becoming more common. Russians commonly use forged credit cards throughout Europe.

Counterfeiting

Ever since money was invented as a means of payment, people have tried to pass counterfeit bills as genuine.[26] U.S. dollars and EU euros are commonly counterfeited. After the fall of the Iron Curtain, the amount of counterfeit money coming from Eastern Europe tripled. Now that photocopying has become very sophisticated and specialized, it is possible for non-experts to produce false banknotes fairly easily. Computer techniques such as scanning are also used for counterfeiting.

Document Falsification

False identity cards and documents have always been subject to fraud.[27] Many employees of financial institutions fail to check customers' identities. Based on police experience, international criminals generally use false or altered identity cards and documents. Since the opening of the Eastern borders and greater mobility, many more people enter Europe with counterfeit identity papers. To hide their real origins, they procure false documents (identify cards, passports, driving licenses) on the black market and use them to cross international borders.

Money Laundering

Drug trafficking was originally considered a national concern, but its international nature quickly became apparent. Law enforcement authorities first began to cooperate internationally via informal dialogues and through Interpol. In 1988, the Vienna Convention established a legal framework for fighting drug-related crime. In 1990, the Council of Europe Convention sought to address money laundering related to all types of crime, drug-related or otherwise (including card and check fraud).[28] Both the G7 and European Union adopted measures to combat financial crime—the former by endorsing in 1989 the forty recommendations of the Financial Action Task Force and the latter by adopting Directive 91/308/EEC on money laundering. Slowly but surely, governments adopted concrete measures and fostered legal and judicial cooperation. Although inadequate at present, it should ultimately have a deterrent effect on money launderers.[29]

Austria was for a time a country of interest for money laundering purposes based on its stable currency, safe economy, liberal foreign exchange policy, and banking secrecy laws that allowed launderers to remain anonymous. Based on economic statistics, the world population spends more money on drugs than on food. Money laundering reached about seventy-three billion Euros a year or half the Austrian gross domestic product (181,80 € in the year 2010). According to the director general of the Swiss National Bank, money laundering is a "breathtakingly vivid description" of the practice by which filthy money is put into a washing machine and clean white money comes out after it is "laundered." By laundering money, profits generated by criminal activities are transported, transformed, converted to, or mixed with legal funds, with the intention to conceal or hide the real origins, types, and disposal of such profits.* The three phases of money laundering are:

1. Placement: channeling cash
2. Adjustment: Changing cash into disposable financial assets
3. Reintegration: "Black" money becomes legal

Austria was criticized heavily by the U.S. and the European Community for its indirect support of money launderers. The consequence was that Austria, now a member of the European Community, introduced laws against money laundering in 1993 and 1994, after which a special bureau dealing with these forms of crime was installed in the Federal Ministry of Internal Affairs. Suspicious transactions must be reported to the bureau by banks. Every year about 1,000 suspicious transactions are reported to the authorities.

Insurance Fraud

Insurance fraud is not a new problem, as Professor Geerds, of the University of Frankfurt am Main, Germany noted.[30,31] Insurance fraud has been committed ever since insurance became available and affects all classes of business all over the world. Insurance fraud is a crime against property. The specific nature of this type of fraud is based on the insurance contract that obligates an insurance company to indemnify (pay) an insured contingent on an uncertain, future event. In cases of fraud, such events are caused intentionally or claimed falsely, a genuine loss is exaggerated, or a contract is unlawful.

Thus, in insurance terms, the event rather than the material property is covered. However, the insured victim expects the insurer to replace the property lost, regardless of the reason for loss. Thus, buying insurance is perceived as a way of undoing damage.

Moreover, many policyholders, particularly those involved in major accidents, expect more than financial indemnification. They want someone who cares and understands, they long for human support and assistance, and need someone hear about their fears and anxieties. Insurers are neither confessors nor psychotherapists, and many policyholders feel their insurance companies have failed them by not satisfying their needs for care, recognition, service, and security. They perceive the companies as materialistic and formalistic and not very helpful in psychological terms. After customers pay insurance premiums for a long period, they react in one of two ways:

* Based on legal definition of money laundering in Austria; see Art. 165 StGB.

1. In the event of a loss, a customer never gets what he expects. The loss occurred despite the payments of premiums and the damage cannot be undone. Claims adjustment and other insurance employees do not provide personal care and attention.
2. After years of remaining loss-free and paying premiums, many people tend to question why they never received anything from their insurance companies.

As a result, they may attempt to get at least part of the money back. The insurance principle and the idea of solidarity underlying the insurance system are difficult for many people to grasp. They do not understand that "a sorrow shared is a sorrow halved." This is due in part to the advertising philosophies of many insurance companies that tend to underline the savings aspects and the "waste not, want not" approach and minimize risk issues.

Recent statistics show that about 3.2 million damage cases were reported to Austrian insurance companies. It is estimated that 5 to 10% of these reports may be fraudulent. That means the extent of insurance fraud may reach nearly €1 billion of which only about 15% can be uncovered as fraud and stopped by insurance companies and reported to police and other authorities.

Sociological and Psychological Aspects of Insurance Fraud

Insurance fraud has been considered from sociological and psychological views by several authors.[32] An interesting paper on the subject by Höfner and Vaughan[31] was based on a study commissioned by the Association of Austrian Insurance Companies. The authors explain the motivations of people who buy insurance. An insurance contract makes them feel safer and frees them to a certain extent of their fears and anxieties. This means that insurance is often purchased as an irrational attempt to overcome existential fears. Policyholders consider their protection against losses and accidents inviolable.

A comparison of insurance fraud with other frequent crimes shows that that hit-and-run driving, shoplifting, tax evasion, and theft are perceived as far more severe and are condemned more heavily than insurance fraud. Other offenses like drug abuse, black marketing, operating a radio or television without a license, smuggling by tourists, and fare dodging were also considered less serious than insurance fraud. The limit above which people feel that real fraud begins is strikingly high. Insurance fraud is regarded as a criminal offense only if it involves €700 to €3,500 or more.

Another interesting paper on the subject was written by Gerhard Schwarz, a docent at the University of Vienna, and describes a study based on multi-dimensional cause research.[33] The study was performed on behalf of the Association of Austrian Insurance Companies in 1987. Schwarz noted that understanding insurance fraud requires a profound insight into the human psyche and the societal dimensions of human action because insurance has an almost religious connotation. Insurance is treated as a substitute for religion and is intended to free human beings from existential fears and protect them against death. Like sacrifices in a temple, premium payments are made to ward off accidents and losses. If a loss or accident occurs, the policyholder recognizes the fallacy of believing that regular premium payments would prevent accidents and thus blames the insurance company. This may result in disappointment with and aggression toward the insurance company. Schwarz compiled the most common explanations given by people who committed insurance fraud:

No one was personally affected.
I paid premiums regularly and want my money back.
My loss was not covered.
It was so easy.
I was in financial trouble.
Someone else suggested it.
I wanted revenge.
I wanted to trick the powerful.
I wanted to help friends.
Everybody does it.
The insurance company was so impersonal.
Fraud is part of the business.
Insurance is like the lottery or gambling.
The idea was implied by the insurance agent.
It's a risk-free way of doing something illegal.
Promises made in the advertisement were not kept.
It's money I didn't have to work for.
It boosted my ego.
It's a cavalier thing to do.

Fraud against European Union

Between 2002 and 2009, the EU had to deal with the problem of implementing the euro and also handle the dramatic increase of white collar crime.[34] It implemented the unité de coordination de la lute anti-fraud (UCLAF), the European Institution to coordinate measures for fighting fraud and corruption, after a report of the highest EU anti fraud institution noted that the union lost about €1.2 billion (2.5 billion German marks) and estimated the real loss five times higher. UCLAF became the Office de Lutte Anti-Fraude (OLAF) in 1999 and is officially charged with protecting financial interests. In 2009, the budget of the EU was about €140 billion of which €1.2 billion was spent in supporting projects. It has been estimated that one-third of the requests were fraudulent and that OLAF covered up about

€50 million as losses by white collar crime and corruption. The weakness of OLAF is that it is an administrative body that has no executive power.

Cyber Crime, Cyber War

At a conference in Vienna, Klaus Jansen, a representative of the German Criminal Investigators Organization stated that, "The citizen, the economy, and the civil society expect that internet shall be a safe place." In reality, the Internet is becoming very dangerous and the new challenge is cyber war.[35] The Stuxnet cyber attack on the atomic reactors in Iran showed how vulnerable states can be. Cyber war is performed by a state, not by an individual or a group. Cyber crime will be a threat for a very long time. Since the 1980s, computer technology evolved, and the past decade saw dramatic changes. The Internet is open to everyone. One estimate is that about two billion people have access to the virtual world. This development opens new chances and dangers.

Computer and Telemarketing Crime

Technological innovations such as the Internet and electronic banking offer new possibilities for committing crimes and transferring illegal profits.[36] The solidarity of democratic societies is endangered by these forms of fraudulent bribery. At present, computer crime is not such an important issue in Austria, unlike other parts of Europe. Computer crime is becoming more of a threat to economic systems. The same can be said for telemarketing crime. All over Europe, using mobile phones to commit computer crimes is a growing problem. Telephone companies suffer enormous damages from this type of crime. Immigrants use this form of computer crime to stay in contact with their home countries. Professor Thomas Bode of the University of Frankfurt in Germany noted at a November 2010 conference that the main aspects of Internet and cyber crime are:

- Fraudulent Internet-shopping
- Computer infections
- Online fraud
- Phishing
- Skimming
- Money laundering
- Pornography

Information Security

Information security seems to be the main goal of functioning governments, public institutions, and administration.[37] As the "Wikileak" case shows, tremendous dangers can arise if certain information becomes public.

Employee Crime

Many crimes against businesses are committed by employees.[38] A 1976 study conducted in Germany by G. Kaiser and Metzger-Pregitzer[39] revealed that 80% of property crime was committed by employees. A 2004 study by Wells and Kopetzky[39] conducted in the U.S. indicated that more than 70% of fraud crime was the work of employees. Theft, fraud, fraudulent conversion, bribe taking, bankruptcy, counterfeiting, computer crime, and espionage are the most common employee crimes. The Association of Certified Fraud Examiners estimated that in 2002, U.S. companies lost 6% of their gross revenue to occupational fraud and abuse. This is the equivalent of $600 billion or about $4,500 per employee.

Price Waterhouse Coopers Profile of Criminal Employees

In December 2005, Price Waterhouse Coopers presented a research study[40] indicating that an enterprise became a victim of white collar or economic crime every second. Offenders were mainly employees who worked several years for a company, functioned in higher management, had no hostile feelings, lacked ethical scruples, and needed money to maintain expensive lifestyles. The two common types of employee crime are embezzlement and sabotage. The complexity and anonymity of computer systems may help criminal employees camouflage their operations. The victims of the most costly scams include banks, brokerage houses, insurance companies—the largest financial institutions.

Very often people guilty of embezzlement have no criminal histories. Embezzlers tend to have issues with their employees, financial problems, and sometimes a simple inability to resist the temptation of a loophole. Screening and background checks of perspective employees can help in prevention but modern laws make some types of screening difficult or even illegal (data protection very often is seen as offender protection). Fired or disgruntled employees sometimes sabotage company computer systems as forms of "pay back." Sabotage may take the form of a logic bomb, a computer virus, or creating general havoc by a number of methods.

The Major Crime Bureau in Vienna that fought fraud cases between 1976 and 2002 and the Austrian Federal Police developed a profile of offenders:[41]

85% amateurs who had no criminal records
12% professionals with background knowledge
3% members of organized crime or terrorist organizations

Continuing Financial Crisis

The full extent of the financial world crisis that started in 2007 is not yet known. It started in the U.S. with criminal speculation that nearly destroyed the economic and financial systems of the whole world. Many European financial institutions lost millions of dollars by investing in highly overestimated American projects. When the financial world learned that the investments were built on sand and not on solid strategies, it nearly was too late. Germany, Ireland, Greece, and other European investors did not exercise due diligence well enough. They trusted the American hype and bought a disaster.

Global Problems, Global Answers

After the financial crisis started in 2007, everyone asked how it happened again in light of the Great Depression of the 1930s. The philosopher Aristotle stated that money has three functions.[42] It serves as a measure for (1) exchange, (2) capital, and (3) ownership. Aristotle also said that, "Capital is the equivalent for fairness because of performance; service money is the equivalent for fairness of needs. … performance, services, and needs are in opposition and conflict." Aristotle was convinced that a third power was necessary to prevent economy from dominating politics. Aristotle was against interest; if money works only for money, there is no ending but infinity. Therefore unlike "real" markets, financial markets will always crash.

As early as twenty years before 2007, some feared a crash because the worldwide ratio of financial markets to real markets was 85:15. When the ratio of financial markets reached 90 to 95%, it became realistic to expect a crash. This was a consequence of the IT markets.[43] In Europe, economic experts determined in January 2009 that the financial crisis[44] occurred because of:

Too much money in circulation
Disregard for risks
U.S. financial policies
Illusion that war doesn't cost money
Hidden inflation factors
Failure to regulate money circulation
Unrealistic U.S. stock price estimates
Failures of rating agencies
U.S. rating monopoly
Lack of efficient controlling mechanisms

Inadequate accounting regulation
Lack of savings
Inadequate real capital
China's excess savings
Wrong interpretations of Keynes
Excessive speculation
Short-sighted oil exporters
Inability to stop consumption
Belief in constantly growing economy
Inability of financing two-class society
Short-sighted planning
Incompetent and dishonest financial advisors
Missed chances during economic booms
Increased efforts of Asian nations
Globalization gap
Demographic diversities between Europe and Asia
Offshore policies
Philosophy of trusting only in consumption
Greed
Lehman Brothers disaster
Gap between euro and dollar
Too much privatization
Stopping of loan policy

Money Deals: Record Highs

The main cause of the financial dilemma is the lack of control of money deals. Each day more than 4000 trillion dollars circle around in foreign exchanges. Despite the financial crisis of 2007, the volume of foreign exchange increased by 20%.[45] It is vital to create mechanisms by which these uncontrolled money deals can be controlled. No efficient regulation by the World Bank, Group of Eight, or Group of Twenty exists to control or stop this practice.

EU Issues

When the EU was launched, Europe became stronger because of the community status. The European Community is the backbone of the new economic power of the continent. With its 500 million inhabitants, the economic, political and social importance of Europe became equal to that of America. But the EU is missing a unified economic policy. Each member state tries to find its own solution and fails. This is the main weakness of the EU. Via the Lisbon Treaty and regular meetings of their governments, EU member countries try to overcome the weakness of the euro. Global problems need global answers. What we see in the European Union is spreading around the world. Although several meetings of the leading economic countries took place, China, India, U.S., and Europe found no acceptable common solution for the financial crisis. As long as they fail, the danger of a new crisis is always present.

Lessons Learned

Practical experiences gained from criminal cases teaches us what works and what does not work. An analysis of international white collar crime cases reveals some general messages.

Changes in Payment Systems

Changes in payment systems bring changes of criminal behavior, particularly in the areas of debit and credit card fraud and counterfeiting. The European banking authorities remain intent on developing new payment systems that are safe and trustworthy. Payment systems are democratic institutions; people place a great deal of trust in them. If the stability of established payment systems cannot be trusted, the democratic way of life cannot survive.

Eurocheque System

In 1968, the Eurocheque system was introduced in the European market. It was an important payment system until debit cards and credit cards became common. Criminals counterfeited checks and check cards and acted internationally.

Bankomat system

The financial sector changed to debit cards, and they are very well accepted by the Europeans who like the idea of using the machines to get cash. This is evident by the increasing number of debit cards issued. Criminals found ways to steal Bankomat cards and obtain the PIN codes of users.

Credit cards

Another trend is more frequent use of credit cards. As a result the credit card industry in Europe is booming as never before. Of course, criminals know how to steal credit card data and use it. Criminal activities, especially by organized crime groups, can heavily compromise and even destroy payment systems. Criminals learn fast. Despite changing payment systems, they adapt very quickly to new systems and resume their criminal activities.

Counterfeit Dollars and Euros

Counterfeit money is created and circulated worldwide. U.S. dollars have always been easy to counterfeit because their security features are very simple. Although the euro has more and better security features, it is also commonly counterfeited.

Weak Banking Systems

After the fall of the Soviet Union, criminals found it easy to found banks in the new democracies and countries in transition. In Russia, for example, organized crime groups own 60% of the banks in Moscow. Between 2000 and 2007, the Council of Europe, UN, and OSCE organized several training seminars in the Balkan region and Central Asia to combat organized crime, white collar crime, financing of terrorism, money laundering, and corruption. One eye-opening fact was the weakness of banking systems in Central Asia. How can you build new democratic structures if people cannot trust your financial structures and banking systems? One important lesson we learned was to teach new democracies how to build stable financial systems. The Austrian Federal Bank helped implement best practices in the Central Asian region.

Money Laundering: Know Your Customer

Important security features to prevent customers from becoming victims of white collar crime are standards in financial businesses. Criminals test financial institutions to determine where they can find weaknesses. A classical modus operandi is to identify themselves as important business men, acting under time pressure and thus have a reason to place so-called "big business" in a rather small financial institution. Sometimes they present excellent recommendations such as business cards of officials or famous local or international society figures. Keep in mind that even international financial fraud cases show similar patterns of criminal behavior. Victims should wonder why they were selected to be parts of this excellent business, but victims don't ask this question although it would have been the best prevention strategy.

Avoiding Risky Business

Very often managers are driven by the desire to accumulate maximum earnings in a short time and don't ask how it is possible to get quick returns of 25% or even more. Being greed driven and relying on an excellent prognosis of financial return, they ignore analytical and critical indicators. Failing to analyze unrealistically profitable situations, particularly in the financial sector, led to dramatic losses by companies and customers. The long-running "419 fraud" schemes conducted by a group from an East African nation are well known, but many other fraud schemes involving counterfeited , fraudulent, and worthless securities represent a promising opportunity to make a lot of "quick money."

Avoiding Employee Crime

Prevention of white collar crime activities has to cover many areas. For example, several studies show a lot of crime happens within companies. Preventing employee crime requires clear policies prohibiting certain activities along with a number of positive actions. For example, risk can be reduced by maintaining a climate that encourages cooperation and good working relationships between management and employees. Other positive steps are implementing open systems and where possible creating job rotation systems that can reduce employee vulnerability to corruption.

We now know how white collar criminals plan, decide, and act. The next step is reducing opportunities for criminals to cheat. The easiest way is to establish a check-and-balance the system that distributes responsibilities and ensures control. Many companies examine backgrounds of employment applicants and monitor performance after hire, but after a time, supervision declines, particularly if management has developed trust in a new employee. That can work as a trap. Trusted employees may have personal problems, addictions to alcohol, drugs, or gambling, or huge debts. Trust and control must be balanced even in cases of trusted employees.

The concept of the satisfied employee is important in business management. An employer has some level of safety if its employers are happy with the company, their jobs, and career potential. It is a well known fact that the most important capital of an enterprise lies in its human resources. Employees who work in stable conditions, who are motivated, and who can develop careers and increase their earnings are much more likely to resist greed and other temptations. Effective management and concern for employees make a company less likely to be vulnerable to criminal activities by employees. Of course, an adequate risk management system, strict standards for employment, restrictions for handling certain materials and documents, and other measures are also required.

Vulnerabilities of Democratic Societies

Today it is easy to travel around the world, use different currencies, a number of debit and credit cards, electronic transfers, and even invest in securities. A fundamental understanding of financial systems is the backbone of democracies and our business and personal lives, as noted at the beginning of this chapter. The fundamental principles of a free market economy are *uberimae fidei* (trust) and *pacta sunt servanda*.

These principles allow people to trust in the system of exchanging money and goods. If this exchange system cannot be trusted, as occurred after the two world wars in the twentieth century, it takes a long time to rebuild trust and establish functioning markets. After more than sixty years of peace in the western world, the onset of the financial crisis in 2007 was shocking. Even the so-called experts did not expect it, and now the world powers must find solutions to prevent a worldwide depression such as the one that occurred in the 1930s. We still face fears of a new financial crisis even though the one that started in 2007 has not ended.

Re-Establishing Ethical Principles

The financial crisis is clearly a result of the decline of ethical principles in the business world. Business is greed driven; the goal, particularly in the financial sector, is to make the most money in the shortest time. A code of conduct can help fight money laundering, and compliance officers responsible for minimizing legal risks can reduce potential for criminal activities. Establishing strict standards and clear responsibilities are other steps for reducing risks along with a company-wide code of conduct. However, these measures can be effective only if representatives of the World Bank and other international public and private financial institutions have the power to investigate and halt illegal activities.

Efficient Police and Justice Systems

The efficiency of current laws and existing penal and legal systems to deter illegal activities is debatable. The huge number of white collar crime cases makes it possible to investigate only large cases that involve huge losses. Efficient police, investigators, prosecutors, and judges are needed to find and prosecute responsible individuals who commit all levels of white collar, financial, and economic crimes. These types of crimes victimize great numbers of people and enormously damage economic systems worldwide. Only well-trained participants in an effective justice system can reduce the numbers of such crimes.

Efficient Prevention Tools

What are the most efficient tools and practices that can help reduce the danger of a new financial crisis? Experts who serve on missions of various international organizations like the UN Crime Prevention Centre, OESCE, the Council of Europe, and OLAF[46] indicate that the only tool for overcoming criminal tendencies is the political will to act against it.

Political Will

The head of the Independent Commission against Corruption (ICAC) of Hong Kong stated in the 1970s that the city (then a British crown colony) was one of the most corrupt areas in the world. Queen Elizabeth II and the then governor of Hong Kong were determined to fight corruption and supported all activities to implement new laws and establish efficient units to fight corruption. Twenty years later, their mission was so successful that Hong Kong is now considered a model for fighting corruption.

Transparency

It is important to convince people that they have strong wills and can overcome weaknesses. One way to transmit this message is government transparency. Every government action, success, and failure should be made known to the public. It took nearly twenty years of transparency to build confidence and trust in Austria.

Control Mechanisms

Laws should function as efficient control mechanisms. The rule of law will be accepted only if it is enforced. Efficient police and justice systems are critical. Information about the apprehension, prosecution, and sentencing of criminals must be disseminated to the public. Cooperation of the police and justice systems with the media and the public is another critical element of combating crime.

Cooperation of Public and Private Sectors

These measures cannot work without solid cooperation of the public and private sectors. A democratic society consists of a network of both sectors. Public institutions were created to serve the private sector. Exchanges of information, cooperation, and openness build resilience against both external dangers and those inside.

Appendix: The Largest Insurance Company Fraud in American History

Rabbi Sholam Weiss, a criminal mastermind from New York, was wanted for racketeering, wire fraud, interstate transportation of stolen property, money laundering, and filing false documents. The charges arose from a huge swindle that netted $450 million in the largest insurance company fraud in the history of the United States. Weiss even sought political asylum in Austria.

The sophistication and scope of the fraud are truly amazing. Weiss looted the National Heritage Life Insurance Company by cheating the Florida-based insurer's oldest policyholders. Weiss, then 46, "jumped bail." The FBI's Wanted poster (Figure 6.2) offered a $95,000 reward for his capture. Insurance regulators provided an additional $25,000 reward. Rabbi Weiss plundered enough loot to allow him a lavish lifestyle as a fugitive. He absconded with $30 million of the insurance company's money and was believed to have found a safe haven among the Israelis. "Weiss's corruption and dishonesty know no end," stated U.S. Attorney J. K. Hunt, in prosecution documents filed in February in Orlando.*

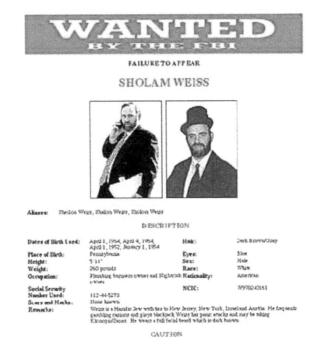

Figure 6.2 "Wanted" poster of Sholam Weiss containing two photos and description.

---

* Edelbacher, M. & Theil, M. (2008). *Kriminalität gegen Versicherungen*. Linde Verlag, Vienna.

Weiss's Gang: Lawyers, Businessmen, and the Gambino Family

Fifteen business executives and lawyers from Arizona, Texas, Illinois, and New York pled guilty or were convicted for participation in the Weiss fraud ring. Authorities say the fraud began in the early 1990s, when Weiss's gang of businessmen and lawyers hijacked the insurer. One was Michael D. Blutrich, a lawyer who owned Scores, a topless club on East 60th Street in Manhattan; the club was then controlled by the Gambino crime family. Blutrich served as National Heritage's attorney. Using a variation on a check-kiting scheme, Weiss and his cronies bought the insurance company in 1993 with a check. After they took control, they simply lent themselves sufficient money to cover the purchase price and forced National Heritage into a web of fraud. They bought junk stocks and mortgages in a series of swindles that cost the insurer hundreds of millions. Much of the money—cash—was never found. Millions more were funnelled into accounts controlled by Weiss.

First Offense: Special Consideration

In 1994, Rabbi Weiss committed his first offense and was indicted on mail fraud charges arising from false claim that more than $1 million worth of bathtubs were damaged in a 1986 fire at his company's warehouse. He was tried in Federal District Court in Manhattan, convicted, and sentenced to eight months in prison. After release to a halfway house, he requested a four-day furlough to observe the sacred Passover holiday at home in Monsey, New York with his family. Of course, federal probation officials readily agreed.

Weiss however, did not fulfill his part of the bargain. Instead Weiss convinced the managers of an Atlantic City casino and hotel owned by former Reform Party presidential candidate Donald Trump to fly him and a youthful female companion by private jet to the resort, where they stayed in a complimentary, $700-per-night suite and wagered $70,000. The rabbi was initially charged with escape for the four-day getaway, but the charges, of course, were dropped by the federal government.

Flight Risk Posts $500,000 Property Bond for Bail

The lawyer who represented Weiss in his most recent proceeding was Joel Hirschhorn of Florida. Long before the Sunday in October when Weiss made his mandated phone call to federal bail officials and then vanished, informed courtroom observers predicted that Weiss would certainly flee. Weiss's flight caused his ex-wife to forfeit her house in Monsey that served as security for the $500,000 bond. How is it possible that the federal government did not know what courtroom observers knew?

At Weiss's Feb. 15, 2000 sentencing (in absentia) for the insurance swindle, Judge Patty Fawsett announced that based on the gravity and repeat nature of his crimes, Weiss would be given a life sentence. Judge Fawsett handed the missing Weiss a massive 845-year prison term by sentencing him consecutively rather than concurrently for the huge number of counts against him. Fawsett also fined Weiss $123 million and ordered him to make $125 million in restitution to the policyholders of National Heritage Insurance which by then was bankrupt.

Apprehension in Austria

Twelve months after he fled the U.S., Sholam Weiss, 46, was captured and arrested in Austria on October 24, 2000. His arrest ended a search that took the authorities across three continents, from some of the world's finest hotels to the slums of São Paulo, Brazil. Police said Weiss had access to as much as half the $450 million he helped steal, and he used some of it to flee. Officials initiated extradition proceedings to return Weiss to the U.S. After his earlier escape, he seldom stayed long in one place. He used prepaid cell phones, mounds of cash, and several false identities to elude authorities in South America and Europe. He also used his Brazilian girlfriend as a front, said officials in the U.S. and Brazil.

Despite Weiss's vigilance, his taste for fine hotels and young women helped officials capture him. Police officials in Brazil, Germany, and Austria, working with the FBI in the U.S. found Weiss by following his twenty-seven-year-old Brazilian girlfriend, whose name was not released by the authorities. Weiss met her at the Vienna train station and took her to an apartment in the fashionable Old Town section. The authorities learned later that he moved into the apartment that day and rented it in the name of his brother-in-law.

One investigator said the FBI believed that Weiss had been in the process of moving from South America to Vienna and was about to establish a new false identity. When the police in Vienna knocked on his door, however, his reaction helped confirm his identity to a team of investigators who had never seen him and were not sure they found the right man. Weiss's immediate reaction was, "I want a lawyer." He did not ask who the investigators were, tell them they were mistaken, or even ask what they wanted. An FBI official praised the efforts of the Brazilian, German, and Austrian police forces who worked together to track Weiss's girlfriend to Vienna.

The Brazilian police official who oversaw the investigation in São Paulo said that five full-time investigators worked with him on the case for several months. They focused on São Paulo's large Jewish community because they suspected Weiss might try to hide there. They also checked the city's finer hotels they thought Weiss would patronize to maintain his lavish lifestyle. The Brazilian federal police sent investigators disguised as mail carriers to some of the hotels to deliver mail addressed to Weiss and found the normally discreet concierges happy to tell what little they knew. This information came from Jorge Pontes, a senior official with the federal police who serves as his agency's liaison to Interpol. He spoke in a telephone interview from Japan, where he was attending an Interpol seminar. Pontes said his investigators tracked Weiss to a hotel in August and obtained telephone records. They found one call to one of the city's poorest neighbourhoods. "It was strange for us, because it broke a little bit of his profile," Pontes said. The call was made to the home of Weiss's girlfriend's mother. This break ultimately led the authorities to Vienna and to Weiss.

The extradition process continues. J.K. Hunt, the assistant U.S. attorney who prosecuted Weiss, said his conviction would make the process clear cut procedurally. "There's $250 million that still needs to be recovered," said Fred Marro, a lawyer representing victimized insurance firms. "From what we've heard, Sholam controls at least that kind of money, and so we're very excited that he's been rounded up."* Sholam Weiss has recently been extradited to the United States.

References and Sources

1. Edelbacher M. (1995). Lecturer at the Vienna University of Economics and Business Administration; each second year a lecture about Financial Crimes or Crimes against Insurances is performed. See Edelbacher/Theil, "*Kriminalität gegen Versicherungen*", Introduction, p. 13. Published by Linde Verlag, 2008, Vienna, (pacta sunt servanda).
2. Ibid. (Uberimae fidei).
3. Costa, A.M. (April 2010). Opening speech. UNODC Crime Commission, Conference on Crime Prevention, Vienna.
4. UNODC Conference on Crime Prevention (April 2010). Vienna.
5. Edelbacher, M., Reither, P., and Preining, W. (1999). *Sicherheitsmanagement*. Linde Verlag, Vienna.
6. International Organization on Migration and UNHCR. (2010). Yearly Report.
7. Sutherland, E.H. (1940). White collar criminality. *American Sociological Review*.
8. Albanese, J.S. (1995). *White Collar Crime in America*. Prentice Hall, Englewood Cliffs.
9. Geis, G. & Meier, R.F. (1977). *White Collar Crime*. Macmillan, London.

* http://www.hoffman-info.com

10. Bachner-Foregger. (2010). *Austrian Criminal Code*, §146ff, pp. 165ff. Published by Manz, Vienna
11. Enste, D. & Schneider, F. (2006). Welchen Umfang haben Schattenwirtschaft und Schwarzarbeit? Ein Versuch zur Lösung des Rätsels. *Zeitschrift für Wirtschaftspolitik,* 86.
12. Glinig, M. & Glinig, G. (2003). Der Internationale Finanzbetrug, Verband *Österreichischer Banken & Bankiers,* 4.
13. http://wikipedia.org/wiki/Bankruptcy, Sept. 11, 2010.
14. http://wikipedia.org/wiki/Bankruptcy, Sept. 11, 2010. ttp://wapedia.mobi/en/ Enron_scandal, September 2, 2010.
15. http://wikipedia.org/wiki/Bankruptcy, Sept. 11, 2010.
16. Edelbacher, M. (2010). Internationaler Finanzbetrug, Verlag Staatssicherheit, Aspang, Wien, 1995; http://en.wikipedia.org/wiki/Inside_trading.
17. Edelbacher, M. (2010). Problem: Wirtschaftskriminalität von der Sensibilisierung bis zu Gegenmaßnahmen, Vortrag an der Akademie der Wirtschaftstreuhänder, Wien. (2007). Bankraubkriminalität, Vortrag. MEPA, Budapest.
18. Rosoff, S., Pontell, H.N. & Tillmann, R.H. (2010). *Profit without Honor: White Collar Crime and the Looting of America,* 2nd ed. Prentice Hall, Upper Saddle River. http://en.wikipedia.org/wiki/Security_fraud,
19. Edelbacher, M. (2010). Problem: Wirtschaftskriminalität. http://en.wikipedia. org/wiki/Pyramid_scheme
20. http://de.wikipedia.org/wiki/Bernhard. Madoff (2010); Standard Presse, Kurier, and other Austrian newspapers, December 14, 2010.
21. Edelbacher, M. (1995). *Internationaler Finanzbetrug,* Staatssicherheit, Aspang, Wien and lectures about Wirtschaftskriminalität (economic crime) at Danube University, Krems and Akademie für Recht und Steuern, Vienna, 1995–1999.
22. Glinig, M. & Glinig, G. (2003). Der Internationale Finanzbetrug, Verband *Österreichischer Banken & Bankiers,* 4.
23. Edelbacher, M. (1995). Internationaler Finanzbetrug, Staatssicherheit, Aspang, Wien and lectures about Wirtschaftskriminalität (economic crime) at Danube. University Krems and Akademie für Recht und Steuern, Vienna, 1995–2009.
24. Ibid.
25. Ibid.
26. Ibid.
27. Ibid.
28. Ibid.
29. Ibid.
30. http://www.statistik.at/web_de/statistiken/volkswirtschaftliche_gesamtrech- nungen/bru.from February 25t, 2012. Source: Statistik Austria , p 97.
31. Edelbacher, M. (1995). Internationaler Finanzbetrug, Staatssicherheit, Aspang, Wien and several lectures at the Danube University and Akademie für Recht und Steuern, Vienna, 1995–2009.
32. Edelbacher, M. & Theil, M. (2008). *Kriminalität gegen Versicherungen.* Linde Verlag, Vienna.
33. Höfner, K. J. & Vaughan, S., Soziologische und psychologische Aspekte des Versicherungsbetruges, 1990, Lecture in Linz, Austria, (Motivation of insurance Fraud) published in Österreichische Versicherungsfachzeitschrift, No 2/1990.

34. Edelbacher, M. (2008 and 2009). Sicherheitsmanagement, Vortrag an der Donau Universität, Krems, OLAF reports, and seminars at European Law Academy, Trier.
35. Jansen, K. (November 19, 2010). The Future of Criminal Investigation. Zukunft der Kripo in Deutschland, Tagung der Vereinigung Kriminaldienst Österreich, Criminal Investigation Service, Vision 2020, Vienna.
36. Bode, T. (November 19, 2010). Internet as Criminalistic Challenge. Das Internet als kriminalistische Herausforderung, Tagung der Vereinigung Kriminaldienst Österreich, Criminal Investigation Service, Vision 2020, Vienna.
37. Ibid.
38. Kaiser, G. & Metzger-Pregizer, G. (1976).
39. Wells & Kopelsky. (2004). Report on Occupational Fraud and Abuse.
40. Metzger-Pregizer, G. Betriebsjustiz – Untersuchungen über die soziale Kontrolle Abweichenden Verhaltens in Industriebetrieben, published by Duncker & Humblot, 1976, Berlin.
41. Ibid.
42. Wells, J. T. & Kopetzky, M. Handbuch Wirtschaftskriminalität in Unternehmen Aufklärung und Prävention, published English in Lexis/Nexis (Occupational Fraud And Abuse) and in German by ARD Orac, Wien. 2006.
43. Schwarz, G. (January 12, 2009). Dominiert die Ökonomie, kommt der Crash, *Der Standard* interview.
44. Ibid.
45. Unterberger, A. (January 3, 2009). Wie konnte das nur passieren? Ursachenforschung zur Finanzkrise das Ergebnis von politischem Populismus, kollektiven Wahr: Nehmungsfehlern und dem Übergewicht Amerikas, *Wiener Zeitung.*
46. Göweil, R. (September 2, 2010). Geldhandel klettert unbeeindruckt auf neues Rekordhoch: 4000 Milliarden Dollar täglich, *Wiener Zeitung.*
47. De Speville, B. Council of Europe Mission to the Balkan Area. Fighting Corruption: The Essential People and Public Awareness Raising and Education on the Dangers of Corruption and Organised Crime.

Cyber Crime and Economic Crime

7

ALEXANDER SEGER[*]

Contents

---

[*] The views expressed in this chapter are those of the author and not necessarily those of the Council of Europe.

Introduction: Ecosystem of Cyber Crime

Crime does not take place in isolation. It is affected by its political, economic, socio-cultural, technological, ecological, and legal or regulatory environment. Crime is shaped by its environment, interacts with it, and influences it. Thus, in many ways, crime and its environment constitute an ecosystem.

Environmental scans[*] help explain, for example, that drug-related crime is a function of globalization, political conditions, historical and socio-cultural factors, and human development.[†] Money laundering is not simply a consequence of drug trafficking; the globalization of the financial system prepared the ground for the laundering of the proceeds of all types of crimes.[‡] The fall of the wall of Berlin in 1989 and the subsequent period of transition of Central and Eastern European countries toward democracy and market economies created opportunities for organized crime and corruption that led to regulatory responses[§] that subsequently forced the "old" democracies of Western Europe to adopt stricter measures in their own countries. Additionally, the September 11, 2001 attacks led to actions to prevent terrorism and considerable reinforcement of actions against money laundering[¶], including the confiscation of crime proceeds, due diligence, expanded supervision, and other preventive measures in the financial sector. These measures were further reinforced in the wake of the recent global financial crisis.

This seems particularly true for cyber crime. The evolution, relevance, and impact of cyber crime can only be understood in the context of the evolution of information and communication technology (ICT) and the consequent emergence of the information or network society.[**] This evolution has

---

[*] The Council of Europe introduced environmental scans in its annual organized crime situation reports from 2001 to 2005. Search also for PEST (analysis of the environment divided into Political, Economic, Socio-cultural, and Technological domains) or PESTEL analysis (of PEST plus Ecological and Legal domains).

[†] See Seger, A. (1998): Entwicklung und Drogen in Asien: Drogenprobleme, Drogenkontrolle und nachhaltige menschliche Entwicklung in Laos, Afghanistan und Pakistan. PhD Thesis, Bonn.

[‡] From an international regulatory perspective, money laundering was first dealt with in 1988 in the United Convention on Illicit Traffic in Narcotic Drugs and Psychotropic Substances. More recent agreements favor an all-crimes approach. See Council of Europe Convention on the Laundering, Search, Seizure and Confiscation of Proceeds from Crime and the Financing of Terrorism (CETS 198) of 2005.

[§] See soft- and hard-law instruments developed by Council of Europe covering money laundering, corruption, organized crime, trafficking in humans, and international cooperation in criminal matters from 1990 onward that apply to all forty-seven European countries; also see monitoring mechanisms such as GRECO and MONEYVAL (www. coe.int/economiccrime).

[¶] Prior to September 11, 2001, the U.S. government planned to reduce its participation in international anti-money laundering efforts, but reversed these plans soon afterward.

[**] Castells, M. (2000).

certainly been the most influential factor and transformed societies world-wide during the past decade. In the information society, "the creation, distribution, and manipulation of information has become the most significant economic and cultural activity."[*] For illustration, it is estimated that Internet use grew by some 445% between 2000 and 2010; some 2 billion people now use it.[†] While penetrations rates are unequal among regions (77.4% in North America, only 10.9% in Africa) and a digital divide continues, all regions have experienced significant growth.[‡]

There is general agreement that the rise of the information society offers unique opportunities to people worldwide in terms of economic development and also in fostering human rights and democracy.[§] ICT changed the ways companies and people do business and offer, buy, and sell products and services. The participatory information sharing of Web 2.0 altered the ways people interact with each other globally with fewer frontiers on a "flat play-ing field."[¶]

Obviously, businesses at all levels are now required to maintain online presences to succeed. The financial sector took advantage of ICT at an early stage to prepare the ground for borderless, around-the-clock global trad-ing and offering of services.[**] Public administrations also function online by offering electronic government services and organizing elections through e-voting. Estonia is very advanced in these respects.[††] In summary, both peo-ple and businesses around the world rely on ICT. As a result public services and infrastructures have also become highly dependent on ICT and this reli-ance makes societies vulnerable.

A major threat arising from the evolution of ICT is cyber crime. Is it not surprising that criminals use ICT to commit crimes and also actively search for vulnerabilities in the systems and exploit them?[‡‡] The evolution of the global information society led to a proliferation of cyber crime to the point that it can be argued that cyber crime and the information society form an ecosystem in which crime continues to exploit new technologies and related

---

[*] This is a widely used and simple definition of "information society." See http://whatis.techtarget.com/definition/0,,sid9_gci213588,00.html
[†] http://www.Internetworldstats.com/stats.htm
[‡] This is also true for Africa with a growth in Internet use of 2.357% in the past ten years and further growth expected from the expansion of fiber optics technology there.
[§] See documentation related to the World Summit on the Information Society (http://www.itu.int/wsis/index.html) and discussions of the Internet Governance Forum (http://www.intgovforum.org/cms/).
[¶] Friedman, T.L. (2006).
[**] With positive but also disastrous consequences.
[††] e-Estonia (http://www.valitsus.ee/?id=5450).
[‡‡] Illustrated by high underground market value of "zero-day exploits," that is, vulnerabili-ties in software that are not known and against which no countermeasures have been taken, so that an attack is likely to be very successful.

developments or morphs to countermeasures in an opportunistic manner.[*] Cyber crime may even be considered an integral part of the information society as reflected in the following definition:

> Post-industrial society in which information technology (IT) is transforming every aspect of cultural, political, and social life and which is based on the production and distribution of information. It is characterized by the (1) pervasive influence of IT on home, work, and recreational aspects of the individual's daily routine, (2) stratification into new classes: those who are information-rich and those who are information-poor, (3) loosening of the nation state's hold on the lives of individuals and the rise of highly sophisticated criminals who can steal identities and vast sums of money through information related (cyber) crime.[†]

This chapter aims to explain the concept of cyber crime, provide an overview of trends and data, demonstrate how cyber crime is an economic offense, and discuss effective practices for countering cyber crime threats.

Concept of Cyber Crime

Cyber crime can be defined in many ways. One could argue that, in essence, cyber crime is not an entirely new type of conduct, but simply an extension of already existing criminal behavior; the only difference is that cyber crime utilizes new technologies.[‡] Another approach is to define it as any crime in which a computer is the agent, facilitator, or target of the crime.[§] This is a broad concept since most crime now involves a computer in some way. The definition could also be limited to cover all crimes targeting computer data or systems. However, this definition would exclude crimes that existed earlier and gained greater impacts through the use of computers, for example, child pornography, fraud, and intellectual property right violations.

It is therefore expedient to apply a definition that covers new types of crime along with old types of crime involving computer use[¶] without being too broad and therefore meaningless. The definition should be sufficiently robust to cover all relevant types of conduct even if technology evolves and

---

[*] See Information Warfare Monitor/Shadowserver Foundation (2010) for a description of the ecosystem of crime and espionage embedded in the fabric of global cyberspace (http://www.nartv.org/mirror/shadows-in-the-cloud.pdf).
[†] http://www.businessdictionary.com/definition/information-society.html
[‡] http://www.britannica.com/EBchecked/topic/130595/cybercrime/235698/Defining-cybercrime
[§] Definition used by Symantec. See http://securityresponse.symantec.com/en/uk/norton/cybercrime/definition.jsp
[¶] Europol. (2007).

cyber crime techniques appear to change constantly. Moreover, the definition should be widely accepted, and finally it should be possible to operationalize and use it, for example, for criminal law purposes.

A definition meeting these criteria became available via the Council of Europe's Budapest Convention on Cyber Crime.[*] On the one hand, the treaty denotes cyber crime as offenses against the confidentiality, integrity, and availability of computer data and systems,[†] that is, offenses against computer data and systems, including:

- Illegal access to a computer system, such as "hacking" (Article 2)
- The illegal interception of the transmission of computer data (Article 3)
- Data interference, that is, the damaging, deletion, deterioration, alteration or suppression of computer data (Article 4)
- System interference, that is, hindering of the functioning of computer systems (Article 5), including denial of service attacks
- The misuse of devices (Article 6)—the production, sale, procurement, or otherwise making available of devices or data (e.g., hacking tools) for purposes of committing the above offenses

Secondly, it comprises offenses committed by means of computed systems, that is "old" forms of crime that produce new impacts through the use of computers:

- Computer-related forgery, that is, conduct resulting in inauthentic data that is acted upon for legal purposes as if it were authentic (Article 7)
- Computer-related fraud, that is, the causing of loss of property to another person by any input, alteration, deletion, or suppression of computer data or the interference with the functioning of a computer system with the intent of procuring an economic benefit (Article 8)
- Child pornography, that is, the production, offering or making available, distribution or transmission, procuring through or possession in a computer system or storage medium of pornographic material that visually depicts a minor (under age 18) engaged in sexually explicit conduct (Article 9)[‡]
- Offenses related to infringements of copyrights and related rights on a commercial scale (Article 10).

---

[*] www.coe.int/cybercrime
[†] The so-called cia offenses.
[‡] This article also covers persons appearing to be minors or realistic images even if no real minor is a victim. Not all countries agree to this and therefore reservations of this article are possible.

The Budapest Convention procedural laws and international cooperation measures apply to any crime involving electronic evidence or committed via a computer system. This provides the treaty with wide scope (see Article 14).

This approach may at first appear too simple in the face of complex crimes. For example, in 2009 and 2010, a widespread phenomenon was the Zeus Trojan horse used to steal banking information. This malware spread primarily through drive-by downloads when Internet users clicked on infected online advertisements. This installed the malware on the user's computer that acted as a robot ("bot") or zombie controllable from a command and control (CC) server operated by criminals.

When the user accessed his bank account online to make a financial transaction, the login credentials and other relevant data were transferred to the CC server. The transaction was intercepted automatically and modified to transfer the money to the account of a "money mule" who made it available for this purpose. From there it was transferred to other accounts and finally cashed out or laundered. The transaction appeared legitimate to the banking computer because the instruction appeared to have come from the accredited user, and the user also received a receipt from the bank that appeared to be correct.* Schemes of this type involved hundreds of victims and millions of euros and dollars.

The COE definition cited above is capable of capturing cases that combine illegal access, illegal interception, data and systems interference, forgery, and fraud.

Although the Budapest Convention was sponsored by the Council of Europe (with forty-seven current European member states), Canada, Japan, South Africa, and the U.S. participated. The U.S. became a full party to the treaty in 2006. A number of other non-European countries are in the process of accession.† Argentina, Australia, Chile, Costa Rica, Dominican Republic, Mexico, the Philippines, and Senegal have been invited to accede. Many more countries used the treaty as a guideline for domestic legislation (Botswana, Mauritius, Senegal, India, Indonesia, Sri Lanka, and others). In short, the concept or definition of cyber crime proposed by the Budapest Convention is widely shared and applied in practice.

---

* See the case documented by M 86 Security (White Paper): Cybercriminals Target Online Banking Customers (August 2010). http://www.m86security.com/documents/pdfs/security_labs/cybercriminals_target_online_banking.pdf Similar cases have been investigated in other countries including Germany and Belgium.

† Council of Europe (2010): Contribution of the Secretary General of the Council of Europe to the Twelfth United Nations Congress on Crime Prevention and Criminal Justice, Salvador, Brazil, 12–19 April 2010 (SG/INF (2010) 4). http://www.coe.int/t/dghl/cooperation/economiccrime/cybercrime/Documents/Reports-Presentations/SG%20Inf%20_2010_4%20-%20UN%20Crime%20congress_ENGLISH.pdf

Tools and Infrastructure of Cyber Crime

Cybercriminals rely on a set of tools and an infrastructure that include several elements described below.

Malware

Malicious software or "malware" denotes all types of software "inserted into an information system to cause harm to that system or other systems or subvert them for uses other than those intended by their owners."[*][†]

- **Viruses**—A virus is hidden code that is activated when its host program is run and it spreads from there to other programs. A virus can simply slow the performance of a computer or damage, alter, and destroy data.
- **Worms**—A worm is similar to a virus but replicates itself without the need for a host program.
- **Trojan horses**—A Trojan horse or other type of spyware may appear to be a legitimate program but has functionalities that disable security systems or contain a key logger that records what the user types including passwords and online banking credentials that may subsequently be transmitted to criminals when the computer is online.

Malware has been around for more than twenty years; the "Morris worm" raised public attention in 1988 when it infected 10% of the then 60,000 personal computers connected to the Internet in less than two hours.[‡] Malware remains the main tool for committing cyber crime and is reported to have evolved into a major industry with a complex economic infrastructure and well-organized and well-funded criminal gangs.[§] Viruses, worms, and Trojans that cripple security applications, download additional malware, infect files, and steal logins, account credentials, and other data are considered the most malicious code samples.[¶]

[*] OECD (2007).
[†] OECD (2007).
[‡] Schmidt, H. (2006), p. 72.
[§] *Sophos Security Threat Report*. (August 2010). p. 28. http://www.sophos.com/security/topic/security-report-2010.html
[¶] For statistics, see Symantec Intelligence Quarterly, April–June 2010. http://www.symantec.com/business/theme.jsp?themeid=threatreport; Microsoft Security Intelligence Report, Vol. 8, July–Dec. 2009. http://www.microsoft.com/security/about/sir.aspx

Increasing numbers of computers are becoming infected.[*] Most computers become compromised through the Internet, for example, by visiting websites that may appear to be legitimate but are infected; visitors may also be redirected to infected pages.[†]

E-mail, particularly spam, is another vehicle for spreading malware, often in connection with fraud schemes.[‡] It is estimated that 75 to 90% of all e-mail traffic consists of spam.[§] It is surprising that most spam can be traced back to a small group of operators.[¶] The main tool for spam and for other types of cyber crime is botnets.

Social networking sites and the number of users expanded considerably in recent years.[**] Social sites are now also used to spread malware and find targets for other forms of cyber crime; as a result they constitute security risks. According to Sophos,[††] social networks have become viable and lucrative markets for malware distribution with Web 2.0 botnets stealing data, displaying fake antivirus alerts, and generating income for criminals.

Botnets

A computer can be infected by malware that turns it into a zombie, robot, or bot; this allows it to be controlled by a third person without the knowledge of a legitimate user.[‡‡] The person who controls the computer can instruct it to send spam messages, spread malware, or act as a proxy to conceal the origin of an attack.

A bot-infected computer is usually connected to a command and control (CC) server from which additional malware is installed, instructions are received, or data is sent. When many of these bot computers are linked and controlled by the same CC server, they form a "botnet" managed by

---

[*] In Germany, it was estimated in 2010 that 43% of Internet users experienced malware infections of their computers. http://www.bitkom.org/65019_65010.aspx According to Symantec, 51% of computers globally experienced malware. http://www.symantec.com/content/en/us/home_homeoffice/media/pdf/cybercrime_report/Norton_USA-Human%20Impact-A4_Aug4-2.pdf

[†] *Sophos Security Threat Report.* http://www.sophos.com/security/topic/security-report-2010.html

[‡] Microsoft Security Intelligence Report, Vol. 8, July–Dec. 2009. http://www.microsoft.com/security/about/sir.aspx

[§] According to Commtouch Internet Threats Trend Report, first quarter, 2010, spam and phishing messages average 183 billion per day. www.commtouch.com/download/1679

[¶] Spamhouse lists about 100 such operations in its Register of Known Spam Operations (ROKSO) database. http://www.spamhaus.org/rokso/

[**] Facebook alone claims some 500 million active users. http://www.facebook.com/press/info.php?statistics

[††] *Sophos Security Threat Report.* http://www.sophos.com/security/topic/security-report-2010.html

[‡‡] See Microsoft Security Intelligence Report, Vol 9, Jan.–June 2010 with detailed analysis of botnets (http://www.microsoft.com/security/sir/).

a "bot herder." They may involve hundreds of thousands or even millions of computers,[*] and some are capable of sending tens of billions of spam or phishing messages per day.

Botnets are thus powerful tools in the hands of organized criminals for spreading spam and malware and intercepting and stealing confidential information. In addition, they can be used for denial-of-service (DOS) attacks. When thousands of computers send requests to the same domain name server[†] at the same time, the system is overloaded and service is denied. DOS attacks can thus be used to paralyze the information infrastructure of an organization, sector, or even a country[‡] while clear attribution is difficult because many thousand systems appear to be the sources of attacks.

Underground Economies

An underground economy usually involves exchanges of goods and services that are hidden from official view.[§] Such an underground economy has now become available on the Internet and has become a critical pillar of the infrastructure of cyber crime. It provides malware and other tools for committing crimes, rents botnets to carry out attacks, develops malware and anti-forensics techniques to avoid detection, and supplies bullet-proof hosting of domains used for criminal purposes[¶] and spam delivery. An underground economy offers a market for stolen goods, in particular credit card or bank account details and other personal information useful for identity-related fraud[**] and drop zones for stolen goods and crime proceeds. In short,

---

[*] Mariposa botnet dismantled in December 2009 consisted of 12 million infected computers.

[†] A DNS server translates a request with a memorable human name (e.g., www.coe.int) into a numeric Internet protocol (IP) address (193.164.229.51) that identifies and locates the corresponding computer system on the Internet.

[‡] One of the best known examples is the attack against Estonia in May 2007.

[§] http://www.encyclopedia.chicagohistory.org/pages/1280.html

[¶] Many bullet-proof domains are reportedly hosted in Eastern Europe and the Far East. For Europe, see report by Spamhouse on the criminal 'Rock Phish' domains registered at Nic.at (http://www.spamhaus.org/organization/statement.lasso?ref=7) http://en.wikipedia.org/wiki/Bulletproof_hosting Registrars and registries often fail to exercise due diligence when domains are registered. The 2010 Octopus conference of the Council of Europe recommended due diligence measures by ICANN, registrars and registries and accurate WHOIS information, and endorsement of the Law Enforcement Recommended Amendments to ICANN's Registrar Accreditation Agreement (RAA) and Due Diligence Recommendations in line with data protection standards (http://www.coe.int/t/dghl/cooperation/economiccrime/cybercrime/cy-activity-Interface-2010/2079_IF10_messages_1s%20provisional%20_24%20Apr%2010.pdf).

[**] *Symantec Intelligence Quarterly.* Apr.–June 2010. http://www.symantec.com/business/theme.jsp?themeid=threatreport

the underground economy offers an economic environment for offenders to organize for cyber crime.[*]

Money Mules

After a crime is committed, the victims have been defrauded, and money has been stolen, criminals must transfer the proceeds online without disclosing or leaving traces of their own identity. This appears to be the most difficult part of economic crime on the Internet. The most common transfer practice is using "money mules" or "financial agents" who open bank accounts or make their own accounts available for transfers of proceeds of crimes. After mules have the funds in their accounts, they receive further instructions to transfer them to other accounts or send them abroad via wire transfer and retain their commissions.[†] Mules may be recruited via e-mail, respond to spam, or access what appear to be legitimate websites offering work at home or financial manager jobs. They may sign formal contracts and deposit copies of ID documents. Not all of them are aware that they are essential parts of a criminal enterprise.

Organized Cyber Crime

The Council of Europe, in its 2004 organized crime situation report, formulated some general hypotheses regarding links between cyber crime and organized crime.[‡] These were validated in the following years and are still valid today:[§]

- ICTs offer anonymity, facilitate logistics, and reduce the risks for organized criminals to be prosecuted. They facilitate remotely controlled operations, covert activities, transnational operations, networking, and encrypted communication.
- The penetration and infiltration of banks and corporations along with online bank robberies via the Internet are far less risky than burglaries in the real world. Modern computer and communication networks have developed specific characteristics that are useful for criminal perpetrators and difficult for prosecutors to overcome. International computer networks offer anonymity to perpetrators

---

[*] G Data Whitepaper on Underground Economy, 2009: http://www.gdata-software.com/uploads/media/Whitepaper_Underground_Economy_8_2009_GB.pdf
[†] http://www.banksafeonline.org.uk/moneymule_explained.html
[‡] Council of Europe (2004).
[§] Extracts from Council of Europe (2005, p. 42–43). The authors were responsible for the preparation of that report.

that can be lifted only if all countries crossed by a communication decide to cooperate.

- ICTs are tools for global outreach and search for potential victims.
- ICTs are likely to change the structure of organized crime, that is, the way members organize to carry out crimes.

Depersonalization of contacts, ease of access, and rapidity of electronic transactions make ICTs attractive tools for money laundering. Organized crime exploits the vulnerabilities of societies, public institutions, businesses, and individuals using the Internet. Exploitation affects not only corporations engaged in e-commerce and business-to-business operations, but also involves electronic theft and phishing. Children are particularly vulnerable.

As economic crime already is a primary activity of organized crime groups, information and communication technologies will further facilitate the commission of new types of fraud. Traditional crimes will have the help of new technologies and morph into electronic bank robberies, cyber extortion and other forms.

Cyber crime does not require control over a geographical territory. It requires few personal contacts and fewer relationships based on trust and enforcement of discipline. In summary, it presents less need for formal organization. The classical hierarchical structures of organized crime groups may even be unsuitable for Internet crime. ICTs favor organizations that are already based on flat structured networking.

ICTs may also change the characteristics of offenders. In the real world legal businessmen engage in organized forms of economic crime. *Modus modendi*, the opportunities offered by ICTs, may tempt legal commercial entities to organize for cyber crime, that is, become organized cyber criminals. The complexity of many cyber crime operations, the infrastructure used, the level of specialization, and the division of labor are all indications of structured organized criminal groups that act in concert to commit offenses to obtain financial or other material benefits.[*]

Internet Fraud

People have many reasons to commit cyber crimes. So-called "script kiddies" may be eager to prove how clever they are and in doing so may create major damage.[†] Pedophiles may use the Internet to pursue their sexual interests by grooming victims or exchanging child abuse materials. Terrorists may use ICTs for

---

[*] As defined in Article 2 of the United Nations Convention on Transnational Organised Crime.
[†] A notorious example is the "I-love-you bug" launched by a student in the Philippines in 2000.

propaganda, recruitment, training and other preparatory acts, target identification, communication, financing and other logistical purposes, or implementing
denial-of-service or other types of attacks against critical infrastructures.[*]

Other politically motivated attacks[†] may include "hacktivism," espionage,
or conflicts via computer systems such as the intrusions and denial-of-service attacks on Estonia in 2007,[‡] Georgia in 2008,[§] the U.S. and South Korea
in July 2009,[¶] the Google intrusion in December 2009,[**] the intrusion into
governmental, business, and academic computer systems in India in 2009,
the Stuxnet worm reportedly designed to sabotage Iranian nuclear power
plants,[††] and the attacks and counterattacks following the release of U.S. State
Department internal documents by WikiLeaks in late 2010.[‡‡] Nevertheless,
it seems that most cyber crime is aimed at generating economic benefits for
offenders. Cyber crime therefore is very much about fraud.

Computer-Related Fraud

Fraud broadly involves intentional deception by which one person causes
loss to another for economic gain. It can be defined as "an intentional misrepresentation of material existing fact made by one person to another with
knowledge of its falsity and for the purpose of inducing the other person to
act, and upon which the other person relies with resulting injury or damage."[§§]

Whether fraud takes place on the Internet or is related to computer systems in any other way should be irrelevant. In some countries, however, the
law requires that a person or a human mind is deceived for a specific conduct

[*] http://book.coe.int/EN/ficheouvrage.php?PAGEID=36&lang=EN&produit_aliasid=2221
http://www.mpicc.de/ww/en/pub/forschung/forschungsarbeit/strafrecht/cyberterror-
ismus.htm http://www.indiajournal.com/pages/event.php?id=6472 http://www.securi-
tydefenceagenda.org/Portals/7/Reports/2008/SoD_110208_cyber.pdf
[†] Also named "Advanced Persistent Theats" or APT. http://www.mandiant.com/ser-
vices/advanced_persistent_threat/. For a brief definition see http://www.damballa.com/
knowledge/advanced-persistent-threats.php
[‡] http://en.wikipedia.org/wiki/2007_cyberattacks_on_Estonia
[§] http://www.registan.net/wp-content/uploads/2009/08/US-CCU-Georgia-Cyber-
Campaign-Overview.pdf
[¶] http://www.guardian.co.uk/world/2009/jul/08/south-korea-cyber-attack   http://
en.wikipedia.org/wiki/July_2009_cyber_attacks
[**] http://www.washingtonpost.com/wp-dyn/content/article/2010/02/03/AR2010020304057.
html
[††] http://www.schneier.com/blog/archives/2010/10/stuxnet.html   http://www.computer-
weekly.com/Articles/2010/11/30/244264/Iran-confirms-Stuxnet-hit-uranium-enrichment-
centrifuges.htm
[‡‡] http://www.cbsnews.com/stories/2010/11/29/world/main7099028.shtml   http://www.
nbcconnecticut.com/news/politics/Lieberman-Among-Many-Caught-in-Suspected-
Wiki-Leaks-Cyber-Attack-111590714.html   http://news.yahoo.com/s/afp/20101208/
tc_afp/usdiplomacywikileaksInternetcomputersecurity
[§§] http://definitions.uslegal.com/f/fraud/

to qualify as fraud. A computer system deceived through the manipulation of data and tricked into transferring money to a specific account may not necessarily constitute fraud. In Germany, for example, a specific article had to be introduced into the criminal code to cover computer-related fraud.[*] This article is based on a specific provision of the Budapest Convention on Cyber Crime of the Council of Europe[†]:

> **Article 8: Computer-related fraud** — Each Party shall adopt such legislative and other measures as may be necessary to establish as criminal offenses under its domestic law, when committed intentionally and without right, the causing of a loss of property to another person by: (a) any input, alteration, deletion or suppression of computer data; (b) any interference with the functioning of a computer system, with fraudulent or dishonest intent of procuring, without right, an economic benefit for oneself or for another person.

Forgery is a related concept. The Budapest Convention requires parties to the treaty to criminalize the following conduct in their domestic legislation:

> **Article 7: Computer-related forgery** — Each Party shall adopt such legislative and other measures as may be necessary to establish as criminal offenses under its domestic law, when committed intentionally and without right, the input, alteration, deletion, or suppression of computer data, resulting in inauthentic data with the intent that it be considered or acted upon for legal purposes as if it were authentic, regardless whether or not the data is directly readable and intelligible. A Party may require an intent to defraud, or similar dishonest intent, before criminal liability attaches.

These definitions and legal provisions help capture a wide range of fraud by not only addressing physical world conduct but also covering the specifics of computer-related forgery and fraud even if technology keeps evolving. Nevertheless, they are too broad to allow for an analysis of fraud and related crime on the Internet.

An organization that has been collecting data on cyber crime and is receiving more than 100,000 complaints per year is the Internet Crime Complaint Center (IC3)[‡] in the U.S. The IC3 has been struggling with the

---

[*] Brunst, P. & Sieber, U. (2010), p. 730.
[†] For the Budapest Convention explanatory report and the status of signatures, ratifications, and accessions, see www.coe.int/cybercrime
[‡] Internet Crime Complaint Center. (2010). Internet Crime Report. http://www.ic3.gov/media/annualreport/2009_IC3Report.pdf

challenge of categorizing types of fraud that make reporting by victims simple and at the same time accommodating the complexity and constant evolution of fraud schemes to achieve meaningful analysis. Until 2008, the IC3
classified frauds into nine categories:

1. Business fraud (including bankruptcy fraud, IPR infringements and
   counterfeit goods)
2. Communications fraud (including theft of IT and communication
   services)
3. Confidence fraud (including action fraud, non-delivery of goods,
   advance fee fraud)
4. Financial institutions fraud (including credit and debit card fraud,
   and identity theft)
5. Gaming fraud (betting and online gambling fraud)
6. Government fraud (including tax evasion, welfare fraud, counterfeiting currency)
7. Insurance fraud
8. Investment fraud (including market manipulation and pyramid
   schemes)
9. Utility fraud

However, this methodology that involved a large number of subcategories
was replaced in the 2009 report to avoid overlap, ensure clearer distinctions,
reduce the number of subcategories, and extend the scope beyond fraud. The
new classification covers seventy-nine complaint types encompassing fraud
and also drug trafficking, intimidation, pornography, terrorism, and a range
of other offenses involving the Internet.

The IC3 in 2009 received 336,655 complaint submissions, of which
146,663 were referred to law enforcement. Most of the referrals concerned
non-delivery of goods and services (19.9%), identity theft (14.1%), debit and
credit card fraud (10.4%), and auction fraud 10.3%).[*] In Europe as well, most
cyber crime reported and recorded by law enforcement is about fraud. In
Germany, for example, more than one-third of computer crimes recorded
in federal police statistics concern "carding" (the use of unlawfully obtained
credit or debit cards). In addition, the German Federal Criminal Police in
2009 recorded more than 50,000 cases of cyber crime of which more than
70% were related to fraud and forgery.[†]

While it is acknowledged that fraud is the most prevalent type of cyber
crime, it remains unclear how to differentiate the many categories of fraud.

---

[*] Internet Crime Complaint Center. (2010). Internet Crime Report. http://www.ic3.gov/
media/annualreport/2009_IC3Report.pdf
[†] http://www.bka.de/lageberichte/iuk/bundeslagebild_iuk_2009.pdf

For example, identity theft is sometimes described as a specific type of fraud separate from carding or account take-over, and sometimes it is limited to the theft of a person's identity, that is, a step before the stolen identity is used to commit fraud. While discussions about the best way to classify fraud involving the Internet will have to continue, for the purposes of this chapter, we assume that identity theft is a constituent of many types of fraud.

Identity Theft

Identity theft may be interpreted in various ways. Some argue that it pertains only to the theft of personally identifiable information (PII). Others consider identify theft to mean that PII is stolen with the intention to commit fraud. Those concerned about legal responses maintain that the possession and transfer of PII of another person with fraudulent intention must be criminalized, particularly if the underground economy is to be targeted.

For example, the U.S. Identity Theft and Assumption Deterrence Act [United States Code, Title 18, Section 1028(a)(7)] imposes punishment on a person who "knowingly transfers or uses, without lawful authority, of a means of identification of another person with the intent to commit, or to aid or abet, any unlawful activity that constitutes a violation of Federal law, or that constitutes a felony under any applicable State or local law."

Others include the theft of PII, possession, transfer or fraudulent intention, and the actual commission of fraud and define ID theft as "fraud or another unlawful activity where the identity of an existing person is used as a target or principal tool without that person's consent."[*] Considering these various approaches, ID theft involves three distinct phases[†]:

1. The obtaining of identity information, for example, through physical theft, through search engines, insider attacks, attacks from the outside (illegal access to computer systems, Trojans, key loggers, spyware, and other malware), or phishing and other social engineering techniques
2. The possession and disposal of ID information, which includes the sale of such information that now plays an important role in the e-underground economy where credit card information, bank account details, passwords or full identities are among the most offered goods

---

[*] Definition proposed by Koops, B.J. & Leenes, R. (2006). http://www.fidis.net/fileadmin/fidis/publications/2006/DuD09_2006_553.pdf
[†] Seger, A. (2007), p. 154. http://www.ispac-italy.org/pubs/ISPAC%20-%20Identity%20Theft.pdf   http://www.coe.int/t/dghl/cooperation/economiccrime/cybercrime/Documents/Reports-Presentations/567%20port%20id-d-identity%20theft%20paper%2022%20nov%2007.pdf

3. The use of ID information to commit fraud or other crimes, for example by assuming another person's identity to exploit bank accounts and credit cards, create new accounts, obtain loans and credit, order goods and services, or disseminate malware

Phishing (fishing for passwords) is one of the most common social engineering techniques used for ID theft. Users are encouraged to disclose passwords, access credentials for online accounts, and other personal information on seemingly legitimate websites. Organizations such as the Anti-Phishing Working Group* record more than 100,000 such attacks every year.

Alternative techniques include smishing (mobile phone text messaging to seek the disclosure of information), spear phishing (targeted phishing of specific persons or groups), pharming (redirection of users to bogus websites), and spoofing (sending an e-mail seeking personal information in the name of an apparently known and legitimate person. However, while phishing and similar techniques are widespread, other forms of theft through illegal access, illegal interception, data interference, attacks against computer data and systems, physical attacks, thefts by insiders, or simply losses of data through negligence are equally important.

After bank account or payment card details, PIN codes or other access credentials, place and date of birth, mailing address, and other personally identifiable data are obtained, the information can be used to commit fraud.

Types of Fraud

Identity theft and fraud in relation to online payments, particularly, payment card fraud, online banking misuse, and account take-over, constitute most computer-related fraud in most countries. Too many types of fraud exist to be detailed here, but we will discuss some of the most common ones.

Payment Card Fraud

The most reported type of payment card fraud involves card-not-present (CNP) payments made via Internet, telephone, or mail order by using genuine but stolen card details. For example, in the United Kingdom, CNP fraud was responsible for more than half of the losses from payment card fraud in 2009.†

Other types of payment card fraud include the use of counterfeit cards that include data from stolen genuine cards. For example, a genuine card is

---

* http://www.antiphishing.org/reports/APWG_GlobalPhishingSurvey_2H2009.pdf
† £266.4 million of total losses of £440.3 million in 2009. See Financial Fraud Action UK. (2010).

"skimmed" and then "cloned." Furthermore, lost or stolen cards can be used for purchases that do not require PIN codes. Finally, a new credit or debit card account may be opened in the name of another person on the basis of stolen ID information.

Online Banking Attacks and Account Takeover

After bank account details and online banking credentials have been stolen through phishing and other techniques, an account can be taken over to make payments or transfer money, often to the account's money mules. Taken-over accounts can also be used to apply for new accounts, loans, new credit cards, or used as mule accounts to receive and transfer money from other criminal operations. Another technique is compromising computers through Trojans that intercept communication between the user and his bank in the course of online payments so that money is transferred to an account different from the intended one.

Mass Marketing Fraud

Mass marketing fraud consists of "fraud schemes that use mass communications media including telephones, the Internet, mass mailings, television, radio, and even personal contact, to contact, solicit, and obtain money, funds, or other items of value from multiple victims in one or more jurisdictions."[*] Variations include advance-fee fraud,[†] 419 fraud,[‡] lotteries,[§] and phony prize winning schemes. Mass marketing fraud is often committed by criminal enterprises that operate globally and create losses estimated at several billion dollars per year.

Confidence Fraud Including Auction Fraud

Because many people purchase goods and services on the Internet and through online auctions, confidence and auction fraud are among the most reported offences on the Internet.[¶,**] Confidence fraud is the misrepresentation of a product advertised for sale or the non-delivery of goods for which customers paid.

[*] According to International Mass-Marketing Fraud Working Group (June 2010). http://www.fincen.gov/news_room/rp/reports/pdf/IMMFTAFinal.pdf

[†] http://www.consumerfraudreporting.org/nigerian.php

[‡] Article 419 of the Criminal Code of Nigeria criminalizes such conduct. http://www.efccnigeria.org

[§] http://www.consumerfraudreporting.org/lotteries.php

[¶] http://www.consumerfraudreporting.org/auctionfraud.php

[**] U.S. Internet Crime Complaint Center lists non-delivery as the complaint most often cited to law enforcement in 2009 (19%). http://www.ic3.gov/media/annualreport/2009_IC3Report.pdf

Investment Fraud Including Stock Market Manipulation

The Internet creates opportunities for investment fraud and stock market manipulation, for example, by online "pump and dump" schemes in which a large volume of low value stock is purchased and subsequently a spam or telemarketing campaign encourages its purchase. When those behind the scheme sell their shares and stop promoting the stock, its price drops rapidly and other investors are left with stock worth significantly less than they paid for it.

Counterfeit Pharmaceuticals

Counterfeit medicines and medical devices represent a criminal market worth billions of dollars. The World Health Organization defines a counterfeit medicine as "one which is deliberately and fraudulently mislabeled with respect to identity and/or source. Counterfeiting can apply to both branded and generic products and counterfeit products may include products with the correct ingredients or with the wrong ingredients, without active ingredients, with insufficient active ingredients or with fake packaging."[*]

Criminal enterprises exploit the opportunities offered by the Internet, namely to trade in counterfeit medicines to generate high profits at low risk and low cost in a global market place. The two main means are:

- Internet pharmacies that often sell substandard, non-approved or counterfeit medicines.[†] The money is paid by customers through online payment systems to banks abroad.[‡]
- Mass marketing fraud or spam messages related to pharmaceuticals reportedly account for the largest share of many billion of spam messages sent daily.[§] Spammers may send messages on behalf of a particular e-pharmacy or act as affiliate advertisers that receive commissions for clicks on a spam message or for actual sales.[¶]

---

[*] http://www.who.int/medicines/services/counterfeit/overview/en/

[†] http://v35.pixelcms.com/ams/assets/312296678531/455_EAASM_counterfeiting%20report_020608.pdf

[‡] See Moneyval typology study on money laundering and counterfeiting (2008). http://www.coe.int/t/dghl/monitoring/moneyval/Typologies/MONEYVAL(2008)22RRepTyp_counterfeiting.pdf

[§] For 81% of the 183 billion spam messages sent per day according to the Commtouch Internet Threats Trend Report Q1 2010. www.commtouch.com/download/1679

[¶] GlavNed reportedly pays a commission of 30 to 40% of drugs sold. http://www.networkworld.com/news/2009/071609-canadian-pharmacy-spam.html?hpg1=bn

Violations of Copyrights and Related Rights

Information technologies and the Internet facilitate the digital reproduction and dissemination of materials protected by copyrights and related rights. For example, with respect to software piracy on the Internet, losses have been estimated to amount to $53 billion for 2008 in direct lost revenues. This does not include the damage caused by unpatched pirate software that facilitates the spreading of malware.[*]

Measures against Cyber Crime and Economic Crime

For many decades, measures to combat economic crime have been pursued. Since the late 1980s, the measures increasingly target crime proceeds.[†] During the 1990s, societies began to devise measures against the emerging threats of cyber crime at domestic and international levels. A milestone has been the adoption of the Council of Europe's Convention on Cyber Crime opened for signature in Budapest in November 2001. Since then, a range of other measures by governments, international organizations, and the private sector have been implemented.

Nevertheless, measures targeting crime proceeds through financial investigations and the prevention and control of money laundering have been largely disconnected from measures against cyber crime. This is now changing. For example, the FATF has undertaken two studies, one on money laundering and terrorist financing vulnerabilities related to Internet payment systems in June 2008[‡] and one on money laundering and terrorist financing through new payment methods in October 2010.[§] In 2009, the Council of Europe decided to undertake a typology study on criminal money flows on

---

[*] http://portal.bsa.org/Internetreport2009/2009Internetpiracyreport.pdf

[†] Reflected in the 1988 United Convention on Illicit Traffic in Narcotic Drugs and Psychotropic Substances by the creation of the Financial Action Task Force in 1989, in the Council of Europe Convention on the Laundering, Search, Seizure and Confiscation of Proceeds from Crime of 1990, and in the Council of Europe Convention on the Laundering, Search, Seizure and Confiscation of Proceeds from Crime and the Financing of Terrorism (CETS 198) of 2005. http://www.unodc.org/unodc/en/treaties/illicit-trafficking.html; http://conventions.coe.int/Treaty/Commun/QueVoulezVous.asp?NT=141&CM=8&DF=&CL=ENG; http://www.fatf-gafi.org/pages/0,3417,en_32250379_32236836_1_1_1_1_1,00.html; http://conventions.coe.int/Treaty/Commun/QueVoulezVous.asp?NT=198&CM=8&DF=&CL=ENG; http://www.coe.int/t/dghl/cooperation/economiccrime/SpecialFiles/FI_en.asp

[‡] Financial Action Task Force. (2008). Money Laundering and Terrorist Financing Vulnerabilities of Commercial Websites and Internet Payment Systems. http://www.fatf-gafi.org/dataoecd/57/21/40997818.pdf

[§] http://www.fatf-gafi.org/dataoecd/4/56/46705859.pdf

the Internet to examine risks, develop indicators and red flags, and identify possible countermeasures.*

The question of criminal money on the Internet was also on the agenda of the global Octopus Conference on cyber crime organized by the Council of Europe in March 2009.† Discussions and information available suggest that in addition to general preventive and public awareness, measures and good practices against cyber crime and economic crime and in particular targeting crime proceeds may comprise the following:

International Standards and Cooperation

A precondition for criminal justice action against cyber crime is that the conduct to be investigated, prosecuted, and adjudicated is defined as a criminal offense. Law enforcement authorities must have the legal power to search computer systems, preserve electronic evidence, and undertake other investigative measures. Because of the transnational nature of cyber crime and the volatility of electronic evidence, authorities must have international cooperation. This also means that substantive and procedural legislation among countries must be compatible and reciprocal. The Budapest Convention provides a solution by requiring states to:

- Criminalize attacks against computer data and systems (illegal access, illegal interception, data interference, system interference, misuse of devices‡) and offenses committed by means of a computer system (including computer-related forgery and fraud§, child pornography¶, and infringements of copyright and related rights**).
- Enact legal procedural measures to enable its competent authorities to investigate cyber crime and secure volatile electronic evidence in an efficient manner (including expedited preservation of data, search and seizure of computer systems, and interception of communications).

---

* The study was carried out by the Council of Europe's anti-money laundering evaluation mechanism (MONEYVAL, www.coe.int/moneyval) in cooperation with the Global Project on Cyber crime and the joint European Union project on money laundering in the Russian Federation (MOLI-RU2). The author of this chapter also served as a lead author of the typology study. This explains similarities between parts of this chapter and sections of the typology study. Only information from publicly available sources has been used here. The study was adapted and published in March 2012. http://www.coe.int/t/DGHL/cooperation/economiccrime/cybercrime/Documents/Reports-Presentations/MONEYVAL(2012)6_Reptyp_flows_en.pdf

† http://www.coe.int/t/dghl/cooperation/economiccrime/cybercrime/cy%20activity%20interface%202009/Interface2009_en.asp

‡ Articles 2–6 of the Budapest Convention on Cyber Crime of the Council of Europe (CETS 185).

§ Articles 7 and 8 of the Budapest Convention.

¶ Article 9 of the Budapest Convention.

** Article 10 of the Budapest Convention.

- Cooperate efficiently with other parties to the convention through general (extradition, mutual legal assistance) and specific provisions (expedited preservation of data, access to stored computer data, interception of traffic and content data, creation of 24/7 points of contact) to assure international cooperation.

Although developed by the Council of Europe, this treaty serves as a global standard, as noted earlier. In addition to most European countries, it has also been signed or ratified by Canada, Japan, South Africa, and the U.S. Argentina, Australia, Chile, Costa Rica, Dominican Republic, Mexico, the Philippines, and Senegal have been invited to become parties, and several other countries on all continents use the Budapest Convention as a guideline for reforming their cyber crime legislation.[*]

Similarly, with regard to financial investigations and measures against money laundering, countries are well advised to strengthen their legislation and take other measures in line with international standards such as the recommendations of the FATF[†] and the Council of Europe Convention on Laundering, Search, Seizure, and Confiscation of the Proceeds from Crime and on the Financing of Terrorism ("Warsaw Convention").[‡]

Cyber Crime Reporting

Public and private sector stakeholders, particularly criminal justice authorities, must have the necessary information to detect cyber crime and determine whether apparently minor fraud schemes are part of a major criminal operation. Reporting systems that provide such information are increasingly utilized. Examples are the Internet Crime Complaint Centre (IC3)[§] in the U.S., MELANI[¶] in Switzerland, and the National Fraud Reporting Centre[**] in the United Kingdom. In the European Union, an Internet Crime Reporting Online System (I-CROS) is being established at Europol. Signal Spam is a public–private partnership in France that allows Internet users to report spam messages that are recorded in a single database that is then used for criminal and administrative investigations. It also serves as a research on enhancing network security and e-mail delivery.[††]

---

[*] See Council of Europe (2010).
[†] http://www.fatf-gafi.org/pages/0,3417,en_32250379_32236920_1_1_1_1_1,00.html
[‡] http://conventions.coe.int/Treaty/Commun/QueVoulezVous.asp?NT=198&CM=8&DF=&CL=ENG
[§] http://www.ic3.gov/default.aspx
[¶] http://www.melani.admin.ch
[**] http://www.actionfraud.org.uk/home
[††] https://www.signal-spam.fr/

Risk Management in Financial Sector

General guidelines for financial sector organizations to manage risk related to money laundering have been available for some time.* Some organizations also designed measures to manage specific Internet-related risks such as the creation of centralized databases to correlate transactions, two-factor authentication, and monitoring for mule account activities. The payment card industry has established security standards for merchants, processors, and financial institutions[†] and risk management guides for merchants.[‡] Commercial websites and Internet payment systems now often pursue proactive risk-based approaches including models for detecting unusual activity.[§]

Due Diligence of Registries and Registrars of Domains

The operation of botnets, the hosting of illegal content, and other cyber crimes is possible only because domain name registries and registrars fail to exercise due diligence when domains are registered.[¶] For example, a registrant is not identified or information entered into the WHOIS database** is not accurate.[††] Some services offer bullet-proof hosting, that is, they protect criminal activities and do not cooperate with law enforcement.[‡‡]

In 2009, law enforcement agents prepared a set of recommendations, "Law Enforcement Recommended Amendments to ICANN's Registrar Accreditation Agreement (RAA) and Due Diligence Recommendations."[§§] The recommendations, among other issues, require ICANN[¶¶] to perform due diligence investigations on all registrars and registries and ensure that they collect accurate and complete data from those registering domain names. In June 2010, the recommendations gained the support of the ICANN

---

* http://www.wolfsberg-principles.com/risk-based-approach.html
† For example, Payment Card Industry Data Security Standard (PCI DSS) and related requirements. https://www.pcisecuritystandards.org/security_standards/index.php
‡ http://usa.visa.com/download/merchants/visa_risk_management_guide_ecommerce.pdf
§ See Financial Action Task Force (2008).
¶ To better understand of registration, see report of Wolfgang Kleinwächter for Council of Europe Project on Cyber Crime http://www.coe.int/t/dghl/cooperation/economiccrime/cybercrime/Documents/Reports-Presentations/2079_reps_IF10_reps_wolfgangkleinwaechter1.pdf
** http://www.whois.net/
†† http://www.icann.org/en/compliance/reports/whois-accuracy-study-17jan10-en.pdf
‡‡ Many bullet-proof domains are reportedly hosted in Eastern Europe and the Far East. For Europe, see report by Spamhouse on criminal 'Rock Phish' domains registered at Nic.at (http://www.spamhaus.org/organization/statement.lasso?ref=7) http://en.wikipedia.org/wiki/Bulletproof_hosting
§§ http://www.coe.int/t/dghl/cooperation/economiccrime/cybercrime/cy-activity-Interface-2010/Presentations/Ws%202/LEA_ICANN_Recom_oct2009.pdf
¶¶ Internet Corporation for Assigned Names and Numbers (www.icann.org).

Governmental Advisory Committee (GAC). The committee encouraged the ICANN board to address these recommendations.*

Specialized Units and Interagency Cooperation

Many countries have established financial intelligence units.† These central authorities receive, analyze, and disseminate information on money laundering and the financing of terrorism, and assist with asset recovery and financial investigation.

In recent years, governments have also begun to create specialized prosecution and high-tech crime police services responsible for investigating and prosecuting cyber crime. Obviously, the better cooperation of authorities responsible for fraud, economic crime, financial investigations, and money laundering with other agencies responsible for cyber crime, the better the chances of success against Internet fraud.

Public and Private Cooperation

Most vital information for combating economic crime on the Internet is held by private sector organizations (banking, payment card providers, online banking services and platforms, and money transmitters) and different types of Internet service providers, domain name registries and registrars, and a wide range of industries, research institutions, and initiatives against cyber crime.‡ Cooperation and information exchange between public and private sectors can therefore achieve major impact. Good practices include information sharing and analysis centers (ISACs) for the financial sector in the U.S.,§ the Netherlands,¶ and other countries. To strengthen cooperation among law enforcement authorities and Internet service providers, the Council of

---

* http://gac.icann.org/system/files/Brussels-communique.pdf
† http://conventions.coe.int/Treaty/EN/Treaties/Html/198.htm
‡ Examples of initiatives focusing on fraud are: The Anti-Phishing Working Group (http://www.antiphishing.org/), a global pan-industrial and law enforcement association focused on eliminating fraud and identifying theft from phishing, pharming, and e-mail spoofing. The London Action Plan (http://www.antiphishing.org/) promotes international spam enforcement cooperation and addresses spam-related problems such as online fraud and deception, phishing, and dissemination of viruses. The participants also open the Action Plan for participation by other government and public agencies and appropriate private sector representatives as a way to expand the network engaged in spam enforcement cooperation. The Messaging Anti-abuse Working Group (http://www.maawg.org/ or MAAWG) was formed to encourage the messaging industry to work collaboratively and successfully address messaging abuses such as spam, viruses, denial-of-service attacks, and other exploitations.
§ http://www.fsisac.com/
¶ http://www.samentegencybercrime.nl/

Europe in 2008 developed guidelines for law enforcement and ISP coopera-tion in the investigation of cyber crime.*

Training

Today, and more so in the future, most criminal activities will involve information technologies and thus yield electronic evidence. Therefore, law enforcement officers, prosecutors, and judges must have at least basic knowledge of cyber crime and electronic evidence. Some may require more advanced training and a few should become highly specialized in certain aspects of cyber crime. In Europe, efforts have been undertaken for several years to harmonize law enforcement training on cyber crime and computer forensics and are coordinated by the European Cyber Crime Training and Education Group (ECTEG).[†]

   Based on the assumption that specific measures are required to enable judges and prosecutors to process cyber crime correctly and make use of electronic evidence through training, networking and specialization, the Council of Europe in 2009 adopted a "concept for cyber crime training for judges and prosecutors" to incorporate such training in domestic training programs.[‡]

Efficient International Cooperation

Cyber crime is transnational as are the criminal money flows from economic crime on the Internet. The international standards such as the Budapest Convention, FATF recommendations, and Warsaw Convention allow coun-tries to cooperate efficiently to preserve volatile evidence. However, countries have not yet fully exploited the opportunities offered by these agreements. For example, based on the experience of the G8 High-Tech Crime Subgroup, Article 35 of the Budapest Convention requires parties to this treaty to estab-lish 24/7 points of contact:

> **Article 35: 24/7 Network**—(1) Each Party shall designate a point of contact available on a 24-hout, 7-day-a-week basis, in order to ensure the provision of immediate assistance for the purpose of investiga-tions or proceedings concerning criminal offenses related to com-puter systems and data, or for the collection of evidence in electronic

---

* http://www.coe.int/t/dghl/cooperation/economiccrime/cybercrime/Documents/LEA_ISP/default_en.asp
† http://www.ecteg.eu/
‡ http://www.coe.int/t/dghl/cooperation/economiccrime/cybercrime/Documents/Training/default_en.asp

form of a criminal offense. Such assistance shall include facilitating, or, if permitted by its domestic law and practice, directly carrying out the following measures: (a) Provision of technical advice; (b) Preservation of data pursuant to Articles 29 and 30; and (c) Collection of evidence, the provision of legal information, and locating of suspects.

(2) (a) A Party's point of contact shall have the capacity to carry out communications with the point of contact of another Party on an expedited basis; (b) if the point of contact designated by a Party is not part of that Party's authority or authorities responsible for international mutual assistance or extradition, the point of contact shall ensure that it is able to coordinate with such authority or authorities on an expedited basis.

(3) Each Party shall ensure that trained and equipped personnel are available, in order to facilitate the operation of the network.

Other important channels of cooperation include Interpol's I-24/7 global communication system and its National Central Reference Points (NRCP) network of designated investigators working in national computer crime units in more than 120 countries. However, many of the 24/7 contact points and NRCP are yet to become fully operational.* A number of other questions remain to be resolved:

- How can the private sector cooperate with law enforcement agencies of other countries?
- What role can networks such as the Egmont Group[†] of financial intelligence units or the CARIN[‡] network of asset recovery agencies play in exchanging financial information related to cyber crime?
- As cloud computing allows increased storage of data and applications on servers in foreign jurisdictions or at unknown locations rather than on individual computer systems, how can law enforcement access and evidence preservation be ensured?[§]

---

* Regarding 24/7 contact points, see http://www.coe.int/t/dghl/cooperation/economic-crime/cybercrime/Documents/Points%20of%20Contact/567_24_7report3a%20_2%20april09.pdf
† http://www.egmontgroup.org/
‡ http://www.europol.europa.eu/publications/Camden_Assets_Recovery_Inter-Agency_Network/CARIN_Europol.pdf
§ http://www.coe.int/t/dghl/cooperation/economiccrime/cybercrime/Documents/Internationalcooperation/2079_Cloud_Computing_power_disposal_31Aug10a.pdf

Conclusions

The threat of cyber crime and other information security risks cannot be overstated in light of the worldwide reliance of societies on information and communication technologies . ICT and the Internet offer criminals unprecedented opportunities to organize and operate a global marketplace at low cost and low risk while criminal justice authorities are bound by agency, geographic, and public–private boundaries that hinder cooperation and must operate with limited skills and resources. Criminals will continue to exploit new technologies, seek vulnerabilities, and adjust to countermeasures. Cyber crime and the information society will continue to function within an ecosystem.

Currently, most cyber crime reported by law enforcement is economic—committed to generate economic benefits. A crucial element of any strategy against cyber crime should focus on the search, seizure, and confiscation of proceeds: following the money. Success can be achieved only by enhanced cooperation of anti-cyber crime, anti-money laundering, and financial investigation agencies, the financial sector, and ICT industries at all levels and across the globe.

International standards such as the Budapest Convention on Cyber Crime, the recommendations of the Financial Action Task Force and the Council of Europe Convention on the Laundering, Search, Seizure and Confiscation of Proceeds from Crime and the Financing of Terrorism provide a common basis for joint action.

References

Brunst, P. & Sieber, U. (2010). Cyber crime legislation. In Basedow, J. & Sieber, U. (Eds). German National Reports to the 18th International Congress of Comparative Law, Washington.

Bundeskriminalamt (German Federal Criminal Police Office). (2010). FIU Jahresbericht 2009. Wiesbaden. http://www.bka.de/profil/zentralstellen/geldwaesche/pdf/fiu_jahresbericht_2009.pdf

Bundeskriminalamt (2010). IUK-Kriminalität. Bundeslagebild 2009. Wiesbaden. http://www.bka.de/lageberichte/iuk/bundeslagebild_iuk_2009.pdf

Castells, M. (2000). *The Rise of the Network Society*, 2nd ed. Oxford, Malden.

Commtouch Internet Threats Trend Report (Q1 2010). www.commtouch.com/download/1679

Council of Europe. (2002). Organised Crime Situation Report 2001. Committee PC-S-CO, Strasbourg. http://www.coe.int/t/dghl/cooperation/economiccrime/organisedcrime/Report2001E.pdf

Council of Europe. (2003). Organised Crime Situation Report 2002. Committee PC-S-CO, Strasbourg. http://www.coe.int/t/dghl/cooperation/economic-crime/organisedcrime/PC-S-CO%20_2003_%207%20E%20OC-Report%20 2002-Provisional.pdf

Council of Europe. (2004). Organised Crime Situation Report 2004: Focus on the Threat of Cyber Crime. Octopus Programme, Strasbourg. http://www.coe.int/t/ dghl/cooperation/economiccrime/organisedcrime/Organised%20Crime%20 Situation%20Report%202004.pdf

Council of Europe. (2005). Organised Crime Situation Report: Focus on the Threat of Economic Crime. Octopus Programme, Strasbourg. http://www.coe.int/t/dghl/ cooperation/economiccrime/organisedcrime/Report2005E.pdf

Council of Europe. (2005). Convention on the Laundering, Search, Seizure, and Confiscation of Proceeds from Crime and the Financing of Terrorism (CETS 198). http://www.conventions.coe.int/Treaty/Commun/QueVoulezVous.asp?N T=198&CM=8&DF=05/12/2010&CL=ENG

Council of Europe. (2008). Guidelines for the cooperation between law enforcement and Internet service providers against cyber crime. Global Project on Cyber Crime, Strasbourg. http://www.coe.int/t/dghl/cooperation/economiccrime/ cybercrime/Documents/LEA_ISP/default_en.asp

Council of Europe. (2009). Functioning of 24/7 Points of Contact for Cyber Crime. Global Project on Cyber Crime, Strasbourg. http://www.coe.int/t/ dghl/cooperation/economiccrime/cybercrime/Documents/Points%20of%20 Contact/567_24_7report3a%20_2%20april09.pdf

Council of Europe. (2010). Contribution of the Secretary General of the Council of Europe to Twelfth United Nations Congress on Crime Prevention and Criminal Justice, Salvador, Brazil. http://www.coe.int/t/dghl/cooperation/eco-nomiccrime/cybercrime/Documents/Reports-Presentations/SG%20Inf%20 _2010_4%20-%20UN%20Crime%20congress_ENGLISH.pdf

Council of Europe. (2010). The Internet domain name registration process from the registrant to ICANN. Global Project on Cyber Crime, Strasbourg. http://www. coe.int/t/dghl/cooperation/economiccrime/cybercrime/Documents/Reports-Presentations/2079_reps_IF10_reps_wolfgangkleinwaechter1.pdf

Council of Europe. (2010). Cyber crime training for judges and prosecutors. Global Project on Cyber Crime, Strasbourg. http://www.coe.int/t/dghl/cooperation/ economiccrime/cybercrime/Documents/Training/default_en.asp

Council of Europe. (2010). Law enforcement challenges in transborder acquisition of electronic evidence from "Cloud Computing Providers." Global Project on Cyber Crime, Strasbourg. http://www.coe.int/t/dghl/cooperation/economic-crime/cybercrime/Documents/Reports-Presentations/2079_reps_IF10_reps_ joeschwerhala.pdf

Council of Europe. (2010). Cloud computing and cyber crime investigations: terri-toriality versus power of disposal? Global Project on Cyber Crime, Strasbourg. http://www.coe.int/t/dghl/cooperation/economiccrime/cybercrime/ Documents/Internationalcooperation/2079_Cloud_Computing_power_ disposal_31Aug10a.pdf

Council of Europe. (2012). Criminal money flows on the Internet: Methods, trends and multi-stakeholder counteraction. MONEYVAL Commitee and Global Project on Cyber Crime. Strasbourg.

Deutsche Gesellschaft für Technische Zusammenarbeit. (1998). Drugs and Development in Asia. http://www2.gtz.de/dokumente/bib/99-0026.pdf

Europol. (2007). High-tech Crimes within the EU: Old crimes new tools, new crimes new tools. Threat Assessment, The Hague. http://www.europol.europa.eu/publications/Serious_Crime_Overviews/HTCThreatAssessment2007.pdf

Financial Action Task Force. (2008). Money Laundering and Terrorist Financing Vulnerabilities of Commercial Websites and Internet Payment Systems. Paris. http://www.fatf-gafi.org/dataoecd/57/21/40997818.pdf

Financial Action Task Force. (2010). Money Laundering Using New Payment Methods. Paris. http://www.fatf-gafi.org/dataoecd/4/56/46705859.pdf

Financial Fraud Action UK. (2010). Fraud the facts: definitive overview of payment industry fraud and measures to prevent it. http://www.ukpayments.org.uk/files/fraud_the_facts_2010.pdf

Friedman, T.L. (2006). *The World is Flat*. New York: Farras, Straus & Giroux.

G Data. (2009). Whitepaper: Underground Economy. http://www.gdata-software.com/uploads/media/Whitepaper_Underground_Economy_8_2009_GB.pdf

Information Warfare Monitor/Shadowserver Foundation. (2010). Shadows in the Cloud: Investigating Cyber Espionage 2.0. http://www.nartv.org/mirror/shadows-in-the-cloud.pdf

Internet Crime Complaint Center. (2010). Internet Crime Report 2009. http://www.ic3.gov/media/annualreport/2009_IC3Report.pdf

Koops, B.J. & Leenes, R. (2006). Identity theft, identity fraud and/or identity-related crime. *Datenschutz und Datensicherheit,* 30, 9. http://www.fidis.net/fileadmin/fidis/publications/2006/DuD09_2006_553.pdf

M 86 Security. (2010). Whitepaper: Cybercriminals Target Online Banking Customers. http://www.m86security.com/documents/pdfs/security_labs/cyber criminals_target_online_banking.pdf

Microsoft Corporation. (2010). *Security Intelligence Report*, 9, Jan.–June. http://www.microsoft.com/security/sir/

OECD. (2007). Malicious Software (Malware): A Security Threat to the Internet Economy. http://www.oecd.org/dataoecd/53/34/40724457.pdf

Schmidt, H. (2006). *Patrolling Cyberspace*. Potomac, MD: Larstan Publishing.

Seger, A. (2007). Identity theft and the convention on cyber crime. In Chryssikos, D. et al. (Eds.), *The Evolving Challenge of Identity-Related Crime: Addressing Fraud and the Criminal Misuse and Falsification of Identity*. UN ISPAC. http://www.ispac-italy.org/pubs/ISPAC%20-%20Identity%20Theft.pdf

Sophos. (2010) *Security Threat Report*, August. http://www.sophos.com/security/topic/security-report-2010.html

Organized Crime, the Mafia, White Collar Crime, and Corruption

8

ARIJE ANTINORI

Contents

Introduction: Comparison of Organized Crime and the Mafia

Before we explore the relationship of the mafia, white collar crime, and corruption, especially in Italy, it is very important to have a clear comprehension of the difference between an organized crime structure and a mafia organization. The differences are shown below:

Organized crime
>   Organized structure
>   Predatory intent
>   Active mobility, no-changing or repositioning of skills
>   Focus on well defined criminal businesses and practices
>   Weakly committed to specific political, institutional, and social background
>   Little interaction with local minor criminals; if required, confined to a specific workforce "rental"; generally weakly plugged into local social context
>   Structure based on binding force of an "agreement" for profit sharing

Mafia organization
  Definitive organization
  Pyramidal or multi-pyramidal and hierarchical structure
  Heavy links to local territory and its political and social background
  Ability to operate simultaneously in different contexts, markets,
    and fields
  Affiliation to the "family" by blood ties
  Top-down internal communication flow

Note that the family tie is the main feature that keeps members together. Another factor is the dogmatic respect of a well-defined "code" involving strong cultural, emotional, and even religious values such as loyalty, respect, and honor.

Other distinctions apply to the Italian context and its peculiar mafia criminal groups. It is important to recognize the difference between the Mafia (with a capital M, typically denoting the Sicilian contingent, better known as the Cosa Nostra) and mafia (with a lower case m), a term that covers all Italian mafia organizations.

Italy presently houses a system of traditional criminal assets such as the Cosa Nostra in Sicily, the 'Ndrangheta in Calabria, the Camorra in Campania, and the Sacra Corona Unita in Puglia. These organizations have developed ties and deal with criminal organized structures outside Italy, particularly in Russia, Ukraine, Albania, Moldova, China, and Nigeria.

The 2008 Eurispes report[*] assesses native Italian mafia wealth around €130 billion. The proof is the flow of funds and interest flooding the wider global money-laundering market where macrocriminal interests converge through "grey finance." The mafia organizations are demonstrating a growing interest in intercepting regional, national, and EU funds.

The Italian public administration system is very complex. It includes many local and national institutions and huge numbers of public servants. In 2009 the Group of States against Corruption (GRECO) of the Council of Europe released its first report on corruption in Italy. The report underlined the increasing percentage of unsuccessful corruption trials caused by the lack of a statute of limitations related to this kind of crime. The report also describes this situation as "a serious fault" of the Italian justice system because it dramatically reduces the efficiency and reliability of criminal law required to fight corruption.

Analysis of international corruption requires thorough comprehension of corruption in toto (its total dimensions along with knowledge of each aspect of corruption (social, economic, cultural), understanding of the

---

[*] Eurispes (2008).

methods used, the legal procedures, and the risk and the prevention contexts. Analysis of corruption also requires greater attention when the factors mentioned above are intertwined with specific mafia interests.

The aim of this chapter is to shed light on the complexity of the mafia scenario. While the mafia is based in Italy, the criminal operations are directed toward exporting its business and organization models inside several European Union countries, especially those in Northern areas. In these countries, a weak awareness of the historical, social, and political roots of this phenomenon leads them to undervalue the seriousness of risks they face. As a result, it is difficult to develop suitable measures such as preventive regulatory, ethical, and political interventions, to explain this criminal organization and relate it to other types of crime.

Evolution of Italian Mafias

The goal of the mafia is no longer to use violence or murder to achieve gain. The intent now is to "buy off" state officials to gain complicity of state officials to produce profits. A look at the institutional bodies in charge of countering mafia efforts by several non-government associations involved in anti-mafia activities show a national system heavily affected by corruption, tax evasion, and illegal economic practices that allow mafia organizations to reinvest large amounts of "black" profits from illegal activities.

In 2007, mafia worth reached €85 billion (about 7% of Italy's gross domestic product [GDP]).* As a result the mafia can be considered the "first Italian company." It ensures work to Southern populations (27% in Calabria, 12% in Campania, 10% in Sicily, and 2% in Puglia) and cost Italy €37 billion—the equivalent of Luxembourg's GDP.† The mafia gradually entered the world of high finance by using its tentacles to penetrate highly profitable enterprises such as refuse disposal, commercial trading, real estate, healthcare, food processing, and other private sectors. It can also be considered a leader in globalized black markets, international drug trafficking, prostitution, usury, extortion, illegal immigration, and human smuggling.

The power of the mafia is widely enhanced and favored by collusion with government officials and political representatives, particularly in the Southern territories. Another important factor to consider is the current weakness of political parties in Italy. They are far weaker than they were in the past. As a result, benefits from political participation have decreased. The loss of power led many politicians to adopt a "look out for yourself" attitude that made corruption far more likely.

---

* Confesercenti (2007). *Le mani della criminalità sulle imprese: X rapporto.*
† http://www.piolatorre.it

At present, the mafias participate in economic and financial crime on two levels: (1) microlevel through control and management of local economic systems; and (2) macrolevel via interconnections with global financial networks. Police forces experience substantial difficulties in determining and locating the line between legal and illegal economic systems, allowing the mafias to increase their criminal influence. This allows them to threaten both the democratic systems of the country and legal markets based on free competition.

The mafia gradually evolved from a system of organized crime into a form of invisible power that uses coercive force. In a democratic political system, coercive power is an exclusive function of the state. In some of the poorer regions of Southern Italy and even in many areas of the richer North, the mafia has virtually replaced the state. After it obtains power, it then dominates the territories, ruling the local criminal elements, infiltrating the social textures, and internationalizing its interests across Europe through legal enterprises and illicit trafficking. The organizations can be defined as "security entrepreneurs" because the state cannot monitor or control them. The mafia metamorphosis has been gradual. It was not achieved by a fierce battle against state institutions as is the case with the drug traffickers of Mexico. The mafia slowly and gradually assumed functions and powers of the state and used them to control its territories. On a local level, this stealing of functions is accomplished through collusion with representatives of administrative bodies and politicians. The *mafiamorphosis* (mafia metamorphosis) followed four steps:

The epidemic—During the 1960s and 1970s, mafia power and networks spread throughout the country.

The strategy of tension—During the 1970s and 1980s, the latent threats became obvious through selective killing.

The massacres—During the 1980s and 1990s, the homicides of Judges Falcone and Borsellino resembled terrorism and showed the anti-state bent of the mafia.

The system within the state—Starting in the 1990s, the mafia constituted a hidden parallel "black system" within the state.

The mafia uses its invisible power of persuasion, conditioning, threats, and subjugation against citizens and companies and traders and managers who live in conditions of economic insecurity due to the global crisis that caused negative impacts in every investment area. The result was the transformation of the mafias into multinational companies that produce wealth through a three-level strategy: (1) using legal companies to hide illegal businesses; (2) mixing legitimate money with dirty money for legal investments; and (3) trafficking in and owning illegal businesses.

A good example of the mafia's strategic transformation is illustrated by the Cosa Nostra or Sicilian mafia. After the 1992 massacres and other violent terrorist attacks against the state, the Cosa Nostra suffered a delayed but strong reaction. Many fugitives who were on "wanted" lists for a long time including the perpetrators of the massacres were arrested. The Cosa Nostra attempted to clean-up its image and change its criminal strategy from widespread violence to a new identity based on low-profile criminal activity. The transformation was intended to (1) gain the support of citizens of Southern Italy; and (2) divert the attention of law enforcement and other anti-mafia institutions. Now the mafia bosses approve the selective use of violence only in extreme cases, usually against affiliates. The mafia, unlike local organized crime groups, assumes the status of a political and social actor and manages the economy via the corruption of the public administrations and local authorities.

"Money for Money"

The mafia economic and financial ecosystem is characterized by a "money-for-money" cycle consisting of (1) accumulating money from illegal activities; (2) using money to pay bribes; (3) creating businesses in new economic sectors; and (4) laundering money to produce capital. These steps consolidate crime, politics, and the economy into a system that approaches the systematic planning of public policies.

Furthermore, the dynamic nature of organized crime groups, especially mafia organizations, is favored by the internationalization of economic and financial services, technological advances, geopolitical changes, and the gap among national legal systems. One of the most significant trends of mafia business and capitalization is certainly environmental concern. In recent decades, a special *ecomafia* (ecological mafia) emerged and now participates in (1) the "concrete cycle" ranging from mining to cement and concrete production and illegal construction in urban and rural areas; (2) the "garbage cycle" of collecting, transporting, and disposal of garbage that causes enormous damage in terms of environment destruction, pollution, and other hazards to public health; and (3) illicit refuse disposal including management of hazardous materials.

The contracts for the construction of public works and services allow the infiltration of crime into public agencies. Some years ago, the mafia started recruiting professionals and managers to cover its dirty businesses, thus acquiring an outward appearance of legitimacy. The mafia continues to approach top university students with the intent of creating the first generation of highly skilled mafia business executives.

An analysis of the relationship between corruption and the mafia reveals warning signals that are useful for understanding the organization and developing countermeasures. The mafia infiltration of many Southern Italy municipal administrations should be treated as a warning about the strength of the mafia in these areas. It is important to underline some key factors related to this development: (1) acquaintances, family members, relationships with people connected in any way to mafias; (2) crime records; (3) illegal activities in the commercial sector; (4) continued failure to deal with illegal construction or garbage disposal issues; (5) illegal investments in public procurements; (6) and lack of government control.

The modern mafia is no longer a predator; it has become an entrepreneur. It controls more than a territory; it manages entire market segments. As a result of the economic crisis, usury is thriving and pollutes whole sectors of the economy. The free market is secondary. Poor quality products are used to construct major public works despite huge costs of construction contracts granted to mafia-controlled businesses. In 2009, the Bank of Italy declared that about €79.4 billion (about 6% of Italy's GDP) was allocated for all competitive bids.[*]

The twenty-first century Italian mafia can be called the "white collar mafia" operating mainly in Northern Italy. Its code of silence is the unchanging factor that links past and present. Assets are spread throughout the four Southern regions although mainly in Sicily. Finally, the mafia no longer infiltrates Italian economic and social structures; it is not integrated within them.

"Jelly System"

It would be interesting to analyze the mafia culture within the context of specific business customs and current economic conditions. Over the years, the mafia profited by disregarding rules and increased its power by involving banks in "dirty deals." Globalization represents another critical factor that helped the mafia expand its shady mix of crime, power, and business into what is known as a "grey area" or "jelly system." It is difficult to determine which operations in the mix are legal and economically stable and which ones are fraudulent because key people in the structures are both legitimate businessmen and undercover mafia representatives.

Especially in Italy, considerable disparity exists in relationships of banks and customers. Restrictions on lending in a difficult economic climate led many individuals to borrow from pawnbrokers. In the current financial crisis, the mafia controls economic and financial systems because it has better cash flows than banks and governments. We can consider the mafia an

---

[*] Mario Draghi, anche straniere, *L'azione di prevenzione e contrasto del riciclaggio*, Commissione Parlamentare d'inchiesta sul fenomeno della mafia e sulle altre associazioni criminali, Roma, 2009.

integrated criminal system based on links of an international organized crime structure, government employees, politicians, law and judicial officers, and others involved in governing.

The stabilization of mafia business through the availability of large amounts of money generated by illicit activities (and then laundered) created a parallel economy held together by centripetal strength. This economy attracts small- and middle-sized entrepreneurs who in the past never would have been involved with or supported criminal activities. The two interconnected components of the illegal ("jelly") economic system are the mafia and corruption. The system expands itself, poisoning the dynamics of competition and polluting the legality of the free market.

The systematic nature of corruption creates a fertile background for a culture that has ancient roots and turned the mafia subculture into a global enterprise. Corruption damages Italian society in terms of self-esteem and trust, and it also damages the international image of Italy. Such negative conditioning inhibits career planning of young people, foreign investments, and trust in institutions by new generations. In short, the mafia drains the vitality and darkens the image of Italy's economic system.

In addition, the low productivity and rampant corruption collapsed the country's economic system, as testified by the ranking of Transparency International, an organization that monitors and assesses transparency in the public sector. In terms of the perceived honesty and corruption, Italy ranked 66th among 178 countries in 2010—four positions lower than in 2009 and twelve positions lower than in 2008.* In fact, Italy ranked below Rwanda and Samoa. The Corruption Perceptions Index (CPI) is recognized as a reputable international corruption measurement and used to identify countries with poor administrations. Using this approach, local economic health is of most interest. Countries are ranked on a score from 0 (highest amount of corruption) to 10. Italy's annual tax evasion is estimated at €100 billion (one-fifth of its GDP), increasingly distributed from north to south. In Italy, media representations of scandals threatens to erode public confidence in its institutions, particularly at a time of serious economic crisis, and the "domino effect" may spread the fear to other EU countries.

During the past decade, the connection of white collar crime, corruption, and the mafia created the "jelly system" based on the oligarchy exchanges by entrepreneurs, wheeler dealers, politicians, law enforcement and other public officers, contractors and the suppliers. The corruption diverts important resources from health, education, development, and research.

---

* www.transparency.org

A strong strategy for combating corruption requires in-depth knowledge of the criminal phenomenon, its dynamics, operation methods, participants, and victims. Corruption is characterized by extreme dynamism and, most important, total invisibility that prevents even superficial knowledge of its operations. It is thus very difficult to develop an effective strategy to combat organized crime and corruption in the economic sector.

Italy has no adequate knowledge base of the economic dimensions of corruption—the costs and losses of public services. No one knows the extent to which public administration officers are exposed to corruption risk. In addition, profiles of criminals and victims are unknown. As a result, it is difficult to determine at what level mafias infiltrate administrations. The complexity of this phenomenon makes it difficult to determine the extent of corruption involving the mafia. Corruption is never visible, unless a single episode becomes obvious and it is exposed. Corruption does not shock the public in the way violent crime arouses public opinion. It is a sad fact that the Italian media system, probably due to information overflow, represents corruption events as gossip, not as crime news.

The few reports about this type of crime underline the complexity of the relationship of white collar crime and the mafia. We need a specific early warning set of indicators. The 2009 *Eurobarometer** estimates that as of 2008 17% of Italian citizens have been the objects of corruptions payoff compared to the European average around 9%. The current Italian context of corruption is characterized by a remarkable number of crimes against public administration that often conflict with case law results.

It is possible to have a clear (if approximate) snapshot of Italian corruption by combining data from various statistical and judicial sources spanning the "clean hands" 1990s counter-corruption investigations to present filling the gap between "old" and "new" types of corruption. Criminal enterprises have developed sophisticated techniques to deflect the attentions of authorities. The procedures needed to make illegal payoffs appear clean are easily diversified, and the following crime behaviors can be identified:

Corruption—A crime against general interests. It can be defined as an illegal contract by a public officer who represents a state and its citizens. The public officer receives on his own behalf or for a third party a remuneration for acting outside his duties. Corruption ensues even if no money or goods are received.

Extortion—This crime is a type of reverse corruption. A public officer abuses his or her power function and forces a subject to give or to promise money or other goods to the officer or a third party in

* http://ec.europa.eu/public_opinion/archives/ebs/ebs_325_sum_en.pdf

exchange for actions against the officer's duties. Extortion constitutes a type of blackmail by a public officer against citizens who have the right to seek services granted by law.

Peculation—A public officer takes possession of other people's property money in the custody of a public office. This is a type of embezzlement against the officer's employer.

According to Professor Alberto Vannucci (2010), illegal payoffs become normal practices and corruption "doesn't dig only public budgets, but produces a dangerous democracy deficit." Often crimes involving corruption require management of huge amounts of money outside the normal bookkeeping systems of enterprises. In 2008 and 2009, one estimate is that corruption grew 229% because of illegal agreements between corrupters and bribers.[*] However the "dark figure" representing the amount of corruption that is never detected is unknown.

Investigation of the mafia reveals alarming combinations of interests of economic interests in Italy and the mafia related to financial and business crime and abuses of authority. Unfortunately, in recent years, the legislature downgraded the importance of such crimes and the number of trials continues to decrease. Law 61 of 2001, also known as the Cirami law, reduced punishments for false statement. The number of sentences between 2001 and 2008 dropped from 419 to 68.[†] An analysis of crime records for 1996 through 2006 revealed that the apex of criminal corruption judgments occurred in 1996 when 1,700 sentences were issued. By 2006, the number declined to 239. This is a shocking reduction indicating that the Italian political–economic system in recent years has been polluted by corruption. The situation in the region of Calabria case is unbelievable. 'Ndrangheta is currently considered the most powerful mafia in the world. It is impermeable and invisible and branches to every area of Calabria including local institutions. Interestingly, criminal statistics reported a weak connection between corruption and the Calabrian mafia.

In 2010, in his judicial year opening speech, Tullio Lazzaro, President of Corte dei Conti spoke of corruption as "a sort of shadow or fog that overhangs and winds the most vital and hard-working fabric of the country." There is, in fact, institutionalization of an illegal payoff system known as *tangentismo*. Illegal payoffs constitute an invisible function that governs and contaminates local administrative policies and mechanisms such as supply procurement, urban planning, licenses, and grant applications creating specific effects:

---

[*] Corte dei Conti. (2010). Relazione del Presidente della Corte dei Conti per l'inaugurazione dell'anno giudiziario. Roma.

[†] Biondani, P. (2010b). Corruzione, la grande beffa, *L'Espresso del Milano*, Sept. 30.

1. Negative impacts on Italian and foreign entrepreneurs who invest their capital in other countries to avoid illegal payoffs
2. Lack of support of young Italian entrepreneurs who take their innovations and training to other countries
3. A negative realization of a self-fulfilling prophecy (defined by sociologists as a prediction that directly or indirectly becomes true) arising from relationship of citizens with public administrators that involve illegal payoffs
4. Delays of or failures to finish public works, resulting in huge cost increases
5. Inadequate representation in a democratic system caused by the inability of citizens to participate, "electoral doping," and unbridled political patronage during election campaigns

The corrupter displays a twisted virtuosity. The systematization of the illegal economic and mafia activities extracts high social and moral costs and creates a market that cannot manage illegality risks or create trusting relationships with individuals or groups. In short, corruption involves the infringement of fundamental democratic values such as (1) transparency because corrupt power must be invisible; and (2) equality because the core function of corruption is to create advantaged relationships and undermine equality in providing services to citizens.

Other major damages from the spread of corruption in a system impact the national economy, politics, national image, and hope for the future. The feeling of impunity and the notion that corruption will not be punished created an "impunity syndrome" that increased the gap between the amount of corruption practiced and the amount reported.

Transparency plays a central role in the corruption struggle. Article 97 of the Italian Constitution states that public administration is organized by law "… so that is the good course and the impartiality insured of it…."* Over time, the good course notions and impartiality assumed different meanings, legislative manipulations, and judicial decisions. The good course notion has become ensnared by efficiency dimensions, effectiveness, and cheapness (the so-called Three Es: efficienza, efficacia, and economicità in Italian) to which we can add a fourth E for ethics. The transparency value is pushing public powers to make their actions public even if they are not expressly cited in the constitution.

Decades ago, the institutional initiatives came from the economic world for the purpose of strengthening administration controls and rationalizing its relationships with public affairs. From an organizational view, widening

---

* La Costituzione della Repubblica Italiana, Sezione II, La Pubblica Amministrazione, Art. 97, *Gazzetta Ufficiale*, 1947. http://www.governo.it/Governo/Costituzione/CostituzioneRepubblicaItaliana.pdf

transparency of public administration has been accomplished somewhat through the computerization and digitization of public records. In 2009, the High Committee against Corruption was eliminated and the Anticorruption and Transparency Service was created*. According to Article 6 of Law 116/2009 citing Article 5 of the UN Convention against Corruption, the service will serve as a national authority to fight corruption, counterfeiting, seizure of goods, usury, recycling irregularities.

The Anticorruption and Transparency Service received economic resources of about €2 million. Its main informative source is the System of Investigation (SDI) section of the Home Office created in 2004. The system receives all reports by crime police organizations such as the Carabinieri, Polizia, Direzione Investigativa Antimafia, Guardia di Finanza, Corpo Forestale dello Stato, Guardia Costiera, Coast Guard, and local police. SDI collects real-time data and utilizes an effective validation system, greatly improving the efficiency and accuracy of corruption data from all sources. Unfortunately SDI does not capture details of corruption incidents; it receives only information reported to the police.

Other sources are not merged into the SDI, utilized by Corte dei Conti, or reported to criminal police. For example, crimes prosecuted directly by judges are not included in the crime statistics of the Ministry of Justice nor are crimes recorded by other authorities and agencies such as the Authority for Public Works. The main problem with using and interpreting data from the SDI system is that the reports of agencies cover specific phases of proceedings (initial report, judgment, sentence or plea bargain). Thus, the SDI contains patchy data, uncoordinated temporal databases, and data entry delays that can exceed a year. All these factors reduce the value of the data and complicate the analysis of the data.

In 1996, the first regulation covering management and destination of seized or forfeited goods was issued. Much later, in 2010, l'Agenzia Nazionale per l'Amministrazione e la Destinazione dei Beni Sequestrati e Confiscati alla Mafia (National Agency for Administration and Destination of Assets Seized and Confiscated to Organized Crime) was created. To date it has recovered about €18 million of forfeited goods—a relatively small portion of the estimated €50 to 60 million annual value of business corruption.†

Patronage Systems: The Ancient Practice of *Do Ut Des*

The symbiotic patronage relationship based on a corruption system has ancient socio-cultural roots. *Gratia* has a double meaning: the favor one

---

* http://www.anticorruzione.it/site/ArtId__789/355/DesktopDefault.aspx
† http://www.associazioneulixes.org/95i-corrotti-restituiscano-cio-che-hanno-rubato/

gains from others and the favor showed to others, based on the Roman custom of *do ut des* (I do so that you do).

The Roman Senate consisted of the *gentes*, founders of the ancient republic. Starting around the fourth century B.C., plebeian gentes were introduced into the *nobilitas*, a closed class of patricians. The *nobiles–gentes* structure served as the ruling class before the development of a city structure and withstood for the Republican and Imperial ages. The structure was impermeable, based on blood lines and sustained relationships between people who guaranteed protection in exchange for goods or services.

Before slavery was a common practice, plebeian *gentes* were working forces. They farmed the lands of nobles and if needed provided military strength. Plebeian *gentes,* like free citizens, were bound by subordination relationships to patricians who gave them economic and other assistance in a Roman society controlled by noble derivation organizations.

A binding relationship of a sponsor and customer was considered a holy agreement based on *fides* or trust (*Fides* were worshipped by Romans as divinities). This bond was the forerunner of customer duty and the plebeians became an inferior class, obstacles to the exercise of justice. By a conspiracy of silence, both sponsor and customer remained committed to handling their own affairs by *fides* and not through the justice system. This relationship called patronage originated in the early Roman community between 900 and 800 B.C. Patronage can be considered a component of Italian cultural heritage that led to modern patronage practices.

The patronage is a useful political tool. *Clientes* must greet and follow patrons in public demonstrations. The chieftain was a political figure, priest, or judge who was trusted to correctly interpret information (written information did not appear until around 500 B.C.). The reciprocal patronage relationship continued through the centuries, contributing to a structured society that placed power and authority in the hands of the aristocracy. The good of the state was equal to the good of the ruling class; thus the interests of the ruling class were protected by the state.

Even though such pernicious relationships are primordial forms of patronage, they differ substantially from current mafia organization relationships. The present relationship of sponsor and state constitutes a patronage system. The modern concept of state good is a major function of political activity and all citizens are expected to respect it. All citizens must submit to state authority and in turn benefit from the state, and we can consider such relationships as corruption crimes. However, mafia power wants advantages; the mafia's goal is to accumulate wealth for a small group exempt from state authority.

Plutarch noted that illegal payoff was a widespread phenomenon of ancient Roman government, especially in the Imperial Age when bureaucratic management was incorporated into the government via the ad hoc creation of *liberti*.* Bribes were used to gain access to some services and/or obtain interviews for high level positions.

Twenty Years Later: "Clean Hands"

In early 1990s, Italy was involved in a judicial ("clean hands") investigation that brought to light a widespread corruption system in the political and financial worlds based on long-lasting agreements between enterprises and political parties. The leaders of the financial world provided funding systems to politicians to obtain public contracts. The new political parties that gave life to the so-called Second Republic disclosed that the corruption in some parts of Italy had environmental characteristics. It was so entrenched that corrupters never asked for favors; they expected favors to be given to them. The usual practice was for a briber to promise and deliver illegal payoffs. Corruption became organized when corrupters and bribers built lasting organizations to conduct illegal transactions over the long term. They used accounting fraud and "black funds" (illegally accumulated money) in their financial maneuvers.

According to Piercamillo Davigo, advisor to the Court of Cassation (Consigliere della Corte di Cassazione), the "clean hands" investigation has not seen the end of corruption. Instead, "The repressive organs practice on criminal deviance the predator function: they improve the species they prey on. We have caught the slowest species, leaving free those faster."[†] In contrast to what happened with other criminal activities such as terrorism and organized crime, corruption warranted special legislation that strengthened investigation tools and the justice system. The legislation that would have allowed judges to take stronger actions was not adopted so *Tangentopoly*, the phenomenon based on the ideology of bribery and it pervasiveness, helped spread the movement for reducing corruption in Italy.

Conclusion

The mafias represent threats far beyond the four areas of Southern Italy where they originated. For about forty years, the Cosa Nostra, Ndrangheta, and Camorra operated in Central and Northern Italy and use these bases of

---

* In Ancient Rome, the *liberti* were redeemed slaves who continued to live in the house of *Patronus*, the master. In return, he expected them to work, respect him, and meet economic obligations.
† Biondani, P. (2010a). *Intervista Davigo:"Sono degli impuniti. L'Espresso Milano.* 15.07.2010.

operation to spread their activities throughout Europe. The mafias played a leading role in crime globalization. They formed in Southern Italy, but it is impossible now to prevent expansion. They focus on business and politics, using intimidation and violence, but permit the state to handle basic functions.

Under mafia domination, market freedom disappears, economic actors become weak, and a crime monopoly forces job markets and companies to adhere to its rules. The mafias exert huge influence on political, social, and economic structures by using fear and violence to achieve their goals. The result is a loss of public trust in the state's power. The mafia then becomes the conflict negotiator and problem solver. Eventually violence is used only when absolutely necessary, and it becomes easy for mafia members to achieve invisibility and blend in with legitimate society.

The Cosa Nostra, Ndrangheta, Camorra, and in a smaller way the Sacra Corona Unita consolidated their national economic and financial dimensions, often cooperating with big foreign criminal organizations. To combat these powerful domestic and foreign criminal organizations, the government and law enforcement officials must accumulation knowledge about the operations of these organizations and find effective ways to handle the charges resulting from illegal investments. Mafia leaders are more afraid of losing their patrimonies than they are afraid of jail. They know that money guarantees comfort for their families and continuity of their organizations. The seizure and redistribution of mafia goods can produce three positive results:

- Weakening of economic power of mafia organizations
- Strengthening of public opinion against mafias
- Assignment of mafia assets to civil society

The Libera, an anti-mafia association, produces various products (flour, pasta, oil, wine, chickpeas, figs, and tomatoes) by cultivating land forfeited by the mafia. Libera sells its products in fair trade markets in some Italian cities. As ex-judge Gherardo Colombo said, "We don't need 'new clean hands,' we need a teachers' army with the purpose to strengthen popular honesty."* From a social and cultural view, it is critical to promote the involvement of the citizenry to awaken their consciences and reawaken legality.

In addition, to exposing the conspiracy of silence around corruption and bribery, now is an opportune time to introduce, as affirmed Pietro Grasso, a national anti-mafia prosecutor, incentives for those who denounce, with the objective of encouraging the fight against corruption crime and implementing

---

* Gherardo Colombo's speech during Day of Legality held by Comitato per la Legalità e la Democrazia di Ravenna and Comitato in difesa della Costituzione di Ravenna, 15.01.2009.

reuse of forfeited assets of criminals. This idea requires undercover operations targeting organized crime, terrorism, drug trafficking, pedophilia, and other activities. The "test of integrity" would be a demand from an undercover officer for money in exchange for performance. The result would be the arrest of an individual who accepts the illegal proposal.

The failure to institute the necessary police and judicial measures to combat corruption may relate to the inability of the police to deal with the amount of white collar crime involving the mafia. Corruption and mafia constitute a socio-cultural system that needs interventions on social and cultural levels with weapons like political will, public opinion pressure, and technological tools. In conclusion, it is important to remember that safety and security are vital in today's societies, and real development cannot proceed without them.

References

Abbate, L. & Gomez, P. (2007). *I Complici: tutti gli Uomini di Bernardo Provenzano da Corleone al Parlamento*. Fazi Editore, Roma.

Amadore, N. (2007). *La Zona Grigia, Professionisti al Servizio della Mafia*. La Zisa, Palermo, 2007.

Amenta, M. (2006). *Il Fantasma di Corleone*. Rizzoli, Milano.

Amenta, M. (2006). *L' Ultimo Padrino*. Rizzoli, Milano.

Antinori, A. (2009). *L 'activité des force de police dans la lutte contre le criminalité organisée de type mafieux en Italie in Cahiers de la Sécurité* janvier–mars 2009 n. 7, Institut National des Hautes Etudes de Securite, FRANCE.

Antinori, A. (2010). *News in fiamme. Fatti e ipostesi sul Caso Rosarno* in *Notizie da Babele - Dall'Osservatorio Carta di Roma*—anno I. Luglio 2010, F.N.S.I., Federazione Nazionale Stampa italiana, Roma.

Antinori, A. et al. (1996). *Il Sogno di Paolo Borsellino: Organizzare la Speranza*. Edizioni Gruppo Abele, Torino.

Antinori, A. et al. (2004). *Raccontare la Legalità. Filosofi e Scrittori si Interrogano su una Parola*, Pironti, Napoli.

Antinori, A. et al. (2006). *Eppino Impastato: Anatomia di un Depistaggio. La Relazione della Commissione Parlamentare Antimafia*. Editori Riuniti, Roma.

Ardita, S. (2007). *Il Regime Detentivo Speciale 41 Bis*, Giuffrè, Milano.

Arlacchi, P. (1983). Morte *di un Generale: l'Assassinio di Carlo Alberto Dalla Chiesa, la Mafia, la Droga, il Potere Politico*. Mondadori, Milano.

Arlacchi, P. (1995). *La Mafia Imprenditrice*. CDE, Milano.

Arlacchi, P. (1996). *Addio Cosa Nostra: Vita di Tommaso Buscetta*. BUR, Milano.

Balazzolo, S. & Oliva, E. (2006). *Bernardo Provenzano. Il Rragioniere di Cosa Nostra*, Rubettino, Soveria Mannelli.

Biondani, P. (2010a). Intervista Davigo: Sono degli Impuniti. *L'Espresso Milano*. 15.07.2010.

Biondani, P. (2010b) Corruzione, la Grande Beffa. *L'Espresso Milano*. 30.09.2010.

Bolzoni, A. & D'Avanzo, G. (2007). *Il Capo dei Capi. Vita e Carriera Criminale di Totò Riina*, BUR, Milano.

Borsellino. P. (2003). *Giustizia e Verità: gli Scritti Inediti del Giudice Paolo Borsellino*, ACFB Editore, S. Elpidio a Mare.

Busà, L. & La Rocca, B. (2006*). L'Usura, le Usure. Tempi, Modi e Luoghi di un Fenomeno Antico e M*oderno, Edizioni Commercio, Roma.

Caruso, A. (2005). *Da Cosa Nasce Cosa. Storia della Mafia dal 1943 a Oggi*, Longanesi, Milano.

Colombo, G. (2009). Speech, Day of Legality, Comitato per la Legalità e la Democrazia di Ravenna and Comitato in difesa della Costituzione di Ravenna.

Confesercenti, S.O.S. (2007). Impresa, Le mani della criminalità sulle imprese, X rapporto, Confesercenti.

Corte dei Conti. (2010). Relazione del Presidente della Corte dei Conti per l'inaugurazione dell'anno giudiziario. Roma.

Crisantino, A. (1989). *La Mafia Come Metodo e Come Sistema*, Pellegrini, Cosenza.

Dalla Chiesa, N. (1976). *Il Potere Mafioso: Economia e Ideologia*, Mazzotta, Milano.

Dalla Chiesa, N. (1993) *Dizionario del Perfetto Mafioso: con un Breve Corso di Giornalismo per gli Amici degli Amici*, Mondadori, Milano.

Dalla Chiesa, N. (2003). *Delitto Imperfetto. Il Generale, la Mafia, la Società Italiana*, Editori Riuniti, Roma.

Draghi, M. (2009). Anche Straniere, L'Azione di Prevenzione e Contrasto del Riciclaggio, Commissione Parlamentare d'inchiesta sul fenomeno della mafia e sulle altre associazioni criminali, Roma.

Eurispes. (2008). Istituto di Studi Politici Economici e Sociali, 'Ndrangheta Holding: Dossier.

La Costituzione della Repubblica Italiana, Sezione II, La Pubblica Amministrazione, Article 97. *Gazzetta Ufficiale*, 1947.

Lupo, S. (2007) *Che Cosa è la Mafia. Sciascia e Andreotti, l'Antimafia e la Politica*, Donzelli, Roma.

Morosini, E. Brambilla, F. (1995). *La Mafia: Economia Politica Società*, Einaudi, Torino.

Mosca, G. (2003). *Che Cosa è la Mafia*, Laterza, Roma. http://ec.europa.eu/public_opinion/archives/ebs/ebs_325_sum_en.pdf

Scarpinato, R. (1975). *Mafia, Partiti & Pubblica Amministrazione*. Jovene, Napoli.

www.governo.it/Governo/Costituzione/CostituzioneRepubblicaItaliana.pdf

www.anticorruzione.it/site/ArtId__789/355/DesktopDefault.aspx

www.associazioneulixes.org/95i-corrotti-restituiscano-cio-che-hanno-rubato/

www.piolatorre.it

www.transparency.org

Rule of Law versus Financial Crime

BOJAN DOBOVŠEK

Contents

Introduction

Europe and the rest of the world face a long-term and far reaching transition of society from the modern era to the post-modern era. The absence of a thorough understanding of this transition is evident from the nature of the discussions pertaining to Europe and its present and future security. Post-modern society is characterized by unpredictable and explicitly contradictory economic, political and social developments (Wicks, 2003). Capitalist society today is characterized by:

1. Economic and political globalization that is becoming increasingly similar to economic and cultural imperialism. It aggravates the polarization between the so-called developed and undeveloped worlds, widens the gaps among different cultures and civilizations, encourages religious fundamentalism and (consequently) terrorism, increases poverty (in the developed and undeveloped worlds), neglects and excludes vulnerable social groups (minorities, youth,

the elderly), and diminishes the possibilities for countries to devise strategies for their own economic and general development and thus face their problems.

2. A neo-liberal capitalist economy that forces its functional, market, and profit logic on different areas of social relations (including areas where it has nothing to offer.

3. Political and economic integration efforts, in particular in European regions, that appeal to common goals and values, multi-ethnic cooperation, coexistence and tolerance, yet at the same time cause troublesome increases in isolationism, xenophobia, populism, and ideological and political (neo)conservatism.

4. Digitalization and informatization of social processes that are changing the foundations of the modern world. We are entering an era known by many names—the information age, digital age, post-industrial age, post-modern age, hypo-modern age, hyper-techno-logical age, and the cyber age.

5. A critical and skeptical approach to social studies that under-mined the authority of the discipline and emphasizes the relativity and limits of its (cognitive) potentials in search of the truth about humans.

6. The appearance of critical post-modern approaches in philosophy that stress the position that ratio should not be defined only as the central progressive force of historical development, but also as a means and tool used throughout history in different, more or less subtle ways by protagonists of different ideological and political backgrounds to dominate and to preserve social positions. Such trends have undermined the foundations of modern enlighten-ment's "big story" about the exclusive role of science and rational-ism in the emancipation of mankind.

7. The transformation of social values and lifestyles that led to exper-imenting with life practices and their increasingly flexible, plural, and atomistic nature. It also strengthened ideological, religious, and moral traditionalism.

8. A number of dramatic discoveries in astronomy, physics, genetics, and medicine that sharpened the contrast between largely liberal ideas about the world and people on the one hand, and more or less dogmatic (conservative) ideas on the other.

9. The appearance of new, complex forms of extremely intensive and far-reaching threats to individual and collective security. Financial crime in all forms represents new threats to individual and collective secu-rity (Kanduč, 4004).

Rule of Law

At this point, it is necessary to look at issues surrounding the most important state institutions that face threats of security and risk in modern society. The discussion shall be limited to the rule of law. The question that arises is the extent to which national parliaments can exert direct and actual influence on global security policy, deal with complex global security problems and challenges in international and supranational political organizations, and protect the security of defense and military associations. The author believes that in their legislative and supervisory functions over both the public and private sectors, national parliaments should play a more active role than they have in the past and must facilitate the necessary structural changes in society needed to curb financial crime.

Organized Crime

When analyzing the trends in modern society, it is apparent that political finances, conflicts of interest, lobbying, and political influence on justice and law-making procedures carry the greatest risk of corrupting the principles and processes of democracy and the rule of law. Endemic corruption destroys fundamental values of human dignity and political equality, making it impossible to guarantee human rights to life, personal dignity, and equality. Because of the possibility of fast and easy profit in the transition processes, corruption as a segment of financial crime exists on a global scale, and we must not allow ourselves to think that it only concerns poor and post-socialist countries.

When exploring how financial crimes are related to other crimes committed by criminal organizations, we must consider that the boundaries and distinctions between organized crime and official public and private institutions are very fuzzy and a great deal of interaction takes place between legal and illegal organizations. Organized crime invests its capital in legal companies, especially into small or medium enterprises, just as legitimate financial institutions invest their capital (Ruggiero, 2001: 65–67). In addition, powerful connections with "innocent companies," political organizations, members of secret organizations, media personalities, bankers, and other powerful people and groups serve as very important means with which organized crime spreads its range, improves its operations, and enlarges its profits.

Rawlinson (1998: 242–246) distinguishes four development phases of the integration of organized crime into legal structures. The first phase is *reactive*. Organized crime acts in situations where it is economically and politically secure and stable, so that it does not have to negotiate with other gangs.

The second phase is *passive assimilation*. Organized crime negotiates with legal structures that need specific services of the "black sector." The legal structures are powerful, and they dictate the conditions of collaboration. The next phase is *active assimilation*. Organized crime penetrates legal structures to the degree where it achieves a dangerous balance between admissible and inadmissible activities, and these activities become more ambiguous for both partners. The last phase is *proactive*. Organized crime is capable of influencing political processes, intimidates all individuals and organizations between it and its goals, and becomes "chameleonic" as it penetrates legal enterprises (banks, political parties, media, and other institutions).

All these phases also apply to legal capital enterprises that maintain relationships with official (political and media) structures. In the last phase, financial organized crime transforms through its networks into the legal sphere and is fighting for state authority. This is the phase characterized by elite organized crime or crime networks. We could say that the crime network is a master of all state areas.

Political scientists are interested in researching this notion. Organized crime is equivalent to the state and cannot be controlled. We can say that organized crime is a fifth branch of state authority. It uses its capital (corruption) to control all other state organizations and institutions including other authority branches and the media. In this phase, the economic and political sectors become dependent on organized crime and that is how organized crime becomes the fifth authority branch and uses its power (corruption and extortion) to exert influence on all the other branches.

Corrupted executives and politicians can also form networks with organized crime representatives to pursue control of the state. Executives and politicians use informal networks to destroy democratic principles. These networks produce great impacts on democratic market development, particularly on the spread of corruption and other forms of financial crime. In this context we can introduce the topic of state capture.

Many economists think that the major cause of corruption is ineffective regulation, but ineffective regulation and corruption are often two sides of the same coin. Usually corruption causes ineffective regulation, rather than the other way around (Lambsdorff, 2007: 9–11). The concept of state capture widens the concept of regulatory capture as an aspect of control of state institutions. This is not necessarily an industrial effort. Capture may be pursued by individuals and groups to further their own interests. It means a narrowing of the concept of regulatory capture; it is an illicit provision of private gains to public officials through informal, non-transparent, and highly preferential channels of access or via blurred boundaries between the political and business interests of public officials. State capture refers to the influence of individuals, groups, or firms within the private sector on the formulation of laws, regulations, and other government policies (the basic rules of the game) by means of illicit and non-transparent provision of private benefits to public officials and functionaries with the intention of gaining a certain advantage (Philip, 2001: 4).

Chowdhury (2004) finds that corruption declines with Vanhanen's democracy index while Treisman (2000) shows that the duration of democracy, defined as the number of uninterrupted years in which a country is democratic, reduces corruption. Borlini (2008: 73) stated that, "Corruption is capable of endangering political and social stability and security, undermining the values of democracy and the rule of law, jeopardizing social, economic and political development." Moreover, both national and international bodies and conferences reached the same conclusion, For example, the Norwegian Bureau for the Investigation of Police Affairs observed that, "Corruption not only distorts the economic system of a country, but also has a negative impact on its political system. Informal networks become a problem when members of such networks choose to ignore rules and legislation and focus on those actions that only benefit themselves and/or fellow members" (Ackerman, 1999: 3). As Ackerman noted, inter-country empirical studies confirmed the negative impact of corruption on growth and productivity. Even when corruption and economic growth coexist, payoffs introduce costs and distortions.

Defining Rule of Law

We support Tamanaha's (2004: 114–127) idea that the rule of law stands in a peculiar state as the preeminent legitimizing political ideal in the world today, without agreement upon precisely what it means.

Consideration of the rule of law is possible in two ways. One approach is research: when each feature of the rule of law appears in the past and then monitoring the development of these characteristics. The second method is thinking about the objectives of the rule of law and then questioning if those objectives are possible to pursue. Such reflection is necessary because the meaning of the rule of law is now described as something good, desirable, and integrated. That is the reason why we have to talk about the rule of law as a specific and very important value.

According to O'Donnell (2004), the rule of law has three crucial features: (1) equality; everyone is treated equally under laws that apply to everyone, (2) clarity; laws must be clear; and (3) publicity; laws must be published and known.

The most important core feature, according to Lord Bingham (2007: 69) is that "all persons and authorities within the state, whether public or private, should be bound by and entitled to the benefit of laws publicly and prospectively promulgated and publicly administered in the courts." Based on this perception, Bingham also proposed eight principles of the rule of law:

1. Laws must be accessible, intelligible, clear, and predictable (everyone should without doubt know what the law is about).
2. Legal right and liability should be resolved by application of the law and not by the exercise of discretion.
3. Laws should apply equally to everyone.
4. Laws must afford adequate protection of fundamental human rights.
5. Court processes must be provided for resolving discrepancies, without costs or delays.
6. Public officials must exercise their (official) powers reasonably, in good faith, for the purpose for which the powers were conferred and without exceeding the limits of such powers.
7. Adjudicative procedures must be fair.
8. The state must comply with its obligations in international law.

Conversely, Tamanaha (2004: 4) stressed that rule of law has three main characteristics: (1) government is limited by the law in that government and state officials must operate within a currently valid positive law with restraints on their law-making power; (2) formal legitimacy through public, prospective laws with the qualities of generality, equality of application, and certainty; and (3) individuals are ruled by law, not by men. Living under the rule of law, it is not to be subject to the unpredictable vagaries of individual. The judiciary must act as special guardians of the law.

Based on the specific historical developments of democracy and the rule of law, several important interpretations are applicable to any discussion on the meaning of the rule of law. Three of the most commonly used and considered (and have the most influence) are the British Rule of Law, North American Constitutionalism, and the German Rechtsstaat (state based on rule of law). The French concept is Separation des Pouvoirs (separation of powers). This chapter will focus on the two mainstream interpretations, the British Rule of Law and the German Rechtsstaat.

German Rechtsstaat

The concept of the Rechtsstaat was formulated in German legal theory in the nineteenth century and based on two principles: Formal Rechtsstaat (the principle of legality, rationality, universality) and Material Rechtsstaat (material principles of protection of the freedoms and rights of individuals). German legal theory and practice later focused on providing formal principles and ignored the material principles of human rights. Some theorists have even argued that the formal principles are in themselves sufficient because formal compliance with procedural rules in adopting legislation is sufficient to ensure validity. Moreover, it is argued that only with these formal procedures is there a guarantee that a substantive law is valid (Cerar, 2009).

A fundamental aspect of Rechsstaat is a connection between the country and the legal system. The primary requirement is that the state's power is limited, and state authorities must always act in accordance with legally defined principles and decisions made in accordance with hierarchically distributed general legislation. This requirement is intended to prevent a police state.

British Rule of Law

The British, during their establishment of democracy, developed the concept of the Rule of Law that, unlike the German concept of Rechtsstaat, does not directly cover the state. This means that the British Rule of Law confers the law with greater autonomy against government policy than does the German Rechtsstaat. Historically, the doctrine of the rule of law had been in place several centuries prior to its formal establishment. If we discuss it in connection with the idea of natural law and limited government, it is essential to know that Britain did not have and still does not have a written constitution. The general principles that serve as a constitution are the results of judicial decisions and precedents (in essence, a judge-made constitution). This distinction is vital to understanding the British Rule of Law concept. Individual rights are grounded in legal precedents that ensure legal certainty. In its original sense, therefore, the Rule of Law does not mean supreme legislative power. It requires that the legislature be subordinated to common law created by the courts (Lauth & Sehring, 2008).

To underline both principles, we can see that the rule of law was formulated as a reaction against state organizations in which the activities of central government bodies are not fixed in advance or identifiable with appropriate legal acts of a representative body. In Continental Europe, the rule of law was established in response to police state governments in which the administration (government) acted in accordance with national interests as perceived by their leaders (principle of rationality). For a police state, according to Pavčnik et al. (2009), internal guidance is sufficient to know how governments have to work. On the other hand, Rule-of-Law governments based on the British model utilize three separate branches of government: legislative, executive–administrative, and judicial.

Modern concepts of the rule of law were established gradually. English and later North American and European continental law contributed the most. According to the modern theory that is generally accepted worldwide, there are no essential distinctions between the European-Continental

Rechsstaat and the Anglo-American Rule of Law. Accepting this assumption as correct, the basic principles that determine the rule of law are:

- Accessibility, equality, clarity, and transparency of the law
- Adoption of laws by the elected representative body and supervised by independent courts and judges
- Binding of the law on all authorities (including administrative and judicial)

Connections of Corruption and Rule of Law

To date, the anti-corruption efforts of the European Union have had very limited effects on countries in transition. The transition and changes leading to a market economy greatly influenced the spread of corruption in the broadest sense. Moral, ethical, and other values were pushed aside in the frenzied race for greater profit by individuals and indeed the whole societies of these countries. Among the factors leading to increased corruption are:

- Political conditions allowing influence of corruption on the rule of law
- Coexistence of old and new elements of political and economic systems
- Failures to comply with laws and weak judiciaries
- Lack of political commitment to reform
- Culture of informality

One characteristic of countries in transition is that old laws and administrative structures prevent the effective functioning of the new laws and administrative structures. Therefore, it is not surprising that the results of research reveal that corruption continues to increase in societies in transition to a market economy and democratic form of government.

The problem of parallel laws and parallel existence of formal structures is likely to decline because candidate countries for accession to the European Union (EU) are adopting European law and order principles and establishing new institutions. But implementation is a problem because of old laws and institutions that remain. In addition, the EU started political processes to reduce corruption. However, in some cases, the opposite effect is occurring. For example, in Estonia and Poland, where the EU seeks decentralization of local governments, corruption has increased (O'Dwyer, 2002: 25–27). In Bulgaria, the assumption is that implementation of the regulations covering lobbying would simply legalize corruption.

Failure to respect laws in Eastern Europe arose during Communist rule and is a major problem that probably will not be overcome in the near future.

Soviet and Eastern European laws may be better written than Western laws, but often they are only partially implemented or not implemented. Moreover, the Communist leaders perceived that they were above these laws—application of the laws was not equal or equitable. Research on the state representative activities showed that in 1997 this problem remained pressing in the Czech Republic, Slovakia, Bulgaria, and the Ukraine.

Although the Communist parties lost their privileged status more than a decade ago, the legal systems in many former communist countries remain under political control. Judges are often appointed by heads of state or parliaments instead of by judicial councils. However, in countries that utilize judicial councils to appoint judges, council members are often politically dependent. Additionally, judges often receive low salaries and are thus susceptible to bribery and other pressures. All these factors act as barriers to effective anti-corruption reforms (Miller, Grodeland, and Koshechkina, 2001).

The main problem is the culture of informality inherited from the Communist era. As noted by Ledeneva and Kurkchiyan (2000: 25), "There are no missing ingredients of legality, but the whole range of practices emerging in the post-Communist environment undermined the ability of legal regulation for its clear operation. Accepting the perspective on the operation of unwritten rules and their understanding could contribute to greater transparency of rules of the game and therefore to increase susceptibility to positive changes and reforms."

State Capture

When analyzing informal networks, it is important to draw attention to the roles and influences of "tycoons" in countries with emerging democracies. In Plato's *Republic* and Aristotle's *Politic,* oligarchy was defined as a form of government in the hands of a few. In the present society, an oligarch is a business or corporate leader who controls enough resources to influence national policy (Guriev & Rachinsky, 2005). Some members of the new ruling class even call themselves barons or tsars and act like the feudal rulers of the past. The *baron* and *tsar* titles are commonly used in Russia and some Western Balkan states (Croatia, Serbia, Montenegro). Modern barons and tsars can form very powerful networks that can influence or even rule the states in which they reside. This constitutes the "state capture phenomenon."

The concept of state capture allows us to categorize individual acts and networks of corruption that are hard to prove into a definite framework of offenses. When defining and analyzing the state capture idea, we analyze how different corruptive activities affect the creation and formulation of laws and regulations. Examples of state capture activities include buying votes in parliament, offering bribes to government officials to influence government regulations, bribes to buy judicial decisions, and illegal funding of political parties. The influence of organized crime is apparent in all these activities. State capture always involves three entities:

- The one who "takes over" from the private or public sphere
- The one "taken over" (the state), particularly its laws, decrees, and regulations
- The one that suffers the consequences (the public).

In essence, a take-over is the use of a country's institutions for private interests (abuses) instead of for the public interest, and activities are conducted via illegal and non-transparent means.

Although the concept of state capture involves powerful oligarchs, it is interesting that "capture" companies are found in wide areas and different sectors of the economy. It is surprising that these companies are generally new to the market. Hellman et al. (2000: 1) remarked, "Many countries start with transition as weak countries, which are not able to ensure basic public goods." Most companies that dominate their markets do not take or offer bribes. Because new companies must be competitive, they have to use the state capture strategy to develop a zone of relative security and secure advantages. Using these questionable business practices greatly increases costs for other companies trying to gain a legitimate share of a market.

Measuring state capture is very difficult because the phenomenon is very complex. One major measurement problem is that regardless of the extensive scope of a take-over, not all the companies in a specific area of endeavor are going to benefit from the capture. In the most extreme cases, a single large monopolistic corporation can create a much larger level of state capture than several less powerful companies that compete among themselves for favors from state representatives. Also, state take-overs can cross borders when foreign companies, investors, or even governments become involved.

There are differences in duration and action in cases in which an individual buys one parliament vote one time, compared to a situation in which one person can make or eliminate laws. Obviously, more harm occurs when someone buys parliament votes during every session than when a single individual buys votes only once. This concept allows us to differentiate *deep* and *shallow* take-overs and *occasional* and *standardized* take-overs. An occasional and standard take-over is less likely to involve direct benefits to public officials. These take-overs operate through informal networks and exchanges and the exchange of money does not play an important role.

Relations in which corruptive demand meets corruptive product and informational symmetry exists between A and C (for example, they have proof of each other's illegal actions) are different from situations in which one party has an advantage and uses it to affect political processes via the media, police, prosecutors, and judiciary, and situations where threats or violence dramatically affect the symmetry of an exchange, the price of goods, or the facility of gaining them. The result is a systematic pattern of domination (Philip, 2001).

These findings show that the concept of state capture has deficiencies and they should be analyzed closely in the future. In transitional countries especially, where distinctions between private and public actions may be unclear, it is hard to determine who is taking over whom. It is also necessary to question whether these actions or non-actions of governments constitute state capture or simply represent unintentional consequence of deficient legislation.

If the verdict is state capture, the next issue is identifying the party who took over and the party taken over. Consider, for example, the model of state capture related to the World Bank. In cases of politically planned efforts to support allies in "seducing" the economy, it is essential to determine whether the action is taken by members of government and their servants (who abuse their own positions for their own benefits on bills of collective interest) or by individual "tycoons" who offer benefits to governments and public officials in exchange for influence (power).

When investigating transitional economics, a common finding is that the economic sector is controlled by state institutions through bank loans. This is not the case in developed countries. The model of transitional countries clearly indicates who takes over and who is taken over. The World Bank, overlooked these important factors related to countries in transition:

- Those who take over and those who are taken over may come from the same social network. Civil servants and politicians may offer their friends different services but may gain no indirect personal benefits.
- Members of government and civil servants rarely differentiate between private and personal matters.

The model of state capture is not appropriate for investigating transition processes and "freeloading" by government allies. Two factors reveal that individuals in transitional economies did not have to use the strategies of state capture and administrative corruption. First, laws and legal foundations were non-existent or were too vague to be effective. Thus, informal networks could take advantage of the weaknesses and turn them to their own benefit. Second, tycoons may not necessarily want to take over state leaders; they may be interested in providing help (Barret, 2004).

More study should focus on how informal networks that pressure states create negative consequences in post-socialist countries and also analyze the role of organized crime groups in these informal networks. Previous measures to repress organized crime through criminal prosecution failed (Dobovšek and Meško, 2008). For this reason, it is essential to increase preventive measures, abolish informal networks, and prosecute their illegal actions. Current preventive measures seek to steer government officials toward an up-to-date criminal policy that endeavors to prevent harmful consequences of crime (Measures Addressing State Capture etc., 2003: 3).

Conclusions

Financial crime is not victimless. When connected with corruption, it undermines the democratic principles that politicians and others should use in their decision-making processes. An epidemic of such behavior creates a general mistrust of state institutions and undermines respect for the rule of law. Various forms of financial crime are widespread in the former Communist societies of Eastern Europe. Research indicates that corruption and financial crime issues have increased in those countries and most citizens blame the increases in financial crimes on the transition to democracy. Financial crime does not simply distort a country's economic system. Political systems are also damaged when members of informal networks choose to ignore rules and legislation and focus on actions that benefit themselves and fellow members. Cultural conditions, such as very strong family and kinship ties, make some societies more prone to financial crime exploitation.

In most countries in a state of transition, legislative turnover is high and state institutions undergo constant reorganization. This is particularly true of Croatia, Slovenia, and the other transition countries of Eastern and Central Europe. Many rounds of government reforms continued through post-war chaos, transition processes, association with the EU, and standardization and harmonization of the existent laws to international conventions. The problems of implementing new and existing legal measures are caused in part by lack of experienced, trained and specialized government workers. This remains a major challenge.

As we have seen, capture denotes a state in which someone uses (abuses) the state (laws and regulations) for personal benefit instead of working for the interests of the public. State capture is achieved by using illicit and/or non-transparent actions. Findings indicate that the current concept of state capture needs to be developed further, especially for transition countries that have no clear boundaries between private and public activities, making it difficult to determine who influences whom.

Informal networks are not dangerous if they are used in positive way, but we must understand the negative aspects of the use of informal networks and the concept of capturing a state government. One important issue still to be determined is how to limit the influence of negative informal networks that are sometimes connected with organized crime or state capture. If state capture occurs, we must try to put the financial crime acts of networks that are hard to prove into a definite framework. Financial crimes affect the creation and implementation of laws and regulations. Examples of such crimes are buying influence in parliament, accepting bribes for ignoring certain regulations or issuing certain judicial decisions, and illegal funding of political parties. The influence of organized crime pervades all these activities.

We can conclude that in transition countries a considerable amount of new legislation has been passed and new administrative structures have been introduced, but enforcement of the laws and legislation is non-existent. Some old laws and administrative structures remain in place. They may serve as a groundwork for future laws because they act as common law and preserve history in those countries. They may be supported by the people who may regard the new laws as foreign and thus not worth obeying. For this reason, government structures and enactment of legislation should be analyzed more closely in the future.

References

Ackerman, R.S. (1999). *Corruption and Government: Causes, Consequences and Reform.* New York: Cambridge University Press.

Barret, L. (2004). The Role of Informal Networks in the Privatisation Process in Croatia, Integrating the Balkans in the European Union: Functional Borders and Sustainable Security, WP 3: The Informal Sector. Working Paper 3. Retrieved 2.5.2005.   http://www.eliamep.gr/_admin/upload_research/874649499_29_RESEARCH.PDF

Bingham, L. (2007). The Rule of Law. *Cambridge Law Journal,* 66 , 67–85.

Borlini, S. (2008). Corruption: The Enemy within and the International Criminal Apparatus against It. PhD dissertation. Milano: Universita Bocconi.

Cerar, M. (2009). Rule of Law. Part 2. Retrieved January 7, 2009, from http://ius-info. ius-software.si/Novice/prikaz_clanek.asp?Skatla=17&id=40285

Chowdhury, S.K. (2004). The effect of democracy and press freedom on corruption: an empirical test. *Economics Letters,* 85, 93–101.

Dobovšek, B. & Meško, G. (2008). Informal networks in Slovenia: a blessing or a curse? *Problems of Post-Communism,* 55, 25–37.

Guriev, S. & Rachinsky, A. (2005). The role of oligarchs in Russian capitalism. *Journal of Economics Perspectives,* 19, 1.

Hellman, J., Jones, G. & Kaufmann, D. (2000). Seize the State, Seize the Day: An Empirical Analysis of State Capture and Corruption in Transition Economies. Policy Research Working Paper 2444. http://www.worldbank.org/wbi/governance/wp1_new.htm

International Crisis Group. (2001). Asia Reports, Kyrgyzstan at Ten: Trouble in the "Island of Democracy" Asia Report 22. Retrieved May 7, 2009. http://www.crisisgroup.org/home/index.cfm?id=1179

Kanduč, Z. (2004). Poznomoderno stanje in družbeno nadzorstvo. *Revija za kriminalistiko in kriminologijo,* 1, 7–8.

Lambsdorff, J. (2007). *The Institutional Economics of Corruption and Reform: Theory, Evidence and Policy.* Cambridge: Cambridge University Press.

Lauth, H.J. & Sehring, J. (2008). Putting deficient democracy on the research agenda: reflections on diminished subtypes. *Comparative Sociology,* 8, 165–201.

Ledeneva, A. & Kurkchiyan, M. (Eds.). (2000). *Economic Crime in Russia.* Kluwer Law International: The Hague, 31–42.

Measures Addressing State Capture in Russia/Ukraine/Central Asia, Helpdesk Query in Helpdesk Reply. (2003). Retrieved February 14, 2005, from Anti Corruption Resource Center. http://www.u4.no/document/helpdesk/queries/query18.cfm

Miller, W.L., Grødeland, Å.B. & Koshechkina, T.Y. (2001). *A Culture Of Corruption? Coping With Government In Postcommunist Europe.* Budapest: Central European University Press.

Norwegian Bureau for the Investigation of Police Affairs. (2008). Annual Report.

O'Donnell, G. (2004). Why the rule of law matters? *Journal of Democracy,* 32, 32–46.

O'Dwyer, C. (2002). Civilizing the State Bureaucracy: The Unfulfilled Promise of Public Administration Reform in Poland, Slovakia, and the Czech Republic (1990–2000). Retrieved June 18, 2009. http://www.escholarship.org/uc/item/23m654p8

Pavčnik, M. et. al. (2009). Pravna država. Ljubljana: G Vzaložba.

Philip, M. (2001). Corruption and State Capture: An Analytical Framework; Department of Politics and International Relations; University of Oxford. Retrieved April 2, 2009. http://www.worldbank.org/wbi/governance/pdf/prague_corrupt_capture.pdf#search='state%20ca

Rawlinson, P (1998). Mafia, Media and Myth: Representations of Russian Organised Crime. *Howard Journal of Criminal Justice,* 37, 4.

Ruggiero, V. (2001). *Crime and Markets: Essays in Anti-Criminology.* Oxford: Oxford University Press.

Tamanaha, B.Z. (2004). History, Politics, Theory. *On the Rule of Law,* 114–126.

Transparency International Corruption Perception Index. http://www.transparency.org

Treisman, D. (2000). The causes of corruption: a cross-national study. *Journal of Public Economics,* 76 , 399–457.

Wicks, R. (2003). *Modern French Philosophy, From Existentialism to Postmodernism.* Oxford: One World Publications.

The Financial Crisis and the Haphazard Pursuit of Financial Crime

10

ROMAN TOMASIC

Contents

Introduction

The global financial crisis has revealed massive financial frauds and misconduct that have long been aspects of our markets but were submerged by the euphoria that dominated these markets in the good times. One aphorism has been used to explain this phenomenon in financial markets: "You only find out who is swimming naked when the tide goes out" (*The New York Times*, 2007).[1] White collar and corporate crimes have long penetrated markets and are very difficult crimes for the legal system to prosecute, let alone control (Gobert & Punch, 2003; Orland, 1995; Simpson & Gibbs, 2007; Levi, 1987; Tomasic, 2000, 2005).

This is especially so where these crimes are of enormous proportions or involve powerful individuals or corporations. Their seeming invulnerability to regulation is enhanced in boom times, and this is further buttressed by powerful political forces supporting corporate risk taking. These political forces have served to muzzle or curtail the activities of enforcement agencies directly through the lack of adequate resources and indirectly by promoting ideologies that legitimize the minimal role of government in markets and industry self-regulation.

The Treasury Committee of the UK House of Commons recently high-lighted the effects of political ideologies in limiting the actions of regulatory agencies that might seek to interfere in markets. It noted that, "Lord Turner [FSA chairman] argued that such a regulatory philosophy was rooted within a political philosophy where the pressure was on the FSA not to scrutinize more closely the business models of the firm. Indeed, Lord Turner pointed out that the FSA had been criticized prior to the financial crisis for being too 'heavy and intrusive' and was under pressure to become even more 'light touch.' This political philosophy, Lord Turner said, was expressed in speeches on both sides of the House of Commons." (House of Commons, Treasury Committee, 2009, p. 11).

Regulatory agencies that challenged such a prevailing political ortho-doxy were thus in danger of attack from all quarters. This was confirmed by the governor of the Bank of England, who emphasized the weaknesses of regulators when he told the Treasury Committee, "Any bank that had been threatened by a regulator because it was taking excessive risks would have had PR machines out in full force, Westminster and the Government would have been lobbied, it would have been a lonely job being a regulator" (House of Commons, Treasury Committee, 2009, p. 12). This political pressure may also be facilitated by governments that compete to create business-friendly financial centers such as London[2] and New York.

Insofar as corporate conduct is concerned, it has proven difficult to crim-inalize catastrophic failure, such as those that led to the nationalization of a number of British banks. The savings and loans crisis of the 1980s in the U.S. revealed unlawful risk taking and looting by bank executives (Calavita & Pontell, 1990, 1991), but few criminal actions; although many banks were closed. The 1990s actually saw a contraction in applying criminal law to white-collar crimes (Simpson, 2002, p. 16). The occasional "rogue" trader such as Nick Leeson (involved in the collapse of Barings) was successfully prosecuted. However, the poor history of enforcement is not surprising based on the limited effectiveness of criminal sanctions in this area.

Criminal sanctions applicable to corporate financial misconduct are not well developed and certainly are not widely used in regard to financial fail-ures, despite the huge amounts of money that may have been lost or misused by such corporate controllers. This is a paradox in light of the prison sen-tences handed down to bank robbers such as Ronald Biggs. The reality is that corporate criminal law does not work effectively in financial contexts, and may well amount to counterproductive regulation (Grabosky, 1995).

Not surprisingly, the limits of law in dealing with large corporate entities such as banks have long been known (Stone, 1975, p. 93; Braithwaite, 1982; Moore, 1987; Tomasic, 1994). Research also suggests that senior corporate managers simply do not see themselves at risk of criminal action, even if they may have breached legal rules.[3] This was made clear by the close relationship revealed recently in the UK between government and the City of London and the appointments of senior bankers and business leaders to manage the policy formulation process.[4] Some leaders of UK financial institutions even become government leaders[5] and senior regulators[6]—a practice that is also common in the U.S.[7]

It has also been difficult in the UK to treat corporate misconduct as a violation of non-criminal legal rules, for example, the fiduciary duties of directors (Tomasic, 2009, pp. 5–9). In this context, the pursuit of corporate misconduct through formal legal means is largely a theoretical question, leading many to argue that corporate law (both criminal and civil) has failed in many areas (Laufer, 2006; McBarnet & Whelan, 1999; Tomasic, 1994, 2006). Its impact has often been more symbolic than real. The system of light touch and principles-based regulation that prevailed in the UK until recent times was a reflection of these powerful political and cultural forces that favored market mechanisms for dealing with corporate misbehavior (Winnett, 2009, p. 1). After decades of restraint on the part of UK courts when dealing with the internal affairs of corporations, prosecutors have generally been reluctant to bring civil, let alone criminal, cases against corporations and their controllers (Tomasic, 2009).

By contrast, the collapse of the Bear Stearns investment bank in the U.S. shortly after the collapse of Northern Rock plc in the UK immediately saw U.S. prosecutors bring charges against former officers of Bear Stearns (Chung, 2008, p. 26; Goldstein, 2008, pp. 22–23). Likewise, after the collapse of Enron and WorldCom, U.S. prosecutors moved quickly to convict their senior corporate officers.[8] More recently, after Bernard Madoff pled guilty, he quickly received a 150-year sentence for his role in a massive Ponzi scheme fraud (Chung & Rappeport, 2009, p. 1).[9] Such actions are extremely rare in the UK. Former chief executives and company chairmen are allowed to retire gracefully, often with very comfortable pensions, instead of facing prosecution.

Too Important to Lose: A Culture of Bribery?

Governments may be persuaded to believe that certain companies are so important to their respective economies that the companies may be shielded from excessive scrutiny. During the recent global financial crisis, many banks were often said to be too big to be allowed to fail, although this judgment is questionable (Kay, 2009b; Stelzer, 2009; Drew, 2009; Stern, 2003). Similarly, efforts by the Labour Government under Prime Minister Tony Blair to protect BAE Systems plc from scrutiny over bribery allegations may illustrate a similar type of over-protectiveness.

Cultures of bribery exist in many industries engaged in international trade; this has been especially evident in the case of one of the UK's largest

exports: arms. BAE Systems plc is a British company and major participant in the international arms trade. It had been involved in the £43 billion
Al-Yamamah contract to sell Tornado aircraft to Saudi Arabia in 1985 and
was subsequently negotiating a new £20 billion contract to sell 72 Eurofighter
Typhoon jets to the Saudis.

It had been suggested that BAE may have paid over £1 billion in bribes to
facilitate these sales (Leigh & Evans, 2007). This led to the launch of a probe
by the Serious Fraud Office (SFO); but various efforts were made to stop this
investigation. A Saudi prince who once served as his country's ambassador
to the U.S. reportedly threatened to stop the £20 billion Eurofighter contract
if the SFO probe continued as it threatened to scrutinize certain Swiss bank
accounts related to the matter. The Saudi prince conveyed his concerns to
senior members of the then Prime Minister's office. These contracts, like
some recent bank failures, were seen as "too big to fail," despite their unfair-
ness to other industry players and the taint they cast on business integrity
and the rule of law in the UK.

In judicial review proceedings before the UK High Court, [10] it emerged
that the Office of the Prime Minister had written to the then Attorney General,
stating that prosecution of BAE was "likely to have seriously negative consequences for the UK public interest in terms of both our national security and
our highest priority foreign policy objectives in the Middle East."[11] Some days
later, the SFO decided to drop its probe of the BAE bribery allegations. The
then SFO head, Robert Wardle, reportedly explained in December 2006 that,
"It has been necessary to balance the need to maintain the rule of law against
the wider public interest. No weight has been given to commercial interests
or to the national economic interest" (Gibb & Webster, 2008, p. 4).

The former Attorney General, Lord Goldsmith, also denied that any
pressure had been placed upon the SFO to drop its bribery inquiry. The
judges in the judicial review observed that the criminal justice system would
be imperiled by the failure of UK officials to respond properly to threats of
retaliation, such as those reportedly made by the Saudi Prince.[12] Six months
after the decision of the SFO not to proceed with its inquiry, an OECD report
again examined BAE–Saudi bribery allegations and was critical of what it
saw as the UK's alleged tolerance of corruption (Leigh, 2008, p. 8). More
recently, Austrian prosecutors announced that they would sue BAE in regard
to alleged bribes paid to several European authorities related to its arms sales
(Leigh, 2009, p. 18). The Al-Yamamah Saudi arms deal is now under investigation by the U.S. Justice Department, suggesting that the U.S. is much more
determined to deal with foreign corporate bribery cases of this kind than the
UK has been until recently (Boxell, 2009, p. 3).

The OECD has also been critical of the failure of the UK to satisfactorily
implement the OECD convention on combating bribery of foreign officials in
international business transactions (Joint Committee on Draft Bribery Bill,

2009, p. 10). Companies such as BAE are keen to appear to have acted fairly, and BAE has sought to change the internal culture that surrounded the 1985 Al-Yamamah affair. To facilitate this, the former Lord Chief Justice, Lord Woolf, was commissioned to undertake an internal review, and his report developed a number of recommendations and principles that should apply to defense companies acting globally (Woolf Committee, 2009). BAE Systems and Lockheed Martin now reportedly have strict anti-bribery procedures (Joint Committee on Draft Bribery Bill, 2009, pp. 9–10).

Interestingly, it was not until recently that action was successfully brought against a UK company that admitted making corrupt payments to foreign officials in Ghana (Evans & Leigh, 2009, p. 13). Until this conviction, "no [UK] company has ever been convicted under the current [bribery] law. ..." (Joint Committee on Draft Bribery Bill, 2009, p. 9).[13] A year after the High Court decision critical of failures to protect the integrity of the UK criminal justice system, two former leading government figures made comments about the difficulties that fraud investigations entailed. Lord Goldsmith, former Attorney General, now working for a law firm, pointed to problems caused by the lack of police resources devoted to dealing with serious fraud allegations that still exist. On the other hand, Lord Goldsmith suggested that serious fraud costs the UK national economy at least £20 billion annually.[14]

Similarly, the former SFO head, Robert Wardle, now also employed by a private law firm, pointed to the frustration experienced by those dealing with serious fraud cases. Wardle noted that companies tended to cover much fraud, not wishing to attract unwanted publicity. Reportedly, Wardle's comments "... highlight years of frustration among those involved in tackling fraud at what they see as a culture of poor intelligence, lack of resources and a shortage of co-operation from corporations unwilling to reveal wrongdoing involving their staff or customers" (Bounds & Peel, 2009, p. 4).

One reason cited for the failures of UK companies to report fraud has been their concern that EU procurement law would bar them from any public works contracts if they reported any such bribery (Peel, 2009b, p. 4). This legal impediment has meant that plea bargaining might be more difficult than it would be in the U.S. However, this attitude may be changing as UK companies have been prompted to implement improved internal anti-corruption practices (Boxell, 2009, p. 3).

The head of fraud investigations at KPMG Forensic was recently reported as saying that the "slow-moving beast of British anti-corruption policy may be starting to show some signs of life" (Boxell, 2009, p. 3). But, as Boxell reports, a KPMG Forensic survey recently noted that 43% of British companies had no anti-corruption measures in place, and 67% of respondents stated that there were places where doing business was impossible without payments of bribes. This KPMG study found that only 35% of UK companies declined to work in other countries because of fear of corruption (Boxell, 2009, p. 3).

The establishment of whistleblower hotlines by many companies, and tougher cross-border investigations by U.S. government agencies looking at industry-wide corruption, seem to have impacted UK companies. As a reporter for *The Financial Times* noted, "Companies had a further incentive to set up better anti-corruption practices after big fines were imposed on Siemens of Germany and KBR-Halliburton of the U.S. for overseas bribery" (Boxell, 2009, p. 3). After a two-year investigation for breaches of the 1977 U.S. Foreign Corrupt Practices Act, Siemens reached a settlement with authorities and agreed to pay about $800 million. It also agreed to pay an additional €395 million to German authorities as a result of paying bribes of about $1.4 billion over a five-year period (Bibazzi, 2009, p. 3).[15]

The concern about the prevalence of bribery in the UK led to efforts to draft a bribery law and publication of a draft bill in March 2009. In its report on the draft, the House of Lords–House of Commons Joint Committee concluded that "the current law has proven wholly ineffective and in need of reform" (Joint Committee on Draft Bribery Bill, 2009, p. 35).

The prevalence of corporate fraud in the UK has been widely discussed and reported(Levi & Burrows, 2008). For example, BDO Stoy Hayward reported that fraud of a managerial kind involving such matters as false financial statements and mortgage-related fraud conservatively accounted for £960 million in the first six months of 2009; in 2008, such fraud is reported to have amounted to £1.2 billion (Masters, 2009a, p. 17, 2009b, p. 19). Recently, the KPMG fraud barometer that measures cases where the fraud charges exceeded £100,000, recorded the highest fraud rate in the UK for the first six months of 2009; it also reported more than 160 cases of serious fraud costing £636 million over the same period. The financial sector produced the largest number of frauds (Hargreaves, 2009, p. 24).

Using another measure, the UK Association of Chief Police Officers estimated the annual cost of corruption in the UK as high as £13.9 billion (Joint Committee on Draft Bribery Bill, 2009, p. 8). While calculations of this kind are always difficult, it has been estimated recently that up to $500 billion in corrupt gains may be paid worldwide as a result of the massive funds made available by governments to facilitate market stabilization during the financial crisis.[16] The World Bank estimated that about a trillion dollars of bribes are paid each year, adding about 10% to the cost of doing business and about 25% to the cost of procurement contracts in developing countries (Joint Committee on Draft Bribery Bill, 2009, p. 8).

Bribery is a corrosive problem that undermines faith in transparent markets and confidence in the rule of law.[17] The UK has been slow to reform its practices and is decades behind the U.S. in its approach to the handling of foreign corrupt payments by domestic companies and their agents. Fortunately, a new bribery bill is a sign of hope that some change may lead to a more fundamental cultural change in the practices of many UK companies.

Financial Crisis as a Catalyst for Change?

Scandals and economic crises usually provide opportunities for reform, but reform efforts undertaken during such periods are often castigated as over-reactions, distortions, or ill-considered measures. The passage of the Sarbanes-Oxley Act in the U.S. after the collapses of Enron and WorldCom (Romano, 2005) was viewed that way, but in reality, it has historically been difficult to reform corporate and securities laws in the absence of the stimulus that crises provide (Davies, 2006, pp. 415–444).

U.S. Treasury Secretary Timothy Geithner alluded to these problems and called for an end to what he described as "dumb regulation." He told a congressional committee recently that, "Every financial crisis of the last generation has sparked some effort at reform, but past attempts began too late, after the will to act had subsided.… That cannot happen this time" (O'Connor, 2009, p. 7).

The U.K.'s Financial Services Authority (FSA) Chairman, Lord Adair Turner, expressed similar sentiments in evidence to the House of Commons Treasury Committee when he argued that regulators needed to develop a culture of independence so that they were not swept along on the tide of the next economic boom and observed that, "The crucial challenge … is to try at least to take the opportunity of this crisis to reinforce institutional mechanisms so that we do not, in 10 to 15 years' time, do it all over again" (House of Commons, Treasury Committee, 2009, p. 12).

Even in the current crisis, frequent calls for restraint have come from banking industry sources keen to limit the degree to which new regulations are introduced (Blankfein, 2009, p. 13; Jenkins, 2009, p. 20; Masters, 2009d, p. 3). Blankfein was the CEO of Goldman, Sachs. The Institute for International Finance, representing over 375 of the world's largest financial institutions, at one stage even argued that it would be "completely wrong" for authorities to impose greater regulation on the financial services industry (Guha & Giles, 2008, p. 1).

The financial crisis that began in late 2007 drew attention to the problems of mismanagement, corporate fraud, and weak corporate regulation. However, little if any attention has been directed to criminal law issues related to the failures of major British banks. There has certainly been much talk of the culture of greed encouraged by the banks and the almost reckless risk taking that some banking business models encouraged (Augar, 2005, 2009a, b; Tett, 2009). However, the closest that we have come to seeking to attribute liability for the banking failures has been to note massive corporate governance failures (Kirkpatrick, 2009). Public outrage has focused on bonuses paid to bank employees, rather the sizes of the losses incurred by failing banks. Most chief executives of UK banks claimed that they were caught completely by surprise by the sudden liquidity crisis that led to bank failures and the need for the injection of government funds to stabilize them.

While bank chairmen and chief executives were prepared to apologize for the distress caused to shareholders, employees, and others by the collapses of their banks, not one accepted personal responsibility for the events leading to the crisis. The CEO of the Royal Bank of Scotland (RBS), Sir Fred Goodwin, offered his "profound and unqualified apology for all of the distress that has been caused." Andy Hornby, the CEO of HBOS, said, "We are extremely sorry for the turn of events that has brought it about."[18] To date, no civil action has been taken against the directors or boards of failed British banks.[19] The failures have also not led to civil actions again the bank directors and executives for the irresponsible risk taking that created these bank failures.

One manifestation of the financial crisis that began in the UK in September 2007 was a liquidity crisis facing financial institutions and businesses. As Warren Buffett reminded us, only when markets collapse or when the metaphorical tide goes out do the weak financial positions of financial players become evident. The financial crisis revealed the enormous risks taken by banks and financial institutions and the effects of the short-sighted bonus culture that drove business activity in recent years. Banks' irresponsible risk taking was found to threaten the safety of the entire financial system leading, as we have seen, to unprecedented injections of public funds (House of Commons, Treasury Committee, 2008).

The crisis also led to regulatory agencies having to reinvent themselves after much criticism for their failures to deal early enough with the causes of the financial crisis in the UK20 and in the U.S. (Summers, 2008, p. 1; Chung & Masters, 2009; Chung, 2009a, p. 6). It also led to efforts to prosecute long-neglected market behaviors such as insider trading and other abuses such as "front running."[21] At the same time, prosecution authorities such as the SFO (Peel, 2009c, d; Bowers, 2009, p. 31), promised to "get tough" with fraud (Peel, 2009c). The FSA's get-tough policy has seen an increase in fines levied (Fletcher, 2009). The culture of self-regulation in the UK has even prompted some companies to question whether the more interventionist approach by the FSA was necessary (Masters, 2009c; Mathiason, 2009b).

Shortly after his appointment as FSA chairman, Lord Adair Turner sought to "wipe the slate clean" as he foreshadowed that the regulator would seek to develop more effective strategies for dealing with banking failures, because, "… we have been doing supervision on the cheap" (Larsen, 2008). In March 2009, the FSA chief executive, Hector Sants, announced that the old much acclaimed "principles-based" approach to the regulation of financial markets was flawed and said, "Historically, the FSA characterized its approach as evidence-based, risk based and principles-based. We remain, and must remain, evidence and risk-based but the phrase 'principles-based' has, I think, been misunderstood. To suggest that we can operate on principles alone is illusory, particularly because the policy making framework does not allow it." Sants (2009) then called for a more intensive supervision of markets: "The the limitations of a pure principles-based regime have to be recognized. I continue to believe the majority of market participants are decent people; however, a principles-based approach does not work with individuals who have no principles."

Like a number of other financial regulators, Sants (2009) was concerned that the FSA lacked credibility and was not taken seriously enough; he warned that people "… should be very frightened of the FSA." This change in attitude was also accompanied by a departure from the old system of "light touch" regulation that characterized business regulation in the city.

In the U.S., the Securities and Exchange Commission (SEC) chaired by Mary Schapiro also indicated that it would seek to be more active as a financial regulator, albeit, subject to its limited resources and the skills levels of its staff (Chung & Ward, 2008, p. 5; Bartiromo, 2009, pp. 13–14).[22] It has now begun to use its "claw back" powers that remained inert since they were introduced in response to the Enron collapse (Chung, 2009f, p. 5). However, the U.S. has significant duplication or overlap in its regulatory architecture that hinders effective action in regard to complex financial institutions that spread across a number of industries and regions. The record until very recently in dealing with long-standing financial frauds such as those perpetrated by Bernard Madoff and Allen Stanford has not been good. These cases will be discussed further below.

It is still early and there is some skepticism about the degree to which this more assertive regulatory talk will translate into more effective action, especially as some agencies like the FSA have been threatened with closure if a change in government occurs (Murphy, 2009, p. 2). However, government efforts to facilitate economic recovery via economic stimulus packages may themselves facilitate corrupt practices, as noted by a number of observers such as the Kroll consulting firm (Masters, 2009e, p. 8).[23]

Sants' call for more intensive supervision was followed by the release in the UK of the so-called Turner Report by the FSA chairman, Lord Adair Turner. Turner's report (2009) sought to identify the causes of the financial failure and to chart a way forward for financial regulation. Turner noted that the previous supervisory approach that led to the collapse was too focused on individual financial institutions and not sufficiently focused on the wider financial system; that approach also merely accepted existing business models and strategies without challenging them. The FSA's earlier regulatory strategy failed to assess the technical skills of bank staffs and relied too much on the capacities of boards and management teams to make appropriate risk decisions. In particular, insufficient attention was paid to bank liquidity risks that "were fundamental to the crisis" (Turner, 2009, p. 87).

Turner went on to call for "more intrusive and more systemic" regulatory supervision, something that he, like Hector Sants, described as "intensive supervision." Turner (2009, p. 88) saw intensive supervision as involving seven key elements that would bring about a "major shift in the FSA's approach":

1. A significant increase in the resources devoted to the supervision of high-impact firms and in particular to high-impact and complex banks
2. A shift in supervisory style from a focus on systems and processes to focusing on key business outcomes and risks and on the sustainability of business models and strategies
3. A shift in the approach to the assessment of approved persons, with a focus on technical skills and probity
4. An increase in resources devoted to sectoral and firm comparator analysis
5. Investment in specialist skills (e.g., analysis of liquidity risks), with supervisory teams able to draw on enhanced central expert resources
6. A much more intense analysis of information relating to key risks
7. A focus on remuneration policies and the integration of oversight of remuneration policies into overall assessment of risk. (Turner, 2009, p. 88)

However, while acknowledging that "[a]chieving high standards of risk management and governance in all banks" was essential, Turner (2009, p. 93) avoided any effort to attribute liability to bank management and bank boards, stating that issues of risk management and corporate governance would be addressed by a Walker review of these matters commissioned by the Treasury.[24] Interestingly, in the U.S., the SEC has not held back in this way and recently forced the board of CitiGroup to commission an external review of its governance arrangements (Guerrera, 2009, p. 1).

In contrast to the FSA, the House of Commons Treasury Committee noted that, "Discriminating between the personal blame that should attach to bank executives and that appertaining to the force of global circumstances is difficult. Yet it is self-evident that some banks have weathered the storm better than others; and some have not required taxpayer assistance to navigate through the credit crunch [italics added]. These facts alone make the charge of management failure impossible to resist. Banks have failed because those leading them failed. Too much criticism has been leveled at the city culture which encouraged excessive risk taking. The banks' boards must also take their responsibility for failing in their duty to establish a culture within their institutions which supported both innovation and risk management" (House of Commons, Treasury Committee, 2009, p. 49).

This would extend to particular reckless actions such as the decision of RBS to acquire the ABN-Amro Dutch bank for over £50 billion, thereby saddling RBS with an untenable debt level. The decision was approved by the RBS board and did not then encounter any significant shareholder opposition. It is also interesting to note that the EU's de Larosiere (2009) report was also critical of boards and risk management within banks.

The Walker (2009) review was released in July 2009 and made thirty-nine best practice recommendations in relation to corporate governance in the UK banking industry. The terms of reference of this review narrowly defined the problem at hand and did not allow for a review of more appropriate legal duties and responsibilities of bank boards or the enforcement of such duties (Walker, 2009, p. 107). Instead, the report focuses on improvements in the professionalism and diligence of bank boards and seeks to avoid a prescriptive approach. Walker recommends that his new principles should be enforced only through the Combined Code on Corporate Governance that operates on a comply-or-explain basis. Walker (2009, p. 8) surprisingly asserted that "the Combined Code of the FRC remains fit for purpose."

This adherence to the old self-regulatory mechanism for corporate governance is curious given that the code failed to have any effect in restraining leading banks that collapsed during the financial crisis. Paradoxically, most companies are able to report complete compliance with the code despite suffering massive corporate governance failures.[25] Although commissioned by government, the Walker review is largely in the tradition of earlier reports such as those of Cadbury and Hicks but focused in this case on the banking industry. The Walker review recommendations deal with:

- Issues of board size, composition and qualifications (Recommendations 1–5), with non-executive directors expected to play a much greater role of challenging executives
- Eight recommendations dealing with the functioning of boards and evaluating them, with emphasis on the roles of the chairman, non-executive directors, and senior independent director (Recommendations 6–13)
- Nine recommendations dealing with the roles of institutional shareholders and the adoption of new principles of stewardship to encourage greater engagement by them (Recommendations 14–22)
- Five recommendations dealing with the governance of risk through the establishment of a board risk committee and its processes (Recommendations 22–27)

- Twelve recommendations dealing with remuneration issues, aimed at achieving a closer link between remuneration and performance and recommending disclosure of remuneration of "high end" executives who are not on the board (Recommendations 28–39)

Walker's final set of recommendations dealing with remuneration is obviously quite critical due to the degree to which bonuses have driven behavior leading to the present financial crisis. The FSA has clearly seen the need to develop clearer rules in this regard, although the tendency of many leading financial institutions, including those in receipt of government funds, to continue to make substantial bonus payments led to concerns about the difficulty of motivating change in this area. Walker's focus on enhancing the roles of non-executive directors and institutional investors is problematic. Board dynamics make it difficult for non-executives to effectively stand up against a strong management team, especially if the chairman supports management. The history of board behavior in recent times illustrates a great reluctance of board members to destabilize a board or "rock the boat" (Leblanc & Gillies, 2005; Lorsch & MacIver, 1989; Huse, 2007).

In regard to enhancing the roles of institutional investors, laudable though this may be at times, it ignores the problem of investor passivity that is well known to researchers in this area. This passivity is related to the significant costs that institutions may incur in taking a more activist position. The stewardship principle ignores the degree to which directors have legal authority for the management and control of a company. Walker also failed to demonstrate how the prevailing pattern of director primacy in Anglo-American corporations will be overturned or controlled.[26]

We have yet to see whether the financial crisis will bring about fundamental changes in regard to the problems that led to the current global crisis. As Timothy Geithner warned, reforms in the wake of financial crises all too often come too late to be effective. One might add that those that do occur are much weaker than might be necessary. Is it then a prospect of "too little, too late" that we see on the horizon? It is really too early to say, but the vital signs are not encouraging.[27]

The costs of the recent financial crisis have been massive and widely shared due to the burden on general taxpayers to fund bank rescues. However, as the tax burden is not equally shared, because many corporations and wealthy individuals can better limit their payments of taxes via off-shore havens, some taxpayers bear heavier cost burdens than others.

Other costs from the financial crisis such as the significant downturn in the economy, insolvencies, and massive unemployment levels contrast greatly with the benefits that individual bankers of failed banks received before and after the collapse (generous bonuses based on short-term gains and generous pensions). This is an astonishing, but not surprising analysis of the costs and benefits arising from this crisis. Not surprisingly, there has been some political concern about the revival of pre-crisis bank bonuses.[28]

Madoff and Ponzimania: The Dark Side of Finance

Among the many frauds to surface after the collapse of the financial bubble of the last decade were a number of pyramid-like Ponzi schemes that seemed to proliferate during the boom years without much concern from regulators and investors. The most dramatic fraud involved New York securities trader, Bernard Madoff. At first sight, the conviction of Madoff in July 2009 for financial fraud and his 150-year sentence seem like signal achievements for the legal system dealing with financial misconduct. However, it took almost two decades for authorities to act after the SEC had many opportunities to intervene earlier and limit the massive $65 billion loss that investors suffered. *The Economist* (2008, pp. 119–120) described the Madoff affair as the "Con of the century," but it was only the most dramatic of many others like it.

Madoff's conviction was not the end of the matter. Efforts were made to convict others who may have been involved in this scandal (Masters & Farrell, 2009, p. 20) and recover lost funds. To use the tidal metaphor used earlier in this chapter to describe a financial crisis, frauds such as those perpetrated by Madoff only became apparent after anxious investors sought returns of their funds due to the liquidity crisis. Most investors found that no funds were left and that they had been duped, usually by someone who appeared to have impeccable credentials and was widely trusted in the business community and by regulators.[20]

Madoff claimed that he alone was responsible for the Ponzi scheme that misappropriated a massive $65 billion. He probably had a small number of direct accomplices, such as immediate family members, but this case was not a massive corporate failure like the unwise expenditure of almost £50 billion by RBS in 2007 in the takeover of the Dutch ABN-Amro Bank that triggered the failure of RBS (BBC News, 2007). While the losses suffered as a result of these two episodes were roughly similar, their legal frameworks were vastly different. There was no suggestion of fraud on the part of RBS in its actions to acquire ABN-Amro, although it was blighted by "the winner's curse" in that it imposed a debt burden that made RBS unsustainable (Thaler, 1992; Anandalingam & Lucas, 2004).

The liquidity crisis simply made funding such a not as transaction unsustainable for RBS (BBC News, 2009; *Business Standard*, 2009). Many of those who invested in RBS and those who left their money with Madoff suffered similar fates—significant declines in the values of their investments or assets. From a consumer protection perspective, those who placed their faith in a reckless RBS and in Madoff suffered considerably, but the law treats these two episodes differently based on the types of corporate misconduct that applied in each instance.

The liquidity crisis also effectively drew attention to Madoff's Ponzi scheme, even though he managed for many years to pass himself off as an esteemed member of the New York and international financial communities. The most extraordinary aspect of the Madoff fraud is that it was allowed to continue for as long as it did without effective regulatory challenge. Like the failure of the FSA to prevent the collapse of Northern Rock by adequate monitoring (House of Commons, Treasury Committee, 2008), the SEC seems to have had only the most cursory interest in Madoff's real activities. Instead, he was often seen as an expert whom even the SEC asked for advice.[30] As a former Chairman of NASDAQ, Madoff achieved high standing in financial markets. He used his "insider" status to lure people to give him their money to invest upon (Gapper, 2008).[31] Some, like James Cox of Duke University, argued that the Madoff case was "the best illustration of the herd instinct that typically overtakes investors" (Chung, 2009b).

Madoff's fraudulent Ponzi scheme started in the late 1980s and continued until December 11, 2008 when Madoff's sons told regulators that their father confessed to them his massive fraud. Madoff's scheme was able to grow large as hedge funds eagerly acted as feeder funds channeling money to Madoff, and they received commissions from Madoff for so doing (Sender, 2008). In addition, numerous European banks lent money to clients to allow them to invest in hedge funds linked with Madoff (RBS and the Hong Kong and Shanghai Banking Corporation [HSBC] in the UK, BNP Paribas in France, UniCredit in Italy, and Santander in Spain). Clients of Japan's Nomura Holdings also suffered from the Madoff scheme (Mackintosh & Mallet, 2008; Clark, 2008; FT Reporters, 2008; Chung, 2009b).

Remarkably Madoff promised and was able to deliver consistently high returns, regardless of changes in the market. When the intermediaries received fees for directing their clients to Madoff, one would have expected that they would have undertaken proper due diligence (Chung & Brewster, 2008). Alas, that was not the case. Many American charities and wealthy individuals were also encouraged to deposit their money with Madoff. He lured investors by a snappy marketing claim that he had a "split–strike conversion strategy" that guaranteed high returns. In fact, he had no such strategy and did not seem to make stock market investments for his clients for at least thirteen years (Caldwell, 2009).

Many other warning signs or red flags were ignored by those dealing with Madoff. For example, the fact that the large fund of money under Madoff's management was audited by the small New York audit firm of Friehling & Horowitz with only one active accountant was unusual. The seventy-year old David Friehling worked for Madoff for some time, was the only partner in the firm, and lived in Miami, not in New York (Chung, 2009c; Wood, 2009).

Many expected that a much larger firm would have been required to undertake such a large audit.

Other auditing problems arose in relation to the hedge funds that recommended that their clients invest with Madoff; arguably, they should have done more due diligence to determine how the recommended hedge funds operated; but this is seen by accountants as a contentious matter as hedge fund auditors would not have been in positions to audit Madoff's own records (Masters et al., 2009).

Madoff was such a successful salesman and marketer that few believed the warnings about his conduct that reached the SEC from time to time. An exposé by Erin Arvedlund in *Barron's Financial Weekly* in 2001 had no impact on confidence in Madoff. The articled noted that Madoff's fund purported to have produced annual returns of 15% for more than a decade. As Arvedlund reported, "Still, some on Wall Street remain skeptical about how Madoff achieves such stunning double-digit returns using options alone. Three option strategists for major investment banks told *Barron's* they couldn't understand how Madoff churns out such numbers using this strategy." Adds a former Madoff investor, "Anybody who's a seasoned hedge-fund investor knows the split–strike conversion [investment strategy used by Madoff] is not the whole story."[32]

Other observers were also skeptical of Madoff's strategy. A former rival, Harry Markopolos, warned the SEC about it for almost ten years, but little resulted from the warnings (Caldwell, 2009, p. 11). Markopolos, a Boston-based securities analyst, reportedly said that it took him only five minutes to suspect fraud after reading Madoff's marketing materials and another four hours or so to develop a mathematical model to show that Madoff's stated returns were not possible (Nasaw, 2009). Markopolos passed this information to the SEC but it was ignored, perhaps due to a lack of current market expertise among SEC staff (Nasaw, 2009, p. 29). Markopolos told a congressional committee that the SEC was unable to deal adequately with the information he provided because the commission was dominated by lawyers and captains of the industry they regulated (Chung et al., 2009b).

Gregoriou and Lhabitant (2009) noted what they describe as a "riot of red flags" that should have triggered regulatory attention to Madoff's dealings. Not surprisingly, even Madoff described his scheme as "one big lie" (Treanor & Clark, 2008).

Much criticism has been leveled at the SEC for not detecting Madoff's fraud and its failure to follow up leads from others in the marketplace. The first such suspicions were passed onto the SEC in 1999. Its enforcement division opened an investigation of Madoff's firm in 2006 and closed it a few years later. The commission also inspected the affairs of Madoff's brokerage in 2004 and 2005, but did not look into Madoff's investment advisory arm until 2006 (Chung, 2009d; Rappeport & Chung, 2009). This is probably because prosecution is a last resort for many regulators (Hawkins, 2002),[33] but they have other strategies.

Although Madoff claimed that he acted alone in operating his Ponzi scheme, what is clear is that the scheme survived more than two decades because of widespread support of Madoff from both investors and regulators across the finance industry. The Madoff case cannot be dismissed as merely the work of a rogue operator. This was recognized by *The Financial Times* that noted the broader responsibility that many others shared for allowing this fraud to continue and flourish as long as it did. It also pointed out that, "Ordinarily, Ponzi schemes like Mr. Madoff's collapse of their own weight within a couple of years because it simply becomes too difficult to pull in enough new money to pay off earlier investors. The recent lengthy boom cycle created unusually fertile conditions for deceit, spawning a wave of frauds. Good times meant fewer investors asked for their money back and the rapid growth of complicated investment products that no one understood made high apparent returns such as Mr. Madoff's seem less implausible" (*The Financial Times*, 2009, p. 12).

These comments extend well beyond Madoff to other fraud cases as well. Similar observations were made in *The Guardian* (2009) after Madoff's conviction: "Until his arrest and ostracism last December, Mr. Madoff was not a fraudster, but a pillar of the Wall Street community. He even served as a chairman of the NASDAQ stock exchange. Besides, to have created such a large scam and kept it going for such a long time required accomplices and blind belief on the part of investors.... Nor was Mr. Madoff a lone rogue.... The problem is that the culture of investment is not so different from that of Ponzi fraud. Swindlers and legitimate fund managers project an image of respectability and stability—and they both make promises about how much money they can make for clients."

The Madoff case throws an interesting light on the fragility of trust in financial markets (*The Guardian*, 2009, p. 28). The Madoff affair was so enormous that it will not come to an end merely with the conviction of its principal actor; victims will pursue years of litigation to attempt to recover some of their lost investments. Regulatory agencies will also need to work to create public confidence in their abilities and show that they are capable of effective action. Most importantly, the Madoff case seriously damaged the idea that markets can regulate themselves without stronger external oversight. The fact that many large banks were suspicious of Madoff but did not act or speak against him also raises questions about the self-regulatory capacity of financial markets and the corrosive power of self-interest.

This problem was also recognized by Alan Greenspan, former chairman of the U.S. Federal Reserve Bank. When speaking before a congressional committee, Greenspan expressed his dismay at the failure of banks to support each other during the financial crisis. He observed that, "[T]hose of us who have looked to the self-interest of lending institutions to protect shareholders' equity, myself included, are in a state of shocked disbelief" (Andrews, 2008). There is therefore much to be said for stronger consumer-oriented agencies to be set up to ensure oversight of financial markets.[34]

Conclusions: Beyond Cost–Benefit Analyses

There has been a long-standing effort in academics and policy debates to achieve higher levels of accountability by corporations. Criminal law has proven a poor instrument for achieving control and its use has been some-what haphazard if used at all against large financial institutions. This chapter sought to review recent episodes in the interactions of corporate law and major market actors, principally corporations and financial institutions. The chapter reviewed recent debates that cast light upon some of the strengths and weaknesses of laws aimed to achieve greater standards of accountability and integrity in markets. The financial crisis stands as a major watershed in recent corporate and financial history because it stripped many market actors of their normal protective mechanisms and shamed regulators to become more proactive. It remains to be seen whether the crisis will also serve as a watershed in corporate legal history.

The chapter began with a discussion of debates about the application of anti-bribery laws to major companies like BAE that engage in international trade. We found that law reform and enforcement in this area have been slow to gain traction and that powerful political and social forces have stood in the way of improved legal remedies. Anti-bribery regulation remains a difficult area for rule of law operation because public policy factors and political forces may stand in the way of effective change. The UK legal system has not fared well in its responses to major cases of corporate bribery.

Second, we moved to the financial crisis. Periods of scandal and market crisis briefly open the door for changes and provide opportunities for questions to be raised about more effective means of achieving corporate accountability and control. This has been especially applicable to banks and financial institutions that were significantly bruised by the crisis. Once again, government has become heavily involved in the crisis through its efforts to maintain market stability and forestall any contagious market collapse as occurred, for example, with the nationalization of banks such as Northern Rock.

The financial crisis directed attention to the internal governance mechanisms and values of modern financial institutions and provoked a strong debate that may impact the shape of the laws and regulatory strategies in this area. However, there is always a danger that when the crisis ends many market actors will simply be tempted to return to their old ways. This is a very natural and difficult tendency to change. The legal system has not been as successful as it may have been in putting in place more effective rules and accountability norms that might have restrained the rampant risk taking that dominated markets during the boom period prior to the crisis.

Third, we discussed one of the darkest episodes in the recent history of stock markets in the form of the Ponzimania that has been found to have been so widespread in recent times. Financial crises sometime uncover large numbers of illegal and fraudulent practices that flourish undisturbed in "normal" times. This crisis occurred as a result of the liquidity crisis that arose during the current crisis and created demands from investors for returns of their capital and investments. We saw a run on British banks; the first was the run on Northern Rock plc in September 2007. We also saw demands by investors for returns of funds invested with securities trader Bernard Madoff in New York that uncovered a massive fraud and the loss of some \$65 billion in investor funds through Madoff's Ponzi scheme.

What was remarkable about this fraud was Madoff's close relations with U.S. regulators and his image as a leading figure of the securities market. The failure of regulatory agencies over many years to deal with this scandal is extraordinary. Equally troubling have been the failures of some banks and other market actors that suspected Madoff's fraud to act more effectively against him. None of these episodes convinces us that the legal system can inspire confidence in its capacities to achieve a greater accountability of major financial institutions and market operators.

The dominance of self-interest and a culture of greed undermined trust in market institutions such as banks, securities advisers, and regulators and the capacities of the legal system. Despite the conviction of Bernard Madoff, more effective monitoring of bank transparency in regard to market actors might have avoided some of the economic damage of recent years. U.S. Treasury Secretary Timothy Geithner and a number of academics have noted over the years the need for a smarter approach to business regulation than the one applied in episodes such as those discussed in this paper. This is especially so in regard to large banks and financial institutions. Ultimately, the recent events call for significant cultural changes within banks and financial institutions—something that may be strongly resisted, as we have seen in the approach to the payment of bribes for offshore contracts.

Notes

1. The corollary of this expression is: "Everyone looks like a genius in a bull market." This points to a troubling attitude that has seen exaggerated risk taking in boom times and critics labeled as somehow insane if they questioned the

prevailing market logic. Many students of financial crises have pointed to the unfortunate fate of those who would challenge the prevailing logic or genius of those riding the bull market (Galbraith, 1990; Kindleberger & Aliber, 2005).

2. Efforts are being made to downplay this priority (Davies & Masters, 2009, p. 2).
3. See discussion of perceptual deterrence research by Simpson (2002, pp. 35–44).
4. This is not, however, new (Augar, 2000; Clarke, 1986).
5. The practice of the appointment of former company and banking industry leaders to the House of Lords and their involvement in making regulatory policy and shaping responses to the financial crisis is relevant in this regard. Mention might be made here of government leaders such as Lord Paul Myners (city minister and former company chairman) and Baroness Shriti Vadera (former investment banker who played a leading role in the rescue of Northern Rock).
6. In the UK, for example, we saw the CEO of the HBOS appointed as the deputy chairman of the FSA, despite having encouraged HBOS to adopt an extremely risky business strategy that subsequently led to the need for government rescue (Eaglesham & Hughes, 2009, p. 2; Treanor, 2009b, p. 33, 2009d, p. 4). A short time later, the UK Treasury moved to take greater control over Lloyds after it was persuaded to take over debt-laden HBOS (Treanor, (2009a, p. 10).
7. See, for example, the appointment of Hank Paulson, a former Goldman, Sachs investment banker, as U.S. Treasury Secretary.
8. Enron CEO Jeffrey Skilling received a twenty-four-year prison sentence that was upheld on appeal. Enron's chairman Kenneth Lay was also convicted, but died two months later and avoided prison. Andrew Fastow, its CFO received a relatively light sentence of six years after cooperating with prosecutors (CBC News, 2006, 2008). The former WorldCom CEO Bernard Ebbers was found guilty of securities fraud, conspiracy, and the filing of false statements and was sentenced to a twenty-five-year imprisonment, although he denied any knowledge of questionable accounting practices. Scott Sullivan, WorldCom's CFO, cooperated with prosecutors and was treated more leniently than Ebbers as his evidence was used to convict the CEO (Masters, 2005; Crawford, 2005a, b).
9. The SEC failed to properly investigate Madoff's affairs for over two decades, despite occasional concerns expressed by other market actors who found Madoff's business model implausible.
10. See The Queen on the Application of Corner House Research and Campaign against Arms Trade and the Director of the Serious Fraud Office and BAE Systems [2008] EWHC 714 (Admin).
11. Extract from the Prime Minister's letter is quoted by the Court in The Queen on the Application of Corner House Research, above, Paragraph 31. This is also quoted by Murphy (2008, p. 4), BBC News (2008), and Gibb & Webster (2008).
12. The Queen on the Application of Corner House Research, above, Paragraphs 170 and 171. Also see Peel (2008, p. 4).
13. The Law Commission has also been critical of problems with the existing UK bribery law and saw it as in need of "rationalisation" (Law Commission, 2008, Paragraph 1.1; Joint Committee on Draft Bribery Bill, 2009, p. 9; www.lawcom.gov.uk/docs/lc313.pdf
14. See report by Bounds & Peel (2009, p. 4).

15. Under the U.S. Foreign Corrupt Practices Act, criminal penalties may be imposed and corporations and other business entities are subject to fines up to $2 million; corporate officers and agents are subject to fines up to $100,000. However, under the U.S. Alternative Fines Act, fines imposed may actually be up to twice the benefit a defendant sought to obtain from making a corrupt foreign payment (*U.S. Department of Justice Lay Person's Guide on the US Foreign Corrupt Practices Act*. www.usdoj.gov/criminal/fraud/docs/dojdocb.html).

16. Estimate made by Transparency International and recently reported by Kroll; also see Transparency International (2009a, b).

17. Similar covert practices such as money laundering and aggressive tax avoidance through offshore tax havens also have similar effects. Unfortunately, it is beyond the scope of this paper to examine these damaging practices (Brittain-Catlin, 2005; Lilley, 2009; Robinson, 1994, 2003).

18. The apologies of bankers were reported by the House of Commons, Treasury Committee (2009, p. 48).

19. The closest we have come is the failed Northern Rock shareholders' action claiming that the bank's assets were appropriated unfairly by the government; see Court of Appeal decisions in (1) *SRM Global Fund LP*; (2) *RAB Special Situations (Master) Fund Ltd* (3) *Dennis Grainger and Others v. Treasury Commissioners* [2009] EWCA Civ 788.

20. FSA has been criticized both through its internally generated review and by external groups such as the Treasury Committee of the House of Commons (Parker, 2009, p. 2).

21. This happened with securities market regulators around the world: in regard to insider trading prosecutions (Hughes, 2008, p. 22; Hughes, 2009b, p. 2; Verkalik, 2009, p. 1; Yu, 2009, p. B6; Mathiason, 2009a, p. 23); in relation to other market misconduct, see Hughes (2009a, p. 17).

22. Nevertheless, the SEC has become significantly more active than it was under the Bush administration (Chung, 2009e, p. 3, 2009g, p. 20). Also in regard to the U.S. Federal Reserve, see Guha (2009, p. 5).

23. Similar patterns of conduct have been noted elsewhere (Lewis, 2009, p. 65).

24. Sir David Walker was the former chairman of Morgan, Stanley and remains a senior adviser to this firm. He was therefore an odd choice to head such a review. In reviewing the Walker Report, Augar (2009b), a former banker and now an industry commentator, was rightly critical of the decision to appoint an insider to review the banking industry. The House of Commons, Treasury Committee (2009, p. 58) was also not convinced that Walker was the right person to undertake this review, saying, "We are not convinced that Sir David's background and close links with the City of London make him the ideal person to take on the task of reviewing corporate governance arrangements in the banking sector."

25. The paradoxical nature of codes, such as the Combined Code, as a way of dealing with corporate governance failures is well known. Both Enron in the U.S. and Satyam in India were hailed for their adherence to corporate governance principles and collapsed shortly after receiving the accolades.

26. See Bainbridge (2008) for a discussion of the director primacy model.

27. Such optimism is not encouraged if we review some of the earlier literature on the manner in which the commercial world structures legal rules to which it is subject (McBarnet & Whelan, 1991; McBarnet, 1991). Insofar as the phenomenon of creative compliance by business that often characterizes business conduct, see McBarnet (1994, p. 73, 2006).
28. See response to FSA's new remuneration code for banks that received public monies (Treanor, 2009c, p. 25).
29. Madoff was not alone in marketing such schemes during the boom years of the 1990s and during the housing bubble. A similar scheme in the U.S. was organized by Sir Allen Stanford; this US$7 billion Ponzi scheme also passed without serious regulatory scrutiny for many years (Clark, 2009, p. 38; Bone et al., 2009, p. 43; Peel, 2009e, p. 1; Chung et al., 2009a, p. 22; Cookson & Peel, 2009, p. 17; FT Reporters, 2009, p. 12; Peel, 2009a).
30. This is a description by one-time SEC official, Edwin Nordlinger (Burrows, 2009, p. 25).
31. For a similar argument about the perceived advantages of insiders, see Kay (2009a).
32. This story was subsequently republished by *Barron's* (2008). See Arvedlund (2009).
33. In regard to the SEC, see Shapiro (1984).
34. Some efforts to move in this direction have been floated in the U.S. (Warren, 2009).

References

Anandalingam, G. & Lucas, H.V. (2004). *Beware the Winner's Curse: Victories That can Sink You and Your Company,* Oxford University Press, Oxford.

Andrews, E.L. (2008). Greenspan concedes error on regulation, *The New York Times,* 23 October. www.nytimes.com/2008/10/24/business/economy/24panel.html?_r¼1&hp

Arvedlund, E. (2009). *Madoff: The Man Who Stole $65 Billion,* Penguin Books, London.

Augar, (2000). *The Death of Gentlemanly Capitalism: The Rise and Fall of London's Investment Banks,* Penguin Books, London.

Augar, (2005). *The Greed Merchants: How the Investment Banks Played the Free Market Game,* Penguin Books, London.

Augar, (2009a). *Chasing Alpha: How Reckless Growth and Unchecked Ambition Ruined the City's Golden Decade,* Bodley Head, London.

Augar, (2009b). Insiders cannot provide answers on finance, *The Financial Times,* 20 July, 13.

Bainbridge, S.M. (2008). The *New Corporate Governance in Theory and Practice,* Oxford University Press, Oxford.

Barron's. (2008). What we wrote about Madoff, *Barron's,* 22 December. http://online.barrons.com/article/SB122973813073623485.html

Bartiromo, A. (2009). SEC Chief Mary Schapiro: the watchdog's new teeth, *Business Week,* 25 May, 13–14.

BBC News. (2007). RBS secures takeover of ABN-Amro, 8 October. http://news.bbc.co.uk/1/hi/business/7033176.stm

BBC News. (2008). UK wrong to halt Saudi arms probe, BBC News, 10 April. http://news.bbc.co.uk/1/hi/business/7339231.stm

BBC News. (2009). RBS shares plunge on record loss, BBC News, 19 January. http://news.bbc.co.uk/1/hi/business/7836882.stm

Bibazzi, M. (2009). Agents and intermediaries: if they are corrupt, you get the blame, *Kroll Global Fraud Report*, 9, 3.

Blankfein, L. (2009). Do not destroy the essential catalyst of risk, *The Financial Times*, 9 February, 13.

Bone, J., Reid, T. & Spence, M. (2009). Cricket billionaire faces 250-year sentence after pyramid scam arrest, *The Times*, 20 June, 43.

Bounds, A. & Peel, M. (2009). Anger will lay swindles bare, says Wardle, *The Financial Times*, 27 April, 4.

Bowers, S. (2009). Serious Fraud Office investigates AIG's London arm after huge losses on loan insurance, *The Guardian*, 13 February, 31.

Boxell, J. (2009). Companies scramble to tackle corruption, *The Financial Times*, 10 August, 3.

Braithwaite, J. (1982). Enforced self-regulation: a new strategy for corporate crime control, *Michigan Law Review*, 80, 1466–1507.

Brittain-Catlin, W. (2005). *Offshore: The Dark Side of the Global Economy*, Farrar, Straus & Giroux, New York.

Burrows, (2009). The SEC's Madoff misery: its 1992 probe raised no red flags, *Business Week*, 12 January, 24–25.

Business Standard. (2009). RBS may post $41 billion loss, biggest ever by a UK firm, 20 January. www.business-standard.com/india/news/rbs-maypost-41-billion-loss-biggest-ever-byuk-firm/346599/

Calavita, K. & Pontell, H.N. (1990). 'Heads I win, tails you lose': deregulation, crime and crisis in the savings and loan industry, *Crime and Delinquency*, 36, 309–341.

Calavita, K. & Pontell, H.N. (1991). 'Other people's money' revisited: collective embezzlement in the savings and loan and insurance industries, *Social Problems*, 38, 94–112.

Caldwell, C. (2009). Madoff's life of make-believe, *The Financial Times*, 14 March, 11.

CBC News. (2006). From collapse to convictions: a timeline, CBC News, 23 October. www.cbc.ca/news/background/enron/

CBS News. (2008). Conviction upheld for Enron's Skilling, CBS News, 6 January. www.cbsnews.com/stories/2009/01/06/business/main4702512.shtml

Chung, J. (2008). Ex-Bear Stearns fund managers are indicted, *The Financial Times*, 20 June, 26.

Chung, J. (2009a). Congress urged to boost SEC funding, *The Financial Times*, 15 July, 6.

Chung, J. (2009b). Half of Madoff loss borne by foreigners, *The Financial Times*, 12 January, 21.

Chung, J. (2009c). Madoff investigation is far from over, *The Financial Times*, 23 March, 22.

Chung, J. (2009d). Regulators censured over Madoff, *The Financial Times*, 28 January, 24.

Chung, J. (2009e). SEC plans money market safeguards, *The Financial Times*, 25 June, 35.

Chung, J. (2009f). SEC toughens stance with first move to use 'clawback' law, *The Financial Times*, 29 July, 5.

Chung, J. (2009g). US authorities file charges over four alleged scams, *The Financial Times*, 26 February, 20.

Chung, J. & Brewster, D. (2008). Feeder funds to be key target of investor lawsuits: focus on level of due diligence, *The Financial Times*, 30 December, 19.

Chung, J. & Masters, B. (2009). SEC moves to rebuild its reputation, *The Financial Times*, 5 August, 20.

Chung, J. & Rappeport, A. (2009). Cheers as Madoff jailed for 150 years, *The Financial Times*, 30 June, 1.

Chung, J. & Ward, A. (2008). Obama signals change with choice of Schapiro, *The Financial Times*, 19 December, 5.

Chung, J., Alloway, T. & Lemer, J. (2009a). The Stanford scandal: why were red flags ignored?, *The Financial Times*, 19 February, 22.

Chung, J., Hollinger & Pignal, (2009b). SEC 'illiteracy' to blame for Madoff failings, *The Financial Times*, 5 February, 21.

Clark, A. (2008). Global trail of victims of the man on 17th floor, *The Guardian*, 16 December, 6.

Clark, A. (2009). US prosecutors charge Allen Stanford with turning bank into $7bn pyramid scheme, *The Guardian*, 20 June, 38.

Clarke, M. (1986). *Regulating the City: Competition, Scandal and Reform*, Open University Press, Philadelphia.

Cookson, R. and Peel, M. (2009). Warning on Stanford in 2003, *The Financial Times*, 27 February, 17.

Crawford, K. (2005a). Ebbers gets 25 years, CNNMoney.com, 23 September. http://money.cnn.com/soo5/07/13/news/newsmakers/ebbers_sentence/

Crawford, K. (2005b). Ex-WorldComCEOEbbers guilty, CNNMoney.com, 15 March. http://money.cnn.com/2005/03/15/news/newsmakers/ebbers/

Davies, P.J. (2006). Enron and corporate governance reform in the UK and the European Community. In Armour, J. & McCahery, J.A. (Eds.), *After Enron: Improving Corporate Law and Modernising Securities Regulation in Europe and the U.S.* Hart, Oxford, 415–444.

Davies, P.J. & Masters, M. (2009). Regulator to soften focus on keeping city's edge, *The Financial Times*, 10 June, 2.

de Larosiere, J. (2009). Report by High Level Group on Financial Supervision in the EU, 25 February, 29–37. http://ec.europa.eu/commission_barroso/president/pdf/statement_20090225_en.pdf

Drew, A.E. (2009). Banks 'too big to fail'? Wrong, *Business Week*, 18 February.

Eaglesham, J. & Hughes, J. (2009). Bankers under fire: opposition queries PM's judgment, *The Financial Times*, 12 February, 2.

The Economist. (2008). The Madoff affair: con of the century, 20 December, 119–120.

Evans, R. & Leigh, D. (2009). Corrupt firm's work found to be defective, *The Guardian*, 8 August, 13.

The Financial Times. (2009). Madoff's demise: world's largest Ponzi scheme was fault of many hands. 30 June, 12.

Fletcher, N. (2009). City watchdog's tough stance earns record £27.3m in fines, *The Guardian*, 8, 23.

FT Reporters. (2008). European banks admit to $10bn exposure in Madoff scandal, *The Financial Times*, 16 December, 1.

FT Reporters. (2009). A sugar-coated show: the Stanford scandal, *The Financial Times*, 4 March, 12.

Galbraith, J.K. (1990). *A Short History of Financial Euphoria*, Whittle Books, New York.

Gapper, J. (2008). Wall Street insiders and fools' gold, *The Financial Times*, 18 December, 13.

Gibb, F. & Webster, (2008). High court rules that halt to BAE investigation was 'unlawful,' a threat to British justice, 11 April. www.timesonline.co.uk/tol/news/politics/article3724411.ece

Gobert, J. & Punch, M. (2003). *Rethinking Corporate Crime,* Butterworths LexisNexis, London.

Goldstein, M. (2008). Bear scandal: a widening probe, *Business Week,* 7 July, 22–23.

Grabosky, P.N. (1995). Counterproductive regulation, *International Journal of the Sociology of Law*, 23, 347–369.

Gregoriou, G.N. & Lhabitant, F.S. (2009). Madoff: a riot of red flags. http://papers.ssrn.com/sol3/papers.cfm?abstract_id¼1335639

(The) Guardian. (2009). Bernie Madoff: just rewards, 30 June, 28.

Guerrera, F. (2009). Regulators make Citi open doors for review, *The Financial Times*, 13 August, 1.

Guha, K. (2009). New rules to expand fed powers, *The Financial Times*, 17 June, 5.

Guha, K. & Giles, C. (2008). Blame us for crisis, say leading bankers, *The Financial Times*, 10 April, 1.

Hargreaves, D. (2009). Ritz fraud helps push cases to record high, *The Guardian*, 20 July, 24.

Hawkins, K. (2002). *Law as Last Resort: Prosecution Decision Making in a Regulatory Agency*, Oxford University Press, Oxford.

House of Commons, Treasury Committee. (2008). *The Run on the Rock,* HC 56-1, Stationery Office, London. http://news.bbc.co.uk/1/shared/bsp/hi/pdfs/25_01_2008runontherock.pdf

House of Commons, Treasury Committee. (2009). *Banking Crisis: Reforming Corporate Governance and Pay in the City,* HC 519, Stationery Office, London, 58.

Hughes, J. (2008). FSA's Dewar signals bold action in stepping up crackdown on insider trading, *The Financial Times*, 6 May, 22.

Hughes, J. (2009a). Ex-Morgan Stanley trader fined £140,000, *The Financial Times*, 27 May, 17.

Hughes, J. (2009b). Six arrested over insider dealing, *The Financial Times*, 28 May, 2.

Huse, H. (2007). *Boards, Governance, and Value Creation*, Cambridge University Press, Cambridge.

Jenkins, J. (2009). Banks fear impact of FSA rule changes, *The Financial Times*, 15, 20.

Joint Committee on Draft Bribery Bill. (2009). Draft Bribery Bill: First Report of Session 2008–2009, Vol. 1, Stationery Office, London.

Kay, J. (2009a). How the 'Madoff twist' entices the financially astute, *The Financial Times*, 18 March, 13.

Kay, J. (2009b). Why 'too big to fail' is too much for us to take, *The Financial Times*, 26 May.

Kindleberger, C. & Aliber, R.Z. (2005). *Manias, Panics and Crashes: A History of Financial Crises*, 5th ed., Palgrave Macmillan, Basingstoke.

Kirkpatrick, G. (2009). The Corporate Governance Lessons from the Financial Crisis, ECD Steering Group on Corporate Governance, Paris. www.oecd.org/dataoecd/32/1/42229620.pdf

Larsen, P.T. (2008). Banking regulator calls for clean slate, *The Financial Times*, 17 October, 1.

Laufer, W.S. (2006). *Corporate Bodies and Guilty Minds: The Failure of Corporate Criminal Liability*, University of Chicago Press, Chicago, IL.

Law Commission. (2008). Reforming Bribery, No. 313, Stationary Office, London.

Leblanc, R.W. & Gillies, J. (2005). *Inside the Boardroom: How Boards Really Work and the Coming Revolution in Corporate Governance*, Wiley, Mississauga.

Leigh, D. (2008). Britain's failure to tackle corruption damned amid new claims against BAE, *The Guardian*, 18 October, 8.

Leigh, D. (2009). Austria set to sue over BAE arms sales, *The Guardian*, 20 June, 18.

Leigh, D. & Evans, R. (2007). BAE accused of secretly paying £1 bn to Saudi prince, The Guardian, 7 June. www.guardian.co.uk/world/2007/jun/07/bae1 (accessed 19 November 2010).

Levi, M. (1987). *Regulating Fraud: White-Collar Crime and the Criminal Process*, Tavistock, London.

Levi, M. & Burrows, J. (2008). Measuring the impact of fraud: a conceptual and empirical journey, *British Journal of Criminology*, 48, 293–318.

Lewis, L. (2009). Chinese bail-out cash heads for Macao casinos rather than Guangdong factories, *The Times*, 20 June, 65.

Lilley, P. (2009). *Dirty Dealing: The Untold Truth about Global Money Laundering, International Crime and Terrorism*, 3rd ed. Kogan Page, London.

Lorsch, L.W. & MacIver, E. (1989). *Pawns or Potentates: The Reality of America's Corporate Boards*, Harvard Business School Press, Boston.

Mackintosh, J. & Mallet, A. (2008). Europe's banks pay price for guarantees, *The Financial Times*, 16 December, 23.

Masters, B. (2005). WorldCom's Ebbers convicted, *The Washington Post*, 16 March, A01. www.washingtonpost.com/as2/wp-dyn/A36896-2005Mar15?language¼printer

Masters, B. (2009a). Corporate fraud losses soar to £960m, *The Financial Times*, 2 July, 17.

Masters, B. (2009b). Corporate fraud rises to £1.2bn, *The Financial Times*, 19 January, 19.

Masters, B. (2009c). FSA's new approach ruffles feathers, *The Financial Times*, 20 July, 21.

Masters, B. (2009d). Investors fear banks will return to old ways, *The Financial Times*, 25 June, 3.

Masters, B. (2009e). Warning of stimulus cash paying for bribes, *The Financial Times*, 22 June, 8.

Masters, B. & Farrell, G. (2009). Blunders sustained Madoff fraud, *The Financial Times*, 13 August, 20.

Masters, B., Pignal, S. & Chung, J. (2009). Plaintiffs take aim at Madoff's auditors, *The Financial Times*, 6 February, 25.

Mathiason, N. (2009a). Do more to stop insider trading, city watchdog warns 'complacent' banks, *The Guardian*, 28 April, 23.

Mathiason, N. (2009b). 'Light-touch' reforms raise fears of new bank disaster, *The Observer*, 14 June, B1.

Moore, C.A. (1987). Taming the giant corporation? Some cautionary remarks on the deterrability of corporate crime, *Crime and Delinquency*, 33, 379–402.

Murphy, M. (2008). Actions 'placed justice system at risk', *The Financial Times*, 11 April, 4.

Murphy, M. (2009). Plan to axe FSA spurs crime warning, *The Financial Times*, 22 July, 2.

McBarnet, D. (1991). Whiter than white collar: tax, fraud insurance and the management of stigma, *British Journal of Sociology*, 42, 323–344.

McBarnet, D. (1994). Legal creativity: law, capital and legal avoidance. In Cain, M. & Harrington, C. (Eds.). *Lawyers in a Postmodern World: Translation and Transgression*, New York University Press, New York, 73.

McBarnet, D. (2006). After Enron will 'whiter than white collar crime' still wash? *British Journal of Criminology*, 46, 1091–1096.

McBarnet, D. & Whelan, C. (1991). The elusive spirit of the law: formalism and the struggle for legal control, *Modern Law Review*, 54, 48-87.

McBarnet, D. & Whelan, C. (1999). *Creative Accounting and the Cross-Eyed Javelin Thrower*, Wiley, Chichester.

Nasaw, D. (2009). SEC attacked for ignoring Madoff alerts, *The Guardian*, 5 February, 29.

(The) New York Times (2007). Editorial: The tide is still going out. 31 August.

O'Connor, S. (2009). Geithner urges end to 'dumb regulation', *The Financial Times*, 25 July, 7.

Orland, L. (Ed.). (1995). *Corporate and White Collar Crime: An Anthology*, Anderson, Cincinnati.

Parker, G. (2009). FSA 'failed spectacularly', say MPs, *The Financial Times*, 31 July, 2.

Peel, M. (2008). Row over national security claim, *The Financial Times*, 11 April, 4.

Peel, M. (2009a). An empire long on claims and short on data, *The Financial Times*, 20 February, 20.

Peel, M. (2009b). Business shuns US-style plea bargaining on bribery, *The Financial Times*, 22 June, 4.

Peel, M. (2009c). Law officer vows fraud crackdown, *The Financial Times*, 4 August, 3.

Peel, M. (2009d). SFO looks for more cases of city fraud, *The Financial Times*, 14 July, 4.

Peel, M. (2009e). Stanford faces $7bn fraud plot charges, *The Financial Times*, 20 June, 1.

Rappeport, A. & Chung, J. (2009). Madoff records put more pressure on SEC, *The Financial Times*, 21 February, 16.

Robinson, J. (1994). *The Laundrymen: Inside the World's Third Largest Business*, Simon & Schuster, London.

Robinson, J. (2003). *The Sink: Terror, Crime and Dirty Money in the Offshore World*, Constable, London.

Romano, R. (2005). The Sarbanes-Oxley Act and the making of quack corporate governance, *Yale Law Journal*, 114, 142–161.

Sants, H. (2009). Delivering intensive supervision and credible deterrence, Speech on 12 March, Reuters Newsmakers Event. www.fsa.gov.uk/pages/Library/Communication/Speeches/2009/0312_hs.shtml

Sender, H. (2008). Feeder's fees may have exceeded norms, *The Financial Times*, 16 December, 23.

Shapiro, S. (1984). *Wayward Capitalists: Targets of the Securities and Exchange Commission*, Yale University Press, New Haven, CT.

Simpson, G. & Gibbs, C. (Eds.). (2007). *Corporate Crime*, Ashgate, Aldershot.

Simpson, S.S. (2002). *Corporate Crime, Law and Social Context*, Cambridge University Press, Cambridge.

Stelzer, I. (2009). If a bank is too big to fail, it must be broken up, *The Daily Telegraph*, 29 July.

Stern, G.H. (2003). *Too Big to Fail: The Hazards of Bank Bailouts*, Brookings Institution, Washington.

Stone, C.D. (1975). *Where the Law Ends*, Harper & Row, New York.

Summers, L. (2008). The pendulum swings towards regulation, *The Financial Times*, 27 October, 13.

Tett, G. (2009). *Fool's Gold: How Unrestrained Greed Corrupted a Dream, Shattered Global Markets and Unleashed a Catastrophe*, Little, Brown, London.

Thaler, R.H. (1992). *The Winner's Curse: Paradoxes and Anomalies of Economic Life*, Princeton University Press, Princeton.

Tomasic, R. (1994). Corporate crime in a civil law culture, *Current Issues in Criminal Justice*, 5, 244–255.

Tomasic, R. (2000). Corporate crime and its regulation: issues and prospects. In Chappell, D. & Wilson (Eds.). *Crime and the Criminal Justice System in Australia: 2000 and Beyond*, Butterworths, Sydney, 259–270.

Tomasic, R. (2005). From white-collar crime to corporate crime and beyond: the limits of law and theory. In Chappell, D. & Wilson (Eds.), *Issues in Australian Crime and Criminal Justice*, LexisNexis, Sydney, 252–267.

Tomasic, R. (2006). The challenge of corporate law enforcement: future directions for corporation law in Australia, *University of Western Sydney Law Review*, 10, 1–23.

Tomasic, R. (2009). Raising corporate governance standards in response to corporate rescue and insolvency, *Corporate Rescue & Insolvency*, 2, 5–9.

Transparency International. (2009a). Kroll Predicts Corruption Costs could Total $500 Billion Worldwide, as FBI Braces for Next Wave of Financial Fraud Tied to Stimulus Spending. http://press-releases.techwhack.com/37879-transparency-international (accessed 19 November 2010).

Transparency International. (2009b). Major Exporters Failing to Curb Overseas Bribery. http://transparency.org/news_room/latest_news/press_releases/2009/2009_06_23_2009_oecd_progress_report

Treanor, J. (2009a). Blank under fire as treasury moves to take control of Lloyds, *The Guardian*, 7 March, 10.

Treanor, J. (2009b). FSA plans £10m in pay rises as Crosby departs, *The Guardian*, 13 February, 33.

Treanor, J. (2009c). Ministers are passing the buck over bankers' salaries, says FSA chief, *The Guardian*, 14 August, 25.

Treanor, J. (2009d). Shown the door: Brown's banker, *The Guardian*, 12 February, 4.

Treanor, J. & Clark, A. (2008). It was all one big lie: $50bn black hole engulfs global funds, *The Guardian*, 19 December, 3.

Turner, L.A. (2009). *The Turner Review: A Regulatory Response to the Global Banking Crisis*, Financial Services Authority, London.

Verkalik, R. (2009). New tightens on insider trading, *The Independent*, 6 April, 1.

Walker, D. (2009). *A Review of Corporate Governance in UK Banks and Other Financial Industry Entities*, HM Treasury, London, 16 July. www.hm-treasury.gov.uk/walker_review_information.htm

Warren, E. (2009). Consumers need a credit watchdog, *Business Week*, 27 July, 76.

Winnett, R. (2009). Brown ordered 'light touch' on bank regulation, says watchdog, *The Daily Telegraph*, 26 February, 1.

Wood, A. (2009). Red flags for investors to heed, *The Financial Times*, 16 February, 5.

Woolf Committee. (2009). Business ethics, global companies and the defence industry: ethical business conduct in BAE Systems plc: the way forward. http://217.69.26/woolf/Woolfreport2008.pdf

Yu, E. (2009). HK sees first jail term for insider trading, *South China Morning Post*, 2 April, B6.

Further Reading

Financial Services Authority. (2008). Internal audit review of its supervision of Northern Rock and FSA management response. www.fsa.gov.uk/pages/Library/Other_publications/Miscellaneous/2008/nr.shtml

Fighting Corruption
The Role of the Media in the Broader Global Context

11

ANTHONY MILLS

Contents

Obstacles and Dangers of Reporting on Corruption

When we talk about the frontline in the fight against corruption, we usually think of law enforcement officials, governments and government agencies, inter-governmental organizations like the United Nations (UN), and non-government organizations (NGOs) such as Transparency International. However the media constitute other crucial actors often overlooked in the anti-corruption battle.

The media across the world are often criticized for making unsubstantiated corruption claims about politicians and others such as corporation executives. It is true that there is often room for improvement in the quest for balance, accuracy, and fairness in reporting. But it is also true that journalists across the world face the risks of death, assault, torture, intimidation, harassment, and wrongful imprisonments for lengthy terms simply because in their mission to acquire and deliver information in the public interest they investigate and unveil corruption. Sometimes corruption comes to the attention of the public only through the work of journalists.

Generally speaking, we think of journalists dying in the act of completing their assignments when they are working in conflict zones or failed states like Iraq, Afghanistan, Pakistan, Somalia and others where governments are in a state of transition. According to the International Press Institute's Death Watch statistics, almost one in five journalists killed in the first six months of

2010 was covering corruption, making it one of the most dangerous subjects in the world to report.[1]

In 2010, the second most dangerous country in the world for journalists was not one of the nations listed above. Instead, it was Mexico, a country that has seen thousands slain in recent years—victims of a brutal stand-off between government forces and ruthless, brutal drug cartels that will stop at nothing to silence journalists. The journalists threatened, assaulted, tortured, and murdered in Mexico are not reporting on the kinds of conflicts associated with heavy losses of journalists' lives as occurred in Iraq. Rather, they are reporting on a multi-billion-dollar drug business facilitated by corruption that spreads its tentacles across the globe. The violent drug kingpins are fully aware of the power of the media, and that is why they seek so consistently to silence reporters' voices. In some instances, reporters have been kidnapped by drug cartels that then forced their media broadcasters to transmit prescribed information. [2]

In Mexico, as in many other countries, the result of this intimidation and murder has been a rise in media self-censorship. The government must realize that it is not in its interests nor the interests of the people governed for the media in Mexico to be silenced. The public in Mexico has a fundamental right to know about the drug violence and the corruption plaguing the country and the efforts of the Mexican government and security forces to stem the tide of violence and corruption. That is why the Mexican government must do everything in its power to identify those who attack and kill journalists working in Mexico.

Another country in the Americas in which the work of journalists has proven extremely dangerous is Honduras. This country has been especially dangerous for journalists who covered corruption and the general breakdown in law and order that followed the 2009 coup. In fact, Honduras was the third most dangerous country in the world for journalists in 2010.[3]

Journalists covering corruption are silenced in other ways too, particularly in undemocratic countries. They are physically attacked, intimidated, harassed, wrongfully imprisoned after unfair trials, and muzzled through the use of criminal defamation laws by those who would rather not hear uncomfortable truths about their involvement in corruption. In tightly controlled China, for example, a recent rise—despite censorship, self-censorship, and threats—in courageous reporting on corruption has occurred along with an increase in the number of journalists who have been viciously attacked. In fact, late in 2010, one journalist who was investigating corruption died in China after being beaten into a coma by a group of assailants. Sun Hongjie, a senior reporter at the *Northern Xinjiang Morning Post*, died in a hospital on December 30, in the Xinjiang city of Kuytun. Six men at a construction site had beaten him up ten days earlier. Colleagues said they believed he was killed because of his investigative work.[4]

In other Asian countries including Afghanistan, reports of top-level corruption and organized crime investigated by journalists have resulted in death or physical harm to the journalists involved in the investigations.[5,6] In Bangladesh, Foteh Osmani, a correspondent for Bangladesh's top weekly newspaper, *Shaptahik 2000*, died from injuries suffered two weeks earlier when unidentified armed assailants attacked him as he was riding on his motorcycle. The newspaper he reported for is known for its investigative reporting on corruption.[7]

In the Philippines, a country in which the press is generally not curtailed by the government, a culture of impunity exists and, of course, relates to the need to build a stable state. For example, Desidario Camangyan of Sunshine FM Radio was shot dead in the Southern Philippines in June 2010. The attackers fled on a motorcycle. Camangyan had been vocal in criticizing corruption. Only three days later another Philippines journalist was shot dead by two men on a motorcycle after he wrote exposés on local politicians in the run-up to local elections.[8]

Various investigative reports have revealed that Russia is a hotbed of organized crime and corruption and also has a particularly bad record on the treatment of journalists who have sought to investigate organized crime and corruption. Since the fall of Communism, dozens of journalists have been slain in Russia. Impunity remains a tragic norm. A prominent business editor known for his investigative reporting was beaten into a coma in an area where a couple of years earlier another investigative reporter was brutally beaten, lost a leg, and is now unable to speak.[9] An editor of the Russian edition of *Forbes* magazine was murdered.[10]

On virtually every continent, journalists who report on corruption and organized crime face terrible obstacles. Across Asia, Africa, and Latin America, a favored tool used by those who seek to silence reporters unveiling corruption is the application of antiquated criminal defamation laws. Generally, such countries do not consider the truth a justification for exposing a corrupt official even though the facts may be very beneficial to the welfare of the citizens. Thus, an article or television report on corruption can be fully substantiated and based on factual evidence, but the authors or producers still find themselves in prison on criminal defamation convictions handed down by judges who are not impartial, and may have been influenced financially or otherwise by the powerful stakeholder who brought the criminal defamation action.

No journalist should face imprisonment on criminal defamation charges. If those who feel they have been unfairly represented or slandered wish to pursue the issue, they should do so through appropriate professional bodies and/or civil compensation where appropriate. In particular, this process should be governed by an integrity-driven judiciary not open to pecuniary or other influences by the very people the judges are supposed to be judging or investigating.

A tragic example of the plight faced by investigative journalists in Africa was the death of a journalist who was denied medical care in prison. Germain Cyrille Ngota Ngota, the managing editor of the *Cameroon Express*, died in prison as a result of inadequate medical care. He had been detained along with two other editors a month earlier and they all faced ten to twenty years in prison for reporting alleged corruption involving a presidential aide and the state-owned oil company.[11]

In Somalia, a country in a state of anarchy in 2010, journalists uncovered a massive corruption scandal that allegedly involved diversion to warlords of World Food Program aid away from the people who were supposed to benefit. Somalia remains extremely dangerous for journalists seeking to cover corruption and other stories.[12]

In the Middle East where independent reporting emerged when Al-Jazeera was founded around 1990, we are witnessing a rapid increase of anti-corruption reporting propelled by online media. However, in many countries in the region, the reaction by the governments in which the alleged corruption occurred has been very repressive. In Tunisia, before the recent revolution in which the president was overthrown, any reporting on alleged corruption linked to the presidential family and its associates met with repression. One prominent journalist who also reported for the French media was charged with crimes, convicted, and imprisoned on charges most observers believed were fabricated. Another reporter was sentenced to four years in prison for reporting corruption in the public sector in the impoverished south of the country.[13]

Journalists across the Arab world are often engaged in online cat-and-mouse games with authorities. For many journalists, the only platform for publication of reports on corruption is the Internet via blogs, Facebook accounts, and similar measures. Unfortunately these investigators are often traced, caught, prosecuted, and sentenced to prison.[14]

In the European Union and other more liberal Western democracies, journalists can generally cover corruption freely, that is, write their stories without the fear and threat of disappearing extrajudicially into state-sanctioned prison black holes, state-sponsored kidnapping, torture, and execution. However, even in liberal Western democracies, the ability of journalists to report freely on corruption must not be taken for granted.

For example, in Italy, where of course the media are free, recently proposed legislation (that thankfully did not pass in its original form) would have significantly reduced the scope for reporting on the content of investigations, particularly on wiretap activities. The efforts to pass the legislation followed enthusiastic reporting on a number of high profile corruption cases. The media would have been barred from reporting on the content of information obtained from wire taps even in high profile cases before the cases went to trial which, in Italy, may take years.

Another impediment to covering organized crime and corruption in Italy comes in the form of threats and violence from criminals. In some cases, it is alleged that corrupt public sector officials are complicit, and in one recent case in southern Italy, a journalist who reported on corruption and organized crime was beaten unconscious as police alledgedly looked on and did not intervene.[15]

In France, secret service involvement in spying on journalists investigating high profile alleged corruption cases has been alleged. If true, it would, of course, represent a breach of France's constitutionally protected right for journalists to keep their sources of information confidential. Journalists reported that their homes and offices had been broken into and the contents of laptops and memory sticks had been stolen. The *Le Monde* newspaper filed a criminal case against "persons unknown," but no information has been made available on the progress of any investigation.[16]

In the United Kingdom a case that came to light that involved the alleged dumping of toxic waste by a British firm on the coast of West Africa. A law firm representing the accused party successfully obtained a so-called super-injunction banning all reporting on the case. The situation only came to light because the issue of the super-injunction was due to be discussed during parliamentary question time, and the law firm sought to have reporting on it in that context banned as well. The ban would have violated the long-standing right of the British media to report on parliamentary matters at any time.[17]

In Slovenia, a Finnish journalist who reported on alleged corrupt arms deals involving the former Slovenian prime minister and a Finnish arms company was charged under criminal defamation proceedings initiated by the former prime minister's lawyer. The journalist was informed that he would be arrested if he returned to Slovenia.[18]

Cooperation of Media, Political Organizations, and Justice Agencies

Free, independent media that holds both private persons and those elected to public office to account before the citizens who voted for them is a fundamental pillar of a healthy democracy. Efforts to stifle such reporting constitute a denial of a fundamental right for citizens, that is, their right to be informed about matters of public interest.

Despite the risks associated with reporting on corruption and the physical harm often inflicted on journalists who expose corrupt stakeholders, the media continue to boldly report on the topic. The media refuse to bow to the tactics of those who will stop at nothing—even murder—to smother truths they find unpalatable. In a global effort to stop corruption, it is absolutely vital to implement a more inclusive approach in which the media's role is both incorporated and respected. This broader vision also presupposes that the media will live up to its responsibilities, particularly in an ethical and professional context.

Of course, journalists should never become too close to their sources including politicians and the anti-corruption officials from whom they obtain information. In the fight against corruption, the media are, in a broader context, allies in public service. Journalists must be included in any strategic discussion of the fight against corruption because of the fundamental role they play in exposing it. Furthermore, despite the mutual suspicion of the media and public officials toward each other, they are on the same side in the battle against corruption. This does not mean that journalists who report on corruption should play the roles of law enforcement agents or other anti-corruption officials. It does mean, however, that the media and public officials must recognize:

- The rights of journalists to investigate and report on corruption
- The value of such reporting in the broad fight against corruption
- Potential deadly consequences for journalists reporting on corruption

It also means that the ability of journalists to continue reporting on corruption must be vigorously defended and strengthened by government and judicial agencies. Journalists must have better access to information. Legislation must provide for the collection and dispersing of information of vital interest to the citizenry. Governments must understand that they owe transparency to the citizens of their countries and this includes openness to media requests for information.

Law enforcement agencies and officials must appreciate that it is actually in their interest and in the interest of the global fight against corruption to behave transparently with the media. Of course, much information is confidential, but the public has a right to know about progress in investigations and about activities in the public interest. There must be greater awareness in official circles that the media play a fundamental frontline role in the fight against corruption and can be helpful to law enforcement agencies, officials, and other public sector groups and intergovernmental agencies and organizations.

The media share a terrible and often lethal burden with the public sector anti-corruption stakeholders, and relationships between journalists and law enforcement and public sector officials fighting corruption are often uneasy.

A degree of mistrust of the media on the part of public sector officials arises from a belief that often journalists, reporters, and television news people are more interested in sensationalism than informing the public on facts of vital interest to the community and irresponsibly reveal sensitive information. The role of free, responsible media is to keep public sector officials "on their toes" while living up to the ethics of journalism and adhering to the values that underpin the profession. This means that confidential, sensitive information is not revealed if doing so is illegal or unethical. It also means not revealing personal information that has nothing to do with relevant issue. In Italy, for example, the task for journalists is made harder because ethical reporting standards, particularly related to wiretap content, are often breached by the media. This creates a sense of righteous indignation among law enforcement and other public sector officials who feel that such actions undermine their anti-corruption efforts.

Public sector officials fighting corruption have a duty toward journalists as well. They must ensure that journalists have access to information and that investigation procedures and outcomes are transparent. Public sector anti-corruption officials who adhere to these standards in their relationships with the media should not be doing so from a sense of obligation. They should acknowledge that the media actually serve a very useful function, and regardless of unethical breaches of information, both sides are in a common fight against corruption.

Most anti-corruption officials and the journalists who investigate and report on corruption work toward the public good, and many journalists and law enforcement officials pay the ultimate price for standing firm against corruption. If law enforcement agencies and public sector bodies tasked with combating corruption are to be transparent and productive and benefit to the maximum from the media's unfettered right to seek and transmit information on corruption, then communications strategies must be in place for anti-corruption officials to use in interacting with journalists. Public officials opposed to corruption must ally with the media and tell their stories to the media, rather than shutting the media out.

Present and Future Media Roles

Battling corruption and those who benefit from it requires courage, a willingness to expose oneself to great personal risk, and the determination to work against huge odds. Those in the media who fight corruption have stories that must be told and the world deserves to hear them. Their stories will benefit the public if told correctly. This is why a holistic approach to combating corruption is so vital. The education and training of police officers, lawyers, and other critical components of the fight against corruption should include those in the law enforcement and legal professions and also those working in the communications areas and those who perform social research such as educators. Interaction and mutual trust are required if these separate organizations and individuals are to be successful. It would be useful for anti-corruption officials to pursue specific training in how the media operate. They must also be sensitized to the fundamental rights of free media and the basic ethical values that must underpin reporting.

We occasionally hear even in the European Union of pressure on journalists to reveal confidential sources. While obliging them to do so may serve a short-term goal of adding information to an investigation, it undermines the ability of journalists to expose corruption through contacts with whistleblowers and other sources. An understanding of the vital roles of confidential sources for journalists would certainly help anti-corruption officials and law enforcement officers more fully understand and value the role of free media in the fight against corruption and also promote democracy ensuring a free but responsible press to assist in handling matters of great importance to the general public.

The media must be more appreciative and aware of the roles of law enforcement and anti-corruption officials in the fight against corruption. Too often, a deep sense of cynicism pervades the media and leads many journalists to approach law enforcement and other officials with the preconceived notion that the officials and judiciary will more likely hinder their investigation rather than provide assistance. In general, media representatives need a greater understanding of the vital roles played by the judiciary, police, and international organizations fighting corruption.

Just as the media seek public sector respect for their rights and activities in fighting corruption, the media must respect the underpinnings of an independent judiciary and committed professional law enforcement officers. It is necessary for all these professionals to be able to work within a legal context without fear of political or economic reprisal. This type of atmosphere constitutes a cornerstone of democracy.

It is clear that momentum for a greater appreciation of the media's role in the fight against corruption is building. Only a few years ago, little if any effort was made to incorporate the media within the broader picture of the common goal of public agencies to serve the public good. The growing sense now is that the media have a vital role to play. Within the parameters of professional and ethical conduct, their role should be promoted and fostered, rather than obstructed and crushed. The state parties to the United Nations Convention against Corruption recently gave the UN a mandate to promote professional and responsible reporting on corruption.[19]

At the same time, it is crucial to translate words into actions. Far too many of the signatory states to the UN Convention against Corruption endorsed the rights of journalists to report professionally and responsibly on corruption but failed to translate their paper pledges into actions within their countries. In many such countries, journalists' efforts to cover corruption are still thwarted at every step, often brutally. Unfair trials and long prison sentences continue.

Journalists, like all citizens, should be governed by impartial and independent judicial systems and enjoy the right to a fair trial. In reporting corruption, they should never be arrested on fabricated charges or charged with sedition or criminal defamation. No authorities anywhere should consider substantiated, journalistically professional, and verifiable reports on corruption as criminal offenses. Unfortunately, in many countries, antiquated laws relating to criminal defamation are still used to snuff out critical reporting, especially on corruption. The wall of impunity behind which the killers, aggressors, and intimidators of journalists who report on corruption hide must be toppled. Unfortunately, for the moment the perpetrators are rarely identified or brought to justice. This must change. Ironically, in some instances corrupt law enforcement officials have the task of investigating the murders of journalists who report on corruption. It is not surprising that their murderers are seldom pursued. In fact, most murders of journalists across the globe, including those targeting reporters investigating corruption, are never solved.[20] Such unchallenged impunity encourages the killers to strike again and again, and makes the broader fight against corruption even tougher.

Conclusion

Despite the difficulties and dangers, journalists in general and those covering corruption in particular have a duty to act professionally and ethically. Unsubstantiated reports on corruption, including those that are the products of political influence on the media serve as ammunition for those who wish to dismiss all reporting on corruption. They make the task for most journalists with integrity infinitely harder. Statutory regulation of the media is not a solution. Voluntary self-regulation and adherence to professional standards, whether in newsrooms or elsewhere, should be the norms for all journalists and others who write about corruption. The public must be able to have faith in the veracity of reports on corruption by journalists. This is why the training of journalists, especially those who cover corruption, is so important and should be backed financially by key stakeholders.

In aspiring to the highest standards of professionalism, journalists covering corruption, often at enormous personal risk, should be secure in the knowledge that they have the support of fellow media professionals and also other sectors on the frontline in the fight against corruption.

References

1. IPI Death Watch Report. Americas surpass Asia as world's most dangerous region for journalists; corruption reporting takes heavy toll. http://www.free-media.at/focus-on/focus-on-corruption/singleview/5060/
2. Freemedia. Three suspects arrested in Mexico journalist kidnappings. http://www.freemedia.at/singleview/5091/
3. IPI. World Press Freedom Review 2010. Focus on the Americas: Mexico and Honduras account for nearly a quarter of journalists' deaths. http://www.free-media.at/singleview/5503/
4. IPI Death Watch Report. http://www.freemedia.at/asia-australasia/singleview/5299/
5. Voice of America. Afghan journalist attacked with acid. http://www.voanews.com/english/news/asia/Afghan-Journalist-Attacked-With-Acid-114202539.html
6. *The New York Times.* Six are held in attack on Chinese investigative journalist. http://www.nytimes.com/2010/12/22/world/asia/22china.html
7. IPI Death Watch Report. http://www.freemedia.at/asia-australasia/singleview/5482/
8. IPI Death Watch Report. http://www.freemedia.at/site-services/singleview-master/5001/
9. *The Daily Mail.* Russian journalist disabled after beating is convicted of slander over corruption probe that saw other reporters attacked. http://www.dailymail.co.uk/news/article-1328448/Russian-journalist-Mikhail-Beketov-disabled-beating-convicted-slander.html
10. Forbes.com. Forbes Russia editor murdered in Moscow. http://www.forbes.com/2004/07/09/cz_sf_0709klebnikov.html
11. IPI Death Watch Report. http://www.freemedia.at/africa/singleview/4903/
12. International Freedom of Expression Xchange (IFEX). Armed groups and politicians behind attacks on journalists says NUSOJ. http://www.ifex.org/somalia/2011/01/12/nusoj_report_2010/
13. IPI. As Tunisian court upholds journalist's sentence, IPI releases report on covering corruption in Tunisia. http://www.freemedia.at/singleview/5033/
14. Reporters without Borders. Arrest of fourth online journalist in 16 months makes Syria the Middle East's biggest jailer for cyber dissidents. http://arabia.reporters-sans-frontieres.org/article.php3?id_article=18939
15. IPI. In Rome, Italian journalists receive threatening letter along with bullets, while in South another reporter is physically assaulted. (http://www.freemedia.at/singleview/5375/)
16. Spiegel Online International. Sarkozy draws ire over media spying claims. http://www.spiegel.de/international/europe/0,1518,727986,00.html
17. *The Guardian.* Trafigura investigation sums up our core values. http://www.guardian.co.uk/sustainability/trafigura-investigation-core-values
18. IPI. Finnish journalist faces jail time in Slovenia over broadcast accusing government of corruption. http://www.freemedia.at/site-services/singleview-master/4488/

19. United Nations Office on Drugs and Crime (UNODC). http://www.unodc.org/documents/treaties/UNCAC/WorkingGroups/workinggroup4/2010-December-13-15/V1056937e.pdf
20. UNESCO. Press freedom: safety of journalists and impunity. http://docs.google.com/viewer?a=v&q=cache:5CMYO7_2X9gJ:unesdoc.unesco.org/images/0015/001567/156773e.pdf+%22press+freedom%22+%2Bimpunity&hl=en&pid=bl&srcid=ADGEEShwsKBfillCiKux4lBWCl59N_wV1YfFhntuG93a-PXTfuVOXyfUcASykp4kEwXaQeToNwzVUuW_2XFCmOKEWc0QMW89a Huu6wklczy_VNO04kJ1C-Ohw6OgxgV5qRS2RjwL4LNhQ&sig=AHIEtbRjK FeYPqn_U59Wdy15fAFNOI2sdQ

Financial Crisis or Financial Crime? Competence and Corruption

12

WOLFGANG HETZER

Contents

Businessmen and Bandits

Public discussion on prevention and prosecution of corruption recently came to be characterized by a surge of infantilism. It becomes apparent that in a number of spheres of society, business, and politics, a sort of make-believe at times even turns into hypocrisy. This becomes evident in the allegation that other competitors also use corrupt practices on international markets and that without paying bribes one never is awarded any contracts. At the same time, one claims the best imaginable quality for one's own products and that one feels committed exclusively to the merit principle.

However, more and more cases show that corruption has become a functional principle even in business conglomerates with tradition and worldwide operations. Some companies are high efficiency centers in which practices of organized crime have become routine in the conduct of business. Corruption in these businesses has assumed a systemic nature, and it is no more possible to deal with it by only sanctions of criminal law.

The damaging effect of corrupt conduct, however, exceeds by far the limits of individual legal interests. Corruption is a major reason for insufficient development and jeopardizes the foundations of any democracy. Considerations should not be limited to the relatively wide meshed grid pattern of criminal law statutes. It is also necessary to include additional perspectives regarding the complex phenomena of corruptive delinquency, especially the extremely challenging phenomenon of financial crisis.

The losses and damages we all face now are not the results of a natural disaster. They are man-made. The question is whether events result from a criminal master plan of a highly specialized "financial mafia" or are we merely confronted with professional incompetence that led whole economic systems and states to a disaster unprecedented in modern history?

Definitions and Deficits

No sufficiently unambiguous and generally recognized definition of corruption exists. Neither German law nor the United Nations Convention against Corruption contains a legal definition. Many attempts have been made from moral, ethical, criminological, political, economic, and regulatory perspectives.[*] In science, corruption is seen as the abuse of a public office, position in commerce or industry, or political mandate for the benefit of another at the instigation of the beneficiary or on the initiative of the office holder with a view to obtaining an undue advantage for either party accompanied by damage or disadvantage to the general public or to an enterprise.[†]

According to another definition, corruption covers all forms of abuse of power aimed to achieve unlawful advantages. This definition is not specific enough because it also covers embezzlement and dishonest dealings and so blurs the boundary with offences against property. In principle, corruption is a situation in which a person who is responsible for performing certain duties pursues improper or unfair advantages for actions or omissions in the performance of those duties. This definition makes clear the essential illegality and danger inherent in corruption. In the performance of duty, the person gaining the advantage is no longer guided by the rules applicable to those duties, but by advantages to which he or she is not entitled. This brings with it the danger that the person gaining the advantage will no longer perform his or her duties properly and damage the employer organization. In short, corruption is an attack on the proper performance of duties through an unlawful relationship of exchange between giver and receiver.

No uniform and fully recognized definition of corrupt conduct exists in the European legal and judicial areas.[‡] The term is used to describe several situations because the traditional designations and terms that differ from

---

[*] Greeve, G. Korruptionsdelikte in der Praxis, 2005, No 1.

[†] Vahlenkamp, W. & Knauss, J. Korruption: Ein unscharfes Phänomen als Gegenstand zielgerichteter Prävention, *BKA Forschungsreihe*, 1995, 33, 20.

[‡] Hetzer, W. General remarks on the fight against corruption in Europe, *NJW*, 2004, 3746.

one language to another cannot always be reconciled. For example, in the European Union treaties and documents, the English corruption was translated into German as *Bestechung* although it means bribery in English and fails to cover all aspects of corruption (bribery, patronage, nepotism, misappropriation of common property, illegal financing of political parties and election campaigns).

The various terms and legal systems give rise to differences both in the legislation governing the bribery of members of parliament, party financing practice, the distinction between corruption in the public and private sectors, and the levels and types of penalties available. Nevertheless, in one special area (protection of the European Communities' financial interests), the beginnings of a legal definition have been proposed. According to the Convention on the Protection of the Communities' Financial Interests, "the deliberate action of an official, who, directly or through an intermediary, requests or receives advantages of any kind whatsoever, for himself or for a third party, or accepts a promise of such an advantage, to act or refrain from acting in accordance with his duty or in the exercise of his functions in breach of his official duties in a way which damages the European Communities' financial interests"* constitutes passive corruption. Each member state must ensure that the acts referred to are criminal offences. The uniform method for combating corruption in the private sector within the EU is to be ensured by means of the Framework Decision of July 22, 2003 that also includes an attempt to define the term.

Whether such definitions are practicable is open to question. The issue is further complicated by the fact that corruption ceased some time ago to be concerned solely with the classic offences of public officials and now includes unlawful conduct in the private sector. In this context, the economic corruption term is more descriptive. While not a term of law, it is commonly used in penal policy, criminal science, and criminology. Essentially it describes dishonest conduct in the private sector that is comparable with conventional corruption by public officials. Economic corruption is said to exist if a private economic operator secretly or covertly receives or requests advantages for himself or another in return for economic conduct by another private economic operator; or grants or offers such advantages to the other party in contravention of generally recognized standards and to the adverse effect of individuals or the general public.† If this description of corruption is correct, economic corruption is thus a type of unwelcome competition in non-performance.

Finally, another common factor of economic corruption and corruption by public officials is that both involve unlawful exchanges of advantages. The

---

* ABI EG. (1998). C326/1, 27 [official journal of European Union].
† Greeve, G., loc. cit. 1.

definition presents both theoretical consequences and practical ones. The quantitative and statistical reality of corruption-related crime is influenced by each state's understanding of the term. The true extent of criminally corrupt conduct cannot be defined as accurately as desirable in Germany or in the other twenty-six EU member states.

To judge by a standard legal commentary on the German Criminal Code, corruption cases do not figure largely in criminal prosecution in Germany. The number of cases, we are told, is small and only a small proportion of those that come to light result in charges. The number of unrecorded cases is high because every corrupt relationship involves offenders on both sides. Nevertheless, the damage caused by corruption is unquestionably very extensive.[*]

It is even more difficult to give a reasonably realistic, comprehensive, and usable assessment of the situation across Europe. Such an assessment should logically be based on meaningful processes to monitor implementation of the relevant provisions. This is, however, a pious hope. The contribution of international organizations to the implementation in sovereign states of the rules developed by the organizations is naturally limited.[†] Nevertheless, incentives for regulatory compliance can be provided through international evaluation of the implementation of international provisions.

Three models have been established: (1) monitoring by the executive body of the relevant international organization; (2) evaluation by a special group of experts; and (3) monitoring by some or all member states of the relevant regime (peer review). However, the implementation of international recommendations on evaluation does not necessarily lead to a reduction in corruption. Firm conclusions cannot readily be drawn in this regard because, in practice, corruption is not even remotely measurable despite the existence of various sets of case statistics and corruption awareness indices.

Whether one of the reasons for this immeasurability is that bribery is (allegedly) a victimless crime in which none of those involved has an interest in detection is open to question.[‡] What we can say, however, is that the assertion that bribery is victimless is pure and proven nonsense because we are all or shall be direct or indirect victims of corruption. In contrast to the Council of Europe and the OECD (Organization for Economic Cooperation and Development), the EU decided not to create specific committees to monitor its anti-corruption rules. No intensive monitoring of the rules, particularly related to private sector corruption goes beyond the mandatory provisions of the Council of Europe and the OECD. Even the EU Convention on the Fight against Corruption makes no provision for implementation review.

---

[*] Fischer, T. (2007). Strafgesetzbuch und Nebengesetze, 5th ed., before Article 298, No. 4.
[†] See Wolf, S. Der Beitrag internationaler und supranationaler Organisationen zur Korruptionsbekämpfung in den Mitgliedstaaten, *Speyerer Forschungsberichte* 2007, 253, 31.
[‡] Wolf, S. loc. cit. pp. 31, 32.

The first protocol to the Convention on the Protection of the Communities' Financial Interests does at least require member states to transmit to the commission the texts of their laws concerning transposition. Against this background, the commission adopted its first report on the implementation by member states of the Convention on the Protection of the Communities' Financial Interests and its protocols on October 24, 2004,[*] and complaints arose about various shortcomings in the implementation of the provisions on bribery in the protocol. These included the fact that member states were hesitant in ratifying the convention and its protocols and had for years showed no interest in considering the commission's proposal for a directive on the protection of financial interests under criminal law.

The directive would have transferred the fundamental provisions of the convention and the protocols to the former first pillar of the structure of the EU and allowed the commission to bring actions against defaulting member states before the European Court of Justice for failure to transpose—an argument that in light of the Lisbon Treaty may need to be discussed. In their second report, the commission members concluded that the harmonization objective of the instruments on the protection of the communities' financial interests has still not been fully achieved formally or materially for all twenty-seven member states.

De facto, the current system of protection operates at several speeds. It results in a mixture of different legal situations in terms of the binding effects of the instruments on the protection of the communities' financial interests in individual member states' internal legal orders. Formally, the system does not produce the desired effective and dissuasive penal protection.[†] Many of the responsible parties in certain "old" member states should remember that when assessing the situations in "new" member states such as Romania and Bulgaria.[‡]

Corruption is one of the oldest and most effective means of social, economic, and state self-organization.[§] Corruption is now one of the most frequently used terms in political debates. For a time it seemed as if European societies recognized an old phenomenon that had for a long time been played down by those in power. With the exception of a few experts, those in powerful positions in government and the private sector in Germany denied the existence of the problem, and some continue to deny the influence of corruption down to the present day. This is true not only in Germany but also in other countries,[¶] but the willingness to recognize the importance of

---

[*] COM. (2004) 709, final of 25.10.
[†] Second report on Implementation, p. 5.
[‡] Bulanova-Hristova, G. (2010). Von Sofia nach Brüssel Korrupte Demokratisierung im Kontext der europäischen Integration.
[§] Claussen, H. R. & Ostendorf, F. H. (2002). Korruption im öffentlichen Dienst, 2nd ed., p. 3: "Korruption gibt es seit Menschengedenken" [corruption has existed since time immemorial].
[¶] Scholz, R. (1995). Korruption in Deutschland, 1995, p. 9

corruption seems to be changing. Corruption is now depicted as a growth sector.* It is no longer an unknown continent to be discovered as a surprise. You can start your journey anywhere and at any time. A panorama of landscapes opens after only a few steps, the path leading time and time again to the courtroom. The courtroom has a topography of its own, but its platforms do not enable all the highs and lows to be measured with sufficient clarity. The idea that there should be a Europe-wide sense of what is and is not fair, of what eases or threatens our co-existence, lies at the interface between naïveté and despair, and is ultimately a paradox.

This is also reflected in "Zwanzig Vorschläge für eine saubere Republik" (Twenty Suggestions for a Clean Republic)† and "Zehn Gebote zur Korruptionsbekämpfung" (Ten Requirements for Combating Corruption), but no patented remedies to end corruption are available. The prioritization of instruments of criminal law does not offer salvation.‡ Corrupt associations in society, business, and politics may reflect a dramatic change in attitude that the crude framework of criminal laws is entirely incapable of accommodating. The same is true of objective structures. Social institutions, political parties, democratic and undemocratic governments, the judiciary, the administration, the police, the military, and business enterprises have formed associations in many countries around the world. Their potential capacity easily outstrips that of conventional criminal associations.

The proposition that a distinction can be drawn between spoils and profit is now sustainable only in fairy tales. The profit-making intentions of economic agents, the ambitions of politicians, the financing requirements of parties, and the greed of public officials have become increasingly interconnected and can no longer be ignored. Their activities create a highly powered form of corruption with which the comparatively simple terminology of criminal law cannot contend.§

When the inner character of a community is shaped by corruptibility, observance of the law degenerates into an object of ridicule. Judicial attempts to overcome this view constitute empty gestures. The uncoupling of work from success and performance from income, which is the corollary

---

* Bannenberg, B. & Schaupensteiner, W. J. (2004). *Korruption in Deutschland: Porträt einer Wachstumsbranche.*

† Leyendecker, H. *Die Korruptionsfalle: Wie unser Land im Filz versinkt*, 2003, p. 273. See also Schaupensteiner, W. J. (2003). Zehn Gebote zur Korruptionsbekämpfung. In *Bundeskriminalamt, Wirtschaftskriminalität und Korruption, Polizei und Forschung*, 22.

‡ Hetzer, W. Strafrecht ist kein Allheilmittel. In: Friedrich-Ebert-Shiftung. (Ed.), *Korruption in Deutschland: Ursachen, Erscheinungsform, Bekämpfungsstrategien*, 1995, 123.

§ See, however, Rzeszut, J. Gerichtliche Strafrechtspflege als Antikorruptionssignal. In Kreutner, M. (Ed.), *The Corruption Monster: Ethics, Politics, and Corruption*, 2006, 345.

of corruption, will destabilize every social system sooner or later. The police and the judiciary cannot sever the associations through illusions.* Nor is it their job to do so. However, fatalistic conjecturing about fundamental human characteristics ("everyone has a price")† must not lead to an apocalyptic arcing of the horizon over "Continent Corruption."

We must make further efforts to get a clear view of the size of this continent, which European integration has made even more extensive. The "long haul" will therefore get even longer. Early crime involved murder and manslaughter. Social differentiation is not just history; it is ongoing. Economic systems originated with robbery, theft, and blackmail—not contracts concluded in good faith. Some things have changed. Civil law moderates the exchanges of goods and services and for the most part, prevents violence. From coercion comes fair competition. From genocide, slavery, and criminal occupation comes colonialism.

From colonialism comes free world trade. From the battlefield comes the Common Market. Against this background, corruption may even be a cultural quantum leap that may lead to a zenith of social, economic, and political development. Modern people no longer have to be annihilated to make way for particular interests. The use of violence has been replaced by temptation.

Payment instructions make declarations of war unnecessary. Money transforms conflict into cooperation. Moral principles are interpreted with flexibility proportionate to the value of the assets changing hands. Questions of power are handled by agreement. The persuasiveness of arguments is of no significance. The day-to-day business of politics offers a broad spectrum of possibilities for the emancipation of entrepreneurial spirit, expertise, and democratic control. The toolbox is full to overflowing and contains well-paid jobs, favors, legislative initiatives, subsidies, and promises of pensions.

In a world in which material prosperity has become the meaning of life and work and income no longer have a discernible connection, corruption is omnipresent. It has a crucial pivotal function. Observance of the law is no longer a modus vivendi for communities as mutually supportive associations. Criminal law provisions to combat corruption may result in a dual paradox. In principle, their ability to steer behavior cannot be guaranteed to the extent necessary because of the indefeasible human constants of greed, openness to temptation, and ambition for power.‡ Criminal law is apparently supposed to appeal to our morality, but it is powerless to change the basic principles of institutions and individuals. Criminal justice does not replace upbringing

---

* Hetzer, W. *Korruption: Legalisierung oder Bekämpfung?* Kriminalistik, 2004, 86.
† Schilling, A. & Dolata, U. (Eds.). (2004). *Korruption im Wirtschaftssystem Deutschland,* 2nd ed.
‡ Androulakis, J. *Die Globalisierung der Korruptionsbekämpfung,* 2007, 479.

and cannot condition the morality of citizens, business leaders, or politicians. Ideally, it protects legal interests through prevention and punishment.

In the case of corruption, however, something else much more important may be at work. The influencing of human behavior that corruption seeks to achieve is always connected with humiliation. As long as those involved will not or cannot understand that conducting a corrupt relationship puts their self-respect at risk, all debate in fighting corruption remains futile. No statement makes an impression if a lack of respect for individual dignity leads to the devaluing of all relationships, the hallmarks of which should be work and loyalty.

The corruptive acceptance of money is an attack on self-respect. Anyone who cannot see this is unlikely to be impressed even by threats of punishment. In that case, only one plea would be plausible: legalize corruption! Whether this would have a detrimental effect on law and order and social justice is open to speculation. If the hypothesis is accepted that corruption has a peace-making impact, such effects of legalization can perhaps be ruled out. In any case, the anarchy of power already appears to have been largely replaced by the order of money. However, that may be the very source of a particular anarchic force that may one day push entire societies back to the beginning of history as described above.

This may be the case when most of those subject to laws understand that their dignity is treated with contempt by a corrupt and subverted social and economic order, by rulers who have been bought, and by a strategically ineffective criminal justice system. In those circumstances, the electorate (the people) will probably resort to means not based exclusively on the rule of law.

This view goes beyond the frontiers of an enlarged European Union.* Thus, in summary, it is safe to say that in all EU member states, the public debate about the extent and risks of corrupt behavior suffers from a lack of comprehensive, reliable, quantitative, and statistical data and the often distorted reporting of sensational individual cases.

An accurate and generically valid empirical inventory of corruption offences remains impossible because of the varied definitions related to these types of crimes. Terminological uncertainties also lead to misconceptions of corruption and make it difficult to achieve a uniform European strategy to prevent and prosecute relevant offences.

In the light of the enlargement of the European Union, the credibility of the European integration project is particularly dependent on the effective control of corruption in all member states. If corruption is to be properly curbed in all of them, the range of penalties available must, irrespective of the different legal systems in operation, be equally effective and continue to

---

* Hetzer, W. EWS, 2003, 489.

be developed across the community (e.g., uniform corporate penalties and confiscation of proceeds of crime).

Corruption must be defined and punished within the ambit of criminal law. Because corruptibility is the latent willingness to accept self-enrichment to the detriment of the community, it constitutes an attitude, a mentality that is particularly prevalent in times of social decline. It should be treated as a cultural and social challenge to the welfare of the EU and countries throughout the world.

Corruption always signals failures of leadership, as is evident in all EU member states where economic interests, personal ambitions, and political objectives are linked. A particular form of corruption that has recently developed is corruptibility as a result of incompetence. Overloaded state bureaucracies rely on the assistance of private individuals who supposedly have special superior knowledge that enables them, to pursue their own economic interests even within a legislative procedural framework. The discussion about the economic prerequisites for and consequences of corrupt behavior in business appears to have taken on a puerile or childlike quality recently. In particular, the comments that other competitors make, for example, on foreign markets ("everyone is doing it" and "contracts cannot be won without the payment of bribes") reflect a childish mentality or a debased sense of right and wrong.

Every society gains the corruption it deserves, just as every democracy finds the appropriate politicians. However, these are by no means exonerations because every individual has freedom of choice in his personal, professional, and political relationships. Unfortunately, individuals often fail to exercise their freedoms or use them with the help of money to obtain advantages to which they are not legally entitled. Corruption is therefore about personal character.

In the present perspective of European policy makers, it has become clear that we need simplified rules on distribution of funds, particularly from public procurements and grants. We must require that beneficiaries, especially companies, raise their standards for preventing fraud. However, we should make their lives easier when applying for public funds. For example, we cannot require that they submit hundreds of pages of documents repeatedly. We should establish databases (white lists) of companies that already demonstrated their eligibilities, capabilities, and results and spare them the need to keep proving themselves.

If product and service providers decide not to apply for public funds due to their past experiences with bureaucratic burdens, their decisions can only foster corruption because those who use corrupt channels are not discouraged by high transaction costs. It is necessary to increase the transparency of these processes since we have not yet achieved it. For example, it is a common practice in the procurement area that envelopes with bids are opened in public, but the prices are not disclosed. This allows various manipulations after the envelopes containing bids are opened. This procedure should be changed and the emphasis should not be on maximum spending, but on the most appropriate bidder.

We should reconsider certain subsidy programs that directly support individual competitors, distort competition, and provide inappropriate discretion in the consideration of applications. We have to prevent conflicts of interest of those who distribute the funds and are the beneficiaries at the same time, e.g., representatives of municipalities who handle structural funds. We should continue devising specific strategies for particular sectors and further motivate potential informants to come forward with information. We need more secure rules for whistleblowers, protection of witnesses, leniency programs similar to those used in competitive policies, and must actively distribute information to the public about attempts to fight corruption.

We need dissuasive and more diversified sanctions such as financial penalties or disciplinary measures. We should not refer every minor case to the judiciary, especially when procedures are lengthy and the results are uncertain. We must improve our cooperation and exchanges of information about fraud among competent authorities in the member states. In addition, we should also continue removing barriers to information exchanges with non-EU partners such as international organizations and other donors.

Market and Mafia

It should not be too surprising to learn that sophisticated forms of fraud exist in the banking sector (prime bank instrument fraud) and are attributable to organized criminality.* The mafia is not an element of Italian folklore. However, organized criminality is a controversial issue, and its existence is subject to debate even in social science and political discussions. We are still far away from a common understanding of the nature or extent of organized crime.

In the Berlin declaration made for the fiftieth anniversary of the signing of the Treaties of Rome in 2007, the European Union (EU) promised to act to counter terrorism, organized crime, and illegal immigration. However, this promise can be fulfilled only if a wide range of demanding conditions is met. One is a clear and valid concept of organized crime that is accepted throughout Europe. It is also necessary to move away from the conception that this form of crime concerns drugs, prostitution, human trafficking, illegal immigration, violence, and mafia culture. Such terms create a specific

* Schorsch, E. *Kriminalistik*, 2007, 236.

form of stigmatization. In the public eye, organized crime is turning into a mythological underworld that conducts its business according to arcane rites and traditions, far removed from civil society and detached from the centers of civil, business, and political life. In some ways, this understanding is comfortable. The mafia consists of other people, foreigners, outsiders who represent outside threats to our well-ordered world and oppress unsuspecting citizens with brute force or corrupt practices.

A glance at any daily newspaper will reveal other views. The news on criminal events at all levels of business, government, and politics should fundamentally change our views of the phenomenon of organized crime. Changes must be made to the criminological *and* criminalistic interpretations of organized criminality. The extremely attractive opportunities for crime presented by funds available in the EU and other public budgets and ongoing changes of the economy and regulatory policies have led to increasingly sophisticated methods of criminal activity. The particularly dangerous proponents of organized criminality adopt a far-sighted, business-like approach. They use commercial methods to identify the highest profit margins and lowest risks.

As a result, organized crime has taken several qualitative steps forward in recent years. It is possible for criminal organizations to increase their systematic exploitation of the welfare system of the EU because of structural changes, control deficits typical of a liberal internal market, the diversity and complexity of the legislative activities, and the corruptibility of elements of the economic, political, and administrative elites in all states. Efforts to define terms are simply expressions of a ridiculous naïveté.

It is becoming clear that we now live in a society in which the meaning of life has been reduced to the pursuit of the maximum profits. Organized crime in such a society has every chance of flourishing. Ultimately, we must assess whether the "gangster principle" has replaced the principles of fair competition in business, the government's commitment to the law, and politicians' mission to protect the common good. Of course, we could believe that the difficulties are founded in the very nature of the matter.[*]

Organized crime is defined as a complex, ramified, often diffuse field of structures, partnerships, and acts that affects many areas. However, reliable information based on empirical evidence of the existence of such a structure is lacking. Thus, myths, guesswork, and speculation are rampant. The law of silence (omerta) is a wide-ranging impediment to reliable empirical findings.

---

[*] Zweiter Periodischer Sicherheitsbericht 15. November 2006 [Second Periodic Security Report], 441. (http://www.bmi.bund.de/nn_122688/Internet/Content/Broschueren/2006/2_ Periodischer_Sicherheitsbericht_de.html). The Organised Criminality and White Collar Criminality chapters in the First Periodic Security Report (2001) provoked critical responses. Hetzer, W., *Kriminalistik*, 2001, 762, 767.

Furthermore, a characteristic of those involved in organized criminality is to maintain "feet in both camps" (one in the illegal camp and one in the legal camp), making it difficult to pursue prosecution effectively.

In this context, it must be understood that organized criminality in its developed form involves more than planning and committing criminal offences. Its personal relationships, connections, and networks exist and operate outside concrete areas of criminality. Organized criminality is characterized by social networks within a residential area, town, region or a country. The networks make it easy to disguise illegal activities.* Based on the few scientific studies available, it is possible to assume, in Italy and other European countries at least, that organized criminality is likely to be protected by way of organizations rooted in tradition.

The Cosa Nostra and the Ndrangheta must only be seen as exceptional cases in a major field of illegal markets and operators. They are the products of specific historical, social, and cultural conditions that cannot be reproduced in any random location. Furthermore, cross-border contacts between those involved in organized criminality do not yet make it reasonable to assume that modern complex criminality, with its rich financial pickings, is largely controlled by powerful, highly organized syndicates.†

It is reasonable to believe that organized criminality is more a matter of professionally organized groups of offenders and networks than of hierarchical structures. These groups are firmly established in all regions and exert intensive influences upon legal markets and social and political structures. This is a reassuring finding in terms of developing criminal policy to combat organized crime.‡

Although it is recognised that a differentiated approach must be adopted toward assessment of the situation in Europe, the conclusion reached was that the mafia and other endemic structures did not have the state, business, or society in thrall to such an extent as to justify any suggestion of a direct risk to the people or to the common democratic good. Against this background, the lack of uniform opinion on whether an official definition of organized criminality is required is hardly surprising.

Germany, for example, has no substantive criminal offence of "organized criminality" to set alongside the organizational crime of "criminal association" (§129 StGB). This situation is therefore different from those in Italy and the U.S. and also from efforts made on a European level to standardize definitions needed to combat organized criminality.§ Germany has a directive on countering organized criminality, but it does not include a sufficiently precise

---

* 2. PSB, pp. 442, 443.
† 2. PSB, p. 444.
‡ 2. PSB, p. 445.
§ 2. PSB, p. 446.

definition of organized criminality.* It describes a phenomenological field of criminal activities.† The principles set down in the directive are intended to help German prosecutors interpret organized criminality as a subcategory of normal criminal conduct in order to condemn specific activities. The principles are not confined to a single offence. They do not offer anything more than a broad-brush orientation framework for investigations.‡

The police criminal statistics (PKS) cannot be used to obtain detailed or conclusive evidence on the number of offences clearly linked to organized criminality, nor do the criminal prosecution statistics fit the bill. These statistics provide data relating only to criminal offences that have been detected or to people who have been subjected to investigations and court actions. However, since January 1998, the statistics kept by public prosecutors have included information on whether investigation proceedings relate to a matter classified as organized criminality.

In contrast to the separate situation reports produced by the German Federal Office of Criminal Investigation (Bundeskriminalamt or BKA), the statistics mentioned apply only to individuals and individual offences. The situation reports and profiles concentrate their coverage on major investigations. It is acknowledged that the categories of statistical evidence are inappropriate for determining threats posed by organized criminality. The investigations do no more than scratch the surface.

Investigation proceedings often start from the premise that a criminal offence has been committed, because this premise seems necessary to obtain the right to initiate proceedings or enforcement measures. Often, by the time an investigation has been completed, it seems appropriate to abandon the case for practical reasons.§

Professional countermeasures by the offenders or the structures that support them serve to "emasculate" investigations that originally seemed persuasive. Tip-offs from informants or undercover investigators usually cannot be combined to constitute sufficient evidence that can be presented at a hearing or trial. These and other circumstances also explain the large gaps among the numbers of criminal offences identified, the numbers of suspects investigated, and the numbers convicted and sentenced. Since 1991, the BKA has produced situation reports on organized criminality. Initially, the statistical data available served as the main source of crime information.

Organized criminality proceedings pending during a period to which a report relates continue to be recorded on the basis of questionnaires based

---

* This is more or less a "mantra of criminal policy." Hetzer, W., *Kriminalistik*, 2007, 251.
† 2. PSB, pp. 447, 448.
‡ 2. PSB, p. 448.
§ 2. PSB, p. 450.

on "official" definitions. The relevant data is subjected to a plausibility check before it is submitted electronically to BKA's central office. Efforts are underway to develop situation reports with more emphasis on the qualitative aspects of criminal situations. Since 1998, a structural analysis format has been used to collect the information needed and the results of the analysis are fed into a situation report.[*]

The structural analysis is used for a qualitative assessment of the group structures existing in Germany. It is also expected to aid investigators in identifying special features of organized criminality and related issues. The ultimate objective is to gain an idea of the scale of the entire phenomenon and facilitate appropriate use of resources. Assessment is intended to evaluate "organized criminality potential" as reflected in the degree of organization and professionalism among groups of offenders.[†]

In summary, organized criminality is not a clearly defined term that can be used to pin down an actual situation. The ability to approach the subject from various angles means that correspondingly different conclusions are reached. Organized criminality is noteworthy for its scope, from traditional gang activity through criminal associations to so-called syndicates. Sophisticated organized criminality is not confined to criminal offences. It is characterized by the establishment and maintenance of stable personal relationships and interpersonal networks. Current empirical research into organized criminality is still not sufficient to provide a completely meaningful and convincing illustration of this form of criminal activity.

Notwithstanding the marked professionalism and internationalization of various groups of offenders, the mafia has not succeeded in establishing a "parallel society" in Germany nor in posing a threat to the foundations of the state, business, and society. International organized criminality does in fact represent a significant potential threat because it attempts to use violence, threats, and corruption to create areas where the rule of law does not apply. The risk of globalized organized criminality is also tied to the globalization of business and the liberalization of markets.

Technological changes such as the Internet[‡] also played parts in internationalizing organized criminality. National counterstrategies have been inadequate for some time. It is now necessary to impound the proceeds from offences committed through organized criminality to prevent the criminal groups from establishing financial bases. The offence-specific approach to criminal prosecution adopted by police and legal authorities does not get to the root of organized criminality. In view of the risks organized criminality

[*] 2. PSB, p. 453.
[†] 2. PSB, p. 454.
[‡] Lippert, F. & Sürmann, H. *Kriminalistik*, 2007, 231.

poses to society, it is necessary for authorities to adopt a business approach including analyses of structures and logistics of criminal groups.

New strategic approaches to assessment must be developed to facilitate risk assessment. The practical approach to assessment must also be intensified and requires immediate and close cooperation of the police and prosecutors. Structural investigation measures are to be used, with due consideration to a corporate approach for uncovering criminal organizations and ensuring that their backers are punished.

Independent scientific research must determine the successes and limitations of increasing European measures of cooperation and coordination. Further harmonization of the legal and operating conditions in EU member states must be achieved to combat cross-border organized criminality. Bilateral agreements can help eliminate the barriers to cross-border prosecution.

Ongoing initiatives at EU and UNO level will serve to establish specifications for forms of conduct subject to punishment, detail the methods of investigation required in national laws, and create increased coordination among investigative authorities. Organized criminality is not the only area where white collar criminal offences overlap. Whether white collar crime is always by definition a form of organized criminality (perhaps even the most sophisticated and dangerous form) remains debatable.

The German government reached a noteworthy conclusion in April 1975. In its draft of a "First Act to Combat White Collar Crime," it emphasized that a legal system that has no compunction in imposing sanctions on the misconduct of an average citizen but all too often had to shoulder arms in the face of manipulation of commercial dealings by intelligence offenders is inconsistent with the principle of all citizens being equal before the law.*

Many subsequent legislative efforts failed to achieve the desired degrees of success. Just as there is no universally accepted definition of organized criminality, there is no accepted and precise definition of white collar criminality.† In essence, considerable concern still surrounds criminality involving unjustified enrichment accrued via the (actual or feigned) production, manufacture, and distribution of goods or exchanges of services required for business purposes. This process considers active economic activity, offences (fraud, false financial statements), and withdrawals from economic activity (bankruptcy offences).

Some of the literature attempts to restrict this broad definition. The practice adopted by Germany's police and courts focuses upon the provisions

---

* Bundestag printed paper 7/3441, 14.
† Lippert, F. & Knorre, U. *Kriminalistik*, 2007, 222; Heissner, S. (2001). Die Bekämpfung von Wirtschaftskriminalität -Eine ökonomische Analyse unternehmerischer Handlungsoptionen [Combating white collar criminality: an economic analysis of options for employers].

of §74c of the German Judicature Act (Gerichtsverfassungsgesetz or GVG). Furthermore, it stands to reason that the forms of white collar criminality are governed by the economic system, economic constitution, social structure, technical progress, and economic trends. Thus, innovations in business and technology will generate new forms of offences.

The list of white collar crime forms is neither complete nor conclusive. The offences include bookkeeping and accounting frauds; tax evasion; insolvency offences; usury and bribery; counterfeit food, beverages, and tobacco; economic espionage; insider dealing; illegal temporary hire of employees; product piracy; and fraudulent commodity futures options. Cases of white collar criminality recorded in the criminal and criminological statistics represent only the "tip of the iceberg." The size of the iceberg remains unknown because much of the research required has yet to be completed. The traditional criminological instruments are largely inadequate for these types of criminal offences. We can only surmise that the undetected amount of white collar crime is large for many reasons:

Lack of or late disclosures of offences
Involvement of legal persons as victims, informers, and accomplices
Lack of social controls
Large proportion (50%) of collective victims (state, social institutions)
Diminution of sense of victimhood among collective victims
Reduced awareness of loss
Reduced willingness to report offences
Large proportion of victim companies
Risk of damage if an offence is reported (e.g., holder of untaxed earnings as victim of a capital investment fraud)
Preference for using civil law methods
Interest in exercising discretion, with a view to possible damage to reputation

Well-founded knowledge about the extent, structure, and trends of white collar criminality is lacking. The current formats of official statistics do not permit recording of white collar offences or reporting is incomplete.* The conclusion is clear, "The information on white collar criminality available at present in the criminal and criminological statistics and in some special statistics cannot be used to provide full and sufficiently reliable details, either in terms of quantity or quality, on the white collar criminality officially revealed."† Consequently, this information is of limited use except as an instrument of planning and information source for legislators.

* 2. PSB, p. 221.
† 2. PSB, p. 222.

White collar criminality is a qualitative problem rather than a quantitative problem[*] and fraud one of the main forms. Appropriate criteria for making a clear distinction between fraud as a white collar crime or general crime are still conspicuous by their absence. The impression is that finance offences account for most frauds and are defined as any forms of offences committed in conjunction with brokering, procuring and extending loans, particularly related to goods, services, and credit.[†]

Since the police criminal statistics include special records for white collar crime, significant variations appear, for example, because the incidence figures are based on complex investigations covering a number of individual cases. However, no clear evidence indicates an upward trend. In general, the figures on white collar criminality recorded by the police do not lead to a conclusion that changes are occurring in undetected areas. The extent of and trends in white collar criminality cannot be determined solely by what happens. Records are based on events reported and what the police find through investigations.

White collar criminality is always characterized by a high level of damage to society, particularly through the material losses it causes. However, there is no reliable information available on this subject. Global estimates have not been supported with sufficient information to verify damages or increases in claimed losses. More variation is present in losses reported for individual areas of the economy. PKS records service as starting points on losses arising from crimes, but they are limited to the incidents reported in specific areas. The statistics record direct losses in value but do not cover consequent damages or indirect losses.

The complexity of investigation proceedings involving large numbers of individual cases can produce exceptionally large variations; in fact, this also occurs when losses are recorded. Loss reports are useful only as initial points of reference. The tendency is to focus on more serious categories of white collar crime losses where relatively few cases generate major losses. However, no clear trend is apparent in losses arising from white collar criminality, probably as a consequence of the recording rules under which the crime and the losses are attributed to the year during which the police investigation was completed.

It appears that intangible losses arising from white collar criminality are more serious than the material losses. Intangible losses include consequent effects of distortions of competition; infection of and knock-on effects upon competitors; associated criminality through assistance by third parties; chain-reaction risks such as economic collapse imposed on law-abiding business partners; health hazards; and reduced confidence among competitors and consumers in certain businesses and even in the prevailing social and

[*] 2. PSB, p. 224.
[†] 2. PSB, p. 227

economic systems. It is difficult, if not impossible, to put a figure on damages that arise from a loss of confidence.[*]

In summary, forms of white collar crimes differ, and the profiles of white collar offenders are very different from profiles of average criminal types. Prevention of white collar criminality is vital to secure the efficiency of the market economy. The public displays a great deal of interest in the effective prosecution of white collar crime. Present police and legal resources are insufficient and specialized expertise is needed, for example, auditing skills to track diversion of profits. Rigorous cooperation of authorities and industry must be developed. Transparency of business practices will improve prevention as will more effective corporate governance in the areas of reporting to regulators, independence of regulators, early warning systems internal controls, and assessments by auditors. Special requirements for international links and globalization of markets would help reduce financial crime.

Hopefully it is now clear that organized criminality is a unique term surrounded by myths, conjecture, and speculation. It has even been called a "form of business."[†] Our context is not limited to the mafia as a historical and modern form of organized crime in Italy.[‡] Organized criminality is a globalized system of uncontrolled and uncontrollable power. The term must be interpreted as a metaphor for various forms of the abuse of power. Organized criminality was found in societies with weak structures, but it now pervades all economic orders and political systems. No level of hierarchy in trade, government, or politics is free of its influence. The ability to distinguish profit from ill-gotten gains now has about as much credibility as a fairy tale.

Tax evasion, corrupt practices, and systemic illegality in commercial enterprises operating worldwide created functional and structural overlaps with organized criminality. While we cannot say that certain companies and governments cover the same ground, ample evidence suggests dangerous clashes involving political party funding, politicians' power interests, corporate profit orientations, and the vulnerability of leading members of trade unions.

---

[*] 2. PSB, p. 232.

[†] Hetzer, W., wistra, 1999, 126.

[‡] A few arbitrarily selected articles from the literature are listed here: Arlacchi, P., Mafiose Ethik und der Geist des Kapitalismus [Mafia ethics and the spirit of capitalism], 1989; Mafia von Innen: Das Leben des Don Antonio Calderone, [Mafia: the inside story: the life of Don Antonio Calderone] 1993; Dickie, J., Cosa Nostra: Die Geschichte der Mafia [Cosa Nostra: the history of the mafia], 7th ed., 2006; Klüver, H., Der Pate Letzter Akt: Eine Reise ins Land der Cosa Nostra [The godfather's final act: a journey into the land of the Cosa Nostra], 2007; Lupo, S., Die Geschichte der Mafia [The history of the mafia], 2002; Saviano, R., Reise in das Reich der Camorra [Journey into the kingdom of the Camorra] 2007.

Corruption has become an important functional principle of the globalized economy.* The use of force is becoming unnecessary. The quiet efficiency of modern white collar criminality that makes it a "capital" risk based on its national importance and international links and organization also means the activities are overlooked. Some people are now asking whether white collar criminality has already become part of the "anarchic shareholder value economy" that favors speculators, restricts long-term capital investment, and renders sustained economic success impossible.[†]

The instruments of criminal law alone are not sufficient to combat conventional organized criminality or white collar crime with the required degree of effectiveness. The requirements include stable guidelines and institutions covering compliance and corporate governance that lend themselves to practical implementation. Ultimately, this will help company charters become more definitive and compliance with statutes and internal standards can be more straightforward.[‡]

The receptivity of certain individuals to legal and moral instruction remains limited. This applies in particular to successful business leaders, power-oriented politicians, and profit-oriented criminals. Criminal law does not provide sufficient mechanisms for their ethical and moral re-education. Thus, an empirically proven logical approach attractive for these individuals should be adopted.

Studies in the U.S. show that honest people do not have to appear as "losers." Institutional Shareholders Services published a study in which the ethical principles and audit results for more than 5,000 companies were investigated. The results indicated that the ten most responsible companies were over 11% more profitable than the ten least responsible. Their share prices were less volatile and dividends higher.[§]

If it is possible to generalize these findings and to allow them to shape actions, the apparently insoluble discrepancy between self interest and the common good may perhaps be reduced to manageable dimensions. It would be possible to dispense with the introduction of a new ethic; reminders of "the good old days" may well be sufficient, even if the ostensibly enlightened and well informed *Zeitgeist* would reject it with horror, simply because of its phrasing. The findings to date produced a number of conclusions.

* Hetzer, W. *Kriminalistik*, 2007, 251, 255. See also, von Armin, H. (Ed.), Korruption und Korruptionsbekämpfung [Corruption and countercorruption], *Publications of the University of Speyer*, 185, 2007; Dolata, U., *Kriminalistik* 2007, 217, 246. On the international aspects of combating corrruption: Wolf, M., NJW 2006, 2735.

† Leyendecker, H. Die grosse Gier-Korruption, Kartelle, Lustreisen: Warum unsere Wirtschaft eine neue Moral braucht [The great lust: corruption, cartels, pleasure trips: Why our economy needs a new system of ethics] 2007, 12.

‡ Leyendecker, H. loc. cit. p. 13.

§ Quoted from Leyendecker, H. loc. cit. 19.

It is not possible to use those methods applied in the official reports to make a sufficiently realistic quantitative or qualitative assessment of the threats posed to society, business, and the state by organized criminality. The established official organized criminality term is insufficiently precise because it functions as a means of discrimination and a legal phrase. Social inertia and economic profit seeking may condense into structures that resemble organized crime. Political party funding requirements and the corrupt submissiveness of state bureaucracies provide organized criminality with opportunities to exercise influence with maximum leverage. Organized crime is also a consequence of the egomaniacal and asocial energies developed by office holders in business, government, and politics to obtain and to defend their positions of power.

Efficient prevention and prosecution of organized criminality by authorities often fail simply because they simply represent a radical expression of a balance of administrative, economic, military and political power. Organized criminality reflects the ethical and moral contradictions of social systems and the living lie of middle-class respectability. White collar criminality is often a sophisticated and very damaging form of organized criminality, the perception of which also suffers because of the ambiguity of definition and the lack of empirical data. Crime in business life reflects the special features of economic systems, technological development, and a level of international integration that allows groups to operate across borders, some of which are no more than refuges for systemic illegality.

Effective prevention and prompt prosecution of white collar criminality is an obligation of social justice even more so than dealing with conventional organized crime. The obligation is frequently not fulfilled because the individual and collective powers of business, government, and politics worldwide attach more importance to self-interest and presumption.

Commerce and Criminality

As already indicated, the so-called financial crisis is perceived as a result of some type of natural disaster: no one could prevent it and no one was responsible or guilty. Just as it is impossible to punish nature, a discussion here about the possibilities of applying penal law to bring bankers, businessmen, and politicians to justice for their illegal behavior is also futile. This is deplorable but not surprising.

Behind the concept of crisis lie individual and collective self-deception, economic interests, and political calculations. Economically minded observers for the most part continue to espouse the view that the financial market crisis is systemic. If you follow that interpretation, no one is at fault except perhaps the politicians who failed to adjust the system's settings correctly. In analysis of trends in criminal law development in times of the financial crisis, the aspect of governing through crime must be considered. States may not be as concerned with making criminal law more effective because they consider political profit more important. A number of damaging consequences arise from such situations in which the end product endangers the rule of law and the principles of democracy.

Crisis has become a keyword in economic and financial policy. Its inflationary use also indicates an intellectual crisis. The word can absolve us of responsibility and produce an almost humble acquiescence to processes supposedly determined by the laws of nature. In any case, media coverage of the financial crisis creates the impression of an organic event not subject to forward-looking control. Such a perception is both misleading and wrong and represents the product of clever media policies.

Many difficult questions arise in the face of a disastrous global financial situation and span a wide range of issues, from economic governance and policies to securities laws. We are now dealing with the most complex issues ever raised in the area of commercial criminal law. Public discussion of the crisis has led to a stupefaction that makes it very difficult to identify those responsible for highly damaging and very dangerous economic developments, and experts are sounding the alarm of "the enemy at the gates."

Richard David Precht, a German philosopher,* noted that the enemy came treading softly, by undermining morals via the ebb and flow of international finance. Precht also states that democracy needs proven and incorruptible experts at the highest levels of government. Only if the best of the best govern, he claims, do people not have to wield the sceptre of power. Furthermore, in the reality of German democracy for example, experts are buried behind piles of unread material, preaching on books that no politician reads, or mired in the everyday life of academia. In contrast, our politicians are like straggling wanderers, their signposts are the lobbyists who freely come and go at the German parliament.

The lobbyists obtain what they want through donations to political parties, consistent friendliness, and present or future job offers. Some political retirees are "elder salesmen" rather than elder statesmen. If insight and an opposing interests collide, the interests will be victorious. Individual and collective self-deception, economic interests, and political calculations can be found behind financial crises. The customary language imputes an episodic nature to the development and pretends that it can be controlled in a process known as crisis management.

* Der Spiegel, October 5, 2009, 74.

Politicians can style themselves as determined and competent protectors of the common good, hoping that those entrusted to their care have short memories or cannot parse the complexity of the subject matter, and maintain their intrinsic trust in political systems. However, the mix of ambition, incompetence, and corruption on the part of decision makers in business and politics created the conditions for international finance to turn into a battlefield ruled by cowardly pirates, overwhelmed office holders, corrupt business people, and criminals—some in the guise of respectable bankers. Again, no force of nature triggered this financial crisis. It resulted from shameful failures at upper levels of management of the public and private sectors.

Many governments simply looked away as a history of state failure developed. Now we suddenly seem to have awoken. The competence of economists is being questioned because they tragically miscalculated despite their great expertise. The world may continue to rush toward its worst economic and social nightmare, as already suggested by the unrest in Greece in 2008. The social market economy is now showing symptoms of a systemic crisis and democracy as a whole appears at risk. Calls for a strong state are heard. Whether we are caught in a genuine economy crisis or merely a financial market crisis is questionable. We can certainly say that the financial crisis was triggered by a triple failure of the U.S.:

- Years of low interest policies (and even negative real-term interest) by the Federal Reserve
- Refusal to regulate financial markets
- Refusal to bail out Lehman Brothers, a bank of "systemic" importance

The debate about the individual causes and the parties responsible began with great hesitation, and questions of culpability under criminal law have not been addressed in any way. A few other factors to consider include:

- Deregulated global capital markets
- Inadequate or faulty regulations
- Excessively generous money supply policies of central banks
- Involvement of governments in lending via public and semi-public banks
- Omissions by management and violations of the duties incumbent on government office holders
- Large numbers of non-performing mortgages arising from massive promotion of home ownership especially in the U.S.
- Failure to modify state regulations to accommodate new financial instruments
- Exploitation of gaps in legislation by banks acting outside existing regulations

- Failure of bank internal risk management systems
- Disproportionate remuneration for bank managers
- Insufficient diversification of risks in securitization
- Lack of experience with new products and inadequate risk assessments
- Arrogance and almost blind faith in the predictive power of mathematical methods and complex estimation procedures
- Underestimation of risk aversion

A discussion of these fragmentary indications that does justice to the subject matter represents only part of a broadly based debate on economic governance. Obviously we cannot deal with all the issues listed above, but some aspects of the economic crisis relating to criminal law should be mentioned. We can start with a few questions.

- Is the damage from the financial crisis an expression of the arbitrariness of natural disasters or a necessary consequence of a combination of a lack of professional competence, continuing political neglect, and criminal energy?
- Did individual and group players in the world's financial markets collude to serve their own motives of enrichment in illegal ways and destabilize entire monetary systems?
- Do we need an internationally coordinated strategy of risk minimization based on criminal law or is risk primarily a question of economic governance?
- Is national criminal law ready for such challenges?
- Will any system of sanctions anywhere impress criminals who colluded globally in a culture of asocial hedonism?
- Are we living in an era in which organized crime has established itself as a way to do business, where governments are reduced to subservient serfdom to highly qualified conspirators?

The most basic question is whether criminal law in its current state or after the implementation of novel penalization strategies is capable of countering risks such as the new types appearing during the continuing financial crisis via prevention and deterrence. Skepticism is in order.

Criminal law is based on unlawful conduct, culpability, and individual attribution. It is the last resort and subsists on derivations from other fields of law. However, criminal law will fail when it deals with the moderation of social, economic, and political processes and systems for the common good. If an assessment of the damage done by institutions and individuals during this crisis becomes possible, certain changes in the functions of criminal law should be debated. The law should include a range of sanctions that can respond to the challenges of systemic crime. Simply too much has happened for society to return to business as usual, particularly in criminal law covering commerce and capital markets. This does not justify an undifferentiated call for the sharp sword of criminal law. That call cannot be heeded in any case if the principle of legality and the code of criminal procedure under the rule of law do not impose liability.

Legality and criminal procedures apply to everyone including those responsible for and acting on behalf of banks before the financial crisis. Nonetheless, it would be wrong to stress only the systemic nature of the financial crisis and fail to determine responsibility under the standards of criminal law. To answer the question of whether certain actions before and during the crisis may be punishable, we must explore the origins of the crisis and precisely define the facts and transactions that may be subject to criminal sanction.

General observations, for example, on breaches of trust, are not helpful without concrete details of what occurred. In public perception, the financial crisis is painted as a natural phenomenon. The idea of ascribing it to the coordinated activities of a criminal caste has met little acceptance, and for that reason no serious investigations of the actions of individual players have been launched. The large bonuses paid to bank managers and the worthlessness of dubious securities raise the question whether a combination of a kleptocratic mentality in banking and immense superficiality also led to the financial crisis.

Actions by regional state banks beyond their public purpose in themselves constitute a breach of duty. The representatives of the state governments serving on management boards never effectively consented to the disastrous business practices of the regional state banks because they own the institutions and have powers of disposition. Any declarations of consent therefore also fall under §266 of the German Penal Code (breach of trust). A gigantic snowballing system granting high interest loans to people who were not solvent began rolling. Real property transactions involving low-income groups became the bases of speculative transactions. The idea was born to turn dirt into gold and ultimately have business activities in the U.S. financed by taxpayers of other nations.

Bankers are the generals of our times. They annihilate money and jobs instead of foreign armies. Criminal law is the only means to beat them—transforming it from the last resort into the sole resort. Supervisory boards hold no sway over them. In the markets, it is customary for the smart players to sell to the dumber players. Whether such actions are punishable as frauds has not yet been sufficiently explored. After a successful initial phase, securitized lending got out of hand to the point where criminal law is the only weapon against it.

Bankers were not allowed to take even minimum risks according to the guidelines of the Basel Committee. In dealing with the fallout from the financial crisis from a criminal law perspective, a greater focus on future legislation must be applied to protection from bankruptcy offences. Basing arguments solely on legally protected property interests and the statutory offence of breach of trust may be anachronistic. For that reason, an emphasis on socially construed, legally protected interests may be a suitable response to neoliberal trends.

When analyzing development trends in criminal law in times of the financial crisis, the aspect of "governing through crime" must be considered. States may not wish to make criminal law more effective and may consider political profit more important. Criminal law must take into account that lending is always a balancing act between making a profit and maintaining security, and that collective constraints weaken awareness of injustice and risks, as revealed by the questionable sale-and-leaseback transactions of the municipalities.

The inventors of new financial products are responsible for the crisis although whether that can be proven through criminal law investigation is doubtful. Such investigations exceed the resources of prosecuting authorities. Instead of making criminal law more stringent, it should be expanded to include new concepts to protect financial interests. In a neoliberal system, the state and criminal law are biased. A lot of criminal law applies to the poor and almost none applies to the rich. The financial crisis proves that companies are not moral and therefore requires control.

Politicians sitting on the supervisory boards of the regional state banks in particular did not protest while the ample profits flowed into the state coffers, although they should have done so in light of the risky financial transactions. Clearly, gross mistakes were made in the course of introducing and maintaining risk management systems. A lack of adequate risk management constitutes a neglect of duty—in essence a breach of duty that serves as an element of the statutory offence of breach of trust. In dealing with the fallout from the financial crisis from a criminal law perspective, evasive transactions are as problematic as physical elements of an offence. They often follow the letter of the law economically but operate against the spirit of the law. Clauses prohibiting evasion of the law that would establish punishability are often lacking.

Offences are like "hot potatoes." Everyone involved claims to have relied on someone else's expertise. No effective criminal law policy exists to cover such collectively incurred risks. Criminal law is an appropriate tool to reduce competitive pressure among bankers. If supervisory regulations were supported by criminal law, employees could cite the relevant precepts of criminal law to superiors when urged to take unwarranted risks. The inability to stand up against risk is enough to assume a pecuniary loss will occur. Introducing existential risk to a systemically important bank poses a threat to the system as a whole and constitutes harm to the legally protected interests of a functional banking system. For this reason covering relevant criminal offences in the Banking Act is appropriate.

The friendly relationships between power and law must end, and management boards must recognize and comply with criminal laws. Fear of criminal law punishment alone is not sufficient because the rich and powerful have far greater means of evading laws, particularly criminal laws. Criminal law policy must deal with the systemic risks and not be reduced to applying existing laws.

What conclusions can we draw from this discussion? The financial crisis was caused at least in part by lack of control, the fraudulent dissimulation of the risks inherent in certain financial products, and a corrupt conspiracy elegantly called "insider trading." It is therefore only logical to call for greater criminal law intervention to protect the financial system. Criminal law will extend further to cover collective legally protected interests implied in the economic system.

It should be clear that the financial crisis is not merely a system failure. It was caused by many offensive actions on the part of decision makers in the banking system. State institutions contributed to the crisis through gross negligence. In Germany, public banks invested more than €100 billion in low quality or worthless U.S. securities. The economic expertise of many banking and political decision makers in Germany and elsewhere was at the same level of the Native Americans who sold Manhattan to European conquerors for a handful of glass baubles and later traded their souls and dignity for a few barrels of whiskey.

To date, no one has drawn the clear and necessary conclusions that the financial crisis is both a political scandal and a specific kind of continued system failure based on incompetence and corruption. We now face a form of organized crime that is extremely dangerous and globally orchestrated. Indeed, the decisive motivations were the rash and totally disproportionate executive bonuses—in reality corruptive payments.

No effective efforts have been undertaken to confiscate these ill-gotten gains from illusory profits of the past. Instead, the practice of securing these gains continues even in the banks bailed out by governments. Unfortunately, the only way to address these conditions in banking by law consists of public criminal investigations that have not gained a lot of ground. Thorough investigation would be in the interest of the banking system to eliminate the appearance of a management kleptocracy. It is time for criminal law, traditionally applied to ordinary individuals to be used against the executives, politicians, and government officials. This type of action is long overdue for those responsible for the financial crisis.

The results of risk taking are evident. The extent of the losses may have been surprising, but their occurrence was not. Even in the regulated zones, banking lived on the edge, with the knowledge and consent of political and economic decision makers. National egoism, human weakness, inadequate laws, insufficient supervision, systematic procurement of benefits via corruption, lack of technical competence, social lethargy, decaying public spirit, and structural failures are only some of the factors that initiated and promoted the greatest destruction of wealth in recent economic history.

The current and continuing disastrous development of the global economy is not an inevitable act of fate; it is the product of political errors, economic incompetence, systemic corruption, and individual criminal energy. The financial crisis term has been used to neutralize and deceive in a public debate that creates the impression that the system of the global financial markets is suffering only a temporary malfunction, and that responsibility imputable under criminal law to certain decision makers is insignificant.

At the origin of the disaster scenario were several U.S. government agencies that led low-income population groups into debt traps by means of welfare state lending policies and thus provoked excessive securitization business with low-quality mortgage-backed securities and credit default swaps. In the U.S., the failure to monitor and control financial systems promoted the emergence of a financial industry that ignored rationality and disconnected from reality by using unrealistic mathematical models to construct structured financial products. This facilitated the emergence of a climate of megalomania and asocial irresponsibility.

In the Anglo-Saxon countries in particular, the decline of conventional industrial production was accompanied by the rise of a capital market culture that pursued profit maximization beyond all economic reason and defied the principles of a social market economy. Yield expectations, profits, and certain types of banking transactions reveal that trade in innovative and structured financial products in particular has degenerated into a system promoting self interest to the detriment of the common good. In Germany, the regional state banks participated in international speculative transactions under the eyes of the politicians responsible. They lacked the necessary expertise and exceeded their coverage resources, thus intentionally and systematically violating the accounting principles of transparency and truthfulness by establishing special purpose vehicles without assets.

Throughout the world, governments allowed the production and use of what Warren Buffet called "financial weapons of mass destruction"—trade in derivatives of all kinds without even minimal impact assessment that over time cast doubt on the ethical foundations of political action. Lloyd Blankfein and other investment bankers inferred that they were doing God's work by maximizing their banks' profits.* Such a claim should have triggered reviews, not only of financial expertise, but also a psychiatric examination of the state of mind that prevailed in the financial industry.

Due to objective conflicts of interests, some rating agencies repeatedly made claims that did not reflect the real economic situations of companies and markets and were instead guided by manipulative wishful thinking. State financial supervision proved unable to prevent certain practices in

---

* *Sunday Times* (London), interview, November 8, 2009. http://spiegel.dewirtschaft/unternehmen/0.158.660075.00html

international financial reporting (incorrect asset reporting and embellished balance sheet data). Because of the amounts of sovereign debt accumulated, the budget policies of numerous EU member states created speculation opportunities for large players in international financial markets that exposed entire national economies to genuine threats.

Under the pressures of Realpolitik,* the financial situation and competitiveness of some national economies in the EU forced the union to undertake a guarantee obligation that could cause it to transform from a traditional community of solidarity into a novel community of liability outside the existing treaty framework, thus imposing unpredictable conditions on the future of European integration. Participation in global financial transactions was increasingly characterized by risky credit creation that distorted competition and allowed participants via leverage to make investments that did not reflect true financial and economic potential. The monetary policies of some central banks and inadequate risk management by numerous financial institutions created conditions under which the financial management of even large investment firms was characterized first by self-delusion and then by manipulative measures that ultimately created suspicions of systematic fraudulent and corrupt behavior.

Globally coordinated initiatives of the financial industry also led to threats to stabilization policies in the real economy. Their dynamics and a destructive force may be too strong to be effectively countered by traditional national and international economic governance. Whether the application of criminal law to individual decision makers in business, finance, and politics will exert appropriate preventive and deterrent effects remains to be determined. The necessary steps to clarify conditions for punishability and define effective sanctions are only now being determined and initiated.

Legislators and Liars

Where, in fact, do we live? And how much time to live is left? What does our world look like, especially after onset of the so-called financial crisis? Who is responsible? Was it anyone's fault that the collapse of the Lehman bank in 2008 pushed the global economy to the edge of an abyss whose depth to date no one has been able to measure?

Does anyone have conclusive information on how far the world was from the edge of this abyss? Where were the competence and political foresight able to deal with the menace of a nuclear fusion in the world economic

---

* Term refers to politics or diplomacy based on power and practical and material factors and considerations rather than ideological notions or moralistic or ethical premises. http://en.wikipedia.org/wiki/Realpolitik

system? Who has to bear the consequences of the most tremendous destruction of assets in recent history? Whose interests facilitated a long lasting orgy of enrichment and who were the beneficiaries?

Did anyone commit a crime in this context? Did the responsible authorities fulfill their duties of oversight? Who were the politicians whose legislation turned capital markets into crime scenes for spreading a particularly dangerous form of criminality?

What professional standards were applied by financial institutions dealing in "structured" products that had no basis in the economy and evolved from the greed of investors and their accomplices? Who advised legislators and what economic interests were pursued? Which ethical principles were and are valid in a society in which even the wealthiest can never get enough?

Of course, we cannot provide satisfactory answers to all these questions. We can only make a rough attempt to recall the most important reasons for the current global economic situation. As a consequence of the crisis, we must contemplate the failure of risk management, future challenges to regulatory policies, and possible systems for criminal prosecution. Too much has happened to simply get back to business in criminal law without addressing economic and capital market crime. We cannot ignore the ongoing devastating crisis. We will have to reflect on who is the sovereign in a country in which constitutional legislators fail to perform their assigned tasks in vital areas.

The involvement of private and profit-oriented interests in the form of internationally networked legal advice groups, in particular in the reorganization of the capital markets, degrades the basic concept of separation of powers to a ridiculous level. Employees of American or British style service companies received millions of euros of taxpayers' money for drafting legislative proposals or writing expert opinions on economic and fiscal issues for the German government. They played an important role in the development of laws that later served as bases for their consulting activities for their large government and commercial clients.

By mutual agreement, governments and beneficiaries transformed objective conflicts of interest into a special form of wrongdoing. International legal advice groups convinced German municipalities to invest in high risk businesses (cross-border leasing, for example). In doing so, the advisors cashed in twice: first for creating the problem and then for finding a (supposed) solution. This represents a breach of ethical codes of not only lawyers. The employees of the ministries responsible for processing legislation, mostly qualified lawyers, should feel concerned and rethink their professional self images. Obviously, they are seen as unable to perform their tasks or participating in a type of "division of labor" that shows contempt for political will and lack of respect for their offices. Is humiliation going to become a management principle?

During some legislative projects related to the capital market, ministry officials were degraded to "copying slaves" for external consultants who were even allowed to use ministry offices and inspect records so that later they could formulate what they considered the will of the people in their own far more comfortable offices. The responsible officials were permitted to make only minor amendments to legislation. Such circumstances serve as breeding grounds for economic and political corruption. The elected representatives of the people will not be able to do anything about this as long the extremely complex legislative processes reduce them to "nodding through" complex law packages at ever shorter intervals.

Perhaps one day, a strategy of tax-financed self-favoritism will solve this "perpetual motion" problem but it will happen at the price of the collapse of democratic legitimacy. The outsourcing of legislation is partly the result of a special type of national bankruptcy. When a government asks companies to solve problems that to an extent have been caused by the same companies' activities to achieve economic success for their private clients, the possibility of collusion must be considered. The combination of government incompetence and commercial expert knowledge can threaten society with destruction that will leave all historic forms of conspiracy far behind.

Along with legality (resistance sanctified by constitutional law), the necessary measures require courage, determination, intelligence, discipline, and ethical and moral motivation. It is highly unlikely that the collusive elements required for conspiracy would be present if courage, determination, and the other qualities listed above were combined with years of government experience. On the other side, i.e., interested business circles and the financial sector in its present state, the absence of the most important ethical and moral elements is obvious.

This does not infer that several national governments cooperated with legal and other advisors as a "mega mafia" to fleece taxpayers turning the economic system into an endless source of enrichment for exclusive cliques of office holders and private power brokers. But the enrichment certainly occurred and it should make us think about who is responsible for a global economy that seriously threatens the livelihoods of many millions of people in Germany and elsewhere around the world.

Are we confronted with structures and processes that possess dreadful power and thus can be dealt with only if we submit to them with the humility of lambs? Are we currently experiencing an institutionalized provocation of all people whose rights and dignity are violated by a very specific mixture of money and law? Whether the existing economic order serves as a further opportunity for antisocial and organized criminal enrichment will depend on the answer to this and other questions. It may be advisable to reconsider whether free, equal, and secret ballot elections will guarantee conditions that render other forms of legitimate self-defense obsolete.

At least to date, elections have not been able to prevent the formation of functional alliances between governments and companies that have highly idiosyncratic views of their responsibilities for public welfare. This is not the only reason it would be interesting to question the prevailing dogma of democratic exclusivity with regard to other ways of interpretation. It is not a matter of prioritizing ideological positions or party manifestos, parts of which after elections are not worth the paper they were printed on before the elections. It is rather a matter of the necessary combination of expertise and legitimacy, and this was the correlation that disappeared during the financial crisis or perhaps even earlier.

Certain rhetorical questions remain. Is the crisis an inevitable process following the laws of nature or did Mammon pronounce a final judgment? Have we all become innocent victims of a financial tsunami or have globally operating marauders made us hostages to their unlimited greed? Did we deserve this crisis because our own interests overshadowed our need to recognize economic realities?

A bank executive asked whether he considered his part in the events that pushed the global economy to the brink of collapse replied that, "It did not depend so much on the behavior of each individual but rather on having the right rules." This enlightening explanation came from Josef Ackermann, CEO of Deutsche Bank. He either did not comprehend the meaning of the question or simply did not want to examine his personal responsibility. Nevertheless, in an interview in October 2009,* Ackermann claimed to have reflected on the causes of the financial crisis and its lessons for the future. This approach inspires a renaming of Robert Musil's *The Man without Qualities* to *The Qualities without a Man* and encourages a new examination of *Crime and Punishment*.

At least, Ackermann admits to several misjudgments. He assumed that every participant in the market only took as many risks as he could bear and that therefore the system remained stable. He would not have expected that some banks pursued such large-scale risks partly outside their financial statements. According to him, the "collective" awareness was not deep enough. Apparently, Ackermann is focusing on errors, not on individual (or his own) guilt and thus the damaged system is defended.

It has been argued that, considering the magnitude of the global financial market, relatively few products were of poor quality, but they certainly affected many people. In keeping with this reasoning, it is difficult to identify bubbles in advance. Banking business presents inherent risks. This is why, especially during the boom times, it is important to maintain a certain level of "risk discipline" or "risk ethics." Moreover, Deutsche Bank and

---

* *Der Spiegel*, October 5, 2009, 74.

Ackermann were seen to have made mistakes but at a very early stage they pointed out systemic difficulties and called for an appropriate solution. There is no reason to collectively wear sackcloth and ashes because most bank employees, in particular in Germany, had nothing to do with the genesis of the crisis. Of course, the "rules of the game" now have to be modified to avoid a recurrence. However, this does not mean that securitized products, financial innovations, or even investment banking will disappear. In the future, the banks will have to hold more equity capital and integrate securitizations into their balance sheets. In addition, derivatives will have to be traded at facilities similar to stock exchanges to reduce the interdependence of banks.

Ackermann noted that banks are among the most regulated sectors of the economy. Only in a few areas, notably real estate financing in the U.S., are rules lacking. Appeals to individual and company morality are not solutions in a competitive society. To a certain extent, wrong incentive systems certainly contributed to the crisis. Other factors such as global imbalances, overly loose monetary policies in the U.S., and expansion of credit are far more important. According to this reasoning, there is no need for a fundamentally different financial system; we need a better one.

As a consequence of the crisis, Deutsche Bank not only plans to couple bonuses to the company's long-term performance and also introduce a "malus system," meaning that a manager would lose a certain portion of his salary if he fails to meet certain expectations in terms of financial performance. But it seems to have no reason to move away from the profit target (25% return on equity before tax). This train of thought makes a discussion with Ackermann about the distinguishability between sense of responsibility and sense of guilt pointless.

The public has started to wonder about the personal qualities of Josef Ackermann, who is considered Germany's most powerful business leader and the one who incurs the most hatred and malice. His social behavior is characterized as discreet and friendly. To date, no one has blamed him for being a fraudster or idiot. He is believed to be a capable and even tax-compliant manager. His performance as a banker is not the focus of criticism. The disapproval relates to the way he stands up for his cause. The question as to what extent he is willing to assume responsibility for the crisis into which his business sector plunged the entire global economy becomes even more significant if the assertion is true that his behavior also decides how people think about the state and the economy.

Surprisingly, the problems started with a success. In 2009, after-tax earnings of Deutsche Bank totaled around €5 billion, with investment banking having achieved the strongest growth due to trading in bonds. That made Ackermann proud. Others see it as proof of the fact that the financial sector simply carries on as it did before the beginning of the crisis and is still "hellbent" on gambling. All imaginable objects of trade on the stock exchange are still subject to high risk bets. One may well ask whether this is reasonable or whether the financial sector should strive first to avoid old and new mistakes by making its own regulatory proposals.

However, this correction requires clarifying what went wrong and who is at fault. Was the cause the failure of individuals or of the system as a whole? Indeed, it seems that Ackermann steered Deutsche Bank through the crisis without its suffering too much damage, but this does not change the fact that he conducted and supported the speculative trades that made the whole system shake.

The debate about Ackermann shows what society expects from its business elite, what it will tolerate, and what it will not accept. This is a particularly important indication, more so because some people consider Ackermann a "figure of hate" or even an enemy. For him, the relation between pure profiteering and the interest in the well-being of his fellow citizens appears to be unproblematic. The financial crisis is not even a fundamental problem for him personally. His institution obviously turned the corner. He is not responsible for the mistakes of others that could survive only with state aid.

The understanding of the fact that the Deutsche Bank also would have collapsed without government support for other bank establishments lies beyond Ackermann's intellectual reach or is deliberately repressed. Both are simple ways to reject all legally or morally justified accusations. The same principle always applies: personal misconduct is irrelevant or non-existent. The market mechanisms of the system failed.

But even Ackermann reportedly finds it "impossible" that many severe cases of speculation resulted in punishment. During a dinner in September 2009,[*] Ackermann had a long conversation about the penal consequences of the financial crisis with Eberhard Kempf, his defense lawyer in the Mannesmann trial. Looking back on this discussion, Kempf (who in his youth was active in the Communist League of West Germany [Kommunistischer Bund Westdeutschland or KBW]) and was known as a "real left-winger" indicated sympathy for the obstinacy in Ackermann's character. However, in Kempf's post-Marxist view, this obstinacy is called intransigence.

Kempf, who, at a certain point became weary of disseminating the KBW's ideas, appreciates the "involvement" of the public that consists of recalling the "natural laws" of capitalism. For example, a higher equity ratio of the banks would make credit more expensive. Above a certain level, a (voluntary) profit limit would cause competitors to "swallow" up the limiting banker in the market.

---

[*] Fleischhauer, J. *Der Spiegel*, April 3, 2010, 57.

Ackermann occasionally addresses the question of whether too much market economy also leads to welfare losses or whether a "rather contemplative" competition could be restored. In spite of his thoughtfulness, he does not seem to have succeeded in truly ingratiating himself with his fellow board members. A few have complained (after leaving the board, of course) that Ackermann and U.S. bankers started to move into executive suites and allow investment bankers to set the tone.

In comparison with their speculation gains, bankers' earnings from the time-honored customer business could only be considered ridiculous. Ackermann does not answer questions on such challenging subjects and apparently members of the Federal Parliament do not blame him for obstructing the work on new rules for the financial sector. However, Ackermann does not contribute anything to these rules either.

We could certainly argue about whether Ackermann is the appropriate demonstration model for a discussion of aspects of the financial crisis that go beyond issues of criminal and civil liability. His more or less charismatic personality does not convince us. It is interesting that Kempf who represents professional elites muses about his sympathy for Ackermann and then discusses yields and impending job cuts without a pause.

At least Kempf, unlike many politicians, knows what he is talking about. He successfully spanned the long way from Communist critiques of capitalism to legal and social philosophy. This is why he is qualified to declare to the rest of the world that anything that is punishable is rude, but not everything that is rude is reason for a criminal proceeding. This is not the place to judge to what extent the mental proximity of Kempf and Ackermann is enhanced by the geographical proximity of their well-located homes in Frankfurt-Westend. More important is the question of what political and systemic consequences are to be drawn.

It is not for lack of imagination that we will refrain from proposing sustainable remedies. However, we can attempt to outline a financial dilemma that seems to be fed from two directions. On one side is an elite problem. For years, business leaders and political decision makers have not understood how much damage their activities and omissions caused or participated (even if unplanned) in a "factual conspiracy" of greed and incompetence. They misled masses of who trusted them and sacrificed the assets of these people to satisfy their socially damaging drives to enrich themselves. For this purpose, they lied, cheated, and embezzled. They systematically accepted bribes and still expected to be respected by their staffs and electorates—a state of mind more likely for analysis from a medical rather than legal perspective.

On the other hand, asset owners were enticed by virtually insane profit guarantees and willingly bet their accounts without question and without turning back, allowing the relationship of the lambs and butchers to solidify. The greed for more and the fear of less created a synergy against which a call for criminal law seems inappropriate. Moreover, the call would be useless if a constitutional criminal procedure law did not impose such liability. This applies without restriction to all parties involved including those who were responsible for banks before the crisis. However, it would be wrong to a priori classify the financial crisis as a systemic crisis in which questions of responsibility may not be raised.

General statements about criminal offences, particularly trust breaches, are useless and have little to do with the financial crisis as long as the issues at stake have not been clarified. It is certainly correct that complex financial transactions serve as breeding grounds for property crimes and complexity per se is not punishable. New forms of financing and investment may certainly offer legal profit opportunities though causing considerable losses to contracting partners and participants in the market.

If financial products pretending to offer solidity (non-existent) or attractive (seemingly) return prospects are constructed more or less in a test tube, their complexity can only be aimed to disguise potential risks. It is possible to design such products to focus on the naïveté, ignorance, or avarice of prospective investors. The connection between complexity and crime has characterized the financial crisis since its onset in 2007. What is disturbing in this context is that this development affected the entire financial market itself and even professional participants were unable to maintain an overview of the risks. They, too, have become victims of this complexity.

Until the crisis erupted, legally protected rights such as confidence in the functioning of the capital market and in the functioning of the credit system had only abstract, theoretical, and synthetic value as concrete forms of threats and damages to these rights developed. The resulting shocks caused a crisis of the confidence in the system for very solid reasons. In addition, the development has been exacerbated by imposing risk on someone else and disguising it as a "rating." The ratings proved too positive and had to be adjusted by their issuers.

The question of whether—and, if so, according to which criteria—rating agencies can be distinguished from bold failures and fraudulent organizations has not yet been answered. Nevertheless, speculation remains legal and part of a bank manager's job and in that regard penal consequences would be absurd. Avoiding criminal liability and glossing over the financial crisis as a systemic problem for which no one is personally liable is not a solution either. The financial crisis triggered an economic crisis that created a social crisis. Globalization has led to a financial casino culture that produced, with dramatic consequences, economic crises, one of which is transnational organized crime that has reached global dimensions.

Corruption played a crucial role in this development. Governments allowed the system and its main actors to get out of control. Without rules, financiers and business leaders turned the system into a general orgy of enrichment. Bankers and asset managers sold their services and their souls to make huge sums of money. Armies of auditors, accountants, and lawyers became mercenaries of legal and illegal industries, covering dirty dealings or giving them airs of legitimacy. Rating agencies and advisory services taught companies how to commit fraud and then gave them clearance certificates. Offshore financial centers accepted money from all sources without question. These activities formed the corrupt core of the crisis.

It is not always easy to define the difference between robbery and creating a bank. A more difficult question is how banks, industrial establishments, auditors, legal advice groups, political parties, and governments differ from criminal organizations. The former president of the Federal Republic of Germany Christian Wulff,* recently stated that the unauthorized destruction of capital was a criminal offence. Does that refer to individual cases of unlawful behavior or products (now under discussion under the minimizing financial crisis terminology) of organized crime?

It would be very interesting to consider the roles of governments within and outside the EU related to the interactions of financial institutions and private companies. The tensions within Europe, the Greek debt, and the desperate situation in Portugal, Ireland, Spain, Italy, and Hungary are currently the main issues in the financial markets. The markets' confidence in Greece disappeared after the revelation that it presented false figures simulating lower debts for years. There are assumptions that investment banks assisted by providing special financial products. This raises the question of whether such collusive practices, if they are proven, should even be considered the most serious forms of organized crime.

Public debate to date has been little more than a trivializing discussion about tricks and venial (minor) sins. This wording is inappropriate in every way. In the public finance sector, large loans are procured in foreign currencies such as dollars or yen, changed into Euros for a certain period (e.g., to pay due obligations), then converted back into the original currency before maturity date. Investment banks made these swaps for years on the basis of fictitious instead of actual exchange rates and thus created credits outside the official debt statistics in both Greece and Italy.

Another question that merits discussion is whether some financial institutions are so big that they are deemed to be "relevant to the system" and must be rescued from their self-inflicted predicaments by the help of taxpayers. In this case, the systemic crisis arose from systemic crime, a special type of delinquency characterized by irresponsibility based on economic incompetence and political negligence and possibly criminal intention. In reality, we are probably confronted with a type of barbarism. The rule of law has degenerated to lip service by people delivering the goods. Fraud and

---

* *Hannoversche Allgemeine Zeitung,* March 2, 2009. http://www.financial.de/news/wirtschaftsnachrichten/2009/03/02

blackmail have become integral aspects of the functions of executives and officials.

Against this background, we should also consider whether a system that allowed such developments may still be relevant. The present global economy has been described by terms normally used after natural disasters. The crisis is often described as a tsunami: unpredictable, uncontrollable, and devastating, despite the willful misconduct of individuals and organizations that caused the economic losses throughout the world. The world of finance, the economy, and political activities contributed to the establishment of a system that entailed risks that were unprecedented in their scope and potential for damage that operated with the consent of public authorities and policy makers.

This alliance of criminals created impacts far more serious than those of a mafia clan. It threatened public welfare and the stability of regions. The destructive force of the structures developed in the financial industry is obvious but the individual and organization-wide responsibility for the consequences remains unclear as do questions of civil liability and criminal penalties. The efforts to date are not encouraging. Several important actors in the global economy cannot be targeted due to ethical or legal considerations. If this situation does not change, the administration of justice will degenerate into a system of social self-defense.

Until a decision is made to develop "revolutionary" transformation measures, we still have plenty of time to think about one other idea. Peter Gauweiler, a member of the German Bundestag, recently called for a decree against extremists and radicals in the banking sector. According to him, the constitution guarantees the protection of property as "property of responsibility."* However, the property of responsibility vanished because of investment banking, hedge funds, and excessive focus on shareholder values. In Gauweiler's opinion, irrational financial speculations undertaken by bankers destroyed more entrusted property than ever. People dealing with the money of others tried to influence fate, replaced the lack of understanding of their investments with ratings, and used special purpose vehicles for profit. They inflated their balance sheets with assets that could not be supported, then calculated their excessive bonuses on the basis of the inflated figures.

Gauweiler thinks that the view that U.S. President Obama put an end to the chatter of financial service providers outside the real economy may be too optimistic an assessment. According to Gauweiler, President Obama's proposal to prohibit credit institutions from conducting non-customer-related, self-interested proprietary trading and transactions that involve hedge funds and holding companies is absolutely correct. Gauweiler considers types of

---

* *Süddeutsche Zeitung,* February 4, 2010, 2.

investment banking that divide up, securitize, and gamble away customer property as "organized betrayal." To put it more simply, financial industries, governments, and politics are domains of organized crime.

Conclusions and Consequences

In April 2011, the U.S. Senate's Permanent Subcommittee on Investigations of the Committee on Homeland Security and Governmental Affairs published its report on Wall Street and the financial crisis ("Anatomy of a Financial Collapse"). The subcommittee notes that in the fall of 2008, the U.S. suffered a devastating economic collapse. Once valuable securities lost most or all of their values, debt markets froze, stock markets plunged, and storied financial firms went under. Millions lost their jobs; millions of families lost their homes; and many businesses shut down. These events cast the U.S. into an economic recession so deep it has yet to recover.

Using internal documents, communications, and interviews, the report attempts to provide a clear picture of activities inside the walls of some of the financial institutions and regulatory agencies that contributed to the crisis. The investigation found that the crisis was not a natural disaster. It arose from trading high risk, complex financial products; undisclosed conflicts of interest; and the failures of regulators, credit rating agencies, and the market itself to rein in the excesses of Wall Street.[*]

In a case study on Washington Mutual Bank (WaMu), the subcommittee focused on how one bank's search for increased growth and profit led to the origination and securitization of hundreds of billions of dollars in high risk, poor quality mortgages that plummeted in value, hurting investors, the bank, and the U.S. financial system. WaMu held itself out as a prudent lender, but in reality, it turned increasingly to high risk loans. WaMu also circulated increasing numbers of its flagship products (optional adjustable rate mortgages or optional ARMs). These high risk, negatively amortizing mortgages from 2003 to 2007 represented as much as half of all WaMu's loan originations.

It joined with Long Beach Corporation and their shoddy lending practices produced billions of dollars in high risk, poor quality mortgages and mortgage-backed securities by qualifying high risk borrowers for larger loans than they could afford; steering borrowers from conventional mortgages to higher risk loan products; accepting loan applications without verifying borrower income; issuing loans at short-term "teaser" rates that could lead to payment shock when higher interest rates took effect later; promoting

---

[*] U.S. Permanent Subcommittee on Investigations, Anatomy of a Financial Collapse Report, April 2011, 1.

negatively amortizing loans that led many borrowers to increase rather than pay down their debts; and authorizing loans with multiple layers of risk.

In addition, WaMu and Long Beach failed to enforce compliance with their own lending standards; allowed excessive loan error and exception rates; exercised weak oversight over third party mortgage brokers that supplied half or more of their loans; and tolerated the issuance of loans with fraudulent or erroneous borrower information. They also designed compensation incentives that rewarded loan personnel for issuing large volumes of higher risk loans and thus valued speed and volume over loan quality.

WaMu's high risk lending operation was also problem-plagued. Its management was provided with compelling evidence of deficient lending practices in internal emails, audit reports, and reviews. Internal reviews of two high volume WaMu loan centers, for example, described extensive fraud by employees who willfully circumvented bank policies. A WaMu review of internal controls to stop sales of fraudulent loans to investors described management as "ineffective." On at least one occasion, senior managers knowingly sold delinquency-prone loans to investors. WaMu's president described its prime home loan business as the "worst managed business" he had seen in his career.[*]

Documents obtained by the subcommittee reveal that WaMu launched its high risk lending strategy primarily because higher risk loans and mortgage-backed securities could be sold for higher prices on Wall Street. They garnered higher prices because high risk produced higher coupon rates than other comparably rated securities, and investors paid higher prices to buy them. Selling or securitizing the loans also removed them from WaMu's books and appeared to insulate the bank from risk.

The subcommittee investigation indicates that unacceptable lending and securitization practices were not restricted to WaMu. Several financial institutions that originated, sold, and securitized billions of dollars in high risk, poor quality home loans that inundated U.S. financial markets followed such practices. The values of many of the resulting securities plummeted, leaving banks and investors with huge losses that helped send the economy into a downward spiral. These lenders were not the victims. The high risk loans they issued served as the fuel that ignited the crisis[†] that led the Office of Thrift Supervision (OTS) to stop the unsafe and unsound practices that led to the demise of Washington Mutual, one of the nation's largest banks.

From 2004 to 2008, OTS identified over 500 serious deficiencies at WaMu, yet failed to take action to force the bank to improve its lending operations and even impeded oversight by the bank's back-up regulator, the

---

[*] Ibid. 2, 3.
[†] Ibid. 4.

FDIC.* Despite the large number of deficiencies, OTS did not once, from 2004 to 2008, pursue an enforcement action against WaMu related to its lending practices or lower the bank's ratings for safety and soundness. Only in 2008, as the bank incurred mounting losses, did OTS finally undertake two informal, non-public enforcement actions. It required WaMu to agree to a board resolution in March and a memorandum of understanding in September, neither of which imposed changes sufficient to prevent the bank's failure.

OTS officials resisted calls by the FDIC for stronger measures and even impeded FDIC oversight efforts by, at times, denying office space and access to records to FDIC examiners. Tensions between the two agencies remained high until the end. Hindered by a culture of deference to management, demoralized examiners, and agency infighting, OTS officials allowed the bank's short-term profits to excuse its risky practices and failed to evaluate its actions in the context of the U.S. financial system as a whole. OTS's narrow regulatory focus prevented it from analyzing or acknowledging until too late that WaMu's practices could harm the economy.

OTS's failure to restrain WaMu's unsafe lending practices allowed its high risk loans to proliferate, negatively impacting investors across the U.S. and around the world. Similar regulatory failings by other agencies involving other lenders repeated the problem on a broader scale. The result was a mortgage market saturated with risky loans, and financial institutions charged with holding safe investments acquiring portfolios rife with risky mortgages. When those mortgagors began defaulting in record numbers and values of mortgage-related securities plummeted, financial institutions around the globe suffered hundreds of billions of dollars in losses, triggering an economic disaster. The regulatory failures that set the stage for those losses were proximate causes of the financial crisis.†

Between 2004 and 2007, Moody's and S&P issued credit ratings for tens of thousands of U.S. residential mortgage-backed securities (RMBS) and collateralized debt obligations (CDOs). Noting the increasing revenue results from Wall Street firms, Moody's and S&P issued AAA and other investment grade credit ratings for most RMBS and CDO securities, deeming them safe investments even though many relied on high risk home loans. In late 2006, delinquencies and defaults occurred at alarming rates. Despite signs of a deteriorating mortgage market, Moody's and S&P continued for six months to issue investment grade ratings for RMBS and CDO securities.

In July 2007, as mortgage delinquencies intensified and RMBS and CDO securities incurred losses, both companies abruptly reversed course and began downgrading hundreds and then thousands of their RMBS and CDO ratings, some less than a year old. Investors like banks, pension funds, and

* Ibid. 4.
† Ibid. 5.

insurance companies that are by rule barred from owning low-rated securities were forced to sell their downgraded RMBS and CDO holdings because they lost their investment grade status. RMBS and CDO securities held by financial firms lost much of their value and investors avoided new securitizations. The subprime RMBS market initially froze and then collapsed, leaving investors and financial firms around the world holding unmarketable and valueless securities. A few months later, the CDO market collapsed as well.

Inaccurate AAA ratings introduced risk into the U.S. financial system and constituted a key cause of the financial crisis. In addition, the July mass downgrades that were unprecedented in number and scope precipitated the collapse of the RMBS and CDO secondary markets, and perhaps more than any other single event triggered the start of the financial crisis.[*]

The subcommittee's investigation uncovered a host of factors responsible for the inaccurate ratings issued by Moody's and S&P. One significant cause was the inherent conflict of interest within the system used to pay for credit ratings. The rating agencies were paid by the Wall Street firms that sought their ratings and profited from the financial products rated. Under this "issuer pays" model, the rating agencies depended on Wall Street firms for business and were vulnerable to threats that the firms would take their business elsewhere if they did not get the ratings they wanted. The ratings agencies weakened their standards. They competed to provide the most favorable ratings to win business and greater market shares. The result was a race to the bottom.

Additional factors responsible for the inaccurate ratings include models that failed to include relevant mortgage performance data, unclear and subjective criteria used to produce ratings, failures to apply updated rating models to existing rated transactions, and lack of adequate staff to perform rating and surveillance services despite record revenues. Compounding these problems were federal regulations that required banks and other institutions to purchase investment grade securities, thus creating pressure on the credit rating agencies to issue investment grade ratings. While these federal regulations were intended to help investors avoid unsafe securities, they had the opposite effect when the AAA ratings proved inaccurate.

Evidence gathered by the subcommittee shows that the credit rating agencies were aware of the problems in the mortgage market, including unsustainable rises in housing prices, the high risk nature of the loans issued, lax lending standards, and rampant mortgage fraud. Instead of using this information to temper their ratings, the firms continued to issue investment grade ratings for mortgage-backed securities. If the rating agencies issued ratings that accurately reflected the increasing risks in the RMBS and CDO

[*] Ibid. 6.

markets and appropriately adjusted existing ratings in those markets, they might have discouraged investors from purchasing these high risk securities and slowed the pace of securitizations.

However, it was not in the short term economic interest of Moody's or S&P to provide accurate credit ratings for high risk RMBS and CDO securities, because doing so would have hurt their own revenues. Instead, their profits became increasingly reliant on fees generated by issuing large volumes of structured finance ratings. Moody's and S&P provided AAA ratings to tens of thousands of high risk RMBS and CDO securities. When the products began to incur losses, the raters issued mass downgrades that shocked the financial markets, hammered the values of mortgage-related securities, and helped trigger the financial crisis.[*]

The financial products developed by investment banks allowed investors to profit from both the successes of RMBS and CDO securitizations and their failures. Credit default swap (CDS) contracts, for example, allowed counterparties to wager on the rise or fall in the value of a specific RMBS security or on a collection of RMBS and other assets contained or referenced in a CDO. Major investment banks developed standardized CDS contracts that could also be traded on a secondary market. They also established the ABX Index that allowed counterparties to wager on the rise or fall in the value of a basket of subprime RMBS securities that could be used to reflect the status of the subprime mortgage market as a whole.

The investment banks sometimes matched parties that wanted to take opposite sides in a transaction and other times took one or the other side of a transaction to accommodate a client. Investment banks also used these financial instruments to make their own proprietary wagers. In extreme cases, they set up structured transactions that enabled them to profit at the expense of their clients.

Case studies of Goldman, Sachs and Deutsche Bank illustrate troubling practices that raise conflict of interest and other concerns involving RMBS, CDO, CDS, and ABX financial instruments that contributed to the crisis. Goldman, Sachs used net short positions to benefit from the downturn in the mortgage market, and designed, marketed, and sold CDOs in ways that created conflicts of interest with the firm's clients and at times made profits on the same products that caused substantial losses by its clients.[†]

The Deutsche Bank case reveals how its top global CDO trader, Greg Lippmann, repeatedly warned and advised his bank colleagues and some of his clients seeking to buy short positions about the poor quality of the RMBS securities underlying many CDOs. He described some of those securities

---

[*] Ibid. 7.
[†] Ibid. 8.

as "crap" and "pigs," and predicted that the investments would lose value. Lippmann was asked to buy a specific CDO security and responded that it "rarely trades," but he "would take it and try to dupe someone" into buying it. He also at times referred to the industry's ongoing CDO marketing effort as a "CDO machine" or "Ponzi scheme."

Deutsche Bank's senior management disagreed with his negative views, and used the bank's own funds to make large proprietary investments in mortgage-related securities that in 2007 had a face value of $128 billion and a market value around $25 billion. Despite its positive view of the housing market, the bank allowed Lippmann to develop a large proprietary short position for the bank in the RMBS market, which from 2005 to 2007, totalled $5 billion. The bank cashed in the short position from 2007 to 2008, generating a profit of $1.5 billion. Lippmann claimed it was the most money made on a single position than any other trade in Deutsche Bank history. Despite that gain, due to its large long holdings, Deutsche Bank lost nearly $4.5 billion from its mortgage-related proprietary investments.[*]

The case studies also illustrate how these two investment banks continued to market new CDOs in 2007, even as U.S. mortgage delinquencies intensified, RMBS securities lost value, the U.S. mortgage market as a whole deteriorated, and investors lost confidence. Both bankers kept producing and selling high risk, poor quality structured finance products in a negative market, in part because stopping the "CDO machine" would have meant less income for structured finance units, smaller executive bonuses, and the disappearance of CDO desks staffs—which is what finally happened.

The two case studies also illustrate how certain complex structured finance products like synthetic CDOs and naked credit default swaps amplified market risk by allowing investors with no ownership interests in the obligations to place unlimited side bets on their performances. Finally, the case studies demonstrate how proprietary trading led to dramatic losses for Deutsche Bank and undisclosed conflicts of interest for Goldman, Sachs. Investment banks were the driving forces behind the structured finance products that provided a steady stream of funding for lenders originating high risk, poor quality loans and magnified risk throughout the U.S. financial system. The investment banks that engineered, sold, traded, and profited from mortgage-related structured products were major causes of the financial crisis.[†] A few excerpts from the subcommittee report reviewed here provoke an irritating question one more time: what is the difference between the banking system, the political establishment, and a mafia organization?

[*] Ibid. 10.
[†] Ibid. 12.

Another question repeated across the U.S. is why, in the aftermath of a financial mess that generated hundreds of billions in losses have no high profile participants been prosecuted? Whether prosecutors and regulators have been aggressive enough in pursuing wrongdoing is likely to long be a subject of debate. They all claim they did the best they could under difficult circumstances but another factor is at work.

Several years after the start of the financial crisis caused in large part by reckless lending and excessive risk taking by major financial institutions, no senior executives have been charged or imprisoned and no collective government effort has emerged. Even worse, former prosecutors, lawyers, bankers, and mortgage employees say that investigators and regulators ignored past lessons about how to crack financial fraud.

As the crisis deepened in spring of 2008 the U.S. Federal Bureau of Investigation (FBI) scaled back a plan to assign more field agents to investigate mortgage fraud. That summer the Justice Department also rejected calls to create a task force devoted to mortgage-related investigations, leaving these complex cases understaffed and poorly funded. Only much later did the Justice Department create a general financial crimes task force. At the same time the regulators failed in their crucial duty to compile the relevant data to build criminal cases. In fact: The same dynamic that helped enable the crisis (weak regulation) also made it harder to pursue fraud in its aftermath.[*]

The former U.S. vice president, Dick Cheney, is quoted as having said that nobody anywhere was smart enough to figure it out or see it coming. He was hardly alone in this assessment. The financial community and the political establishment kept asking the same rhetorical who-could-have-known question and tried to suggest that the financial crisis was akin to the attacks of September 11, 2001—catastrophic and almost impossible to foresee. That is definitely not true.[†]

We are left with even more questions without answers. How do governments deal with individuals who do not tell the truth? What are the reasons for making false statements? Are we dealing with stupidity or fraudulent activities? Can justice ever prevail if big money, political power, and criminal energy are involved?

The statements of Preet Bharara, the U.S. attorney in Manhattan in May 2011 might have led to a conclusion that prosecutors were finally getting tough on the illegal behavior that helped bring about the financial crisis, but this too is probably an illusion. The target of Bharara's wrath was Mortgage IT, a small operation Deutsche Bank bought in 2007. The authorities cite

---

[*] Morgensohn, G. & Story, L. No prosecutions of top figures, in Financial Crisis. http://www.nytimes.com/2011/04/14/business/14prosecute.html?adxnnl=1&ref=homepage&src=me&adxnnlx=1302883351-D5XYwN/7u/XENNAtFx6MFA

[†] Nouriel, R. & Mihm, S. (2011). *Crisis Economics*, 1.

eight years of alleged fraud, but the complaint filed did not single out one Mortgage IT representative as a wrongdoer. It appeared that this faceless corporation somehow defrauded the government without human help. Stunningly, although Bharara's office concluded that Mortgage IT executives "knowingly, wantonly, and recklessly lied to federal officials, it decided that none of the executives deserved jail time. The U.S. attorney initiated a civil case, not a criminal proceeding and the only remedy prosecutors could seek was a sum of money which was a tap on the wrist considering that Deutsche Bank revenues in 2010 exceeded $42 billion.

When asked why no criminal charges were brought, Bharara said, "Every lie is not a crime." Five years after the start of the financial crisis, the right question is whether any lies amount to crimes. They certainly do not constitute crimes for financial executives. As long as prosecutors fail to pursue criminal actions against financial executives, their message is that crime pays.[*]

As long as no serious criminal investigations are initiated, no answers to the above questions will be forthcoming although several facts and conclusions have emerged. In the U.S., the Financial Crises Inquiry Commission was created to examine the causes of the financial and economic crisis. In its report published in January 2011, the commission intended to provide a historic accounting of what brought the U.S. financial system and economy to a precipice and to help policy makers and the public better understand how this calamity occurred.[†] The first and one of the most important conclusions was that the crisis was avoidable. The commission made a number of points clear:

> The crisis was the result of human action and inaction, not of Mother Nature or computer models gone haywire. The captains of finance and the public stewards of our financial system ignored warnings and failed to question, understand and manage evolving risks within a system essential to the well-being of the American public. Theirs was a big miss, not a stumble. While the business cycle cannot be repealed, a crisis of this magnitude need not have occurred. To paraphrase Shakespeare, the fault lies not in the stars, but in us.[‡]

Another conclusion was that widespread failures in financial regulation and supervision proved devastating to the stability of the nation's financial markets: "The sentries were not at their posts, in no small part due to the widely accepted faith in the self-correcting nature of the markets and the ability of financial institutions to effectively police themselves."[§]

---

[*] Nocera, J. You call that tough? *New York Times*, May 7, 2011. http://.ny.times. com/2011/05/07/opinion/07nocera.html?_r=1&ref=joenocera&pa

[†] Financial Crisis Inquiry Report (FCIR), Final Report of National Commission on the Causes of the Financial and Economic Crisis in the United States, January 2011, XI.

[‡] Ibid. XVII.

[§] Ibid. XVIII.

The commission does not accept the view that regulators lacked the power to protect the financial system. From its perspective, they had ample power in many arenas and chose not to use it. The report clearly states that dramatic failures of corporate governance and risk management at many systematically important financial institutions were key causes of the crisis. Many of these institutions grew aggressively through poorly executed acquisition and integration strategies that made effective management more challenging. The institutions and credit rating agencies embraced mathematical models as reliable predictors of risks. Too often, risk management became risk justification. Finally a combination of excessive borrowing, risky investments, and lack of transparency put the financial system on a collision course with crisis.[*] The government was unprepared and its inconsistent response added to the uncertainty and panic in the financial markets.[†]

The Commission found a systemic breakdown in accountability and ethics.[‡] An erosion of standards of responsibility exacerbated the crisis. However, it would be too simplistic to pin this crisis on mortal flaws like greed and hubris. The commission rightly stressed the failure to account for human weakness as a relevant factor. It cited human mistakes, misjudgements, and misdeeds that resulted in systemic failures.

A crisis of this magnitude requires the work of more than a few bad actors. At the same time, the breadth of this crisis does not mean that everyone is at fault. The commission places special responsibility on public leaders charged with protecting the financial system, those entrusted to run regulatory agencies, and the chief executives of companies whose failures drove the nation and the rest of the world to crisis: "Tone at the top does matter and, in this instance, we were let down. No one said no."[§]

In addition the collapsing mortgage-lending standards and mortgage securitization pipeline lit and spread the flame of contagion and crisis. Many mortgage lenders set the bar so low that they took eager borrowers' qualifications on faith, often with a willful disregard for borrowers' abilities to pay. As irresponsible lending using predatory and fraudulent practices became more prevalent, the Federal Reserve neglected its mission to ensure the safety and soundness of the nation's banking and financial system and protect the credit rights of consumers. It failed to build a retaining wall before it was too late. The Office of the Comptroller of the Currency and OTS, caught up in turf wars, pre-empted state regulators from reining in abuses.[¶] Over-the-counter (OTC) derivatives also added significantly

---

[*] Ibid. XVIII, XIX.
[†] Ibid. XXI.
[‡] Ibid. XXII.
[§] Ibid. XXIII.
[¶] Ibid. XXIII.

to the crisis. The enactment of legislation in 2000 to ban the regulation of OTC derivatives by the federal and state governments was a key point in the march to financial crisis.[*]

The failures of credit rating agencies were essential cogs in the wheel of financial destruction. The commission found that the three agencies were key enablers of the financial meltdown:

> The mortgage-related securities at the heart of the crisis could not have been marketed and sold without their seal of approval. Investors relied on them; often blindly.... This crisis could not have happened without the rating agencies.... You will also read about the forces at work behind the breakdown at Moody's, including the flawed computer models, the pressure from financial firms that paid for the ratings, the relentless drive for market share, the lack of resources to do the job despite record profits, and the meaningful public oversight. And you will see that without the active participation of the rating agencies, the market for mortgage-related securities could not have been what it became.[†]

The commission addressed key questions related to capital availability, excess liquidity, and the roles of Fannie Mae and Freddie Mac. It found that low interest rates, widely available capital, and international investors seeking to put money in real estate assets in the U.S. were prerequisites for the creation of a credit bubble:

> Those conditions created risks, which should have been recognized by market participants, policy makers, and regulators. However it is the commission's conclusion that excess liquidity did not need to cause a crisis. It was the failures outlined above—including the failure to effectively rein in excesses in the mortgage and financial markets—that were the principal causes of this crisis.... The government-sponsored enterprises (GSEs) had a deeply flawed business model as publicly traded corporations with the implicit backing of and subsidies from the federal government and with a public mission.... In 2005 and 2006, they decided to ramp up their purchase and guarantee of risky mortgages, just as the housing market was peaking. They used their political power for decades to ward off effective regulation and oversight, spending $164 million on lobbying from 1999 to 2008. They suffered from many of the same failures of corporate governance and risk management discovered in other financial firms.... The GSEs participated in the expansion of subprime and other risky mortgages, but they followed rather than led Wall Street and other lenders in the rush for fool's gold.[‡]

[*] Ibid. XXIV.
[†] Ibid. XXV.
[‡] Ibid. XXVI.

The conclusion is clear. The government failed to ensure that opportunities matched the practical realities on the ground. Witness again the failure of the Federal Reserve and other regulators to rein in irresponsible lending.* In its inquiry, the commission found dramatic breakdowns of corporate governance, profound lapses in regulatory oversight, and near-fatal flaws in the financial system. A series of choices and actions led the U.S. toward a catastrophe for which it was ill prepared. One of the last conclusions is one of the most important : "The greatest tragedy would be to accept the refrain that no one could have seen this coming and thus nothing could have been done. If we accept this notion, it will happen again."†

* Ibid. XXVII.
† Ibid. XXVIII.

Preventing Another Financial Crisis: Roles of Control Mechanisms

III

MAXIMILLIAN EDELBACHER AND MICHAEL THEIL

Introduction: Preventing Another Financial Crisis: Roles of Control Mechanisms

In the face of the current financial crisis and the damage it caused, many call for preventive measures to assure that a worldwide financial crisis will not happen again. Recalling the past, and in reference to the current situation, it certainly appeared that the controls placed on the financial institutions during the great depressions of the 1930s and those instituted afterward were believed sufficient to assure that another financial collapse would never happen. Thus it was believed that everything was under control before the outbreak of the current disaster. Is it credible to say that the new measures in effect up to this point are sufficient for the future? Section III of this book, the final part, is devoted to alternative approaches to think about the problem and several suggestions for approaches that can be used to avoid worldwide financial disasters in the future.

In its dimensions and its dynamics, the current financial crisis is certainly an exceptional situation. It is no wonder, therefore, that we do not dispose of recipes for dealing with it immediately. While every situation may appear unique, it is possible to understand it on a more abstract level and hopefully be able to make some generalizations about financial crises. This describes the aim of this section.

In Chapter 13, "Dealing with Insurance: What Can be Learned," Theil describes and reflects on the working methods and instruments of insurance companies. Compared to other economic entities, the core business of an insurance company is to assume risks, often large ones, from other companies, organizations, households, and individuals and maintain a balanced risk portfolio. Closer analysis shows that many of the working methods and instruments are available exclusively to insurance companies. Furthermore, their ability to analyze and arrange risks is unique. Suggestions relevant for non-insurers are straightforward: do not take risks that you are unable to analyze thoroughly and for which you lack the necessary instruments to reasonably control the outcomes of the risks. If you do otherwise, failure will be inevitable.

The role of the press and the police as allies in detecting and investigating organized crime is the subject of Chapter 14 by Dobovšek and Mastnak. Based on their research, they conclude that both detectives and investigative reporters often are active in uncovering the same illegal activities pursued by organized criminal groups However, they generally complete their investigations in different working modes and under differing rules. For example, media reporters may make conclusions that fall short of judicial standards. However, they often have access to information that is concealed from police investigators. Also, press investigations may reveal facts that give new directions to stalled police inquiries or may renew attention toward old inquiries in which the public lost interest.

In Chapter 15, "Human Factors Analysis; How to Build Resilience against Financial Crimes," Felsenreich analyzes the current financial crisis from a "depth psychological perspective" to better understand the group dynamics of power systems and the people who form financial power systems and make corruption of the systems possible. He concludes that safety cultures are the only guarantors that can make financial industries more resilient.

It is often argued that the financial crisis was made possible because of powerful influences of the banking sector upon politics, thus leading to insufficient regulation and control of financial institutions by governments. In Chapter 16, Noussi applies lessons learned from institutional reforms in developing countries to the issue of stronger oversight of the financial sector. She explains how the tremendous influences of the financial industries on government leaders can be curtailed. She argues that stronger regulation and control are hard to achieve; instead a more promising approach is to show banking institutions that they will benefit from a more transparent environment. In her view, results from analyses of developing economies suggest that such openness presents advantages for all market participants.

"Business Angels" who participate actively in private enterprises may be of help in environments that are vulnerable to illegal practices by large market participants. In Chapter 17, Fath explains how experience experts in the financial world who work side by side with their clients may exercise influence on the financial industry to follow good business practices. These experts can help new entrepreneurs in decision making and in particular advise them how to avoid taking large risks.

In Chapter 18, "Legislative and Programming Initiatives to Prevent and Control Financial Crimes in the United States," Kratcoski contributes a discussion of the role of legislation in the aftermath of the 9/11 terrorist attacks on the U.S. The major piece of legislation created by congress was the USA

Patriot Act of 2001. Title III of the act covers international money laundering abatement and anti-terrorism financing. It exerted the most direct effects on preventing and controlling some of the financial crimes most closely associated with organized crime, white collar crime, and terrorism. However, many of the measures and programs adopted to prevent financial crime were implemented in piecemeal fashion and require further adaptation and development before an integrated strategy and operational plan are in place. Otherwise, some of the programs will be of questionable value. Kratcoski also reports significant progress and notes that many programs show positive results.

Chapter 19 by Edelbacher, Theil, and Kratcoski summarizes the past, present, and future of financial crime. The authors draw on the material presented in the various chapters to illustrate how various natural or man-made situations created a crisis that upset the normal pattern of everyday life and security and suggest actions required to allow society to regain some sense of normalcy. These lessons learned from past experiences can be very helpful in overcoming and adjusting to present day crises, whether natural disasters (floods, earthquakes, hurricanes, drought) or man-made situations (aftermath of war, economic depression, financial crisis).

We presently have the technology and vast sources of information to help us predict future disasters with some accuracy. We can determine positive and negative outcomes likely to arise from a political or financial course of action. We may not be able to prevent natural disasters, but human and financial losses may be lowered substantially if appropriate research, planning, and program implementation are completed.

Dealing with Insurance
What Can Be Learned

13

MICHAEL THEIL

Contents

Introduction

During the recent financial crisis, people who had up to that point invested in stocks and other financial products were caught shocked when they realized how quickly their money could be lost. Well meaning advisors, after the fact, told them that they should have known more about risk and how to deal with it. In this chapter, we will shed light on ways to deal with risks prudently, that is, in a manner by which a decision maker can survive economic losses.

Taking risks is one of the principal characteristics of enterprises. This concept is most valid for insurance companies whose main purpose is to assume risks that other economic entities do not wish to bear and whose principal factor of production is equalization of risks by forming a suitable portfolio of insured risks over time. These two characteristics make an insurance company a prototype risk bearer that other economic entities might use to learn the essentials of risk taking and use the information to their advantage.

In this chapter, we will first discuss the character of the insurance business. The difference between pure and speculative risks is an important starting point. Next, a discussion of the principles of insurance pricing will shed light on the cost drivers and mechanisms of insurance production. Because of the wide variability in the extent of risk transfer from an insured to an insurance company, common forms of insurance will be described. Knowing the motives for insurance regulation can demonstrate the importance of a well-working industry that benefits society and the economy on the one hand and the various reasons its functioning is threatened on the other hand. While it is safe to say that insurance markets usually serve their purpose under most circumstances, in certain situations such as compulsory insurance, legal interference is necessary. A discussion of the characteristics of ideally insurable risks not only shows which properties are essential, but also, and perhaps even more importantly, the problems that arise if these requirements are not met.

It is worth noting that all insurance companies are large institutional investors. Premiums for all lines of insurance are usually necessarily paid in advance. For that reason it is desirable for insurance companies to invest premium funds until they are required to pay claims. However, investment is not the core business of insurance. Moreover, since safety is an important target, insurance companies are not comparable to other investors. This chapter discusses what non-insurers can learn from the basics of the insurance business. The final section is devoted to concluding remarks and an outlook.

Basic Principles

Distribution of Risk

Insurance is a financial agreement that redistributes the costs of unexpected loss (Dorfman, 1994; Trowbridge, 1975). The insurer (insurance company) concludes contracts (risk transfers) with a large number of parties (insureds) and operates on the basis of the mathematical law of large numbers. This core technique aims at reducing variation, thus making expenses for compensation more calculable. Since insurance plays an important role in society, it operates under special laws that regulate access to the market, reporting, supervising and facilitating the business, for example, by allowing the building of reserves as other economic entities are allowed to do.

Insurance involves both pure and speculative risks. Pure risks present only a possibility of loss. The converse speculative risk may produce a gain or loss. The objection commonly raised against this distinction is that it has no definite zero point, that is, whether a result is considered a gain or loss may depend on a given situation. Thaler and Johnson (1990) found that gaining first and losing later during a visit to a casino is different from experiencing losses from the beginning of a gaming session, and both situations utilize different decision patterns.

Tversky and Kahneman (1981) elaborated a theoretical basis for this behavior and called it *framing*. For example, whether a glass is half full or half empty is a matter of view (frame). The prospect theory (Kahneman & Tversky, 1979) is built around the related concept of reference points that serve as a basis for the reasoning of a decision maker.

The insurance situation, however, is different (Theil, 2002). In the most basic case, both alternatives (paying a premium and bearing uncertain loss) are framed as negative deviations from a reference point. In other words, the analysis of insurance by distinguishing pure from speculative risks makes sense since there is general agreement on the position of the reference point.

Principles of Pricing

Risk transfer impacts insurance premiums. A premium consists of specific elements: (1) a net risk premium calculated on the basis of individual loss exposure, (2) a security loading to absorb variance, (3) a loading to cover costs that are not directly risk-related, (4) a profit margin, and (5) taxes.

Fair Premiums

An insurance premium is actuarially fair if based on individual expected loss. A premium calculated on this principle has advantages for insured and insurer, but it is not always feasible to develop actuarially fair premiums. The result may be over- or under-pricing relative to individual risk and the insurance pool may become less predictable (and consequentially more expensive if higher security loadings and reserves become necessary). Poor risk allocation (adverse selection) may even ruin insurance companies.

To explain the importance of an actuarially fair premium, the following example is widely used. Consider a market with two insurance companies and a large number of insurance buyers. Company A charges premiums based on individual expected loss. Company B charges an average premium based on collective expected loss. Let us assume that at the beginning, policyholders are randomly and evenly distributed between the two companies. At the end of each period, contracts must be renewed. Insurance buyers thinking that they pay more than their individually fair premium will switch to Company A. Since all A's insurance contracts are calculated on the basis of individual loss exposure (the company's portfolio is called structurally neutral), A is not negatively affected by the switch. Company B is affected because its remaining policyholders have relatively high loss expectations, forcing B to raise premiums to the new average. This procedure repeats itself at the end of each period. Ultimately Company B will leave the market or go bankrupt.

Taking the individual expected loss as a starting point for premium calculation has the additional merit that it can induce risk-reducing or risk-avoiding behavior on the part of the buyer. In fact, as a starting point of risk management, insurance companies rewarded the implementation of risk reduction or risk avoidance measures of policyholders by reducing premiums. It is obvious that such incentives work best when pricing is a matter of individual expected risk.

Another possibility to induce risk avoidance or reduction and reduce premiums is to cut off loss distribution at its lower end by agreeing upon deductibles. In practice, that means insureds pay their smaller losses. This technique again requires calculation of premiums on the basis of individual expected risk.

On the other hand, a complete transfer of risk from insured to insurance company is widely suspected to generate additional risk, usually referred to as "moral risk" that implies that a policyholder has a higher expected risk when he carries insurance against it. Although little empirical evidence indicates this interrelation, insurance companies try to counter such effect by including deductibles in their insurance agreements. It should be noted that this concept also applies to reinsurance contracts concluded between reinsurers and primary insurers, where (unlike other insurance contracts) both parties are highly knowledgeable about risk and risk transfer.

Security Loading

Security loading is intended to provide for the variations of losses inevitable in every portfolio. It can be shown (Karten, 1991) that without security loading, an insurance company will go bankrupt. The reason for this lies in so-called long tail risks that have very small probabilities and very high loss potentials. Security loadings can be replaced by reserves. A new insurance company would require higher security loadings than an insurance company that already has sufficient reserves.

Forms of Insurance

Different forms of insurance are often developed because full insurance (complete transfer of risk to insurer) is unfeasible. One reason is that complete transfer may result in unintended consequences. Another is that premiums for full transfers are often prohibitively high. Therefore, the parties try to find a more suitable solution. Different forms of insurance vary the amounts of risk transfer and risk premium as a solution to the problem.

Full insurance—As noted, full insurance means a complete transfer of a risk to an insurer. A contract can include deductibles that limit the insurer's liability for low and moderate size risks. The result of deductibles, of course, is not a complete risk transfer.

Limited transfer of risk—By setting a maximum sum insured, risk transfer is modified at its upper limit, that is, for large, improbable risks. Basically, the two common forms are used. The first is agreement on a specific sum of money for indemnification. No matter how large a loss actually is, the insurance company will pay only the specific sum in compensation. Settlement of damages is easy and therefore economical, resulting in a reduction in premium. The second type of contract compares an incurred loss to the sum insured and indemnification is calculated proportionally.

Regulation

To guarantee that insurance companies can deliver their services consistently over very long periods and protect consumers, insurance markets are highly regulated (Dorfman, 1994). In practice, companies must meet special requirements before starting an insurance business. After licensing, they must submit reports containing more information than required from other types of businesses. In case of problems, insurance authorities may close an insurance company or, because cessation is not necessarily in the interests of the insureds, the authorities may continue a business. To prevent malpractice, consumer protection organizations and state authorities may initiate class actions—a situation not typical for other businesses.

Compulsory Insurance

Society has many reasons to have certain risks insured (Dorfman, 1994). Legislation requires insurance for some activities. A widespread example is liability insurance for drivers of automobiles. We might ask why drivers do not purchase insurance voluntarily (Theil, 2002). Eisenführ and Weber (2003) provide a number of reasons for legislation to require this action. First, many drivers overestimate their abilities. In short, they admit that driving a car has a risk but other drivers are more prone to these risks. This behavior has been termed "illusion of control" and "overconfidence bias" and is widespread and stable. Second, car accidents may involve immediate and consequential damages. The former may be obvious; the latter are systematically underestimated and usually more serious. The reason may be a mental mechanism that removes indirect consequences from further consideration.

Both dynamics are common and consistent, and it is practically impossible to overcome them. In fact, evidence indicates that they may be reduced but only to a very small extent and for a very limited of time. Both factors are believed to be reasons for market failure in the field of insurance.

Ideal Insurable Risks

To insure a specific risk, certain characteristics must be determined. Several compilations of relevant properties have been developed (Berliner, 1982). Since this section is about explaining the basic principles of risks and not about how to insure them, a simple treatment will suffice. Therefore, we will limit our discussion to the five important factors of chance, independence, estimation, concreteness, and size. Related requirements are never fully met. Instead, insurers have to decide to what extent deviations are tolerable. In the next section, we discuss reasonable levels of tolerance for non-insurers.

Chance Events

To be insurable, risks must be driven by chance rather than deliberately. This means that neither contracting party is in a position to make a loss happen or to rule it out completely. If one party can influence risk, it acquires an unfair advantage over the other party. Real chance events are rare. In fact, they exist in very specific and ideal settings only, for example, tossing a coin or playing dice or roulette (in a fair way, we have to add). Absolute chance is not a requirement for being insurable. Rather, it is sufficient that neither of the two contract parties can cause a loss to occur or influence the characteristics of a loss. For example, certain forms of life insurance pay in case of the death of an insured—a certainty for mortal humans. Uncertainty about the time of death is sufficient to satisfy the chance requirement.

In some situations, an incident is uncertain and loss size is certain. Deficiencies in which chance is lacking are usually dealt with by individual insurance contracts, insurance contract law, or insurance company regulators. However, imperfections remain, for example, when one party has much more information about the risk insured and conceals the information from the other party (asymmetric information) or in cases of insurance fraud.

Independent Events

Clearly, matters become much more contrived if risks are not independent of each other. We may think of a disease that spreads; one incident (a person catches the disease) increases the probability of additional incidents so that other people are more likely to contract the disease. Another example is when one incident affects several insured entities, for instance, several vehicles insured by a single insurer are ruined during a hailstorm. In both cases, the probability distribution of one loss is not independent from those of other losses. In other words, neither loss size nor loss probability or both of a single risk insured are independent from other risks.

Violation of independence constitutes a dangerous situation that allows losses to spread almost without limit. Measures that can be taken are separation, for instance, to isolate certain groups or risks such as ill persons, allowing multiple insurers in a market, and modifying insurance mechanics.

Estimation of Probabilities and Loss Sizes

From the view of an insurer, risk estimation is necessary to ascertain whether a specific risk fits its pool of written risks and also to determine the premium. On the other hand, the decision to insure against a particular risk or pursue another measure depends on estimated likeliness and loss size. Point estimates and whole probability distributions would be desirable.*

These estimations are, of course, difficult and also subject to a number of errors and biases (Theil, 2003). The situation is somewhat easier for an insurer because it has data, availability of risk pools, and advice from reinsurers and thus can afford analysis of lesser known risks.

---

* Point estimates refer to a single loss size and its related probability. Probability distributions describe a whole range of loss sizes.

Concreteness

Concreteness determines whether a risk is specific or general. One of the most important functions of an insurance contract is to define the transferred risk sufficiently. To serve this purpose, the parties can agree about the qualities of a risk (types of losses, exclusions, and other factors and the quantities (deductibles and limits). Although not completely ruled out in theory, insurers are reluctant to write policies that appear too general. This makes some risks practically uninsurable; the most popular example is entrepreneurial risk.

Size

Since the capacity of an insurance company (capital and/or its ability to find reinsurance) is limited, it can write risks only to a particular extent. If size is exceeded, the insurance company may suffer a technical loss or even become insolvent. Even if capacity would allow insurance of a large specific risk, the resulting high variation in expected claims hinders effective risk balancing and the company should reject the proposed contract. In essence, this is the mirror image of the most important motive of an insured for purchasing insurance. Some risks are simply too extreme to bear, making risk transfer desirable if not necessary. Insurance companies have access to the reinsurance market, giving them a method for dealing with problems of risk size.

Lessons to Learn from Insurance

Risk Management

Today, the term *risk management* is widely used in the financial sector to describe techniques to deal with financial risks. Originally, the purpose of risk management was significantly different (Mehr & Hedges, 1963, 1974). It was introduced as a concept of lowering insurance premiums by lowering risk and focused on pure risks. Risk management is intended to eliminate, reduce, or transfer exposure to risk. Insurance is the standard for transferring risk exposure. Elimination and reduction can then be implemented in combination. The most important feature of risk management is its original focus on pure risks.

Much later, the risk management concept was extended to speculative risks. At first glance, this appears attractive. A vast number of instruments to analyze and manage risks seemed ready to be utilized in the world of speculative risks. It should be noted (Theil, 1995) that even in the second decade of the twentieth century, a similar model was developed in the German scientific literature (*Risikopolitik* or risk politics). This theory proposed that an enterprise can be managed from the perspective of risk by avoiding the most dangerous exposures and finding entrepreneurial success in taking the most suitable risks. However, this approach never proved sufficiently applicable in practice.

In a similar manner, widening risk management to speculative risks also creates extensive problems. Risk management is widely used in dealing with financial risks measured by money standards and implementing financial measures. In this regard, two main concerns must be mentioned. It has been already proven difficult to reasonably apply risk management techniques to pure risks. A widespread problem, for example, is that some risks are easy to analyze because they can be measured by money. Other risks such as loss of life, disease, and damage to good will tend to be very difficult to analyze and thus become inappropriately measured or even neglected.

A similar problem involves comparing risks for which we have good statistical knowledge and those for which knowledge and insight are lacking. Moreover, since many risks have to be dealt with simultaneously, the complexity soon becomes overwhelming. Finally, even though we still do not completely understand the phenomenon, there appear to be profound differences in perception and as a result the handling of pure versus speculative risks. The major problem is that the implementation of risk management as a management tool creates the impression that all possible risks are controllable. That is certainly never true, and the misconception becomes more dramatic if risk management is extended to speculative risk.

Risk Communication

Risk management was first intended for relatively large companies that could afford to build sufficiently large knowledge bases. Smaller businesses and households depend upon advice from others. Even with the best of intentions, risk advice is not easy to give. Even with a limitation of pure risk, communication is impeded by many errors and biases (Eisenführ & Weber 2003).

This fact is well known in insurance theory and practice, and it is naïve to think that these problems simply vanish when the focus is broadened. To the contrary, since complexity and incompatibility issues grow in size, the related problems grow in importance. Financial risk management has now gone one step backward in that it concentrates on financial risks and financial measures. The core problems remain:

Complexity, is likely to be reduced since the focus lies on a reduced number of risks.

Risks may even increase, since the area is dominated by money as the standard measure, which leads to neglecting risks that are difficult and not measurable in money.

Differences in perception of positive versus negative developments.

A brief look into how people deal with risk reveals that some kinds of risk are routinely neglected or underestimated. As noted above, this is one of the core reasons for compulsory insurance, that is, forcing people procure insurance is intended to protect them and others against severe financial consequences of loss. Conversely, non-experts may freely buy financial products that may involve financial consequences including the total loss of capital. This means legislators place responsibility on those who buy such products; he who buys such products must also bear possible negative consequences.

Since taking this responsibility is difficult, consumers demand more protection and more information. This approach is naïve since evidence indicates it will not serve its intended purpose. For instance, Tversky and Kahneman (1981) argue that decision makers make simplified comparisons of alternatives, so-called minimal accounts, to reduce cognitive strain. Decision makers follow especially radical ways of simplification in situations where their expertise is limited (Hogarth & Kunreuther, 1997, Kool et al., 2010, Croy, Gerrans & Speelman, 2010). Risk communication therefore has significant limitations that cannot be ignored.

Risk Transfer

Insurance transfers risk from an insured to an insurance company. We have seen above that this transfer is not necessarily complete; risk transfer is limited in many situations. However, the largest fraction of risk is transferred by insurance. Other financial agreements also involve some risk transfer, but the transfer is not the core element and the most important reason to have the agreements. If a person is granted a loan by a bank, part of the risk that the loan taker becomes insolvent is transferred to the bank. Similarly, if someone buys shares in a company, part of the risk of company bankruptcy is transferred to the buyer. Note that the direction of risk transfer depends on the nature of the financial agreement.

Pricing

The core element of an insurance premium is the individual expected loss. In a situation with speculative rather than pure risks, what would be the analogue? It is difficult answer this question. Much empirical evidence has been found that positive and negative deviations from a reference point (gains and losses) are perceived asymmetrically. This situation is well described by the value function of prospect theory in which gains are weighed less than losses (Kahneman & Tversky, 1979). In addition, Tversky and Kahneman (1992) also propose that the decision weights derived from the probabilities of outcomes differ depending on whether the outcome is a gain or loss. Others (Einhorn & Hogarth, 1987; Thaler, 1985) extended these findings to more realistic situations with indistinct probabilities and simultaneous gains and losses.

In summary, their results agree in that reference dependence is the crucial factor for assessment, that is, the way loss is seen in comparison to gain depends on the given situation and thus the view may vary. Thus, both individual and general standards for putting gains and losses in relation to each other are lacking. These concerns are not critical if one stays in the sphere of only gains or only losses, thus making pure risks (those with only loss potential) more simple to perceive than speculative risks (those with loss and gain potential). Apart from the statistical foundation discussed below, finding an appropriate price for insurance is considerably easier.

However, pricing of financial products is handled differently, mainly through interest risk sharing and fees (Geneva Association, 2010). To present some examples, a borrower is responsible for repaying the credit and related interest; in addition he has to pay to present some examples: a borrower is responsible to pay back the credit and related interest; in addition, he has to pay fees; an investor participates in the risks the company of which he buys shares; intermediaries of this contract claim fees. Part of this is risk related; for instance, a (small) part of the interest claimed, or fees that are proportional to risk. Below we will discuss whether being risk-related in this respect means the same as in the context of insurance. Considering the distinction between pure and speculative risks, we already know that there must be a difference. Concerning other properties of risk, we will analyse risk from the perspective of the characteristics of ideally insurable risks.

Insurance Companies

The main competence and, therefore, the main reason for existence of insurance companies is their unique capability of dealing with risks other economic entities are unable or barely able to handle. In particular, the core techniques that insurance companies employ to manage risk are risk selection, risk pooling, building of reserves, and further transfer of risk.

Non-insurers consist mainly of companies, organizations, and consumers that engage in activities other than insurance and thus do not have insurance data at their disposal. As a straightforward consequence, their ability to deal with risk is expected to be systematically weaker than the abilities of insurance companies. Very large organizations may come close to a situation that allowed them to exploit the mathematical law of large numbers. For instance, their sales may be large enough to produce sufficient cash flow to cover compensation required by warranties, but even the largest companies most probably do not utilize such arrangements to cover product liability.

However, non-insurers of any size cannot organize risk pooling as insurance companies do (Mugler, 1979). Smaller organisations, companies, households, and consumers fall far short of such capabilities and thus cannot balance risks in their own portfolios. To the contrary, they may be overburdened by having to deal with risk in a reasonable way.

Chance Events

We may assume some financial risks have chance properties if we look at the contracting parties' abilities to influence future developments, although in some cases it is hard to speak of chance events. Consider a small investment in a large company. The investor will have no influence on the company's business and usually receives limited information about its activities. The position of the company's administration is that it makes the decisions that influence future events and apart from publicly available information, only the company has internal information at its disposal.

If one cannot speak of chance events from the perspective of the parties involved in business, dealing with risk becomes much more contrived. The availability of risk information to only one party becomes decisive, resulting in a one-sided situation. Ex post, it may result in court action (when one party claims that relevant information was concealed by the other party). Ex ante, one of the standard measures of legislation is to demand the disclosure of all relevant information. Even if this information was properly understood, which we may reasonably doubt, it is subject to significant errors and biases.

Apart from differences in availability of information, Thaler and Johnson (1990) found that whose money is involved also makes a difference. They analyzed situations in which decision makers used their own and other people's money. When the decision makers' own money was at stake, their decisions were more prudent and less risky, contrary to a situation when they used other people's money. We may take that as an indication of the lack of chance events and the fact that influence is exercised asymmetrically.

Independent Events

Concerning independence, we noted above that it is difficult to determine whether risks are independent. This problem is more pronounced for insurers because they pool risks, but it is also a problem for non-insurers. Consider a fire spreading in your neighborhood or an avalanche or a mudslide destroying a community. Insurers can take several measures to reduce if not eliminate this problem.

First and foremost, insurers are experts in the field of risk. They systematically gather information about risks in general and about risks in their portfolios in particular. General risk information may be available to other economic entities as well. Portfolio risk information is definitely not available. In addition, insurers can limit their liabilities based on the nature of an event. For example, an insurer can exclude natural disasters, cover only events within a specific period, or limit the amount of compensation (setting limits of coverage, implementing deductibles). All of these limitations are included in insurance contracts that put the insurer in a more powerful position than the insured. From a technical view, the risk is transferred only in part; in most cases only a small fraction of the risk remains with the insured.

Insurers can also transfer all or most of the dangerous segments of risks through reinsurance contracts. The reinsurance market is exclusively accessible to insurers; other economic entities do not have such instruments at their disposal.

If risk is not independent, and if we lack the required instruments, risk tends to become unmanageable quickly. A review of the internal operations of an economic entity may reveal that the lack of independence of risks may imply that many of its risks produce losses that usually exceed its financial capabilities. Furthermore, lack of independence may result in indirect losses in addition to direct loss. Such cause–consequence-chains are extremely difficult to analyze; moreover, it is practically impossible to make adequate provisions against such losses. This leads to the conclusion that risk is only measurable in isolated systems (Haller 1975). We learned from the recent financial crisis that risks are not independent, and the crisis arose from multiple risk failures (Geneva Association, 2010). The ACCE Working Group assigned to study the credit crisis noted several factors that contributed to it:

Credit risk—The tail risk of default was underestimated although dealing with long tail risks would be the core competence of insurance companies. This error was magnified by multiple repacking and leveraging involved in the structured credit markets and by the assignment of overly optimistic ratings by credit rating agencies.

Liquidity and maturity risk—Contrary to widespread assumptions, markets became illiquid. Assets are difficult to value without liquid markets. Insurance companies maintain liquidity through adequate premium calculation and adequate reserves; insurance in an assessment system can even work on a balance of in- and out-payments.

Counterparty risk—The perception of counterparty risk has risen
sharply and raised concerns about the massive credit default swap*
markets. We can safely assume that we will find behind the misper-
ception the same errors and biases inherent to pure risk perception;
to counter such problems, insurance companies must do business on
a sound statistical basis.

Market, systemic, and concentration risks—These risks were underestimated and shown to be correlated. Insurance companies can
reinsure parts of their written risks by constantly controlling for
cumulative risks.

Correlation risk and volatility—Past assumptions about correlations
have been rendered useless, at the same time price volatility acts
countercyclically.

Reputational, legal and operational risk—The use of off-balance sheet
conduits and structured investment vehicles exposes banks to reputational and legal problems arising from their implicit and explicit
commitments.

Warehousing or pipeline risk—The possibility of using financial institutions for on-selling exposures suddenly stopped. This is roughly
equivalent to a situation where no reinsurance is available. Usually,
reinsurance leaves some risk with an insurance company, so that business is necessarily done prudently.

Enterprise risk—Explosive growth of complex financial instruments
made large, complex financial institutions too big to fail. For a number of reasons, such growth rates are unusual in the insurance field.

These intertwined effects intensified the problems that would also have
been severe in isolation. If we want to learn from insurance, separation of
risks is the alternative.

Estimation of Probabilities and Loss Sizes

Estimation of both loss probabilities and loss sizes is subject to a number of
problems. Intense research on this topic has shown that both lay people and
experts are prone to error and to bias (Theil, 2003).

The asymmetrical natures of many loss distributions further aggravate
this problem. A loss distribution usually shows what is called "a long tail"—
we have small and medium size losses to expect and very few very large ones.
If distributions were symmetric, we could hope that errors and biases would

---

* The purpose of CDR is to transfer and transform risks of credit defaults.

be relatively evenly distributed around a mean value, thus balancing our miscalculations. This, however, is not the case, and the danger of very large, very rare events puts an entire economic entity at risk.

An insurer's situation is more favorable; it has considerably more loss experience than other businesses and can determine the extent of loss it will assume for an insured. The insurer, however, faces additional risk stemming from taking over and pooling loss distributions. The risk can be broken down into three parts (1) the residual risk of chance that is inevitably a part of any loss distribution; (2) the risk of error related to the decisive characteristics of the loss distribution (risk causes and consequences); and (3) causes and consequences that were determined correctly and changed over the duration of a contract.

To counter these technical risks of insurance, an insurer can conduct research to learn more about risk. Some parts of risk, however, will always remain, making security loadings and reserves inevitable. Without such measures, the probability of insurer bankruptcy would be almost certain. The building of reserves and more strict provisions of capital use are set by legal systems exclusively for insurance companies to make their survival likely.

Economic entities must be large enough and specialized enough to have sufficient risk expertise. Insurers turn to reinsurance companies to acquire more knowledge about risks. Bearing this in mind, it is naïve to think that other economic entities would be capable of judging financial risks properly.

Concreteness

Since concreteness is determined in an insurance contract, the insurer has considerable advantage. We noted above that entrepreneurial risk is usually not insurable, which brings us to the difference between *pure* and *speculative* risks. Pure risk assumes some loss probability; speculative risk involves a chance of gain or loss. The difference may appear arbitrary. Nevertheless, insurance law usually rules out gains from insured losses, thus making the point that the motive for and utility of insurance is safety, not monetary gain for the insured.

In cases of speculative risk, these things are more contrived from a perceptual view, as discussed above. Putting this aspect aside and focusing only on the influence that the parties can exercise on contract design and provisions, we can expect that less knowledgeable economic entities face substantial disadvantages. This is one of the most important reasons insurance brokers are widely seen as intermediaries and must fulfill certain obligations to inform insurance buyers. The "best advice" principle also constitutes legal responsibility for insurance brokers, an obligation not imposed in other businesses.

Size

The role of size is essentially the same for insurers as it is for non-insurers. Size makes a difference to an economic entity, and the difference is crucial. Insurance companies usually are large. As a result, their risk bearing capacities are usually greater than those of many other economic entities.

Many very large non-insurance companies also have considerable risk-bearing capabilities. However, even if they engage in risk balancing procedures as insurance companies do, they still lack the ability to build technical reserves and have no access to the reinsurance market to further transfer risks. Haller (1975) puts considerations of risk size in perspective: a risk that endangers survival of an individual or an organisation must be avoided since there is no reasonable way to deal with such risk.

Conclusions

To deal with risk successfully, it is necessary to have unbiased data and know the size of the economic entity. In this context, developing a foundation for decision making for a risk management situation should be based on the ability to distinguish successes that occur by chance from those that result from willful acts. Such a policy should succeed. In case of an extreme event, an economic entity should survive if it has effective risk management, and smaller losses should not force it to change its plans dramatically. We learned that judgment of risk is subject to a number of errors and biases and knowledge of risk requires expertise. Therefore, acquiring unbiased knowledge is definitely a major undertaking. Finally, size plays an important role in protecting resources and balancing risks.

A further complication is that these issues are interrelated. Size alone is no advantage if judgment of risk is biased—the larger the size, larger the problem. Insurance companies can utilize unique techniques and measures. No other business field has the core capabilities of risk pooling and balancing, combined with specific possibilities for building reserves. Only insurers have access to the reinsurance market. In addition, the market power of insurance companies is often so great that they can refuse to cover risks that do not seem to fit their portfolios.

While we can learn from insurance companies, it is not feasible to attempt to replicate their ability to deal with risk. Attempting to imitate their roles as investors is also not advisable. One reason is that insurance companies follow a specific structure with security at the top and this is not common for other economic entities. In addition, insurance companies are not known for their success in other economic areas. In fact, if insurance companies fail, which rarely happens, the reason for failure is generally the result of risky investment decisions, not because of their insuring risks.

American International Group (AIG), one of the largest primary insurers in the world, is an example. Very large companies may be able to pool and balance (presumably rather) small parts of their risks. That is, they may be able to acquire sufficient knowledge about the risks and aggregate an adequate number of comparable risks. However, because they cannot build adequate reserves and transfer the risks to reinsurance companies—two measures that are used to reduce insurance technical risk—a comparatively higher level of risk will remain.

Similarly to insurance companies, very large companies may exert considerable market power, allowing them to avoid certain risks entirely or at least in part. The analysis of insurance companies reveals that pure and speculative risks are perceived and treated differently. Therefore, a promising approach is to split risks into pure and speculative parts and treat them separately. In practice, such division of risk is mostly undertaken when negotiating contracts. In such negotiations, market power is certainly helpful.

In many other respects, large companies remain vulnerable. Even implementation of a risk management system, does not necessarily imply that they will achieve a lower level of exposure. Their risk identification and assessment can still be subject to errors and biases. The complexity of large entities adds to the problem instead of reducing it. Unlike smaller economic entities, decisions in large companies are made by groups rather than individuals. There are indications that group decisions may be more risky than individual decisions. Moreover, in the modern world, shareholders' desires for profit are very pronounced. This pressure may lead management to take greater risks and refrain from implementing costly risk assessment mechanisms that could reduce profits.

This kind of thinking may be aggravated by myopia, since large companies present reports of their economic standing at least yearly and usually quarterly. Long tail risks usually have longer time horizons.

As we have seen recently, size can be helpful when companies become "too big to fail." That means that the costs of their risky investments and other activities that turned sour were transferred to other companies or to taxpayers. The recent case of Ireland shows how such developments may spread (*Economist*, 2010): Irish banks that suffered mainly from bad loans were supported by the Irish government and consequently by the Irish taxpayers. The burden proved too high, making it necessary for Ireland to be covered by an "international umbrella." As a result, large parts of the original risks taken by Irish banks have been spread to taxpayers all over Europe.

Small economic entities (small businesses and households) remain at the low end of the risk scale based on their abilities to deal with risk. They lack sufficient expertise to deal with risks and do not have sufficient market power to eliminate risks via contract negotiations. At the same time, considerable risk is shifted to these groups. One might recall, for instance, the opting out of the state pension system during the Thatcher administration in England (Schulz, 2000). Privately run pension funds do not necessarily fare better for those entitled to pensions in the future. Funds may go bankrupt, thus ruining the expectations of income for those who retire under the system. Similar considerations apply for comparable constructs.

For a catastrophic risk—one that is likely to endanger the ongoing existence of an economic entity—Matthias Haller (1975) developed a clear strategy, essentially an imperative to avoid such risks but risk avoidance is not that easy, as we have seen. It is unclear whether people who may be affected by catastrophic risk are able to identify these risks as catastrophic. There are many reasons to believe that they cannot do so. In addition, the conflict between myopic shareholders and long-sighted risk managers should lead individuals to choose safe means and opt against profits in the short run.

References

Berliner, B. (1982). *Limits of Insurability of Risks*. Prentice Hall, Englewood Cliffs, NJ.

Croy, G., Gerrans, P. & Speelman, C. (2010). The role and relevance of domain knowledge, perceptions of planning importance, and risk tolerance in predicting savings intentions. *Journal of Economic Psychology*, 31, 860–871.

Dorfman, M. (1994). *Introduction to Risk Management and Insurance*. 5th ed. Prentice Hall, Englewood Cliffs NJ.

Economist. (2010). Ireland's woes are largely of its own but German bungling has made matters worse. 397, 12.

Einhorn, H. & Hogarth, R, (1987). Decision making under ambiguity. In Hogarth, R. & Reder, M. (Eds.). *Rational Choice: The Contrast between Economics and Psychology*. Chicago, 41–66.

Eisenführ, F. & Weber, M. (2003). *Rationales Entscheiden*. Berlin.

Geneva Association, ACCE Working Group on Credit Crisis. (2010). The global crisis: how could it happen? *Geneva Reports: Risk and Insurance Research*, 3: 21–43.

Haller, M. (1975). *Sicherheit durch Versicherung?* Bern.

Hogarth, R. & Kunreuther, H. (1997). Decision making under ignorance: arguing with yourself. In Goldstein, W. & Hogarth, R. (Eds.). *Research on Judgment and Decision Making: Currents, Connections, and Controversies*. Cambridge, 482–508.

Kahneman, D. & Tversky, A. (1979). Prospect theory: an analysis of decision under risk. *Econometrica* 47, 263–291.

Karten, W. (1991). Das Einzelrisiko und seine Kalkulation. In Gross, W., Müller-Lutz, H.L. & Schmidt, R. (Eds.). *Versicherungsenzyklopädie*, Band 2, 4. Aufl., Gabler, Wiesbaden, 199–221.

Kool, W. , McGuire, J., Rosen, Z. & Botvinivk, M. (2010). Decision making and the avoidance of cognitive demand. *Journal of Experimental Psychology*, 139, 665–682.

Mehr, R. & Hedges, B. (1963). *Risk Management in the Business Enterprise.* Homewood, IL.

Mehr, R. & Hedges, B. (1974). *Risk Management: Concepts and Applications.* Homewood, IL.

Mugler, J. (1979). *Risk Management in der Unternehmung.* Wien.

Schulz, J. (2000). The risks of pension privatization in Britain. *Challenge,* 43, 93–104.

Thaler, R. (1985). Mental accounting and consumer choice. *Marketing Science,* 4, 199–214.

Thaler, R. & Johnson, E. (1990). Gambling with the house money and trying to break even: the effects of prior outcomes on risky choice. *Management Science,* 26, 643–660.

Theil, M. (1995). *Risikomanagement für Informationssysteme.* Wien.

Theil, M. (2002). *Versicherungsentscheidungen und Prospect Theory. Die Risikoeinschätzung der Versicherungsnehmer als Entscheidungsgrundlage.* Wien.

Theil, M. (2003). The value of personal contact in marketing insurance: client judgments of representativeness and mental availability. *Risk Management and Insurance Review,* 6, 145–157.

Trowbridge, C. (1975). Insurance as a transfer mechanism. *Journal of Risk and Insurance,* 42, 1–15.

Tversky, A. & Kahneman, D. (1981). The framing of decisions and the psychology of choice. *Science,* 211, 453–458.

Tversky, A. & Kahneman, D. (1992). Advances in prospect theory: cumulative representation of uncertainty. *Journal of Risk and Uncertainty,* 5, 287–323.

Police Detectives and Investigative Reporters Working Hand in Hand against Organized Crime

14

BOJAN DOBOVŠEK AND MATIJA MASTNAK

Contents

Introduction

Because of swift technological advances, societal control mechanisms in the modern world are unable to deal with modern social pathology. The law is not the most efficient instrument to regulate the undesired conduct of a person or a society. Police and prosecutors alone cannot curb some forms of financial crime (organized crime and corruption). For example, experience shows that ordinary law enforcement agencies are ineffective in deterring corruption while investigative reporters are probably among those best placed to deal with it (Dobovšek & Mastnak, 2009).

Sometimes transnational organized crime—elite organized crime and crime networks—can also penetrate state institutions. Both economic and political sectors become dependent on organized crime (Dobovšek, 2008). As investigative journalism is an extraordinarily informal mechanism of control that deals with deviancy and deviants and oversees state mechanisms of control, government, and politics (watchdog activities) (Pečar, 1994), it can disclose the criminal and corrupt activities of criminal networks. Therefore in good investigative journalism, a reporter or media house must conduct an independent investigation, free from of influence of state institutions (Bešker, 2004).

Investigative reporting is characteristically limited to democratic societies (more so, than other types of journalism). With the democratization of political systems it is possible to pursue a special journalistic investigation method called investigative reporting (Košir, 1995). Democracy is founded on a number of principles, including the accountability of elected representatives and civil servants to the people. Ideally, many mechanisms should guarantee this, but even the best systems may be abused. Experience shows that when wrongdoing does take place, investigative journalists are among those best placed to expose it, and to ensure that justice is done (Knight, 2001). Investigative reporting is therefore, or at least should be, the final safety net to catch the societal anomalies that elude formal controls by the police, the legal system, and other government entities.

Investigative Reporting and Criminal Investigation

The first task of the investigative reporter is to uncover concealed information. Combining several definitions (Dobovšek & Mastnak, 2009; Gaines, 1994; Šuen, 1994; Benjaminson & Anderson, 1990; Ullmann & Honeyman, 1983), we note the following characteristics of investigative reporting:

- It produces a story that is an original work of the reporter rather than a report on a public agency's investigation.
- It reveals facts that some deliberately tried to conceal.
- Concealed facts are important to the public.
- Reporters or media investigate stories independently.
- Reporters use special methods.

The work done by investigative reporters is distinct from apparently similar work done by police, lawyers, and other regulatory bodies in that it is not limited in scope, legally restricted, or bound by public transparency (de Burgh, 2000). On the other hand, investigative reporters can and do use methods and techniques similar to those used in formal crime investigations. Further similarities between investigative reporting and police work relate to planning investigations (Dobovšek & Mastnak, 2009).

When a reporter receives a tip, his first task is to check it. Before any real investigation is started, an investigative reporter or a detective must conduct a preliminary investigation. Of course, the preliminary investigation of a reporter is not the same as that conducted by a detective. While the preliminary investigation of an investigative journalist starts by evaluating an object of investigation to eliminate obvious mistakes* (Obad, 2004), a preliminary criminal investigation involves three sets of tasks—coordination, evidence collection, and other investigative activities; Brandl (2004). A journalistic investigation is concluded when the reporter has collected enough facts to answer the same seven basic questions that guide criminal investigations: Who? What? When? Where? Why? How? With what? (Šuen, 1994; Žerjav, 1994).

Investigative methods are more strictly defined in criminal investigations than in investigations undertaken by reporters. Therefore, to draw a clear line between criminal investigation and reporting investigation, the methods of investigative reporting should be precisely identified.

It is somewhat paradoxical that while the investigative reporters are not authorized by the law to investigate and are thus limited in some ways, they have more freedom to operate. Due to this paradox, it our thesis is that a journalistic investigation starts when a criminal investigation has stalled. If this thesis is correct, we can ask ourselves what forms do cooperation between reporters and police and other law enforcement officials take. We would also like to point out that investigative reporters will be effective in conducting investigations only if they are sufficiently qualified and skilled.

Methods

A pilot study included five in-depth interviews with investigative reporters and five with police detectives. All interviews were conducted in person in August 2010 at locations chosen by the interviewees. Each interview lasted thirty to forty-five minutes and was recorded on tape.

The investigative reporters interviewed work for different media. The first respondent works for public television, the second for POP TV (highest share of viewers in Slovenia), the third works for the daily *Delo* newspaper (second highest daily circulation in Slovenia), the fourth works for the daily *Dnevnik* newspaper (third highest daily circulation), and the fifth works for the weekly *Mladina* magazine. Two of the police detectives interviewed work on financial crimes, the third is assigned to organized crime, the fourth to property crime, and the fifth is in the section for special techniques.

This research focused on interactions between reporters and police officers and on the methods, techniques, and working processes of investigative reporters and police detectives. Collected data were analyzed by an interpretative method.

---

* This is a basic examination that at times can be conducted by obtaining information at a library.

Results

State of Development of Investigative Reporting in Slovenia

Research question—In your opinion, how developed is investigative reporting in Slovenia?

The consensus among the investigative reporters was that investigative reporting in Slovenia is poorly developed. One respondent said that investigative reporting in Slovenia was not the same as investigative reporting known in western countries. "In the best case, we have disclosure journalism, which has some elements of investigative reporting, but that kind of journalism cannot be qualified as investigative reporting. Investigative reporters do not have enough resources for proper journalistic research. They especially do not have enough time. The main reason for this situation is the fact that all media in Slovenia are in a bad economic situation."

Two reporters emphasized the false impression that indicates how a lot of investigative reporting is conducted. One interviewee said, "A lot of stories published in newspapers or broadcasted on television seem investigative, but in reality most of these stories were served by political parties."

Conversely, four police detectives were convinced that investigative reporting is well developed in Slovenia. Two respondents said that investigative journalism was "in full swing in recent years." One detective answered, that there was no investigative reporting in Slovenia. "It is a pity, that we do not have investigative reporting. Some journalists represent themselves as investigative reporters, but I think they are not. At least in the way they should be. Our investigative reporting has too many similarities with yellow papers." Detailed analysis shows that other detectives understand investigative reporting only in the context of tabloids.

All police detectives said that investigative reporting is needed and mentioned different reasons. One common reply was that investigative reporting is needed because otherwise "filthinesses" would remain hidden. We noticed one particularly interesting answer: "Because of the very high standards of evidence in our courts, many criminals avoid conviction. And the only way for justice to be served, is to expose his or her conduct in public."

Methods, Techniques, and Working Processes of Investigative Reporters and Police Detectives

Research question—What methods do you use?

The answers cover methods, techniques, and components of the working process of investigative reporters and police detectives. We analyzed their answers and compiled them into working process trees for both groups. As shown in Figure 14.1, many similarities between journalistic and criminal investigations are apparent.

Both processes start with acquiring information. Police detectives gather information in two ways: (1) as a result of their activities such as patrolling, and (2) after notification of an incident by informants, victims, state entities, or other parties. Journalists follow the same information gathering processes or on occasion encounter suspicious information while browsing databases (their own activities) or sometimes receive tips, for example, from police detectives or other sources.

Before a "real" investigation gets started, information must be verified. An investigative reporter can verify information with an expert, or with informal contacts with police personnel, or other state employees (prosecutors, inspectors, etc.). Police detectives can verify information among other ways by observing suspects or engaging informants.

A follow-up investigation by a police detective at first glance does not have many similarities with a journalistic investigation. Reporters do not have statutory powers to carry out covert operations or interrogate suspects. However, interviews with politicians in front of a camera sometimes resemble interrogations. Both investigative reporters and police detectives utilize interviewing and both groups confirmed that interviewing is one of the most useful tools of an investigation.

Other differences also exist. For example, police detectives have the authority to arrest. A criminal investigation usually lasts longer than a journalistic investigation. A journalistic investigation can sometimes end by publishing compromising documents. For better understanding of the working process of the investigative reporter we include an excerpt from one of the interviews:

> When you are known as an objective investigative reporter tips are coming from all directions. First you have to pick up a tip, which can bring up relatively important information to the public. Then follows the verification of the tip with my informal contacts among the police detectives. It is better to verify with two different sources within police. These two sources must not know that you have contacts with both. Then follows an interview with the "target" (you publish that interview). After that, you have an interview with the opposite side. After that, another interview with the "target" follows. The public soon notices the questions he or she answered unconvincingly. It is then time for an editorial. After publishing an editorial, usually more whistleblowers get in touch with you. Possessing a document is always a bonus. But often there is a problem. By publishing certain documents you risk a disclosure of your source. Trust is all you have. You do not have the privilege to betray someone's trust, especially that of a police detective.

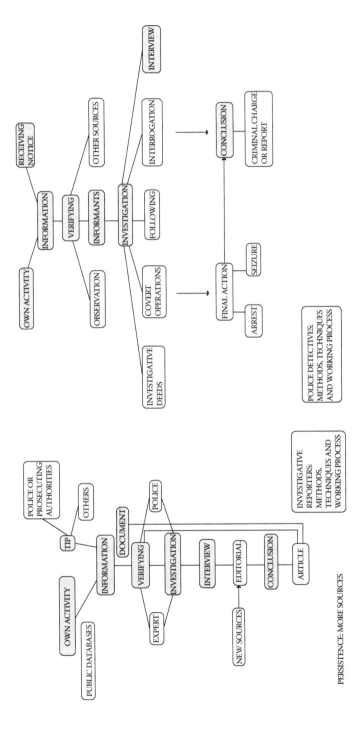

Figure 14.1 Investigation flowchart.

Interactions of Investigative Reporters and Police Detectives

Research question—Investigative reporters: How do you contact police detectives? Police detectives: Are you familiar with informal contacts between investigative reporters and police detectives? To research this topic effectively, many sub-questions were needed. Police detectives in Slovenia have no formal contacts with journalists. Police officially communicate with journalists only through public relations representatives.

All five journalist respondents said that this communication was very poor. One respondent said, "There is a complete media blockade in Slovenia. The only way to get familiar with certain issues is through informal contacts within police." All police detectives said they were aware of such informal contacts but did not utilize them. Police detectives warned us that any information about investigation given to a reporter without authorization constitutes a violation of the law. On the other hand, the investigative reporters taking part in the survey all claimed that there are no investigative reporters that do not have informal contacts with police detectives. The detectives and the reporters share the opinion that large numbers of informal contacts and whistleblowers exist among police officers (Figure 14.2).

The reasons police detectives are motivated to participate in such interactions are different from the reasons of investigative reporters. Investigative reporters usually have informal contacts with police detectives to get stories. Three journalist respondents said they used contacts mainly to verify information or to obtain confirmation of document authenticity.

The whistleblowers among police detectives can be divided into four groups. The first group is motivated by revenge and includes officers who angry, for example, for not getting promotions. The second group consists of detectives with high integrity that cannot tolerate wrongdoing; investigative reporters said that these whistleblowers are the most reliable sources. The third group is politically motivated; the fourth group consists of detectives who feel powerless. They are convinced that certain persons avoid

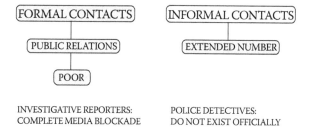

Figure 14.2 Contacts between police detectives and investigative reporters.

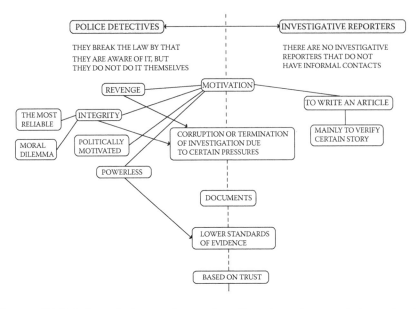

Figure 14.3 Informal interactions of police detectives and investigative reporters.

punishment due to improper laws. The only satisfaction they can get is informing the public about criminal behavior.

Whistleblowers from the first and the second groups betray information when they notice corruption within the police or when an investigation is terminated due to pressures from above. In these cases, police officers with integrity must deal with a moral dilemma and choose between giving information to the media (for which they are not authorized and thus break the law) and reporting irregularities (risking their jobs while knowing that their actions are futile). Long-term interactions between police detectives and investigative reporters are based on trust (Figure 14.3).

Similarities and Differences

> **Research question**—Police detectives: What are the advantages and what are the disadvantages of your investigation compared to a journalistic investigation? Investigative reporters: What are the advantages and disadvantages of your investigation compared to a criminal investigation?

Police detectives said that the statutory powers were their most important advantages over investigative reporters but also noted that these powers also represent their largest disadvantages. Their legal authorization to use such powers also brings strict supervision (Table 14.1).

Table 14.1   Comparison of Police and Reporter Investigations

	Police Detectives	Investigative Reporters
Advantages	Statutory powers	Lower standards of evidence
		More trusting witnesses
		Quicker path to documentation
Disadvantages	Statutory powers	Statutory powers
	Less funding	Fewer resources (money, time, databases)
		Knowledge of law, criminalistic skills
View of aims	Same	Similar

Police detective respondents were convinced that investigative reporters had more money to use for conducting investigations. Respondent investigative reporters thought otherwise and believed they had fewer resources (money, time, databases). Another disadvantage of journalistic investigation according to the journalists is their lack of statutory powers. Four of them said they were not skilled in understanding the law.

The answers of the police detectives revealed certain advantages of journalistic investigations. Witnesses are often more trusting when talking to journalists and journalists sometimes have quicker paths to documents. One respondent said, "For example, for someone working for the Foreign Office wanting to reveal some documents compromising a superior official, it is a much quicker way to contact a journalist. Police detectives have to do everything legally. A journalist can often publish such documents the next day." One journalist also said that police detectives must find proof of crime whereas reporters are free to report on what they learn, even if it falls short of judicially recognized standards of proving illegality.

The police detectives said that investigative reporters had the same aims as the police. The investigative reporters were of the opinion that the aims of police detectives were "similar."

Conclusions

One of the main distinctions between criminal and journalistic investigation is that while investigative reporters lack statutory powers and are somewhat limited in their work, they have more freedom with which to conduct an investigation. It is also true that only government investigators must find proof of crime. Reporters are free to report on what they learn, even if it falls short of judicial proof standards. This latter distinction is probably even more important than the former as the investigative reporters can be also concerned with what is harmful to society (even though it may not be illegal).

Pilot study findings suggest that a journalistic investigation starts when a criminal investigation reaches a dead end. This is a speculative statement. To confirm this hypothesis, a further and broader survey among investigative reporters and police detectives is required. However we can reasonably believe that the number of informal contacts between investigative reporters and police detectives is considerable. One of the reasons, according to the claims of investigative reporters, is that formal contacts are very ineffective and the only way for the investigative reporters to learn about certain issues is through informal contacts with police.

Experience shows that ordinary law enforcement agencies are ineffective in deterring corruption and other complex forms of crime. Investigative reporters are probably among those best placed to deal with corruption, but the pilot study suggests that in Slovenia they are insufficiently qualified and skilled.

Another interesting topic for research would be the problem of funding for investigative reporting. Proper investigative journalism is expensive. Only a few media houses in the world are willing to provide resources for deep investigations. In Slovenia, the general belief is that public television should support investigative control on a larger scale, but that presents the danger of increasing the political influence of the news, which might then disseminate propaganda instead of objective information.

References

Benjaminson, P. & Anderson, D. (1990). *Investigative Reporting*, 2nd ed. Ames, Iowa State University Press.

Bešker, I. (2004). Osnovni pojmovi. In Bešker I. & Obad O. *Istraživačko novinarstvo*. Zagreb, Medijska Agencija HND.

Brandl, S.G. (2004). *Criminal Investigation: An Analytical Perspective*. Boston, Pearson.

de Burgh, H. (2000). *Investigative Journalism: Context and Practice*. London, Routledge.

Dobovšek, B. (2008). Economic organised crime networks in emerging democracies. *International Journal of Social Economics*, 35, 679–690.

Dobovšek, B. & Mastnak M. (2009). In Meško, G., Cockroft, T., Crawford, A. & Lemaître, A. (Eds.), *Crime, Media and Fear of Crime: Investigative Reporting versus Transnational Organised Crime*.

Gaines, W. (1994). *Investigative Reporting for Print and Broadcast*. Chicago, Nelson-Hall. http://www.rthk.org.hk/mediadigest/20020415_76_21467.html

Knight A. (2001). *Online Investigative Journalism*. *Ejournalist 1(1)*. Retrieved April 15 2010. http://ejournalist.com.au/vlnl/inv.pdf.

Košir, M. (1995). Istraživačko novinarstvo. *Medijska istraživanja: znanstveno-stručni časopis za novinarstvo i medije*, 1, 43–51.

Obad, O. (2004). Metode u istraživačkom novinarstvu. In Bešker I. & Obad O. (Eds.). *Istraživačko novinarstvo*. Zagreb, Medijska Agencija HND.

Pečar, J. (1994). Preiskovalnemu novinarstvu na rob. *Teorija in praksa*, 31, 859–863.

Šuen, M. (1994). *Preiskovalno novinarstvo*. Ljubljana, Fakulteta za družbene vede.

Ullmann J. & Honeyman S. (1983). *The Reporter's Handbook: An Investigator's Guide to Documents and Techniques.* New York, St. Martin's Press.

Žerjav, C. (1994). *Kriminalistika.* Ljubljana, Ministrstvo za notranje zadeve RS, Izobraževalni center.

Human Factors Analysis
How to Build Resilience against Financial Crimes

15

CHRISTIAN FELSENREICH

Contents

Introduction

The financial markets changed dramatically, not only in the years of the so-called financial crisis that started in 2007, but in the ongoing liberalization of the markets over past decades. One example is restoration of speculation tools after lifting of a ban arising from the 1919 crisis along with globalization and technical innovations that put the entire system in a very vulnerable situation. The magnitude of the money supply led segments of the financial markets to depart from their traditional, conservative, and "boring" roles. They didn't want to see themselves as guarantors for sustainable developments because making big money was "sexy."

The role change did not result from a coincidence. Most of society wanted top-down changes that would increase changes to participate in a "winning game." Another factor was the breakdown of socialism in the late 1980s that gave this economical liberalization process an ideological boost. Traditional economists who were skeptical and warned of failure were replaced by new-style analysts. Such changes are (and always were and will be) invitations for innovative people, winners, risk takers, and unscrupulous marketers (the description depends on perspective) to assume leading roles and determine new goals and competition levels. Thousands of ambitious, young and smart individuals saw chances for careers in finance by creating products that had only one goal: leveraging profits.

To explain the erosion of financial organizations, it is necessary to review the whole picture, particularly the human factors that serve as the major puzzle stones that show the motivations of people at all levels of the financial system. A systemic view reveals that the sub-prime mortgage crisis and crash of Lehman Brothers were symptoms, not problems. The transformation of the financial sector to a toxic structure was the end point where a domino effect toppled the whole system.

Years earlier, undesirable investments were bundled off to smaller organizations that had little understanding of the broad problem. They were caught up in the illusions of AAA investment ratings like the citizens in the "Emperor's New Clothes" fairy tale.

Stephan Schulmeister,* a well known Austrian economist, called these modern emperors the finance alchemists. One of the most famous was Bernard Madoff. Like all alchemist sagas, his story started when he was recognized as a finance genius when in truth he was a thief. The revelation of his Ponzi scheme that created the largest finance scandal in U.S. history put the 72-year-old former chairman of the NASDAQ market in jail for 150+ years. The press now calls Madoff the Satan of Wall Street.

Madoff's activities led to the death of Jeffrey Picower, a friend who was suspected to be involved in the financial schemes and the suicide of Madoff's son who worked as a trader for his father. Bill Foxton, a British soldier, shot himself because of the loss of his life savings to Madoff.† Other dramas involved celebrities, retirees who lost retirement funds, and organizations and individuals whose investments had no value. The story achieved Shakespearean tragedy dimensions.

How could something like this happen? Did anyone have suspicions? What were authorities like SEC doing or not doing? In brief, Madoff played hard, committed real crimes, got caught, and is getting what he deserves. However, that summary serves as a reaction to a symptom. The entire picture of the financial crisis remains undetected. Few people, even those in the highest ranks of finance and government saw the problems with the "Madoff

---

* Schulmeisterspricht von, *Finanzalchimisten*, ORF-News online, 2010.
† Army major kills himself over Bernard Madoff fraud debts, Adam, S., *The Telegraph* online, 2009.

spirit" that infiltrated most of the financial world run by the emperors and their subject workers.

Madoff did not work in a vacuum. He and his allies maintained the myth while they conducted daily business for years. Irving Picard, the court-appointed trustee who oversees assets seized from Madoff, some of which were Austrian investments handled via a feeder system established by Madoff that became the biggest such scheme in Europe. The losses totaled more than $9 billion and directly involved the Herald Fund of the private Bank Medici in Vienna; but also prime funds of the biggest Austrian bank—the Bank of Austria and with them, one of the biggest banks in Europe—their holding company UniCredit. Tax oases such as the Cayman Islands also played roles in the game.

According to Picard, Bank Austria's reputable and powerful long-term head, Gerhard Randa, personally intervened to expedite a bank license for Bank Medici in 2003. Picard also claims that Bank Medici lacked an infrastructure and was a "de facto-daughter" of Bank Austria. Of course, all involved parties deny wrongdoing: "With vehemence (and all juristic power) we will hold against the accusations; we only did "normal" bank works and we got victims of Madoff's criminal acts."*

The Central African-Bank for Development (BDEAC) in 1999, based on a recommendation of Bank Austria, invested about €16 million in the Austrian bank's prime funds. The non-profit African bank desperately needed to fight poverty and to build infrastructures for the poorest of the poor. In 2009, BDEAC received a notice from its "co-victim," Bank Austria, that the money had vanished.†

Anicet G. Dologuélé, the president of the Central African-Bank for Development continues to work for the return of his bank's funds by petitions to Austrian authorities. At the other end of the winner-and-loser continuum, John Paulson who headed a hedge fund "earned" about $4 billion by transactions involving "scrap" from allegedly reputable finance organizations. He gambled against clients of Goldman Sachs who held acid (worthless) paper at the beginning of the subprime crisis. Paulson was Goldman's long-term business-partner and "helped" Goldman create products including the Abacus Fund. Paulson brought in bad loans against which he bet. Suspicion is strong that Goldman directly speculated against its customers. In a settlement with the U.S. Securities & Exchange Commission (SEC), Goldman was required to pay a $550 million fine (a record fine, but still farcical in context) in the summer of 2010 for providing incomplete investor information—not

---

* Klage "mit aller Vehemenz" bekämpfen, ORF News online.
† Primeo-Schatten reichen bis nach Afrika, Renate Graber, *Der Standard* online.

for wrongdoing. Paulson's machinations are subject to judicial action. Both parties to this scheme claim they did only normal bank work.[*,†]

The world is facing complex problems, starting with both the detectability and the uncertain definitions of insider trading and white collar crime. It is impossible to gather sufficient resources to prosecute all this criminal or suspected criminal activity and close all the loopholes that led to the crisis. Strengthening the authorities and legal structures will not solve the problem. From the perspective of this chapter, the first priority is not to detect culprits that created this huge loss of accountability, values, and social responsibility.

A systems approach is required. Albert Einstein noted that evildoers weren't the problems; the majority of people (the system) that let them operate are the problem. Focusing on upgrades of the judiciary and executive systems is a reactive approach. A proactive approach that remains active is required and it means understanding and correcting the financial system.

The financial markets endured a number of catastrophes in recent history, for example, the Asian crisis of 1997 and the dot.com bubble in 2000. Those incidents should have made clear what a credit crunch and loss of trust would mean, but the world did not learn. A new reactive approach known as bank rescue was pursued. That taught us that system banks were too big and important for the government and the public to let them fail. The problem was handed over to taxpayers and as a result banking is no longer a private enterprise.

The only answer can be an essential paradigm-change accepted and honored by the entire finance community. The finance industry, like chemical production and nuclear power plants, should be categorized as a high risk environment that must be made failure-free for society. While risk management is not new in the financial world, the external control mechanisms such as regulatory agencies and law codes are not nearly as proactive as they should be.

Internal risk management activities including the engagement of rating agencies and use of their mathematical models provided delusionary feelings of security instead of help. The protection tools of the financial sector are little more than very sophisticated fig leaves. A parallel may be seen in the aviation industry that was seen as a high-risk environment until the 1970s. (It is still seen as a high-risk environment, but ongoing human factor innovations transformed the perspective to a high safety environment.) Technological innovations did not produce sufficient progress in the area of flight safety. The industry adopted a safety culture that included systemic

---

[*] Die gewonnene Wette des John Paulson, Wadewitz, F., *Zeit* online, 2010.
[†] Goldman Settles With SEC for $550 Million, *New York Times* online, 2010.

and human factors-based risk management procedures that transformed air transportation into a very safe environment. It is unrealistic to think that such measures could be directly implemented into financial systems but some principles are applicable.

Finance industries are used (or misused) as political tools and are also in power positions that allow them to impact politics in ways that support their interests (profits). The largest operators who make the most profits represent the biggest stumbling blocks to the required changes. The intent is not to fight against finance industries. We must support finance operations that are interested in conducting fair business for the future. The current disaster is man-made, not an act of nature or deity. For that reason, humans are responsible for finding solutions. We have to start to make the financial world more resilient.

Resilience

According to Wikipedia, resilience is generally the ability to recover from (or to resist being affected by) some shock, insult, or disturbance. *Resilience engineering* describes the latest developments in the areas of human factors and system safety. Eric Hollnagel, an opinion leader in the field, noted in his 2006 book that, "The performance of individuals and organizations must at any time adjust to the current conditions (Hollnagel et al.)." That means an organization must be able to find proactive answers to threats (external) and errors (internal) and deal with realities that are often seen as unchangeable constraints.

According to systemic thinking, large changes are rarely accomplished from outside an organization. Changes are achieved internally and usually apply to an organization's internal structures. Here lies the main power of a resilience engineering approach. It focuses on the inner growth of an organization—the personal growth of the people within the organization. That requires examination of the psychological and sociological aspects of hierarchies (leaders and followers), group dynamics, personality styles, mass phenomena, feedback culture, motivations, and the subconscious drivers that underlie all these criteria.

A basic premise of resilience engineering states that the knowledge of threats and errors already exists within the organization. *Drift into failure** and *normalization of deviance*[†] are other important concepts. If there is

---

* "Drift into failure" is a phrase based on the theory of practical drift" in Scott A. Snook's 2000 book titled *Friendly Fire*, pp. 179–201.
[†] Diane Vaughan used the "normalization of deviance" phrase in her 1996 book, *The Challenger Launch Decision*, pp. 62–64. She describes the erosion of NASA's safety culture that led to the 1986 space shuttle disaster.

no systemic perspective to detect threats and errors and eliminate them, practical and social erosion will take place. An organization drifting into failure is slowly pushed or is pushing itself into an abyss. Normalization of deviance is a subconscious social process (group dynamic) by which involved people perceive drift as a normal process—another parallel to "The Emperor's New Clothes."

Other important concepts are interactive complexity and tight coupling.* The first involves classification of the many operational threads that can challenge an organization. Other issues are the inherent domino effects and the speed of a domino effect. Resilience involves a combination of both issues. Risk specialists know that the financial industry is highly complex, interactive and coupled.

The subprime crisis at the start led to an international financial crisis that expanded to a world economic crisis and now operates as a state debt dilemma; the end is not in sight. This represents a convincing argument for classifying the finance world as a high-risk environment in the human factors tradition. This indexing is also helpful for implementing the same shared mental model.† The lack of a common goal for implementing financial safety because of different interests of partners and clients is a big stumbling block on the way to making the financial industry more resilient.

Other factors are the necessity to create foresight‡ to overcome hindsight bias§ and avoid a culture of production¶ where protection is underestimated and/or pseudo risk managements denying human factors are implemented. The major strength of a resilience approach results from analyzing and optimizing the social realities of organizations in a process known as implementing synergetic hierarchies in which leaders play dominant roles.

Sidney Dekker, another mastermind of resilience engineering, emphasizes the need to ask who holds the power in organizations (2007). The

---

* Charles Perrow used terms first in a complexity/coupling chart in *Normal Accidents: Living with High-Risk Technologies*, 1999, pp. 96–100. Perrow said nothing about finance organizations. He cites traditional high risk environments like mining, military, rail, chemical industries, marine, space, aviation, or nuclear power plants along with not-admitted ones, the financial world plays no role as a critical infrastructure in his chart. It appears that nothing changed since then. Today the breakdown of the banking system is often compared to a nuclear meltdown—the complex/coupling worst-case-scenario.

† The "same shared mental model" is often used in resilience approaches although it is not a component and its original is unknown.

‡ The "create foresight" concept appears in Hollnagel, Woods & Leveson's "*Resilience Engineering: Concepts and Precepts*" 2006, p. 6.

§ "Hindsight Bias" is a chapter in Sidney Dekker's *The Field Guide to Understanding Human Error*, 2006, pp. 21–28. He argues that everyone in the role of investigator has to step into the shoes of those *inside* the tunnel—the practical, social, or emotional situation that produced the unwanted outcome. The perspective from the outside is never sufficient to completely explain an inherent problem.

¶ "Culture of production" is another phrase from Vaughan's *The Challenger Launch Decision*, pp. 196–237.

superiors determine the organizational culture and also serve as symbols of the social and emotional constellations of the subordinates and surrounding context (society, political system). Leadership and management commitments to giving safety top priority are the linchpins for making the financial world more secure. Safety culture is an umbrella term for all activities involved in achieving security. A safety culture is different from a production culture, and safety activities must be bundled to avoid a drift into failure and the normalization of deviance.

Safety cultures can also be defined as spaces for optimizing outcomes and can serve as proactive trails to achieve the proper balance with production and protection; they must also be just.* They have to focus on proactive methods and deal with accountability when unwanted outcomes occur.

This point is crucial in a finance industry context especially in the state of the industry today. While safety (just) cultures deal with non-punitive models, they do not argue against punishment in general; their ideology is a passionate plea for not seeing judicial or regulatory activities as preventive safety mechanisms. A concentration of unjust behavior, such as financial crime, must be seen as the unfortunate end of an erosion process by which an entire industry drifted into failure.

However, understanding the thinking model of resilience and the process required to implement a safety culture involves more than key words and catch phrases. It requires a deep look into the theory and philosophy of human factors and system safety whose roots lie in the old enmity of high reliability theory and normal accident theory. The path to resilience can be seen as a trail through these two belief camps to find an integrative source. One model that clarifies the process of balancing production and protection is the control value square portraying the motivation trap (Figure 15.1; Felsenreich, 2007).

High Reliability Theory (HRT) and Normal Accident Theory (NAT)

HRT can be seen as a theory of compensation (an individual can "make it" if he or she is clever enough and has a real desire). HRT focuses on human will, motivation, and the ability to succeed. It is strongly positive and based on the premise of working hard and learning to achieve success. The concept appears beneficial in that it enhances positive attitudes and may bring benefits to employees, organizations and society. The problem is the one-dimensional nature of the concept that induces an illusion of control.

---

* Just cultures are described in Sidney Dekker's *Just Culture: Balancing Safety and Accountability,* 2007.

Control-Value-Square

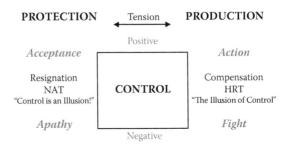

Figure 15.1 Control value square.

Normal Accident Theory (NAT) may be interpreted as a theory of resignation not only bringing impossibility, failure, fate, and even subconscious thinking that drives behavior without our knowledge into the game, but giving them a prominent place. It induces resistance and for that reason is considered negativistic—as a form of revenge by HRT followers aimed at NAT treatment of control as an illusion (Figure 15.1).

Control Value Square

The control value square[*] states that the two positive attitudes for control (based on NAT and HRT) are action and acceptance (Figure 15.1). They stand in opposition to one another. To achieve the idea of a value square, the positive charge must be integrated into the negative one, and a balance must be achieved between compensation and resignation. If one of the values becomes too strong, the organization goes to the sharp end of the continuum. Action and acceptance degenerate to apathy or fight. This concept may appear strange, for example, what is positive about resignation and what is negative about a fight? Resignation can produce positive effects. For example, an airline pilot can decide not to take off or land, perform a go-around because of a missed approach caused by crosswinds, or divert to another airport for safety reasons. The initial intention was abandoned but the acceptance (resignation) led the pilot to find an alternative and take action. In essence, he achieved a safe balance between two positive antagonists.

---

[*] Schultz von Thun (1989) uses the value square to depict his communication model. He puts the positive attitudes of communication (truthfulness and effect awareness) into opposition. The corresponding negative terms are bluntness and façade. *Miteinander Reden: Stile, Werte und Persönlichkeitsentwicklung*, p. 45.

The problem in definition and practice is deeply rooted in high-achieve-ment, Western-oriented societies and this leads to a fight orientation. The winners are the role models who are defined as having strong wills and extraordinary abilities. The general tendency then is to see fighting as posi-tive and giving up as negative—something only losers do. According this social concept the winners want to focus only on what is possible.

Motivation Trap

The motivation trap is based on a single dimension: "more of the same" even-tually becomes counterproductive. To a certain point motivation (the assump-tion of having control) is helpful because it empowers an individual or a group, and empowerment brings positive energy for pursuing success and avoiding failure in an operation but motivation remains one-dimensional. The positive attitude eventually becomes counterproductive because acceptance of uncer-tainties (technical, organizational, social) is not part of the concept.

What causes a harmful denial of practical limits leads to fight and drift into failure. The motivation trap is an internal mechanism that appears when a think-positive myth is unleashed in an effort to make the impossible seem possible. The entire financial industry became addicted to a productivity pathos and deeply ensnared in a motivation trap.

Josef Ackermann, head of Deutsche Bank, serves as a good example. He rigidly adhered to a 25% rate of return and rejected a recommendation to limit the remunerations of bank managers to €500,000 annually. In an interview with an online economics publication he argued that, "This rate is not the expression of greed, but a statement that the Deutsche Bank wants to be in the club of the best banks in the world." He also said, "One does not become the best [managers] for this amount of money."* While he made no mention of how the 25% return should be achieved, the questions for the future are what are the best banks and who are the best managers?

Such (one-dimensional) approaches need risk-managements that supports this kind of bank-industries self-pictures (and interests). To the outside but also to the inside, everything is done to keep up an image of a safe (high reli-able) branch. But it's a typical (pure) HRT-approach (*The Illusion of Control*) where so called modern bank-risk-management is always producing *more of the same*: More (exacter) mathematical models; more (highly educated) risk-personal; more (sophisticated) hard ware (computers) and soft ware (risk-man-aging-programmes) and so further on. It is so staying highly mechanistic and addicted to (additional) automation—denying the human factor.

---

* Ackermann braucht kein Geld "Würde mich schämen," N-TV online, 2008.

The 2008 financial crisis provided many examples. Lehman Brothers achieved a triple A rating on a Friday and collapsed on Monday. The French Societé General bank lost approximately €5 billion through actions by Jérôme Kerviel, one of its employees. The institution claimed it had no knowledge of its Delta One top traders' speculation and called Kerviel a "terrorist." Kerviel stated in court that the bank acted "like pimps sending their subordinates to prostitution."*

One of Austria's largest banks, BAWAG PSK, had to be sold because of wild speculation in the Caribbean several years earlier. In 2009, Austria also nationalized the Hypo Group Alpe Adria Bank because of years of loan mis-management and political activities. "Acid" (valueless) loans totalled €8.5 billion, and the Austrian taxpayers must bear the cost.† In Germany, Gerhard Gibrovsky, former head of risk management and a member of the managing board of Bayerische Landesbank received a prison sentence in January 2011 because of involvement in a scandal arising from a bank deal with Bernie Ecclestone of Formula 1. Gibrovsky transferred $50 million from Mauritius and the Caribbean to his private Sunshine Foundation in Austria and gave the risk manager title a new meaning.‡ Finally, based on EU stress test findings, the Anglo-Irish Bank had a sufficient capital base in July 2010. In November 2010, the bank collapsed and about €35 billion are needed to recapitalize it. That amount represents a fifth of Ireland's GDP. Commentators wrote about the situation as "What a misinterpretation."§

Protection and production are different qualities. It is not possible to insert protection into an organization as a one-time event. Protection needs an ongoing holistic approach driven by the collective will of all involved, not by the will of a few leaders, to allow detection of uncertainties and threats.

Recall what Sidney Dekker said about the necessity to focus on those holding the power and how much power sharing they practice. The picture in the financial industries is not a positive one. Power holders included Deutsche Bank's Ackermann, Richard Fuld of Lehman Brothers, Henry Paulson of Goldman, Sachs (not a relative of John Paulson) who was a U.S. government official at the time of the Lehman crash and put Fuld, an old rival, to the sword. Lloyd Blankfein of Goldman, Sachs pronounced that "banks do God's work."¶ Sean Fitzpatrick of Anglo-Irish made his bank into a self-service out-let for the richest men in Ireland and helped push the whole country to the abyss.**

---

* Jérôme Kerviel: Allein gegen die große Bank", Balmer, R., *Die Presse,* online. 2010.
† Systematische Misswirtschaft bei Kreditvergabe, Oswald, G. & Graber, R., *Der Standard,* 2010.
‡ Gefängniszelle statt Royal Suite mit Seeblick, Peltsmeier, H., FAZnet, 2011.
§ In der Geiselhaft der Banken, Schnauder, A., *Der Standard,* 2010.
¶ Goldman Sachs will nicht gegen Kunden gewettet haben, Reuters online, 2010.
** Mächtige Clans im Hintergrund, ORF News online, 2010.

All these leaders were more or less "one-man shows."

This is not said to blame these people. Greed and addiction to power are not criminal offenses. They are personality characteristics and, if taken to extreme, constitute personality disorders. Blame applies only to criminal activities. It is necessary to understand the mechanisms that lead to hierarchies consisting of almighty leaders and conformist followers. Analysis must involve individual and collective psyches and inherent group dynamics. A depth psychological perspective with a focus on the (individual and collective) subconscious drivers is needed.

Depth Psychological Perspective[*]

Gareth Morgan (1986) wrote about a myth of rationality that "helps us to see a certain action as legitimate, credible, and normal, and hence avoid the wrangling and debate that would arise if we were to recognize the basic uncertainty and ambiguity underlying many of our values and actions."[†] The deep will of individuals and groups to maintain the myth of rationality (illusion of control) is from a psychological perspective very understandable. It helps stabilize and structure the inner and outer worlds, but it can become counterproductive (Figure 15.1).[‡] It denies and excludes individual personalities and interactions (group dynamics) and the counterpart of rationality: emotionality.[§] The integration of emotionality means to follow a holistic approach which is not only a path of cognitive will, but is also a path to create emotional space. A depth psychological perspective deepens NAT and should help us understand the two strong oppositional belief camps (NAT and HRT) and the effort to overcome the motivation trap. To do so, it is necessary to focus on the individual and collective levels of the subconscious.

Individual Level—Understanding the subconscious is necessary to understand defense mechanisms (Freud, 1937).[¶] Defense mechanisms such as repression, denial, and other unwanted cognitive and emotional reactions become more important as pressure is put on the psyche. Internal pressure

---

[*] Depth psychology in this context means a psychology that works with the concept (or existence) of an unconscious mind and not a substitute for Alfred Adler's individual psychology or Freud's psychoanalyses. The intention is to distill a complex theory into simple terms in limited space.

[†] Gareth Morgan, *Images of Organization*, 1986, p. 135.

[‡] This one-dimensionality can also be seen in the work of one of the main representatives of HRT, Gene Rochlin, specifically two articles: Self-Designing High Reliability Organizations (1987) and Safe Operation as a Social Construct (1999).

[§] Thinking without feeling is impossible; they constitute a unit.

[¶] Sigmund Freud originated the concept of defense mechanisms. His daughter, Anna Freud, clarified and refined them.

arises from belief systems* of an individual's culture. Both types of pressure are crucial to reality. Assuming that pressure is linked with hierarchical level in an organizational context, the steeper the hierarchical gradient, the more likely an individual is to revert to his or her defense mechanisms. The "cleverness of the psyche" to protect one's integrity, security, and status causes humans who would under other circumstances (synergetic hierarchic structure) follow their normal healthy impulses to resist inconsistencies (like threats) remain silent (utilizing a defense mechanism) instead of standing up and saying "no." This follows Felsenreich (2007) who said, "We only understand if we stand the consequences."

Collective Level—Watzlawick and Beavin (1980) said, "One cannot not communicate." Extending the statement to groups, "One cannot not get into relationships." Relationships form whether we want them or not on private and professional levels. The qualities of those relationships are strongly linked with the inherent space. If people are allowed to express their thoughts and feelings to each other freely, they have an adult to adult encounter.

Two important terms of depth psychology are regression and transference. On a group level, non-functioning adult to adult relationships are affected when one person slips into the parent role and the others take on the child role (regression). Regression triggers defense mechanisms. This is crucial to understand because the unwanted cognitive and emotional reactions described above are stored in the subconscious. They are not gone; they work in the background and produce what are called transferences[†]

In depth psychology, transferences are problematic because of the inability of negative thoughts and feelings to disappear. As a result the thoughts and feelings are transferred (subconsciously) to other non-involved[‡] or involved persons[§] who are not able to endanger integrity, security, and status.

The "cleverness of the psyche" becomes even more problematic. In addition to addressing feelings and thoughts to the wrong persons, transference subconsciously reverses the situation. This means that positive thoughts and feelings are transferred to those in parent roles and negative thoughts and feelings are transferred to colleagues who try to confute this dynamic by speaking up. The outcome of such transferences sets up a "devil's circle" in which the power and control of the leaders (parents) increases and the power of the subordinates (children) decreases. The self-preserving unbalance caused by numerous transferences can be defined as the conformism of

---

* Belief-systems in depth psychology are learned do's and don't dos.
† Depth psychology transference is a defense mechanism used here as an umbrella term.
‡ Examples of transference to non-involved persons are: (1) a person has trouble in her job and transfers her anger to her life partner, or (2) a person loses money through speculation on easy markets and increases his hatred against refugees in his country.
§ The dilemma is that if they are not transferred to others they could easily become self-destructive (e.g., depression).

a collective subconscious and it leads to the hen-or-egg question. Do people conform because they face strong hierarchies or do they create strong hierarchies by their conformist behavior? From the perspective of this chapter, the activators of these negative group dynamics are external constraints. One of the goals of this chapter is to shed light onto human interactions and explain the psychological background that creates leaders and followers.

Transactional Analysis

Transactional analysis (TA), a basically depth psychological theory developed by Eric Berne, a psychiatrist in the late 1950s, depicts content in a psychological model. It focuses on human relationships and analyzes human *transactions* according to their ego states.* Transactions consist of the communications and behaviors caused by thoughts and emotions of humans or groups of humans. The ego state model categorizes psyches into adult, child, and parent levels. The adult ego state is characterized by integration (conscious levels of thinking and feeling). The child ego state is based on feeling (emotionality). The parent ego state exhibits a level of thinking (rationality).

Transactions that represent a functioning relationship between adult people should be independent of their roles as leaders or followers and conducted on an adult-to-adult level. This does not deny the need for hierarchies or infer that a parent ego state or child ego state is negative. On the contrary, hierarchies and leadership are necessary for controlling subordinates and necessary aspects of supervision. A certain amount of childish trust is good in following situations. However, leadership and trust should be integrated in the adult ego state.

Integration means that inherent thoughts and feelings (even negative ones) are conscious and both sides of a situation show awareness and share definitions of the different roles. This represents space for reflectiveness (absence of transference).† Leadership is determined through competence and not through personal ego (leading is a form of giving). This dynamic is called a synergetic hierarchy (Figure 15.2).

Steep hierarchy is determined through the presence of transferences and allows no space for reflective behavior. The superior party has (boundless) power and control over subordinates who are forced to conform to or rebel

---

* Berne, E. (1964). *Games People Play*: (The Psychology of Human Relationships,) 23–32.
† Absence indicates minimized transferences; they are always valid in human relationships.

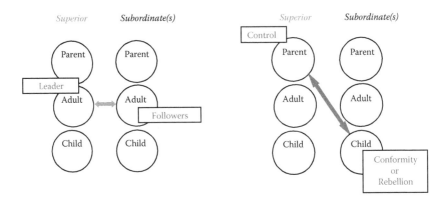

Figure 15.2 Synergistic hierarchy versus steep hierarchy.

against the leader and the system. *To rebel means to face conflict what requires a tremendous amount of (personal) power and integrity in a steep hierarchy.*[*]

The consequences for *so-called* whistle blowers are horrendous. German psychotherapist and author Heinz Peter Röhr (1999) states that, "One has not only the boss as opponent but the whole follower system."[†] After transference, a group dynamic settles in. Conformists fulfill the wills of superiors and do not fight against problems. They fight whistle blowers who reveal problems. Blowers have no chance of success in a steep hierarchy. Conformist followers achieve all the success. If a whistle blower is in a high position, his or her inner and outer conflicts reach the point where he or she quits or is fired.

At the time of its crash, Lehman Brothers had debts exceeding $600 billion. Despite that, it held an AAA rating; the results of an Ernst & Young audit were positive. [Ernst & Young is one of the world's leading accounting firms; its motto is "Quality in everything we do."[‡]] Ernst & Young was accused of helping to mask Lehman's financial disaser. By the way, Ernst & Young earned about $100 million with Lehman from 2001–2008. One major flaw of Lehman's was its lack of internal critical voices. High ranking manager Matthew Lee in May 2008 warned the managing board about Lehman's "perverted repo-105 transactions." According to the SEC report, Ernst & Young was involved and representatives spoke with Lee personally. Ernst & Young and Lehman's managing board together found that Lee's warnings were baseless and Lee had to leave the company a few days later.[§]

A self-reflective culture arises from people who ask non-conforming questions. Without such questions, a culture becomes pseudo-reflective and a nor-

---

[*] Rebellion is seen here as idealistic. The rebel's aim is not to assume a power position, but to focus the benefit of the effort on the entire organization.
[†] Narzissmus: Das innere Gefängnis, 165–166.
[‡] Ernst & Young Homepage. http://www.ey.com/ (retrieved March 2, 2011).
[§] Zahlungsunfähigkeit verheimlicht, ORF News online, 2010.

malization of deviance and a drift into failure is a logical consequence. The drivers for all these dramas are also deeply embedded into society and into the collective subconscious. They are visible in the interactions and relationships of low-ranking people (employees, voters, spectators, job applicants) towards higher-ranking leaders (owners, managers, politicians, sports figures).

Depth psychologist Erich Fromm (1968) explains the core of these often ambivalent but stable relationships. It is the powerful attraction normal, healthy people (with tendencies toward self-doubts) feel toward people with omnipotent self images—in other words, the trust of the first group in the excellence of the second.[*]

The increasing speed and complexity of the modern world also create instability, and we see a renaissance of the strong dualistic transference involving the hero (strong leader, rescuer, role model) and the antihero (whistle blower, culprit, victim, scapegoat) along with the transfers (or projections) of hopes, dreams, frustrations, anger, hatred, etc. The modern world needs leaders, rescuers, and role models (super father figures). Super father figures can also be included in the theories of TA. The major exponent, Thomas Harris (1967)[†] explains the concept of so-called life positions. *As bases for functioning (balanced) adult to adult relationships, the life position should be "I'm OK, you're OK".* However, Harris states that most humans lack self-esteem and exhibit that lack by feeling that other people are better, smarter, prettier, more successful, etc. *They hold the life position "I'm not OK, you're OK".* This can be very painful on a personal level. It induces transference from the everlasting child position and demands heroes. The activity is harmless and is actually positive because it induces hope.

What is problematic is the interaction with the minority of humans who are driven to fulfill the role of the hero and who internalize the opposite life position, i. e., "I'm OK—You're not ok!" TA notes that developing this position is very basic. A small child can develop the position subconsciously based on whether he or she is treated well. (Traumatized) adults who adopt this attitude are traumatized and can no longer transmit positive feelings towards others. This can be seen as a revenge toward the collective for the suffering and as a compensative act to never again experience the (painful) dependencies of childhood. The "I" is important; the "you" gains importance only if it supports the interests of the "I." Trust is lost and real relationships are no longer feasible (known as the anti-social script).[‡] The script leads to narcissistic personality that eventually becomes a full-blown disorder.

---

[*] *The Heart of Man: Its Genius for Good and Evil,* German version, pp. 76–77.
[†] *I'm O.K, You're O.K.: A Practical Guide to Transactional Analysis.*
[‡] Building a personality (or personality disorder) is a complex action. Every life script is produced as a reaction toward the social environment (for example, frustration as pictured in Maslow's pyramid) and also as a learned behavior such as socialization in a mafia context.

One famous expert on personality disorders, Otto F. Kernberg, a professor of psychiatry and the director of the New York Presbyterian Hospital (2004), describes people with severe narcissistic personalities as showing a remarkable lack of empathy and deep emotional disinterest in others. This chronicle of inner emptiness unleashes the paradox of an overblown ego that has a significant need for ongoing ego boosts. However, the need is never filled because relationships that vitalize people are not possible, and the need is significant. Narcissistic personalities gain their power from competition, not from solidarity.

Narcissists exhibit remarkable self-confidence and no sense of indebtedness. They assert rights to command and cheat. Behind an attractive façade is a personality that is cold and inexorable.* Based on this disconnection of real emotions, narcissistic personalities are free of fear and also compassion. Emotions are substituted by images. Inconsistencies are seen as challenges presented by ignoramuses. Driven narcissistic personalities can be remarkably convincing in selling genuine or questionable products. Their constant quest for "the big feeling" leads them to pursue superlative aims (wealth, fame); they are totally goal oriented. Long-time acquaintances and friends are "scared off" because the narcissist requires 100% loyalty and disagreement is absolutely prohibited.

Organizational and Societal Context

Some of these characteristics are desirable for organizations. Strong leaders who have no fear and high levels of self-esteem are goal oriented, and seen as rational and positive. They are ready to execute "tough" decisions usually related to innovative changes. It is paradoxical that a deficit (from a psychological perspective) is seen as strength in the "real world." Psychologists acknowledge that narcissism as a personal style can have tremendous innovative power. Indeed, people driven by superlative pretensions who followed their "fantastic" ideas brought positive progress to the world.†

Is suffering the major impetus for innovation or do we have alternatives? The answer probably lies in our collective subconscious where thousands of years of suffering are stored. Competition and winning are the dominant drivers in our professional world and losers represent inevitable by-products. Heinz-Peter Röhr (1999) states that we live in a narcissistic society, where self love—the healthy essence of narcissism—is strongly perverted.‡ This works in both directions. The absence of self-esteem is as problematic as an overblown ego that compensates for subconscious inferiority feelings. From this

---

* Aggressivity, Narcissism and Self-Destructiveness, German Version, pp. 76-80.
† More often (e.g., war scenarios) it led to terrible disasters.
‡ Narzissmus: Das innere Gefängnis, p. 155.

perspective, it appears that narcissistic leaders and conformist followers are products (and thus victims) of a greater systemic imbalance pictured in a male-dominated society.

The intention of this chapter is not predominantly to focus on cultural history, although it is of interest because human factors and system safety via protection bring the female principle into the game.* These life-protective efforts are archaic in the matriarchic tradition of giving and affirming life. Production as the counterpart can therefore be classified as male following the patriarchal tradition of hunting, conquering, and taking collateral damage. The dual approach of culprits and victims and winners and losers† while protection follows a holistic approach.

A depth psychological perspective shows that in principle resilience based on human factors and system safety is far more than only a tool for classified high-risk environments. This view answers various questions about the interactive complexities of organizations and about the whole of society today. From this view, the unbalanced male and female forces are causes of the increasing group dynamic problems because unjust behavior determines unfair goals and competition levels. It makes the devil's circle visible and understandable with its ongoing and self-preserving loss of trust and lack of reflectiveness where anti-social behavior becomes normative.

From this (humanistic) perspective it is easy to call a drift into a failure a "drift into anti-sociality." The trail to understanding failures in organizations leads automatically to deeper social issues: Organizational misbalances are social misbalances. What happened in the financial world (and still happens) can be classified as strongly narcissistic. In recent decades, Wall Street built a parallel world with its own rules and values removed from the needs of the real world. For example, hedging was devised to create a risk management instrument and it has become a perverted betting tool.

Determining whether such developments are criminal is not the aim of this chapter, but the financial world certainly made a fluid transition from normal competitive behavior to financial crime. The leaders in the finance industry and mafia archetypes display some similarities. They confidently operate in their own worlds characterized by anti-social ideologies and behaviors. Operating from power positions built in the past, they maximize their profits with little or no effort that benefits society. The handful of people in the inner circles enjoy perverse wealth and increasingly totalitarian power.

Financial crimes, like other white collar criminal activities reveal aggressive behavior via veiled threats instead of guns and knives. The soldiers in this war are well educated, well mannered, often handsome, eloquent, and well dressed. Their arms consist of their financial powers, insider relations,

* Both men and women have these qualities.
† This dualism is depicted by our criminal law system (guilty or not guilty).

and the law that sits firmly on their side through lobbying to impact regulation and loyal jurists who scan the legal systems to find loopholes.*

As in the mafia, there are super father figures in the top-positions of
financial industries. While these top managers are effect-aware and diplomatic toward the public (in contrast to the media-shy "real" godfathers) with
exceptions such as the "god's work" citation), they are often sharp-edged
and blunt in dealing with the inner organization. Shortening Adam Smith's
theory to the first part, they express cynical (Darwinist) ideas such as "Those
social-romanticists will never understand how the business world really
works." Or "Eat or be eaten—that's how it is." "Those people criticizing us
should focus on their own personal problems and get their jealousy under
control." "No risk, no fun. And by the way, we are only doing our job. So
what?"

Other aspects or types of super fathers include those playing the roles of
good but strict fathers who picture themselves as carrying the load of ensuring the further existence of projects, the whole entire company and so thousands of jobs or even the prestige of national icons on their shoulders. They
have minimal understanding of those who are unhappy with general developments. Their attitudes (rationales) are that a leader has to do what a leader
is paid to do, to be commercially successful means to…, or others in the field
already….

It can be said that the first super father figure types are much closer to
what can be defined as financial criminality. They are primarily acting from
their narcissistic and anti-social personality-styles while latter (the good but
strict fathers) are reacting to the reality the first super fathers created. From
this perspective, it is easier to understand how business realities (not only in
the world of finance) are constituted and how the devil's-circles begin to run.
The pressure from the top results in intensified threats and constraints until
everyone in the field is "part of the game." As pictured in the Control Value
Square and the Motivation Trap, over time smaller financial organizations
are forced (or feel forced) to take additional risks to (paradox) save their own
futures.

However, the discussion of totalitarian leaders and their conformist followers and personality problems should not be moralistic. It is not about
stigmatizing people. In particular, the style of the second super father type
cannot be labelled as entirely antisocial. It also cannot be said that followers are (as a personal style) "weak." It can be said that organizations under
high constraints (or under assumed constraints) are subconsciously in

---

* Ernst-Wolfgang Böckenförde states: "The free, secularized state lives from preconditions
he himself cannot guarantee." Strategic respect of statutes without ethical motivation
will erode the whole democratic structure of a civil society. Verheerende Wirkung auf die
Rechtskultur, Werth, W., *Morgenjournal* ORF online, 2011.

danger of assigning the wealth to problematic personalities who install Steep Hierarchies. This installation happens mostly out of noble intentions, i.e., to act in the best interests of the whole organization and in the hope of gaining control over the constraints and threats. So it's about understanding why and how un-constructiveness as a group-dynamic is settling in and why and how on a relationship-level this becomes automatically (subconsciously) justified.]

The general (systemic) totalitarian tendencies can be also seen in a recent EU-wide survey conducted by the University of Bielefeld (Germany): About a third of Germans prefer authoritarian types of government; the number exceeds 40% in Great Britain and France and 60% in Portugal and Poland.[*] This alarming result pictures the increasing inner-child hopes of people that their present problems will be managed if a super father figure leader assumes charge. The reality that results from such wishes can be seen in history books.

The methods by which politics deals with finance industries are very sensitive and shocking. Former Federal Reserve chief Alan Greenspan in January 2008 signed a contract to work as an analyst for Paulson & Co. hedge funds.[†] After the crash, congress invited John Paulson to provide advice on how to deal with the financial crisis. Congress and the press treated him like a star. No one asked whether the guru "earned" billions a few months earlier.[‡]

We are reminded of the principle of finding a thief to catch a thief. Josef Ackermann is a powerful example. He and John Paulson devised financial products[§] and engaged also Greenspan as an investment banking analyst for Deutsche Bank in 2007.[¶] The role both Ackerman and Greenspan played in advising European Community organizations is, to put it mildly, problematic because what Ackermann doesn't say is that it's not about Ireland or Greece: The billions from European central banks in the form of the so called rescue-parachutes should again save the ones who, through hair-raising risk-taking, brought the whole problem into the world.

This is not a plea to let EU partner countries or their banking systems fail. It is a plea to examine the psychological and sociological questions. What banks learned from the crisis they produced imposed no consequences for past behavior and no impacts on future activities. And what should the people who have to pay for it learn when Jean-Claude Trichet and Angela Merkel & Co. presents those who helped create the disaster (as) the masterminds to find ways out of the crisis. One critic commented that, "We are hostages

[*] EU-Studie: Jeder Dritte wünscht sich starken Mann, ORF News online, 2011.
[†] Greenspan joins NY hedge fund, *Financial Times* online, 2008.
[‡] Wall-Street-Legende im Zwielicht", Kuls, N., *Frankfurer Allgemeine Zeitung* online, 2010.
[§] Ibid.
[¶] Jobwechsel: Greenspan berät die Deutsche Bank, *Die Presse* online, 2007.

of the banks.* However, only middle-rank employees such as trader Jérôme Kerviel are taken to court and found guilty for organizational disasters. The 33-year old Kerviel was sentenced to five years in prison (two on probation) and required to repay €4.9 billion to his former employer, Société Générale.

Sociologist Diane Vaughan states that this phenomenon is typical for a culture of production. "Middle managers are most likely to be held accountable because they made the decisions ... and left 'twisted in the wind' while more powerful administrators ... who had acted years earlier in ways that influenced the outcome are not.... People at both the top and the bottom of the hierarchy escape."[†] This finding becomes all the more interesting as court testimony reveals the working practices and organizational culture at Société Générale.

Witnesses reported shocking safety deficiencies, uncontrolled growth, and excessive demands. A *Der Spiegel* article stated that more than seventy explicit warnings about Kerviel's reckless trading were ignored.[‡] Another marker indicating the improbability that the reactive judicial system will be of help in the financial crisis is a *Wall Street Journal* article stating:

> The U.S. government's investigation into the collapse of Lehman Brothers Holdings Inc. has hit daunting hurdles that could result in no civil or criminal charges ever being filed against the company's former executives.... SEC officials have grown more worried they could lose a court battle if they bring civil charges.... The key stumbling block: the Repo 105 accounting move, while controversial, isn't necessarily illegal.... In a statement, Ernst & Young said the firm stands "behind our work on the Lehman audit and our opinion that Lehman's financial statements were fairly stated in accordance with the U.S. accounting standards that existed at the time."... Lawyers [of all four former Lehman executives] previously have denied any wrongdoing related to Repo 105. Fuld told lawmakers he had "absolutely no recollection whatsoever of hearing anything" about Repo 105 at the time of the transactions.[§]

Fuld claimed he had no idea what was going on in his company and no judicial action will make him accountable. The logical conclusion based on the two accounts is that a Lehman middle manager will be presented to the court as a scapegoat. While sarcasm (along with anger and rage) is deeply understandable, it has no bearing on the problem. This is one of the most difficult parts of a "New View on Human Error."[¶] It strongly argues

---

* In der Geiselhaft der Banken, Schnauder, A., *Der Standard*, 2010.
† *The Challenger Launch Decision*, 1996, p. 409.
‡ Einer zahlt alles, Seith, A., *Der Spiegel* online, 2010.
§ Lehman Probe Stalls; Chance of No Charges, Eagelsham, J. & Rappaport, L., *Wall Street Journal* online, 2011.
¶ The "new view on human error" is a paraphrase from Sidney Dekker's *Ten Questions about Human Error: A New View of Human Factors and System Safety*, 2005.

for overcoming blame. Viennese psychologist and psychotherapist Karl Kriechbaum (2010) stated that humans "mean no harm" despite the terrible things they do; they are not able to behave in another way. They act according their personal scripts. If a script has a strong narcissistic (egoistic, power-addicted) component, they will be anti-social. One cannot expect a narcissistic person to "feel" accountability because accountability is not part of the narcissistic personality.

This is not said to excuse persons such as Fuld & Co or Jérôme Kerviel, who definitely displayed a form of pathological gambling. Without doubt, it is necessary to have legal systems in place that will protect society from the harm those criminals create. It is much more essential, especially for high risk environments, to do everything possible to root out the flawed systems that permitted the criminals (acc. their personal dramas) to operate. Structured approaches must be developed and implemented so that it will never again be necessary to issue seventy warnings at Société Générale to help the organization to realize that it's at the brink of disaster.

The "New View" cited above does not focus on fault. On that basis, a systemic problem allowed the financial crisis to happen, and we are back to the hen-or-egg problem involving financial crime, legal system, and social imbalance. What should be done if the problem arises at the highest ranks of society? What should be done if entire organizations or segments of society adopt mafia-like structures?

These self-preserving circles composed of anti-social narcissistic personalities have the power to dominate their conformist followers whom Kriechbaum calls passive narcissists because they seek protection under their potent masters' umbrellas.[*] A human factors and system safety perspective would focus on the healthy aspects of business and support those who are open to change. Even people in high ranking positions are unhappy with the newest developments.

Resilience should be built into organizations like banks, regulators, and rating agencies to allow them to detect and eliminate role and loyalty conflicts. This requires cultural changes, particularly on the part of decision makers who will have to use their dominance and self-confidence in positive ways. The financial industry must reframe accountability from synergetic hierarchies.

Synergetic Hierarchy versus Steep Hierarchy

The subconscious process of constituting and running steep hierarchy relationships that represent the dark side of will and discipline is universal. Constraints are detected as threats to an organization and feared. The

---

[*] Der Mensch mit Eigenschaften: Unsere Programme, unsere Umwelt und unsere Zustände bestimmen unser Leben, 2010, p. 11.

collective anxiety creates the need for a strong, confident super father figure who will make success, no matter how difficult, possible if all the lower ranks follow his instructions. He advocates closed ranks and sets goal achievement as the highest priority. Time for reflecting on behavior or other non-goal perspectives is seen as a waste of resources.

A type of pseudo-reflectiveness develops based on following the goals set by leaders. Whistle blowers are seen as burdens—handicaps to the collective striving for success and threats to morals. The social closeness promoted by the system is characterized by fear, one-dimensionality, and dualism—a culture of conformism.[*]

The conscious processes of constituting and running synergetic hierarchy relationships (the positive sides of will and discipline) are also universal. Even under high constraints the organization is aware of "*The Illusion of Control*" which means that the collective feels its reflex for "closed ranks" and quick fixes, but is developed enough to reflect this reflex. The synergetic hierarchy appreciates that the most needed resources for reaching sustainable goals are relationships based on "yes" and "no." A certain amount of dissent is encouraged and appreciated. Adult-to-adult levels of encounters are guaranteed and people are taken seriously. Empowerment and power sharing are seen as creating positive action systems that foster individual strengths and the balancing of different interests through bundling healthy social feelings in the interest of all involved parties. This creates fairness and collective accountability.

This path of synergy follows the paradox that a person in a rush should go slowly; in other words, in high stress situations, good decision making involves diverse opinions and negotiation. Power sharing is seen as a working tool for knowledge sharing. Nonetheless, the hierarchy remains untouched (the concept involves balancing power, not eliminating it). Decision making authority remains in the hands of leaders because they hold the responsibility. Decisions are made as transparent as possible. Sceptical subordinates are expected to accept the reality of decisions and execute them. This system promotes self worth. Social closeness is based on trust and determined through multi-dimensionality, holism, and hierarchical clearness and constitutes a culture of resilience or safety culture.

Safety Culture

Organization errors can cause tremendous damage by destroying human lives and health, quality of life, economies, and the environment. The

---

[*] The essences of these relationship phenomena were described in 1921 in Freud's book about mass psychology paradox. Freud states that love plays a prominent role in constituting steep hierarchies. *Massenpsychologie und Ich Analyse*, pp. 48, 49, 55, 58.

resulting losses for organizations are often horrendous. Expensive legal settlements, loss of trust and good will, economic losses, damage to reputation, and other negative impacts can be ruinous. A recent example is the BP oil spill in the Gulf of Mexico in 2010.

Human Factors and System Safety

Aviation is a very safe transport system. Based on mileage, a passenger's chance of involvement in a commercial aircraft accident is about on the same as the chance faced by a railroad passenger. Vehicle traffic is 20 times more life threatening according to the European Transport Safety Council (2003) despite the complexity of the commercial effort.

The aviation industry is subject to strict regulation and high standards of safety and employs advanced automated technology. Despite these efforts, human errors cause up to 80% of aircraft accidents (the remainder are due to technical failures). This statistic clearly shows that achievement and high level performance (the optimum balance of production and protection) is guaranteed only if the human factors are known. In addition to technological factors, sociological and psychological factors come into play. Human factors such as rest requirements, organizational structures denoting responsibilities, group dynamics, personality styles, feedback mechanisms, and motivations are only some of the human issues that must be considered.

In general, it can be said that aviation follows an eclectic approach (not ideologically narrowed by following a single psychological or sociological school). Human factors and system safety are part of flight training and human factors seminars for flight and other personnel (e.g., air traffic controllers) (and) are mandatory and regulated through authorities in most of the countries. Such seminars cover incident statistics, new scientific findings, safety-related skills, team building, and personal interactions. Group members share their experiences from incidents and this indicates a level of transparency on the parts of companies and the industry. Participants learn from the failures of others. Aviation can be seen as a role model. Despite its competitive philosophy, accident information is disseminated to the public.

Errare Humanum Est—This Latin phrase translates as "To err is human." Worst case scenarios are at the top of a human error pyramid as shown

below. The smallest (worst) group at the top of the pyramid covers serious accidents. As seriousness decreases (toward the bottom of the pyramid), the frequency increases. Modern error management shares Cicero's perspective that human error is unavoidable. As shown in the error pyramid above, the few worst case scenario accidents at the top are preceded by many smaller incidents or near misses. Utilizing the knowledge of small incidents and near misses to avoid worst case scenarios is the main goal of an error management program. The continuation of the Latin expression is *sed in errare perseverare diabolicum* (but to insist on the error is diabolic).

System Approach—To attempt to achieve a failure-free enterprise, it is necessary to reframe the handling of errors from a person approach to a system approach. The person approach is an obsolete concept that human error is the primary cause of incidents; the culprits must be identified because they produce waste. Warnings, mandatory refresher training, suspensions, and other punishments along with more rigorous regulations and control mechanisms are the logical consequences. Punitive measures represent an understandable human reaction to error (lack or loss of control) but are not usually successful because they do not deal with the basic dynamics that lead to unwanted events.

The system approach treats human error as a symptom, not a cause. Mishaps are considered consequences of underlying problems of an organization. Dealing with the problems requires focus on an entire system—hardware and software designs, the efficacy of processes and regulations, the presence of role and goal conflicts, and production pressures.

Professor Rene Amalberti of IMASSA (France's institute for aerospace medical research) defined in his presentation at the Airbus Human Factors Conference in 2005 in Madrid that based on under-usage of a (fatal) risk of 10^{-4}, a transition to a system approach must take place. To clarify his point, a (fatal) risk of 10^{-4} equates approximately to risks from road traffic and medicine in general. A value of 10^{-2} would be very unsafe (equivalent to mountaineering in the Himalayas); 10^{-6} is ultra-safe (nuclear industries). The level for civil aviation is between 10^{-5} and 10^{-6}; 10^{-7} is according Amalberti's a level that does not require intervention because there is no chance (progressive curve). In other words, there is always "space for fate"—there is no form of intervention that will enable us to realize an accident-free enterprise (see Table 15.1). Control is an illusion!

Non-Punitivity—The core element of a system approach is non-punitivity. This means that individuals on the sharp end of the error chain (who "produced" the negative outcome) are not automatically made accountable. On the one hand, this helps explain the interrelation that created the adversity and is necessary to avoid future mishaps. On the other hand, it has an ideological impact because the understanding-process is seen as having a higher value than the punishment of the person who (allegedly) caused it.

Table 15.1   Model: Recombination and Use of Information from Reporting Systems, Amalberti 2005

Frequency				
10^{-2}	10^{-3}	10^{-4}	10^{-5}	10^{-6}
Next accident will repeat previous accidents		Next accident recombines parts of past accidents or incidents using same precursors		Next accident is unique; context is new; details may evoke past "micro accidents" not considered consequential

An automatic enmity exists between culprit and prosecutor and the culprit will try hard to be exonerated. This enmity leads mostly to loss of trust. Anger, fear, and stigmatization (black sheep phenomenon) prevent any kind of cooperation. It is paradoxical to speak about accountability when the accountable participants are forced to leave or are otherwise punished. Even if the incident affects an end to normal cooperation, replacing the person can create problems such as the loss of that person's knowhow, uncertainty about the successor, and potential loyalty-conflicts. Accountability via a system approach acquires a sustainable meaning. The belief system focuses on individual accountability and subsequent punishment is not productive. Consistent rehabilitation measures and preventive activities that keep the error from being reproduced make sense for all the parties involved.

Incident Reporting Systems—Installing a reporting system is the next logical step after acceptance of the concept that top-down control is an illusion, especially in large organizations. Management can obtain effective safety-related information only if it makes the need for subordinates to report incidents plausible. Incident reporting systems can be open, anonymous, or partially anonymous (e.g., de-identified through safety-personal). An interactive phase of implementation (including all involved) revealing intentions, possibilities, and limits is mandatory. An incident reporting system should be relevant to the needs of all involved and reporting should include incidents and near-misses. Threats and errors should be identified and eliminated. A safety manager should handle reported incidents. Large organizations require safety departments.

Safety Cultures in Finance Industries—The positive effects of implementation of a safety culture are high performance through identifying threats and errors as well as sustainable and transparent rehabilitation of made errors. Other positive results are the strengthening of solidarity and employee identification with mission and organization that increase motivation, leading to improved productivity and work environment. Sustainable prosperity is guaranteed.

The organizational goal is creating and preserving an environment that minimizes the risks of errors. Critical questioning and reflection by personnel at all levels is required relating to routine and other operations. A determination of how much centralization or decentralization is required to ensure safety. The result should be a same shared mental model by which all people in an organization follow maximized consistent communications and operational methods. The main challenge of implementation is initial scepticism about the real intentions of such projects. Building mutual trust requires time, and management commitment to the changes is an absolute necessity.

Financial operations have no alternatives. The failure to focus on human factors will cause safety measures to fail. Risk management, as it is practiced today, is obviously not effective. A human factors and system safety approach should be the base on which mathematical models bring the desired results. Such an approach endangers the powerful elites and they will resist. Other challenges are bank secrecy for protecting sensitive data versus needed transparency.

Management commitment is a precondition to implementation of a safety culture. After management is committed, the six steps are:

1. Disseminate information about intentions, goals, and concepts.
2. Categorize organizational structures based on complexity/coupling and determination to centralize or decentralize.
3. Classify errors and define threats.
4. Determine which threats and errors should be eliminated and the extent of resources that can be provided and will yield a return of investment.
5. Install a non-punitive organizational culture; work on group dynamics, hierarchies, communications, feedback, and incentives.
6. Implement reporting systems; assign (or hire) safety manager or build safety department.

Conclusions

Peer Steinbrück stated in an interview that he thought "We can do what we want, we have no chance, the whole entire system will collapse."* Steinbrück should know because he was Germany's minister of finance and a member of the G8 emergency negotiation team when Lehman Brothers crashed. To date,

---

* Article, Als ich das hörte, brauchte ich einen Stuhl," Szigetvari, A., (DER) Standard."

the system has not collapsed but if Steinbrück was correct, the current disaster represents the last severe incident before a worldwide worst-case-scenario.

Despite the serious threat, those who have vital interests in preventing changes continue to get what they want. For example, according to the media, John Paulson broke his own $4 billion earning record in 2007 and made $5 billion in 2010. The source of the money is "a top secret of the media-shy star" but certainly arose from investments in gold index funds.* The politicians and the public seem to have forgotten the passionate pleas of Nikolas Sarkozy who demanded "a total change" from finance industries in his opening speech at the 2010 World Economy Forum.†

IWF chief Dominique Strauss-Kahn who in the meantime had to quit his job because of his very personal scandal in 2011 described the ongoing bonification practice as something that: "seduces the finance branch to (new) white collar crimes"‡ While many people continue to show very little interest in the future developments in financial operations, billions of taxpayers' dollars and euros are used to "save" financial organizations whose leaders continue to construct artificial bubbles through speculation. This feeds the impression that both individuas and communities are carelessly ignoring these developments and thus playing with the futures of this generation and those to follow. Prevention is everyone's responsibility.

One conclusion could be that society simply gets the bank managers and politicians it deserves. This chapter reveals that the public (normal people, employees, but *even* smaller financial institutions) are caught in a devil's circle. They are *on a personal and organizational level part of a fight against* those threats and constraints an over-powerful "elite" who follows its own interests (*while keeping up a self-image of high performers*) brought into the world. Regardless of possible criminal issues, the paper shows that the ongoing constitutions of those social realities (unbalances) are not simply human nature (and inevitable anyway), but an erosion that can be named as *Drift into Failure and Normalisation of Deviance*. What also implies that "something" can be and should be done against it.

The first step is to categorize financial businesses as high risk environments. The second is to install a safety culture. The examples covered in this chapter show what happens when safety is ignored, supervision is flawed, and risk management models deny human factors: the industry pushed itself toward collapse after following illusions of control and getting caught up in the motivation trap. Despite "modern" bank risk management, disaster occurred in the name of production and protection was absent—another indication that a

* Der Milliardenmann, Braumberger, G., FAZ net, 2011.
† Es schlägt die Stunde der Mahner, Goffart, D., Knipper, H. & Riecke, T., Handelsblatt online, 2010.
‡ IWF Chef: Rückfall bei Skandalboni, ORF News online, 2011.

focus on human factors and system safety are desperately needed for financial organizations.

One of the core statements of this chapter is that it makes no sense to stigmatize people. It's about understanding how even mafia-like structured parts of the finance-branch with their almighty leaders work and how they follow a stringent way of encounter that is not positive for society. The recurrent theme of this chapter is developing human relationships and that requires an understanding of their feelings, thoughts, and beliefs and how people react with each other. Knowledge based on depth psychology can be of great help in explaining these socio-technical and organizational interactions in general and provide information about mishaps.

A safety group is invaluable for building and keeping real teams running through loyalty in which the right amount of reflective enmity is reflected. Simple acceptance of the existence of the "myth of rationality" would bring organizations a step further and allow them to reflect from other angles. Investing in safety cultures characterized by integrative safety departments (that have the psychological knowledge) is a good investment in the future. Safety departments endowed with sufficient resources can find and avoid one of the biggest social threats on organizations: the conformism that narrows vision and fosters pseudo-reflection. A safety group is invaluable for building and keeping real teams running through loyalty in which the right amount of reflective enmity is reflected. Instead of leaders whose personal needs force them to abuse their positions, leaders in a safety culture are selected to accept limits and to focus on sustainable development.

We as a society are at a point where we should open categorical discussions about which direction the world should follow on both ideological and practical paths. Our past hunger for more exhibited by the increasing speed and complexity of business endangers entire systems and nations. This chapter attempted to explain the inevitable man-machine interface what means that every development of technology has to be adapted onto human (psychological, social, and political) needs. It follows the perspective of humanistic psychology which postulates that the next necessary and useful step for society's development lies not so much in the outside (increase of technique) but in the inside (personal growth). We must deal with one of the most serious modern threats: the collective belief in the need for full speed operation and unlimited liberalization of financial market that led to a collective breakdown of trust and relationships. We are facing what Freud called *thanatomania,* a condition in which every structure we have built will be endangered and ultimately destroyed.

This chapter is a plea for a strong civil society wherein we stop projecting our hopes for a better and safer future onto, in some extent, anti-social, narcissistic persons. We should follow Freud's approach to detect individual and collective subconscious drivers and makes them conscious in the interest of whole social systems.

If current financial industries do not reframe and rebalance protection and production, back away from maximizing, and pursue sustainable optimization, they will destroy the stability and social balance the western world created after World War II. Hopefully, Einar Mar Gudmundsson, author and initiator of Iceland's "cooking-pot revolution" who cited Iceland as the experimental laboratory for the world economy crisis, will be proven incorrect. If Gudmundsson is correct, the world's political leaders will have to adapt the plea of Iceland's prime minister when he announced in fall 2008 that Iceland collapsed under a debt load more than twelve times the national budget: God save Iceland!*

References

Newspapers and Periodicals

Ackermann braucht kein Geld "Würde mich schämen," October 18, 2008. N-TV online. Retrieved December 12, 2010. http://www.n-tv.de/wirtschaft/meldungen/Wuerde-mich-schaemen-article29711.html

Als ich das hörte, brauchte ich einen Stuhl: Interview with Peer Steinbrück on the occasion of his book "Unterm Strich". October 9/10, 2010, p. 14. Andras Szigetvari. Der Standard.

Army major kills himself over Bernard Madoff fraud debts. February 13, 2009. *The Telegraph* online. Retrieved February 16, 2011. http://www.telegraph.co.uk/finance/financetopics/ bernard-madoff/4603017/Army-major-kills-himself-over-Bernard-Madoff-fraud-debts.html

Der Jahrhundertfehler: Gorillas Spiel, November 2009, *Der Spiegel* online. Retrieved February 1, 2010. http://www.spiegel .de/spiegel/print/d-64497194.html

Der Milliardenmann. January 29, 2011. *Frankfurter Allgemeine Zeitung* online. Retrieved February 25, 2011. http://www.faz.net/s/RubD16E1F55D21144 C4AE3F9DDF52B6E1D9/Doc~E7FBB8906885F489FBEAE352DAA49D0FA~A Tpl~Ecommon~Scontent.html

Die gewonnene Wette des John Paulson. April 17, 2010. *Zeit* online. Retrieved February 25, 2011. http://www.zeit.de/wirtschaft/2010-04/goldman-sachs-paulson

Einer zahlt alles. October 5, 2010. *Der Spiegel* online. Retrieved February 2, 2011. http://www.spiegel.de/wirtschaft/0,1518,721401,00.html

Es schlägt die Stunde der Mahner. January 27, 2010. *Handelsblatt* online. Retrieved November 14, 2010. http://www.handelsblatt.com / politik/international/davos-es-schlaegt-die-stunde-der-mahner;2520123

EU Studie: Jeder Dritte wünscht sich starken Mann. March 11, 2011. *ORF News* online. Retrieved March 11, 2011. http://www.orf.at/stories/2046991/

---

* Island in Sicht, Horst Christoph, *Profiles*, 2010.

Gefängniszelle statt Royal Suite mit Seeblick. January 24, 2011. *Frankfurter Allgemeine Zeitung* online. Retrieved March 2, 2011. http://www.faz.net/s/RubEC1ACFE1EE274C81BCD3621EF555C83C/Doc~EBEEC123B3D4C46D7B68024AA8D372AC1~ATpl~Ecommon~Scontent.html

Goldman Sachs will nicht gegen Kunden gewettet haben. April 7, 2010. *Zeit* online. Retrieved December 12, 2010. http://www.zeit.de/wirtschaft/unternehmen/2010-04/goldman-sachs-wetten

Goldman Settles With S.E.C. for $550 Million. July 15, 2010. *New York Times* online. Retrieved February 20, 2011. http://dealbook.nytimes.com/2010/07/15/goldman-to-settle-with-s-e-c-for-550-million/

Greenspan joins NY hedge fund. January 15, 2008. *Financial Times* online. Retrieved December 14, 2010. http://www.ft.com/cms/s/6ccb18b8-c2fb-11dc-b617-0000779fd2ac,html

In der Geiselhaft der Banken, Andreas Schnauder. November 23, 2010. *Der Standard*, p. 28.

IWF Chef: Rückfall bei Skandalboni. *ORF News* online. Retrieved February 21, 2011. http://www.orf.at/#/stories/2043434/

Island in Sicht. Christoph, H., *Profil* . 2010.

Jérôme Kerviel: Allein gegen die große Bank. June 8, 2010. *Die Presse* online. Retrieved December 2, 2010. http://diepresse.com/home/wirtschaft/international/572018/Jrme-Kerviel_Allein-gegen-die-grosse-Bank

Jobwechsel: Greenspan berät die Deutsche Bank. August 13, 2007. *Die Presse* online. Retrieved March 4, 2011. http://diepresse.com/home/wirtschaft/economist/323294/Jobwechsel_Greenspan-beraet-die-Deutsche-Bank?_vl_backlink=/home/wirtschaft/index.do

Klage mit aller Vehemenz bekämpfen. *ORF News* online. Retrieved December 17, 2010. http://www.orf.at/stories/2030532/2030538/

Lehman Probe Stalls; Chance of No Charges. March 12, 2011. *Wall Street Journal* online. Retrieved March 13, 2011. http://online.wsj.com/article/SB10001424052748703597804576194871565429108.html

Mächtige Clans im Hintergrund. *ORF News* online. Retrieved November 12, 2010. http://www.orf.at/stories/2025087/2018209/

Primeo-Schatten reichen bis nach Afrika. December 12, 2010. *Der Standard* online. Retrieved January 30, 2011. http://derstandard.at/1291454915125/weltweite-verluste-primeo-schatten-reichen-bis-nach-afrika

Schulmeister spricht von Finanzalchimisten. *ORF News* online. Retrieved September 24, 2010. news.orf.at/stories/2016131/2016144

Systematische Misswirtschaft bei Kreditvergabe. August 16, 2010. *Der Standard*, p. 9.

Verheerende Wirkung auf die Rechtskultur. February 10, 2011. *ORF News* online. Retrieved February 10, 2011. http://oe1.orf.at/artikel/269234/

Wall-Street-Legende im Zwielicht. April 20, 2010. *Frankfurter Allgemeine Zeitung* online. Retrieved December 25, 2010. http://www.faz.net/s/RubD16E1F55D21144C4AE3F9DDF52B6E1D9/Doc~E5D992A453E8C4ECD9B69406EF6DC28F2~ATpl~Ecommon~Scontent.html

Zahlungsunfähigkeit verheimlicht. *ORF News* online. Retrieved December 20, 2010. http://www.orf.at/stories/2032070/2032071/

Books and Papers

Berne, E. (1964). *Games People Play: The Psychology of Humans Relationships*. New York: Penguin Books.

Dekker, S.W. (2005). *Ten Questions About Human Error: A New View of Human Factors and System Safety*. Mahwah, NJ: Erlbaum.

Dekker, S.W. (2006). *The Field Guide to Understanding Human Error*. Hampshire, UK: Ashgate.

Dekker, S.W. (2007). *Just Culture: Balancing Safety and Accountability*. Hampshire, UK: Ashgate

Felsenreich, C. (2008). About Loyalty and Resilience: Why a New View on Human Error should Focus on the Dark Sides of Basically Positive Human Attitudes. Master's Thesis, Lund University School of Aviation.

Felsenreich, C. & Kriechbaum, K. (2008). *Politik-Analyse, Politik Therapie. Interaktives Fehlermanagement*. Wien: Kriechbaum Verlag

Freud, A. (1937). *The Ego and the Mechanisms of Defense*. London: Hogarth.

Freud, S. (1921). *Massenpsychologie und Ich-Analyse*. Leipzig: Internationaler Psychoanalytischer Verlag.

Fromm, E. (1964). *The Heart of Man: Its Genius for Good and Evil*. New York: Harper & Row.

Harris, T.A. (1967). *I'm OK, You're OK: A Practical Guide to Transactional Analyses*. New York: Harper & Row.

Hollnagel, E., Woods, D.D. & Leveson, N. (Eds.) (2006). *Resilience Engineering: Concepts and Precepts*. Hampshire, UK: Ashgate.

Kernberg, O.F. (2004). *Aggressivity, Narcissism and Self-Destructiveness in the Psychotherapeutic Relationship: New Developments in the Psychopathology and Psychotherapy of Severe Personality Disorders*. New Haven: Yale University Press.

Kriechbaum, K. (2010*). Der Mensch mit Eigenschaften: Unsere Programme, unsere Umwelt und unsere Zustände bestimmen unser Leben*. Wien: Kriechbaum Verlag.

Morgan, G. (1986). *Images of Organization*. Beverly Hills: Sage Publications.

Perrow, C. (1999). *Normal Accidents: Living with High-Risk Technologies*. Princeton, NJ: Princeton University Press.

Rochlin, G. (1999). Safe operation as a social construct. *Ergonomics*, 42, 1549–1560.

Rochlin, G., La Porte, T. & Roberts, K. (1987). The self-designing high reliability organization. *Naval War College Review*, Autumn 1987.

Röhr, H.P. (1999). *Narzissmus: Das innere Gefängnis*. München: dtv.

Schultz von Thun, F. (1989). *Miteinander Reden, Band 2: Stile, Werte und Persönlichkeitsentwicklung*. Hamburg: Rowohlt.

Snook, S.A. (2000). *Friendly Fire: The Accidental Shootdown of U.S. Black Hawks over Northern Iraq*. Princeton: Princeton University Press.

Vaughan, D. (1996). *The Challenger Launch Decision: Risky Technology, Culture and Deviance at NASA*. Chicago: The University of Chicago Press.

Watzlawick, P. & Beavin, J.H. (1980). Einige formale Aspekte der Kommunikation. In Watzlawick, P. & Weakland, J.H. (Eds.). Bern: Huber.

Stronger Oversight of the Financial Sector

16

Lessons from Institutional Reforms in Developing Countries

KATHARINA NOUSSI

Contents

"Remember this crisis began in regulated entities…. This happened right under our noses."

Paul S. Atkins, former member, U.S. Securities & Exchange Commission, 2008*

"The lessons we have to learn from the financial market crisis are clear: we need a new regulatory framework for financial markets that contributes to more responsible behavior on the part of all financial market participants."

Wolfgang Schäuble, Federal Minister of Finance, Germany, May 19, 2010[†]

---

[*] Wilmarth (2009: 967) citing Drew (2008).

[†] Effective Financial Market Regulation after Pittsburgh: Achievements and Challenges, International Conference, Federal Ministry of Finance, Berlin, May 2010, http://www.g20.org/Documents2010/05/201005_Germany.pdf (accessed 01 March 2011).

Introduction

The global economy is currently experiencing multiple crises that particularly affect the global poor.[*] Concerted action and political commitment are urgently needed to achieve institutional reform at the global, regional, national, and local levels. However, many observers would agree that reforms addressing financial regulation, climate change, trade policies, or democratic accountability are difficult births, often embracing too little substance and occurring too slowly.

This chapter will examine efforts to reform financial regulation and oversight as a response to the recent financial market crisis that started in mid-2007. However, the lessons can equally be applied to other contentious reform processes such as climate change, trade policy, and democratization. The first section of the chapter will briefly review the origin, reform proposals, and achievements to date relating to the global financial crisis. Another section of the chapter will take an unusual approach to the study of private financial sector reforms in industrialized countries by reviewing experiences with public finance reforms in developing countries. The chapter will also discuss current scholarship on institution building stemming from democratization and state-building theories, particularly the theory of rational choice institutionalism. Finally, it will propose a human rights-based approach to development as a possible strategy for reform-minded groups and concludes with a discussion of prospects for financial reform.

Financial Market Crisis: Origin and Necessary Reforms

The global economy is currently experiencing the most severe financial crisis since the Great Depression.[†] The crisis devastated global financial markets and triggered a world-wide recession.[‡] Global stock market values declined

---

[*] Addison and Tarp (2010) identify three distinct but interrelated crises: (1) the financial crisis, originating in the global North, but also affecting the global South via reduced demand and lower prices for their exports, reduced private financial flows, and falling remittances; (2) climate change and the growth in greenhouse gas emissions; and (3) despite a global commitment to the millennium development goals (MDGs), malnutrition and hunger are on the rise, propelled by the recent inflation in global food prices. We would add others: the crisis caused by rising illegal activities such as drug trade and human trafficking; the crisis caused by authoritarian regimes that inhibit public finance transparency and corruption control. The related public distrust may lead to public revolts such as the recent events in the Arab world. Finally, the crisis in Japan started a renewed debate about the dangers of atomic energy.

[†] Wilmarth (2009: 966) citing Brunnermeier (2009), Claessens et al. (2008), Gregg (2009), Bernanke (2009).

[‡] Wilmarth (2009: 967) citing: Faiola (2009), Gregg (2009), Slater (2009).

by $35 trillion during 2008 and banks and insurers reported $1.1 trillion of losses through March 2009.[*] Seventeen large universal banks account for more than half of those losses, and nine either failed, were nationalized, or required government-funded life support.[†]

Central banks and governments in the U.S. and European Union (EU) responded quickly to the crisis and provided $9 trillion of support to these and other financial institutions.[‡] It is generally agreed that large complex financial institutions were the primary private sector catalysts for the destructive credit boom that led to the subprime financial crisis. Their enormous losses reveal the stunning failures of financial regulatory agencies.[§] The agencies imposed light regulation of commercial banks, lighter regulation of investment banks, and little or no regulation on the 'shadow banking system,' hedge and private equity funds, and bank-created special investment vehicles (SIVs).[¶]

It is generally agreed that the current global financial crisis resulted in large part from major systemic failures: "a failure to put appropriate systems in place, a failure to make systems work properly, and a failure to foster the integrity of systems" (Thynne, 2011: 1). According to the analysis of the Financial Stability Board (FSB),[**] the crisis revealed that financial oversight institutions, particularly as they relate to the so-called systemically important financial institutions (SIFIs), must be reformed in four key areas:

1. Unambiguous supervisory mandates and independence as well as access to the appropriate quality and quantity of resources
2. A full suite of powers available to all national supervisors to execute on their mandate
3 An improved set of standards for supervisors, the quality of which must reflect the higher complexity of the financial system and the firms that comprise it, including the integration of better micro and macro risk detection processes
4. A stricter assessment regime that consistently drives supervisors to high quality work and alerts authorities to potential weaknesses in their oversight processes earlier (FSB, 2010b: 7)[††]

---

[*] Wilmarth (2009: 963, 966).
[†] Wilmarth (2009: 963, 968).
[‡] Wilmarth (2009: 963, 966).
[§] Wilmarth, (2009: 1046).
[¶] Crotty (2009: 564).
[**] The FSB was established in April 2009 as the successor to the Financial Stability Forum with the objective to coordinate at international level the work of national financial authorities and international standard setting bodies. http://www.financialstability-board.org (accessed 03 March 2011).
[††] See also FSB (2010a).

The question posed in this chapter is why have these oversight systems not been in place before the crisis and what are the critical factors for success in bringing about reforms? According to Tomasic (2011: 7) the massive financial frauds and misconduct revealed by the crisis (and long present in our markets) could occur because white collar crime is extremely difficult to prosecute.* The seeming invulnerability of some of the most powerful individuals and corporations to prosecution and regulation is enhanced in boom times and supported by political forces favoring corporate risk taking. After a period of seemingly global agreement that this crisis marks the end of financial liberalization,[†] as the world economy recovers, financial stakeholders are again questioning the need for regulatory and supervisory reforms.

On May 19, 2010, Wolfgang Schäuble, Federal Minister of Finance of Germany[‡] stated:

> However, as the immediate impact of the crisis wanes and the world economy recovers, the momentum for reforms risks letting up. Some financial institutions are again generating large profits, thanks not least to the vast government intervention deployed to rescue them. As a result, market players are increasingly questioning the need for regulatory and supervisory reforms.

Tomasic (2011:7) shows that bankers strongly influence governments and market ideology. He refers among others to the close relationship that emerged in recent times in the UK between the government and the City of London such as the appointment of senior bankers and business leaders to lead the policy formulation process. Sometimes, leaders of UK financial institutions become government leaders and senior regulators—a practice also common in the U.S. as Epstein and Carrick-Hagenbarth (2009) in their analysis of the linkages of academia, private financial institutions and public institutions demonstrate. Crotty (2009) equally points out the fact that between 1998 and 2008 in the U.S., the financial sector spent $1.7 billion in federal election campaign contributions and $3.4 billion to lobby federal officials.[§]

---

* Tomasic (2011: 7) citing: Gobert and Punch (2003), Orland (1995), Simpson and Gibbs (2007), Levi (1987), Tomasic (2000, 2005). When analyzing the criminalization of corporate conduct in the UK and the U.S. over the last thirty years, Tomasic (2011: 8) citing Simpson (2002: 16) shows how it has proven very difficult to deal with, let alone control, catastrophic failures of corporate conduct. The 1990s saw a contraction in the use of criminal law for white collar crimes. The introduction of legal reforms to fight the payment of bribes by UK companies in regard to off-shore contracts was strongly resisted for years.

[†] For a change of the global discourse see Crotty (2009: 575) quoting senior Financial Times columnist Martin Wolf (2009): "The era of financial liberalization has ended."

[‡] Effective Financial Market Regulation after Pittsburgh: Achievements and Challenges, International Conference, Federal Ministry of Finance, Berlin, May 2010, http://www.g20.org/images/stories/canalfinan/eventante/02germany.pdf (accessed 29 March 2012).

[§] Crotty (2009: 577) citing Wall Street Watch, 2009 :17.

The political pressure by the banks was also facilitated by governments, particularly those that competed with each other to create business-friendly financial centers such as London and New York (Tomasic, 2011: 8). Thus, the influence of the financial sector in politics cannot be underestimated. Tomasic pointedly summarizes that:

> These political forces have served to muzzle or curtail the activities of enforcement agencies either directly, through the lack of adequate resources, or indirectly, by promoting ideologies which legitimize the minimal role of government in market agenda preference for industry self-regulation (Tomasic, 2011: 7).

As an example how the prevailing political orthodoxy could not be challenged by regulatory agencies, Tomasic (2011: 8) quotes the governor of the Bank of England who emphasized the weaknesses of regulators as follows

> Any bank that had been threatened by a regulator because it was taking excessive risks would have had PR machines out in full force, Westminster and the Government would have been lobbied, it would have been a lonely job being a regulator.[*]

This leads to the conclusion that the introduction of stricter financial regulations and the bringing about of profound cultural changes within banks and financial institutions might be a difficult task as it will be strongly resisted by market actors and political forces benefitting from the current system.

Crotty (2009)[†] analyzes the assumptions of and empirical evidence on the theoretical foundation behind the New Financial Architecture (NFA)[‡] that he believes is among the roots of the crisis.[§] The claim of neoclassical financial economics is that free financial markets minimize the possibility of financial crises and the need for government bailouts.[¶] Although one might think that

---

[*] Tomasic (2011:8) citing the governor of the Bank of England who holds the Treasury Committee (House of Commons, Treasury Committee, 2009:12).

[†] As Crotty (2009) notes, he has taken this section from a much more detailed analysis of these structural flaws (see Crotty, 2008).

[‡] "New financial architecture" refers to the integration of modern financial markets with light government regulation introduced since the 1980s (Crotty, 2009: 564).

[§] "After 1980, accelerated deregulation accompanied by rapid financial innovation stimulated powerful financial booms that always ended in crises. Governments responded with bailouts that allowed new expansions to begin. These in turn ended in crises, which triggered new bailouts. Over time, financial markets grew ever larger relative to the nonfinancial economy, important financial products became more complex, opaque and illiquid, and system-wide leverage exploded. As a result, financial crises became more threatening. This process culminated in the current crisis, which is so severe that it has pushed the global economy to the brink of depression" (Crotty, 2009: 564).

[¶] Crotty (2009: 564) citing Volcker (2008) for a summary of this narrative and Crotty (2008) for an analysis of the assumptions.

the recent crisis delegitimized this doctrine, this is not clear. On the one hand, Crotty (2009) believes that many of the most influential supporters of the neo-liberal financial system, including Alan Greenspan, changed their stand. On the other hand, quoting among others Nobel Laureate Paul Krugman, Crotty questions the commitment of the Obama administration to bring about profound change as he believes the president's advisors are known critics of regulation, having "spent their entire careers opposing it" (Crotty, 2009: 577).

The reformers, of course, paint a brighter picture. Sven Andresen (2010), secretary general of the Financial Stability Board (FSB), believes that "regulatory reform is proceeding" at several places and levels today. The "new system-wide oversight arrangements" put in place include the U.S. Financial Services Oversight Council, the European Systemic Risk Board, the IMF-FSB Early Warning Exercise, and the Financial Stability Board (FSB). "Major jurisdictions and regions are reforming their regulatory and supervisory structures to strengthen responsiveness to systemic risks, improve coordination and close gaps." Principles have also been agreed internationally on how to expand "the regulatory perimeter to encompass hedge funds, OTC derivatives and credit rating agencies." Finally, "cross-border oversight" for so-called systemically important financial institutions (SIFIs) is being put in place (Andresen, 2010: 40).

In general, since the outbreak of the crisis, an unprecedented global coordination and reform commitment has been initiated by the G20.* However, many challenges remain, as the FSB itself admits in its last report to the G20 (FSB, 2011). It thus remains to be seen whether public pressure to reform will surmount the influence of the financial market players. Adam S. Posen, a senior fellow of the Peterson Institute for International Economics and external member of the Monetary Policy Committee of the Bank of England, in a statement at an international conference organized by the German Ministry of Finance in May 2010 in Berlin, captured the main points of this chapter:

---

* The Group of Twenty (G20) consists of the finance ministers and central bank governors of nineteen countries: Argentina, Australia, Brazil, Canada, China, France, Germany, India, Indonesia, Italy, Japan, Mexico, Russia, Saudi Arabia, South Africa, Republic of Korea, Turkey, United Kingdom, United States of America. The European Union, represented by the rotating council presidency and the European Central Bank, is the twentieth member. To ensure global economic fora and institutions work together, the managing director of the International Monetary Fund (IMF) and the president of the World Bank, plus the chairs of the International Monetary and Financial Committee and Development Committee of the IMF and World Bank also participate in G20 meetings on an ex-officio basis. The G20 thus brings together important industrial and emerging-market countries from all regions of the world. Together, member countries represent around 90% of global gross national product, 80% of world trade (including EU intra-trade) as well as two-thirds of the world's population. The G20's economic weight and broad membership give it a high degree of legitimacy and influence over the management of the global economy and financial system. http://www.g20.org/about_what_is_g20.aspx (accessed 11 April 2011).

What this ... leads to is a different overall philosophy for financial regulation. We need more rules and less discretion. In fact, we need big, dumb, blunt, binding simple rules for financial institutions to adhere to. I think the reason we saw so many bank supervisors fail in so many different ways was because there is no way to keep supervisors who have discretion from being captured or being scared to have things go wrong on their watch. Better to have very stiff rules and not subject the supervisors to a test of will. On both the micro-supervision and what is now called 'macro-prudential' sides, I want to see a lot less room for ad hoc judgments. There is a lot of talk about creating systemic risk committees, be that within the European System of Central Banks, in the U.S. or elsewhere. Just imagine what kind of lobbying would go with those committees, and what kind of uncertainty will hang over financial markets as a result.[*]

The G20 focuses political attention at the technical level on the creation of "colleges" of supervisors that can share information across borders on a confidential manner so as to create early warning systems (Matthews, 2010: 564–565 citing G20 and FSB communiqués). However, these informal mechanisms fail to address the enforcement issue. There exists no obligation to compel enforcement. The general empirical question to be addressed in this chapter is how to create a sincere political will for reform nationally and internationally in order to design and implement binding oversight systems and rules.

Ultimately, the reform of the financial sector comes down to increasing public accountability and control, which by its very nature will be resisted by groups benefitting from the current system, as power holders rarely cede power voluntarily. The chapter will now look at the experiences with reforms of public finance accountability in developing countries. This somewhat unusual approach is based on the idea that these countries can offer experiences with the introduction of highly contentious reforms. Many developing countries operate under semi-authoritarian regimes whose social order is built on corruption and patron–client networks. The introduction of stricter oversight of public finances is by definition strongly resisted in such countries, but under which conditions have reform efforts been successful?

Public Finance Oversight in Developing Countries

Corruption and the misuse of public funds are threats to human security. First, state capture, bias, and the malfunctioning of oversight institutions are threats to human security in the broader sense of human well-being. The

---

[*] Posen (2010: 22–23).

United Nations Convention against Corruption (2005: ii) states in its foreword that:

> Corruption is an insidious plague that has a wide range of corrosive effects on
> societies. It undermines democracy and the rule of law, leads to violations of
> human rights, distorts markets, erodes the quality of life and allows organized
> crime, terrorism, and other threats to human security to flourish.

When public finances are diverted or lost, they are not used to improve
education or health services and thus damage the fight against poverty, particularly in the poorest countries, and increase human insecurity. Second,
demands for more public accountability, transparency, and democratic
reforms may lead to more direct forms of physical violence as we have seen
recently in North Africa and the Middle East Region.

The UN Convention against Corruption also stresses that corruption
undermines democracy. It is undisputed that public finance oversight is an
important feature of democratic systems. The concept of democracy can be
defined from minimalistic or broad perspectives, all of which share the basic
principle of rule by the people.* For the current purpose, we need a broad
definition such as:

> Democracy is a social system that creates responsiveness to citizen
> interests and polices corruption. Therefore democracy requires not
> only elections, but also effective political institutions (North et al.,
> 2009a: 56).
>
> Public accountability is the hallmark of modern democratic gover-
> nance. Democracy remains a paper procedure if those in power can-
> not be held accountable in public for their acts and omissions, for
> their decisions, their policies, and their expenditures (Bovens, 2007:
> 182).

The past decade has seen a significant paradigm shift in the mechanisms
to deliver aid to developing countries and in the objectives of aid. During the
1980s and 1990s, the donor community conditioned aid delivery among others
on the reduction of national spending. That led to widespread privatization,
cuts in public services, and drastic downsizing of bureaucracies. Today, the aid
community stresses the need for good governance and in this context supports
the training of civil personnel and strengthening of state institutions. Thus,

---

* There exists no consensus on the concept of democracy. There are nearly as many definitions of democracy as scholars who study it. The definition of democracy has been one of
the most widely debated and contested issues in the history of political philosophy.

after fostering reductions of state institutions during the 1980s and 1990s, the aid community today stresses the need for institution building.

Particularly democratic institutions that should guarantee horizontal and vertical accountability often do not work properly and are subject to donor reforms. Such institutions, however, face a difficult challenge. Their task is to assert themselves against powerful forces within the state that would rather like to keep privileges and would like white collar crime to stay undetected. Oversight agencies (anti-corruption authorities, supreme audit institutions, the judiciary, and ombudsmen) often fail to investigate abuses of power in the public or private bodies over which they exercise jurisdiction for reasons of both elite capture and political bias.* The budget process is particularly prone to capture and rent seeking.† These factors make public finance control extremely difficult.

Supreme audit institutions (SAIs) such as auditors general and courts of audit were created to conduct external audits of public finances. External auditing is not an end in itself; it is a component of a regulatory system of public finance oversight that includes internal auditing, parliamentary reviews, public debate facilitated by the media, judicial prosecution, and other mechanisms. Most crucial to the operation of SAIs is their independence. Joseph Moser, president of the Austrian Court of Accounts and secretary general of the International Organization of Supreme Audit Institutions (INTOSAI) stated that:

> Only an independent external government audit function—in conjunction with professional staff and methodologies—can guarantee an unbiased, reliable and objective reporting of audit findings. The independence of Supreme Audit Institutions is therefore of primary importance for the transparency of public administration. It furthermore safeguards and sustains the efficiency of the control functions of Parliaments, thereby strengthening public trust in government institutions (INTOSAI, 2009: 1).

The crucial importance of the independence of SAIs is also reflected in the *United Nations General Assembly Resolution* A/RES/66/209, adopted in December 2011, which stresses that SAIs need to be *independent and protected against outside influence in order to accomplish their tasks objectively and effectively*. While SAIs exist in most states, recent studies and data reveal major weaknesses in government auditing in many countries. For example,

---

* See Goetz and Jenkins (2005) for a detailed discussion of the meanings of *capture* and *bias*.
† Economists often define rents as *excess returns* above *normal levels* in competitive markets. More specifically, rent is "a return in excess of the resource owner's opportunity cost." (Tollison, 1982 cited at http://en.wikipedia.org/wiki/Economic_rent#cite_note-4, accessed 11 April 2011).

de Renzio (2009) analyzed PEFA* data and stated that, "Although most countries fare quite well in regard to the initial stages of the budget process, their performance gradually deteriorates when one looks at predictability and control in budget execution, accounting, recording and reporting, and external scrutiny and audit."

A survey by the International Budget Partnership (IBP, 2010: 6) confirms these findings of generally weak SAIs: "The overall strength of SAIs is relatively weak. Among 94 countries assessed in the 2010 Survey, the average score for questions on the strength of SAIs was just 49 of 100. Only 24 of the 94 countries surveyed have strong SAIs while 32 countries have weak SAIs."

Andrews (2010) differentiates in his study of public finance management (PFM) reforms in Africa between various performance leagues. Some countries are making more progress than others. Still, as Andrews noted, certain findings were typical for most African countries:

- Budget preparation processes are comparatively stronger than budget execution and oversight processes across all African countries.
- African PFM systems generally suffer from an implementation deficit; laws and processes may be in place but seldom affect behavior.
- Processes that involve multiple players are weaker.

These findings are in line with many other authors' conclusions.[†] They all criticize the largely technical approach used to reform budget institutions in poor countries by bilateral and multilateral development agencies. Positive experiences with reforms often result from political economy approaches that emphasize a systemic approach to reform.

If an SAI is not independent, the focus of reform can not only lie in improving the internal governance of the SAI: "Existing reforms face limits that can only be overcome with adjustments in reform approach; with less focus on pushing reform technicalities and more on creating 'space' in which reform takes place, less concentration of engagements with small sets of actors and more on expanding engagements, and less emphasis on reproducing the same reform models and more on better understanding what context-appropriate reforms look like," (Andrews, 2010: ii).

---

[*] The Public Expenditure and Financial Accountability (PEFA) Program started in 2001 as a multi-donor partnership intended to "to strengthen recipient and donor ability to (i) assess the condition of country public expenditure, procurement and financial accountability systems, and (ii) develop a practical sequence of reform and capacity-building actions." One important tool of the PEFA is the development of assessment reports of country performances; see www.pefa.org (accessed 06 March 2011).

[†] Allen (2008, 2009); Santiso (2006, 2009); Pretorius & Pretorius (2008); Shah (2007); Stapenhurst et al. (2008).

In sum, current scholarship including the recent World Bank (2010) analysis of SAIs in the Middle East and North Africa region concludes that the political economy of reform is crucial to its success. "Ultimately the success of efforts to build the capacity of the audit body will depend on whether the parliament is prepared to utilize the auditor's report" (World Bank, 2010: 33).

O'Donnell (1993, 1998), who, in some ways originated the concept of accountability, argued that integrity and transparency in government require that state agencies of horizontal accountability interlock and overlap in a systemic fashion. Diamond (2009: 303) elaborates on O'Donnell's argument: "Interlocking authority allows different agencies to become reinforcing, so that, for example, an audit agency uncovers fraud, a countercorruption commission imposes civil penalties for it, the judiciary presses for criminal penalties, and an ombudsman stands by to investigate and report if any piece in the process breaks down or needs assistance."

In summary, this section demonstrated that public finance oversight is considered an important feature for development and democracy and has given an overview of the current state of affairs. The overall conclusion is that although institutions may be de jure in place, de facto they often do not work properly. Furthermore, reform experiences have shown that despite the importance of technical aspects of reform, political will ultimately conditions reform success. The next section discusses the elements needed for favorable political environments to emerge.

Theories on Institution Building

Three main approaches apply to understanding institution building in developing countries (Krasner, 2009). First, modernization theory (Lipset, 1959; Przeworski et al., 2000; Boix & Stokes, 2003; Sachs, 2005, 2008; Inglehart & Welzel, 2008) argues that economic and social development through urbanization, value changes, and education will lead to a demand for democratization. The lesson drawn from this strand of theory would be to take a socio-economic development approach that supports growth and may lead in the long term to public demand for accountability.

The second approach stresses that states must first build effective democratic institutions to develop. The debate about institutional capacity emerged after the influential comparative studies of democratic transitions by Linz and Stepan (1996), the World Bank's "The State in a Changing World" report (1997), and the work of Fukuyama (2004). Fukuyama explains that while it was necessary to limit the scope of state functions in poor countries, it was a mistake to also reduce state capacity. This strand of thinking is based on the early work of state theorists such as Huntington (1965, 1968) and Tilly (1992).

The essence of the institutional capacity theory is that development will occur only if states succeed in building effective autonomous institutions able to organize politics. Thus, building accountability and effective oversight is understood as a prerequisite for socio-economic development. The mainstream of development policy today follows this institutional capacity approach and stresses the need for capacity building of state institutions, particularly those guaranteeing horizontal and vertical accountability that generally show poor performance in aid-dependent countries. Capacity building is provided in the form of technical assistance such as training programs and infrastructure grants. However, the success of this technocratic approach on institution building is disputed. Some argue that, although capacity building is crucial during the reform process, if it is provided in a political vacuum, it only creates "empty shell institutions."

The third approach agrees with the institutional capacity theory that institutions are prerequisites for development but criticizes the capacity building approach. This group of scholars emphasize the politics (political processes and power games) behind the pol...ities (political institutions), as well as the difficulties of transferring effective institutions to weak states. The new stream of research on democracy and capitalism applies what Krasner (2009) called "rational choice institutionalism" and others called an "integrated political economy approach" (North et al., 2009b: 269) or "new structuralism" (Iversen, 2006: 617) to understanding how institutions develop. Common is the interest in looking at the socio-economic conditions behind the institutions to understand their creation and mode of functioning. Typical questions are why some institutions of public accountability work effectively and others do not, and what structural conditions facilitate pacts for sustainable democratic reforms.

Before this chapter discusses the main ideas of the "rational choice institutionalism theory," I will summarize the main insights so far in this chapter, on how effective regulation and oversight within the context of the new financial architecture might develop. According to the insights from modernization theory, an enlightened and demanding public would be the prerequisite for effective reform. This is, of course, a huge topic of current scholarly debate.

Some scholars claim that the current capitalistic financial system lost its legitimacy. Based on the periodic occurrence of major financial crises and economic recessions, the public will organize and demand more regulation, accountability, redistribution, and may even call for an end of the capitalist system. Others are more skeptical and cite two arguments against that idea. First, politics and the media are often heavily influenced by financial elite groups and thus a total change of discourse is not likely. Second, even if most people are skeptical of the current financial system, they may not necessarily believe a different system will perform better.

The financial crisis of 2007 triggered huge public outcry and calls for reform. The G20 were compelled to make economic recovery and reform of the NFA its top priority. However, as the effects of the crisis are slowly overcome, so is the coverage of the reform progress in the media. Public interest is already decreasing. It has also become clear that building stronger financial oversight and redistribution such as the introduction of a tax on financial transactions is not a technical matter of policy formulation but a political issue. Holders of power rarely relinquish control to the poor and less powerful. Consequently, contrary to the assumption of the theory of institutional capacity, financial regulation and oversight cannot be autonomous as the groups benefitting from the current system must be embedded in the oversight institutions to make them work and be sustainable. Under what conditions do privileged groups accept deals that will cause them to make concessions?

This chapter will now try to develop insights based on rational choice institutionalism. While modernization theory and institutional capacity theory believe in economic and political development if only the assistance is provided, this approach negates that political development is a linear process. The essence of this stream of thinking is that individuals and groups act according to their available options, and therefore the results of political deals are always open and not linearly defined. One of the latest books on this line of thinking is *Violence and Social Orders* by North et al. (2009b). The authors base their theory in part on the influential study of democratic transitions by Acemoglu and Robinson (2006).

Acemoglu and Robinson developed a framework that demonstrates when and how elites find it in their interest to concede power to non-elites. North et al. (2009b) developed this framework further by arguing that the elites are not a unified group; rather, they compete and even go to war against each other. Therefore they cannot intentionally decide to do anything, let alone to share power with non-elites. The contribution of North et al. (2009b) to the democracy and transition literature is the theory that corruption and personalized political and economic institutions preserve political order and prevent violence among elite groups in developing countries. Thus, reforming accountability institutions must be a deeply political endeavor, not a technocratic matter. The political order of a society must change, and the change necessitates political deals between the elite groups and perpetual organizations in order to develop sustainable democracies.

Based on extensive historical analysis, North et al. (2009b) explain that the transition from authoritarian to democratic structures must be consistent with the logic of the current social order. To trigger a transition, it is important to create preconditions that convince the elites that it is in their own interest to transform personal and privileged deals among themselves into impersonal laws so that all elite group members are treated the same way. In a second step, elites will transform their unique and personal rights to impersonal rights for all citizens. North et al. (2009a, b) call these pre-conditions for increased impersonal exchanges the "doorstep conditions." They are:

- The rule of law among elites (the objective is to separate personal identity from privilege and thus contribute to new ways for imper-sonal exchange and trade).
- The development of perpetual elite organizations in the private and public domains (sophisticated organizations that last and are not tied to a specific person; this increases impersonal exchange as one can count on the firm or public entity to last and is thus more inclined to invest in or trade with the firm or entity or take on its regulations).
- The consolidation of political control over the military (to prevent the spread of violence among various groups and achieve stability for investment and political development).

Democracies can also develop otherwise (e.g., through revolutions) but in these cases they are often not stable. The main feature of sustainable political orders is that they must be self-enforcing and pareto-improving. "Democracy endures only if it is self-enforcing. It is not a contract because there are no third parties to enforce it. To survive, democracy must be in a state of equilibrium at least for those political forces which can overthrow it: given that others respect democracy, each must prefer it over the feasible alternatives" (Przeworski, 2006: 300, citing Przeworski 1991).

This logic of a self-enforcing equilibrium contradicts the theorem that democracies develop from constitutions.* Constitutions are necessary but in the sense of coordination, that is, they pick one equilibrium from among several.† Democracy survives not by exogenous rules but for endogenous rea-sons. Democracies are self-enforcing because it is in the incumbents' interest to be moderate; otherwise they face a threat of rebellion.‡

---

* "Constitutions are not necessary because democracy survives not because of exogenous rules but for endogenous reasons, they are self-enforcing. The rules that regulate the functioning of a democratic system need not be immutable or even hard to change. When a society is sufficiently wealthy, the incumbents in their own interest moderate their distributional zeal and tolerate fair electoral chances. Democratic governments are mod-erate because they face a threat of rebellion. Democratic rules must be thought of as endogenous" (Przeworski, 2006: 320–321 citing Calvert, 1994, 1995).
† Przeworski (2006: 321 citing Hardin, 2003).
‡ "This logic of a self-enforcing equilibrium is consistent with John Locke's discussion of the right of rebellion in his Second Treatise of Government. Locke stipulates a set of con-ditions that can justify rebellion; each of these conditions is tantamount to a violation of the basic constitutional structure of the polity" (Krasner, 2005: 81 citing Weingast, 1997).

Other authors applying a similar framework of elite networks and their role in development are Khan (2005, 2006), Fisman (2001), Meisel and Ould Aoudia (2008) and the new research on authoritarianism such as Haber (2006) and Magaloni (2008). To summarize, the third theoretic framework called rational choice institutionalism argues that politics is central to development processes.[*] The current proposed policy options stemming from these insights, according to the analysis of Krasner (2009) vary substantially, from abolishing aid altogether (Moyo, 2009) to altering external incentives (Collier, 2010) and supporting local initiatives (Easterly, 2006).

This section reviewed three theories on institution building from the democratization, state building, and development scholarship. The first theory subsumed as modernization theory believes in strengthening public demand for accountability. The second focuses on building institutional capacities. The third puts politics at the heart of the issue and concludes that democratic reforms will endure only if they are self-enforcing and thus Pareto-improving. Otherwise they will not be accepted. In the context of democratization processes, demands for reform that are not embraced by all elite groups as the best available options will lead to violence, repression, or in the case of a public revolution, it will be followed by a renewed dictatorship.

Public demand for reform and institutional strengthening may thus not be sufficient strengthening for financial market oversight. Reforms must also be Pareto-improving and thus be embraced by the powerful institutions and groups benefitting from the current system. Otherwise reforms will not be accepted or will be too shallow or too little too late as some observers believe.[†] Overt political repression and violence will not arise in the democratic countries of the OECD but we already see the rise of extremist parties and social movements (to the left, right, and as religious terrorism). This chapter has shown that public demand for stronger financial oversight is crucial to reform success, but it also argued that enduring reforms must be gradually developed and unfortunately can succeed only if they are embraced by all elite groups and thus all major financial actors in the world. Sven Andresen, secretary general of the FSB stated:

> Three things have been important in getting us to where we are now. First, the recognition that, in a closely integrated system, we all sit in the same boat. Second, the political leadership in agreeing on objectives and timelines for substantial reform, including through the G20 process. Third, the establishment of mechanisms, such as the FSB to hasten and coordinate the policy

---

[*] See Schouten (2008), Unsworth (2009, 2010), or Leftwich & Sen (2010) for recent accounts of the debate.

[†] http://mises.org/mobile/daily.aspx?Id=5060 (accessed 03 March 2011). http://www.guardian.co.uk/business/2010/sep/14/banking-reforms-too-little-too-late (accessed 03 March 2011).

development needed to meet these objectives. Based on these pillars, and
with continued resolute political leadership, I am quite confident that we will
be able to move forward to achieve a strengthened global financial system.
(Andresen, 2010: 41)

To conclude, while technical and organizational capacities including guaranteed and secured resources of oversight agencies are required
to allow regulators to act with confidence and courage, political economy
factors such as the leverage of public demand for reform linked to the
legitimacy of the financial architecture and the options available to various
privileged groups ultimately impact the success of reform. Crucial, according to North et al. (2009b), is an understanding of the relationships among
various financial market actors.

Understanding the problem in terms of a conflict between elites and the
masses (Acemoglu & Robinson, 2006) is not sufficient. The conflicts among
various elite groups are just as important for implementing change. Thus the
main question is how can financial reforms be Pareto-improving and self-
enforcing? Perhaps reforms will be successful and sustainable only if SIFIs
find it in their own interest to make concessions.

Human Rights-Based Approach to Development

One comprehensive approach in line with the idea that politics is central to
development is the human rights-based approach to development (HRBA).
The concept was developed by UN agencies as a result of the 1997 Programme
for Reform whereby Kofi Annan, then UN secretary general, called on all
entities of the UN "to mainstream human rights into their various activities
and programs within the framework of their respective mandates."*

This chapter argues that a HRBA may be an adequate policy response
to institution building understood from a rational choice perspective. An
HRBA to development considers politics central to development processes.
It starts its assumptions and development interventions from the perspective
of individuals and their choices on one hand and in the strengthening of the
role of international, national, and local institutions on the other. The HRBA
works toward strengthening the capacities of rights holders (particularly dis-
criminated groups) to make their claims and duty bearers (particularly state
authorities) to meet their obligations.

The HRBA treats the attainment of development goals and the fulfill-
ment of human rights as two sides of the same process. It adds legitimacy
to development objectives by transforming the language of needs to a

* http://hrbaportal.org/?page_id=2127 (accessed 06 March 2011).

language of rights. It also introduces the analysis of the responsibilities of various actors and imposes accountability for failures within an institutional framework:

> A human rights-based approach is a conceptual framework for the process of human development that is normatively based on international human rights standards and operationally directed to promoting and protecting human rights. It seeks to analyze inequalities which lie at the heart of development problems and redress discriminatory practices and unjust distributions of power that impede development progress. (OHCHR, 2006: 15)

There are significant differences between a rights-based approach and an economic approach to development:

> For many economists, any attempt to posit and enforce a human right to basic services is either fanciful or counterproductive, or both. Human rights theorists counter that economists are too quick to hide behind the impracticality of realizing rights, particularly economic and social rights, when in many cases violations are primarily the result of explicit political decisions rather than resource scarcity or other physical or institutional limitations (Seymour & Pincus, 2008: 388, citing Donnelly 2003: 29).

Despite these profound disagreements, authors such as Gauri (2004) and Seymour & Pincus (2008) believe that both approaches share similarities and are in fact complementary. Both approaches have their origins in enlightenment thought and are committed to the autonomy of the individual and his or her choices.[*] The HRBA to development can direct the tools of economics to contribute to the attainment of human rights that are articulated in international law. On the other hand, economic understanding and tools are important for human right defenders to pursue their goals more effectively (Seymour & Pincus, 2008: 404). The two different views can even be reconciled regarding the concept of accountability.

The economic approach views processes of account giving instrumentally. From a HRBA view, account giving facilitates development processes and is also part of the objective of development per se. Normative

---

[*] "Whether the focus is on rights or preferences, the individual reigns supreme, with all the methodological advantages and disadvantages that this implies for the study of society. Economists recognise that the rational agents who motivate their microeconomic models could not freely express their preferences without the prior realisation of at least some rights. That set includes property rights, the realisation of which, as with rights more generally, assumes the prior existence of the required legal infrastructure to establish and protect them. For their part, rights advocates know that individuals cannot realise their rights without access to a minimum level of income" (Seymour & Pincus, 2008: 388).

micro-economic theory on the other hand has as objective to expand choices to consumers, both because choices raise utility directly and because competition among providers increases social welfare. Therefore, account giving is critical in an economic approach but does not have intrinsic value. It could in principle be reconciled with authoritarian styles if they had the same goals (Gauri, 2004).

However, both the HRBA and the economic perspective to development are skeptical that electoral politics and market rules alone will provide sufficient accountability for the effective and equitable provision of services. Both approaches recommend wider access to information, more local organizations for more local organizations, stronger advocacy, and changes in governance to strengthen the positions of service recipients and rights holders respectively (Gauri, 2004).

According to the HRBA, effective institutional reforms in highly contentious areas such as financial sector oversight can only be achieved if the general public identifies its rights and claims them. Furthermore, the oversight of the international financial sector must be embedded in a system of public accountability based on international law. However, which international law are we talking about? The need for greater clarity of rights and responsibilities in the cross-border financial sector is clear, particularly with respect to failed institutions.

Matthews (2010: 557) notes that customary public international banking law is currently being developed as standards are set by the G20. "In other words, the G20 is creating a path by which informal standards can gain the force of law by incorporating the work of informal bodies into formal treaty-based entities with real authority to act at the global level" (p. 556). Finally, the IMF as an enforcement agency is developing a range of mechanisms to compel enforcement by its member states (e.g., revision of Article VIII and the Memoranda of Understanding; see Matthews, 2010: 572). This development of a first customary law can succeed if supported by the public and codified into international law. Only then will it be possible to effectively hold duty bearers such as governments and SIFIs accountable without relying merely on voluntary early warnings by colleagues and superiors.

Summary and Conclusions

This chapter started by investigating the assumption that the subprime financial crisis with all its effects on the global economy resulted from financial crimes. A number of studies verify this hypothesis and suggest that these white collar crimes were only possible because of the political ideology in place, the powerful influence of the banking and financial sectors in politics, and insufficient regulation and control. Current efforts for reforming financial control and regulation among the G20 and beyond have been criticized as "too little too late."

The intent of this chapter was to analyze why stronger regulation and control of the financial sector are hard to achieve and what can be done. We took the unusual approach of looking at the poorest countries, some of which do not even have financial sectors in place. The chapter reviewed empiric evidence of reform in public finance auditing in aid-dependent countries. The main lessons from auditing reforms is that they are only effective if they are holistic, strengthen the whole system of democratic control, and the public demands accountability.

I reviewed the scholarly debate on democratic institution building in developing countries. Public demand and institutional capacity are important. However, for democratic institutions to work effectively and be sustainable, the social order must change. The current order cannot be understood without analyzing the issue of violence and how it is currently contained. Thus, contrary to what we may want to see, oversight institutions cannot be completely autonomous from the groups they must control. Oversight must include the elites or they will not be effective.

Oversight institutions must also enjoy a high degree of independence; otherwise they will be strongly biased and easily captured by powerful elite groups. To conclude, for these institutions to be effective, it must be in the interest of privileged groups to make democratic concessions and thus concede power to oversight institutions. The most promising condition for democratic reform to develop and endure is organizational proliferation by which elites create rules and institutions to improve and regulate competition among them to prevent violence. Financial market regulation requires a solution that is pareto-improving and self-enforcing.

This chapter argues that strengthening the transparency, accountability and regulation of the financial sector will only be possible if the main market players are put into a position where it is in their own interest to agree to such reforms. This could be the case if the losses faced by financial criminals are high, legal prosecution is consistent and severe, public bailout of financial losses is unlikely, and public outcries and demands for greater transparency and oversight are loud and persistent. Finally, this chapter proposes reform-minded groups to take a human rights-based approach to advocate for institutional reform. This requires strengthening the capacities of the public to claim rights (through education, awareness raising, alliance building, networking, etc.) and to locate responsibilities within a system of public accountability in order to help duty-bearers to meet their obligations.

References

Acemoglu, D. & Robinson, J.A. (2006). *Economic Origins of Dictatorship and Democracy*. New York: Cambridge University Press.

Addison, T. & Tarp, F. (2010). The Triple Crisis: Finance, Food, and Climate Change. Working Paper 2010/01, World Institute for Development Economic Research (UNU-WIDER).

Andresen, S. (2010). Effective financial regulation after Pittsburgh: achievements and challenges. Speech at International Conference, Federal Ministry of Finance of Germany. Berlin, May. http://www.g20.org/Documents2010/05/201005_Germany.pdf (accessed 01 March 2011).

Allen, R. (2008) Reforming fiscal institutions: the elusive art of the budget advisor. *OECD Journal on Budgeting*, 3, 1–9.

Allen, R. (2009). The Challenge of Reforming Budgetary Institutions in Developing Countries. IMF Working Paper.

Andrews, M. (2010). How Far Have Public Financial Management Reforms Come in Africa? HKS Faculty Research Working Paper Series RWP10-018, Harvard University, John F. Kennedy School of Government: Cambridge, MA.

Boix, C. & Stokes, S.C. (2003). Endogenous democratization. *World Politics*, 55. 517–549.

Bovens, M. (2007). Public accountability. In Ferlie, E., Lynn, L.E. & Pollitt, C. (Eds.), *The Oxford Handbook of Public Management*. Oxford: Oxford University Press, 182–208.

Collier, P. (2009). *Wars, Guns and Votes: Democracy in Dangerous Places*. London: Bodley Head.

Crotty, J. (2009). Structural causes of the global financial crisis: a critical assessment of the new financial architecture. *Cambridge Journal of Economics*, 33, 563–580.

De Renzio, P. (2009). Taking Stock: What do PEFA Assessments Tell Us about PFM Systems across Countries? Working Paper 302, Overseas Development Institute, London.

Diamond, L.J. (2009). *The Spirit of Democracy: The Struggle to Build Free Societies throughout the World*. New York: Times Books/Holt.

Easterly, W. (2006) *The White Man's Burden*. New York: Penguin Press.

Epstein, G. & Carrick-Hagenbarth, J. (2009). Financial Economists, Financial Interests and Dark Corners of the Meltdown. Working Paper 239, University of Massachusetts, Political Economy Research Institute, Amherst.

Financial Stability Board (FSB). (2010a). Intensity and Effectiveness of SIFI Supervision: Recommendations for Enhanced Supervision.

Financial Stability Board (FSB). (2010b). Reducing the Moral Hazard Posed by Systemically Important Institutions. Recommendations and Time Lines.

Financial Stability Board (FSB). (2011). Progress in the Implementation of the G20 Recommendations for Strengthening Financial Stability. Report to G20 Finance Ministers and Central Bank Governors.

Fisman, R. (2001). Estimating the value of political connections. *American Economic Association*, 9, 1095–1102.

Fukuyama, F. (2004). The imperative of state building. *Journal of Democracy*, 15, 17–31.

Gauri, V. (2004). Social rights and economics: claims to health care and education in developing countries. *World Development*, 32, 465–477.

Goetz, A.M. & Jenkins, R. (2005). *Reinventing Accountability: Making Democracy Work for Human Development.* Basingstoke, Palgrave Macmillan.

Haber, S. (2006). Authoritarian government. In Weingast, B.R., Wittman, D.A. & Goodin, R.E. (Eds.), *The Oxford Handbook of Political Economy.* Oxford: Oxford University Press, 693–707.

Huntington, S.P. (1965). Political development and political decay. *World Politics* 17, 386–430.

Huntington, S.P. (1968) *Political Order in Changing Societies.* New Haven: Yale University Press. (A new edition with a foreword by Francis Fukuyama was published in 2006.)

Inglehart, R. & Welzel, C. (2008). *Modernization, Cultural Change, and Democracy: The Human Development Sequence.* Cambridge: Cambridge University Press.

International Budget Partnership (IBP). (2010). *Open Budgets. Transform Lives.* Washington: IBP.

INTOSAI. (2009). Lima Declaration and Mexico Declaration. General Secretariat, Vienna. http://www.intosai.org/blueline/upload/englisch.pdf (accessed 03 March 2011).

Iversen, T. (2006). Capitalism and democracy. In Weingast, B.R., Wittman, D.A. & Goodin, R.E. (Eds.), *The Oxford Handbook of Political Economy.* Oxford: Oxford University Press, 601–623.

Khan, M. (2005). Markets, states, and democracy: patron-client networks and the case for democracy in developing countries. *Democratization,*12, 704–724.

Khan, M.H. (2006). Governance and development. Paper presented at World Bank and DFID Workshop, Dhaka.

Krasner, S. (2009). State development, state building and foreign aid. Speech at Stanford University. http://cddrl.stanford.edu/events/state_development_state_building_and_foreign_aid/ (accessed 10 October 2010).

Krasner, S.D. (2005). The case for shared sovereignty. *Journal of Democracy* 16, 69-83.

Leftwich, A. & Sen, K. (2010). Beyond institutions: institutions and organizations in the politics and economics of growth and poverty reduction- a thematic synthesis of research evidence. http://www.ippg.org.uk/8933_Beyond%20Institutions.final%20(1).pdf (accessed 05 February 2011).

Linz, J. & Stepan, A.C. (1996). *Problems of Democratic Transition and Consolidation: Southern Europe, South America, and post-Communist Europe.* Baltimore: Johns Hopkins University Press.

Lipset, S.M. (1959). Some social requisites of democracy: economic development and political legitimacy. *American Political Science Review,* 53, 69–105.

Magaloni, B. (2008). Credible power sharing and the longevity of authoritarian rule. *Comparative Political Studies,* 41, 715–741.

Matthews, B.C. (2010). Symposium: International law and the economic crisis. Emerging public international banking law? *Chicago Journal of International Law,* 539.

Meisel, N. & Ould Aoudia, J. (2008). *Is Good Governance a Good Development Strategy?* Paris: French Development Agency.

Moyo, D. (2009). *Dead Aid.* London: Allen Lane.

North, D.C., Wallis, J.J. & Weingast, B.R. (2009a). Violence and the rise of open-access orders. *Journal of Democracy,* 20, 55–68.

North, D.C., Wallis, J.J. & Weingast, B.R. (2009b). *Violence and social orders: A conceptual Framework for Interpreting Recorded Human History*. New York: Cambridge University Press.

O'Donnell, G. (1993). On the state, democratization and some conceptual problems: a Latin American view with glances at some postcommunist countries. *World Development*, 21, 1355–1369.

O'Donnell, G. (1998). Horizontal accountability in new democracies. *Journal of Democracy*, 9, 112–126.

OHCHR (Office of United Nations High Commissioner for Human Rights). (2006). Frequently Asked Questions on a Human Rights-Based Approach to Development Cooperation.

Posen, A.S. (2010). Shrinking financial institutions and imposing rules on supervisors. Speech at International Conference, Federal Ministry of Finance of Germany. Berlin, May. http://www.g20.org/Documents2010/05/201005_Germany.pdf (accessed 01 March 2011).

Pretorius, C. & Pretorius, N. (2008). Review of Public Financial Management Reform Literature. Department for International Development (DFID) Evaluation Working Paper EV698, London.

Przeworski, A. (1991). *Democracy and the Market: Political and Economic Reforms in Eastern Europe and Latin America*. New York: Cambridge University Press.

Przeworski, A. (2006). Self-enforcing democracy. In Weingast, B.R., Wittman, D.A. & Goodin, R.E. (Eds.), *The Oxford Handbook of Political Economy*. Oxford: Oxford University Press, 312–328.

Przeworski, A., Alvarez, M.E., Cheibub, J.A. & Limongi, F. (2000). In Przeworski, A. (Ed.). *Democracy and Development: Political Institutions and Well-Being in the World, 1950–1990*. New York: Cambridge University Press.

Przeworski, A., Stokes, S.C. & Manin, B. (1999). *Democracy, Accountability, and Representation*. Cambridge: Cambridge University Press.

Sachs, J.D. (2008). *Wohlstand für viele. Globale Wirtschaftspolitik in Zeiten der ökologischen und sozialen Krise*. München: Siedler.

Sachs, J.D., Rennert, U., & Schmidt, T. (2005). *Das Ende der Armut. Ein ökonomisches Programm für eine gerechtere Welt*. München: Siedler.

Santiso, C. (2006). Banking on accountability? Strengthening budget oversight and public sector auditing in emerging economies. *Public Budgeting & Finance,* 26, 66–100.

Santiso, C. (2009). *The Political Economy of Government Auditing: Financial Governance and the Rule of Law in Latin America and Beyond*. London: Routledge.

Schäuble, W. (2010). Speech at International Conference, Federal Ministry of Finance of Germany. Berlin, May. http://www.g20.org/Documents2010/05/201005_Germany.pdf (accessed 01 March 2011).

Schedler, A. (Ed.). (2006). *Electoral Authoritarianism: The Dynamics of Unfree Competition*. Boulder, CO: Lynne Rienner.

Schouten, P. (2008). Theory Talk 21. Stephen Krasner on Sovereignty, Failed States and International Regimes. http://www.theory-lks.org/2008/10/theory-talk-21.html (accessed 01 March 2011).

Seymour, D. & Pincus, J. (2008). Human rights and economics: the conceptual basis for their complementarities. *Development Policy Review*, 26, 387–405.

Shah, A. (2007) *Performance Accountability and Combating Corruption*. Washington: World Bank.

Stapenhurst, R. (2008). *Legislative Oversight and Budgeting. A World Perspective*. Washington: World Bank.

Thynne, I. (2011). Symposium introduction: the global financial crisis, governance and institutional dynamics. *Public Organization Review*, 16, 1–12.

Tilly, C. (1992). *Coercion, Capital, and European States, 1990–1992*. Cambridge: Blackwell.

Tomasic, R. (2011). The financial crisis and the haphazard pursuit of financial crime. *Journal of Financial Crime*, 18, 7–31.

Tollison, R.D. (1982). Rent seeking: a survey. *Kyklos*, 35, 575–602.

United Nations. (2005). *United Nations Convention against Corruption*. Vienna: United Nations Office against Drugs and Crime.

Unsworth, S. (2009). What's politics got to do with it? Why donors find it so hard to come to terms with politics, and why this matters. *Journal of International Development*, 21, 883–894.

Unsworth, S. (2010) An upside view of governance. http://www2.ids.ac.uk/gdr/cfs/ pdfs/AnUpside-downViewofGovernance.pdf (accessed 01 March 2011).

Weingast, B. (1997). The political foundations of democracy and the rule of law. *American Political Science Review*, 91, 245–263.

Wilmarth, A.E. (2009). The dark side of universal banking. *Connecticut Law Review*, 41.

World Bank. (1997). *The State in a Changing World*. Oxford: Oxford University Press.

World Bank. (2010). *Public Financial Management Reform in the Middle East and North Africa: Overview of Regional Experience*. Report 55061-MNA, World Bank, Washington.

Business Angels
Can They Help to Prevent Another Financial Crisis?

17

CLEMENS FATH

Contents

Introduction

The financial crisis that started in 2007 is considered by many scientists and economists to be the worst financial crisis since the Great Depression of the 1930s. The crisis was triggered by the collapse of the United States housing bubble followed by a liquidity shortfall in the U.S. banking system, resulting in the collapses of large financial institutions, the bail-out of banks by national governments, and downturns in stock markets around the world.

Many causes of the financial crisis have been suggested and numer-ous proposals to prevent future crises have been discussed. However, no amount of monitoring of economic and financial indicators would have enabled any regulator to keep under control the human behavior that led to excessive risk taking by financial institutions. What drove these banks to excessive risk taking? We all know that it was the greed of individuals to earn more and more cash.

Research in the informal venture capital market[*] has been fashionable since the early 1980s because informal venture capital is seen as an important stimulus for the economic development of a country. Informal venture capi-talists, also called *business angels*, are well known as important stakeholders for potential high-growth ventures. Empirical research indicates that busi-ness angels contribute with funding and bring added value to the ventures in which they invest. They play a vital role for the development and growth of new ventures in terms of the financial capital they invest and the entrepre-neurial skills, expertise, and personal networks acquired throughout their professional lives.

This chapter discusses the various value-added benefits and presents a model that explains under which circumstances the cooperation between a business angel and an entrepreneur is successful.

From the analysis of twenty-seven Austrian cases we can learn that a fit between the dimensions of the supply (*business angels*) and the demand (*entrepreneur)* is most important. Critical dimensions for this fit are the quantity and quality of the involvement of the business angel, the atti-tude of the entrepreneur toward cooperation, and a need for management services in the venture. These dimensions are integrated in a model that describes the performance-influencing factors of a venture backed by a business angel. Finally, the chapter discusses which findings can be derived from the analysis of the described value-added services to prevent another financial crisis. Obviously, business angels share their experiences, act as sparring partners, and bring entrepreneurs "back down to earth." They provide coaching and consulting services that may allow bank employees, investment companies, rating agencies, and other financial entities to pre-vent another financial crisis.

---

[*] Informal venture capital is defined as investments by individuals (informal investors or business angels) of unquoted equity capital in ventures that they do not operate; their expected reward is an eventual capital gain.

Value-Added Services of Austrian Business Angels: An International Comparison

Overview of Research Findings

The author completed a review of the results of studies from the United States, Canada, Australia, Japan, Singapore, Great Britain, Germany, Finland, Norway, Sweden, and Austria to obtain the data to analyze the effects of value-added services on the economy of countries and regions. Comparative works of Brettel et al. (2000), Gaston (1989), Mason (1991 & 1992), Kelly (2000), Landström (1993), Mason and Harrison (1993 & 1995), and Stedler and Peters (2003) formed the basis for the analysis.

To provide a clear explanation, the value-added services of business angels are classified into subcategories based on the formal–juridical role of the business angel within a company: (1) the types of value-added services (tasks performed); (2) quality of value-added services (value of tasks performed); and (3) quantity or time intensity (frequency or amount of support) of value-added services provided to entrepreneur.

Formal–Juridical Role

The role of the business angel depends on his or her formal–juridical position in a company. Business angels perform various functions (participate in management, sit on advisory or supervisory boards) without filling formal positions. International research studies indicate that business angels generally pursue very active, hands-on management roles. For example, 60% of the investors in the study of Mason and Harrison (1996) were members of the board of directors of the companies (two served as chairmen) and 40% held no formal-juridical positions in the companies.

Types of Value-Added Services

A sample of Austrian business angels (n = 27; Fath, 2004) shows a similar distribution (Table 17.1). Most of those interviewed (67%) were members of supervisory or advisory boards, 13% acted as a managers or co-manager, and 20% said they filled no formal–juridical positions. According to Harrison and Mason (1992a), Ehrlich et al. (1994), Freear et al. (1995), Brettel et al. (2000), Ardichvili et al. (2000), Haines et al. (2002), Hemer (2002) and Stedler and Peters (2002), the value-added services of business angels vary widely. In fact, their contributions may be large enough to change the direction of a company. This is in line with the statement of Kelly (2000), who confirms

Table 17.1   Value-Added Services of Austrian Business Angels to Portfolio Companies

Rank	Type of Value-Added Service	Number Contributing to Specific Areas
1	Strategic advice	24 (88%)
2	Contact mediation	21 (77%)
3	Coaching and sparring in decisive situations	18 (66%)
4	Consultation in financial matters	17 (62%)
5	Marketing support	14 (51%)
6	Support in human resource management	10 (37%)
7	Provision of start-up expertise	10 (37%)
8	Provision of industry expertise	6 (22%)

Note: Total participants = 27.

that the importance of the role of a business angel is context-related and can change over time. A review of the literature and research on value-added services of business angels and findings from the interviews of Austrian business angels resulted in the following categorization:

- Consulting services related to formulation of company's strategy
- Mediation of contacts ("door opening")
- Coaching and sparring to aid decision making
- Financial monitoring
- Operational functions (marketing, human resource management, etc.)
- Triggering start-up and providing consulting services during start-up

Except for a few small differences, the results of the interviews of Austrian business angels corresponded to the results of the studies from Ehrlich et al. (1994) and Harrison and Mason (1992b). The great importance of mediation of contacts for Austrian angels is obvious. The four most frequent contributions in the study of Ehrlich et al. (1994) were (1) communications with other investors, (2) financial monitoring, (3) acting as a "sounding board" and (4) consulting services focusing on company strategy.

In the study of Harrison and Mason (1992b), the activities indicating the greatest importance were: (1) development of company strategy, (2) operating as a "sounding board," (3) financial monitoring, and (4) development of marketing plans or supervision of operative performance. Ehrlich et al. (1994), Harrison and Mason (1992b), and others reveal that a large proportion of business angels play important roles in developing and implementing company strategies. Their expertise comes into play when they serve as coaches and introduce new perspectives and skills in various business disciplines.

The advice of a business angel can be of great value to a company in the process of a strategic reorientation. The author's research indicated that strategic advice was of the highest importance. Business angels usually have access to tight networks of contacts built over the courses of their careers. Such networks of contacts with decision makers in the industrial and financial worlds and with experts like lawyers, tax advisers, and consulting firms can be useful to an entrepreneur developing a company. The results of our research confirm the assumption of Brettel et al. (2000) that the value-added contribution through mediation of contacts is of greater importance in Germany than in other countries, also for Austria.

Coaching and Sparring Partner in Decision Making

Business angels often act as coaches or "sounding boards" (Ehrlich et al., 1994) and thereby transfer their general business experience and ideas. The entrepreneur accepts the business angel as a person with whom he can discuss everyday problems and share the burden of making all decisions. Entrepreneurs often feel alone. A business angel allows them to reflect on decisions and discuss problem areas of the company.

The results of the Austrian research work suggest that the greater the insecurity about the future demand, prices, and customer preferences, the more business angels can contribute to the development of a company. Thus, the entrepreneur can benefit from the business and life experience of an angel. The task of the business angel is to act as a constructive consultant and demonstrate what is practical and feasible and what is not.

Financial Monitoring

Private investors who supervise their investments merely by joining supervisory or advisory boards and receive regular reports are passive investors, not business angels. In addition to financial monitoring, business angels usually support entrepreneurs with a range of services that fall between passive investment on the one side and co-management on the other. The financial monitoring of a business angel is similar to that performed by other investors (reviewing and discussing budgets and plans; Mason & Harrison, 1996). Entrepreneurs usually send monthly financial reports to business angels who compare them with original budgets and/or business plans. Entrepreneurs may also provide angels with market results or technical progress reports. The results of the Austrian study have shown that the cooperation between business angel and entrepreneur builds trust and eventually reduces the entrepreneur's burden of writing financial reports and following other control measures.

Table 17.2   Operational Activities of Business Angels

Activity	Percent
Developing marketing plan	64
Motivating personnel	56
Interfacing with other investors	61
Providing contacts with customers	56
Developing product and service techniques	53
Evaluating product and market opportunities	61
Replacement of management team member	52
Assistance with short-term crises and problems	58
Management recruiting	47
Development of products and services	58
Help in obtaining sources of debt financing	42
Help in obtaining sources of equity financing	56
Providing contacts with suppliers	39

Source: Harrison, R.T. & Mason, C.M. (1992b). *Frontiers of Entrepreneurship Research*, 388–404. With permission.

Operational Functions

In some cases, business angels also execute operational tasks and support the entrepreneur in relevant areas like marketing, personnel management, accounting or legal matters, negotiating, and moderating change. Table 17.2 lists operational activities of British business angels. The percentages indicate business angels (n = 36) who indicated that they actively executed the respective tasks listed. The author's research indicates that Austrian business angels predominantly support entrepreneurs in the areas of marketing, finance, and personnel management (Table 17.1).

Trigger for Start-Up

The results of the interviews with Austrian business angels revealed that some companies would not have been started without the support of business angels. Therefore, the business angel may act in a supporting function that influences a start-up decision.

Consulting During Start-Up

Our research reveals that in several cases business angels actively participated in and supported managerial activities during start-ups. They helped create business plans and continued to participate by offering assistance in the development and implementation of the plans. For example, they helped to find suitable office space and wrote job descriptions.

Quality of Value-Added Services

The quality of value-added services touches on an area that has to date been neglected in international research. Only the study of Harrison and Mason (1992) notes that entrepreneurs at times are not totally satisfied with the quality of value-added services provided by business angels. The quality of the services provided depends on the specific needs of the company.

On the basis of the results of interviews of the Austrian business angels, clearly the contribution of the provided value-added services depends on the knowledge and experiences of business angels. If a business angel can provide good contacts with potential customers, suppliers, banks, and other entities and has leadership experience, start-up expertise, and the ability to advance a company, an entrepreneur can derive great benefit. However, the services of a business angel may not contribute to a company and add value and may, in fact, be a burden if the angel pursues a negative course that leads to an undesirable trend, for example, by following a misleading or unclear strategy.

Quantity of Value-Added Services

By definition, a business angel is not a passive capital investor who only takes part in advisory meetings and plays no role in management. Depending on how a business angel defines his role, he can strongly influence a company or exert very little influence. Landström (1992) differentiated active and passive business angels.

The contributions of passive business angels, for example, are limited to support on advisory boards, sharing contacts, or acting as mentors or sparring partners. Very active business angels exercise their functions by acting as co-managers who support development of a company in an operative way. In most cases, this very active participation is executed only for a short period and somewhat informally. A substantial time must pass before the importance of value-added contributions is recognized.

The time spent by German angels varies between one to three days per month (Brettel et al., 2000), totaled about twelve hours per month for Swedish angels (Landström, 1993), and one or two days per week for British angels (3i Group plc, 1994). Neiswander (1985) reports that U.S. business angels devote on average five hours per week during the first six months of their investments and thereafter spent three to five hours per week. The results of our research are in line with the findings of studies reported in the literature. On average, Austrian angels (n = 27) reported that they spent four to five, days per month working for their portfolio companies.

Development of Model to Demonstrate Value-Added Contributions

According to Landström and Olofsson (1996), entrepreneurs continuously argue that the experience of business angels is of even higher value than pure financing although the conditions under which the contributions of business angels really add value to a company are debatable. Which factors decide whether a business angel really contributes to the success of a company? The conditions that help a company achieve additional value (beside financial capital and improved equity capital ratio) depend on a series of factors. A two-phase model (Figure 17.1) describes how success factors of business angel investments become effective. The model is based on the fit concept of the configuration approach (Mugler, 1998), various empiric research results (Barney et al., 1994; Busenitz et al., 1997; Rosenstein et al., 1993; Sapienza et al., 1996), and on the contingency-based model of Wijbenga et al. (2003).

Phase 1: Fit as a condition for a successful cooperation — Does a business angel fit to the specific entrepreneur, the environment, and the company? This is the main issue in the pre-investment phase (phase 1) during which a business angel makes his investment decision. The analysis of the observed cases supports the thesis that different fit categories between an angel on one side and the variables (environment, company, entrepreneur)on the other determine whether the match of a certain business angel with a certain entrepreneur in a certain environment in a certain company is likely to succeed.

"Fit" is defined as the result of a mutual coordination process (Mugler, 1998) between two or more variables intended to optimize the relationship

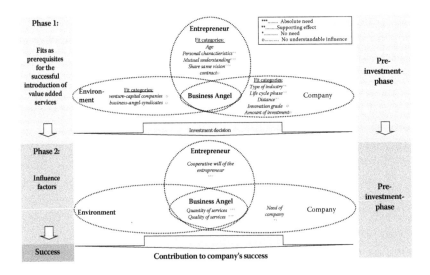

Figure 17.1 Two-phase success factor model.

between the variables. A good fit is seen as a prerequisite for a successful contribution of value-added services. As an example, consider a business angel experienced in a certain market. This factor increases the value of the cooperative effort and is a requirement for a successful contribution of value-added services. The business angel will have a better understanding of the demands and problems of the company.

Phase 2: Factors of influence — If the necessary conditions for a successful cooperation (phase 1) are present, the arrangement progresses to phase 2 (post-investment) based on certain factors of influence:

- Quantity of value-added services: Does the business angel have enough time to support the entrepreneur or the company?
- Quality of value-added services: Does the business angel have the abilities needed by the entrepreneur or the company?
- Cooperation will of entrepreneur: Is the entrepreneur generally willing to openly accept the value-added services of the business angel or is he interested only in the financial aspects of the cooperation?
- Need of company: Are value-added services the business angel can provide really needed by the company?

Quantity Factor

The analysis of the research on Austrian business angels has shown that the appropriate time intensity or depth of service provided is far more important than the amount of time spent. The right fit between the time capacity of a business angel and the needs of an entrepreneur or the needs of the company is decisive. The business angel should allow enough room to maneuver and adjust the services to fit the needs of the entrepreneur.

For example, a typical trait of an entrepreneur is the need for independence (Klandt, 1984, 120) that could be endangered by a business angel who interferes too much. Busenitz et al. (1997, 175) explain that this "overinvolvement" may be obstructive for the development of a company. However, a business angel should make available a minimum amount of time to actively support the entrepreneur or the company. Sapienza et al. (1996) indicated that the profit contribution of the value-added services introduced by venture capital companies[*] strongly depends on the frequency of on-site support or the number of hours a venture capital investor spends at the company.

---

[*] Venture capital companies invest their shareholders' money in start-up companies and other risky but potentially profitable ventures. The work of business angels is usually informal; the work of venture capital companies is institutionalized.

Quality Factor

The quality of the introduced value-added services, for example, the quality of the network contacts a business can make available to an entrepreneur or special knowledge of a business angel about certain areas of a company can vary significantly. If the business angel can establish valuable contacts with banks, investors, customers, or suppliers and open doors that were previously closed, the access to the contact network of the business angel adds significant value to the company. The same is true if the business angel increases the strengths of the entrepreneur (e.g., as a sparring partner) or can equalize the weaknesses of the entrepreneur (e.g., lack of business administration skills) and make a positive contribution to the development of a company. This relation was noted by Rosenstein et al. (1993) who argued that the profit contribution of the introduced value-added services depends primarily on the knowledge and experience of the venture capital investor.

Cooperation Will of Entrepreneur

The cooperation will of the entrepreneur is an absolute requirement for a successful contribution of value-added services (Barney et al., 1994). If the entrepreneur judges the value-added services of the business angel as valuable to him and his company and if he is interested in more than the capital provided by the business angel, the stage is set for a successful contribution. Some of the Austrian business angels in our research noted that entrepreneurs welcomed their services as useful contributions during the pre-investment phase. However, in the post-investment phase, the cooperation of the business angel was seen as a negative involvement in management operations. Wijbenga et al. (2003, 244) explain that the entrepreneurs who have a personal characteristic known as internal locus of control are rather willing to cooperate with venture capital investors, because they view value-added services more openly and are more receptive to advice, improvements, and suggestions.

Company Needs

If the value-added services of a business angel based on his experience and expertise are not the services urgently needed by the company, no positive contribution to development will likely occur because of this misfit. Based on the resource-oriented approach, Wijbenga et al. (2003, 241) see a profit contribution if the value-added services add to the available resources of the company. For example, if a company lacks expertise in business administration because the entrepreneur's education and focus are on engineering, the investment of a business angel experienced in managing start-up companies is a reasonable supplement of resources. Wijbenga et al. (2003, 239) argue that "the success of growth companies strongly depends on the personality of the entrepreneur or his industry, strategy and management experience. Should the entrepreneur have weaknesses in these areas, the value-added services are especially valuable as a supplement to the available abilities of the entrepreneur. Entrepreneurial fit relates to directing the venture capital companies' value-contributing activities such that they align with the entrepreneur's features. A proper alignment enhances the portfolio company's performance."

Success Factor Model

The factors of influence are shown in a success factor model described in Figure 17.1. The single fit categories or factors of influence determine the success or failure of cooperation with a business angel. They also determine whether the business angel investment (in addition to financial capital) can contribute to the positive development of a company. This model is based on the assumption that a good fit of variable groups is a prerequisite for a successful contribution of value-added services in the post-investment phase. Because not all fits are equally important, the single fit categories and successful factors were weighted as follows:

Number of Stars	Extent of Need
3	Absolute need
2	Supporting effect
1	No need or no understandable influence

The described weighting is an attempt to highlight the importance of single fit categories for the contribution of value-added services. It is not about showing that cooperation with a business angel can succeed only if every single fit category reaches optimum. It should demonstrate that some factors are more important than others and that single factors that appear not important may exert influence on overall cooperation.

To explain the relationships in the success factor model, the "mutual understanding" fit category is described as an example. If business angels are asked to name the key factors of a successful cooperation, mutual understanding, sympathy, and trust are cited most. A harmonious relationship of both actors is vital in crisis situations. If mutual understanding is absent, the result is a misfit and both parties should carefully reconsider another arrangement, for example, status as a minority investor with standard rights of information (Riding et al., 1995; Mayfield, 2000).

The importance of "interpersonal aspects" for the contribution of value-added services was stressed by Sapienza et al. (1996, 464) who state, "In some cases, where the relationship is really a solid one with management, we can add a lot more than just money. In those cases where we don't have a good relationship, when we don't have rapport, there is just nothing we can do."

Higashide and Birley (2002) empirically prove that an emotional conflict of the personalities of the entrepreneur and venture capital investor has a negative influence on the development of a company. A mutual understanding is required for the introduction of value-added services into the post-investment phase. In such a case the entrepreneur will not reject the inputs of the business angel and allow the angel sufficient time. Because of the great importance of mutual understanding, the model fit value is three stars (absolute need).

Conclusions

Sometimes it is useful to consider other areas, different disciplines, or research fields to incorporate new ideas into an existing field of research. This approach was used in this chapter. At first sight, business angel financing (usually focusing on start-up ventures or small companies) and the huge financial industry involving complex derivative spin-offs appear to have little in common.

However, this chapter shows that business angels can provide guidance in unstable situations (like a start-up or crisis situations) by providing value-added services. Their expertise is helpful in supporting decision making processes whenever an entrepreneur faces complex and unusual tasks. They also have the potential to reduce the risk potential of a company, particularly through coaching and consulting.

Employees of banks, investment companies, and rating agencies would benefit from such expertise and perhaps prevent another financial crisis. The existing players in the financial industry are well advised to increase their focus on new ways to reduce financial risks in their businesses. Simple quantitative measures such as adding staff to internal control departments are not sufficient. The focus should be on the quality of all levels of management of an organization.

The introduction of financial angels with extensive experience in public and private financing may be one of many measures required to reduce the inherent risk in the financial industry. As in the success factor model, a first step should ensure that the role and task of a financial angel fits into the existing structure and process. Financial angels can contribute to improve the soundness and financial behavior for public and private financial institutions if management supports the approach, the financial angel has sufficient experience, and the angel has the necessary rights and power to change the financial structure and processes.

References

3i Group plc. (1994). *Angel Investors*. London, 3i plc.

Amatucci, F.M. & Sohl, J.E. (2004). Women entrepreneurs securing business angel financing: tales from the field. *Venture Capital*, 16, 181–196.

Ardichvili, A., Cardozo, R.N., Tune, K., & Reinach, J. (2000). The role of angel investors in the assembly of non-financial resources of new ventures. *Frontiers of Entrepreneurship Research*, 2000, 483–504.

Barney, J.B., Busenitz, L., Fiet, J.O. & Moesel, D. (1994). Determinants of a new venture team's receptivity to advice from venture capitalists. *Frontiers of Entrepreneurship Research*, 321–335.

Brettel, M., Jaugey, C. & Rost, C. (2000). *Der informelle Beteiligungskapitalmarkt in Deutschland*. Gabler Verlag, Wiesbaden.

Busenitz, L.W., Moesel, D.D. & Fiet, J.O. (1997). The impact of post-funding involvement by venture capitalists on long-term performance outcomes. *Frontiers of Entrepeneurship Research*, 174–188.

Ehrlich, S.B., DeNoble, A.F, Moore, T. & Weaver, R.R. (1994). After the cash arrives: a comparative study of venture capital and private investor involvement in entrepreneurial firms. *Journal of Business Venturing*, 9, 67–82.

Fath, C. (2002). Business–Angels–Finanzierungen: ein Literaturüberblick. *Journal für Betriebswirtschaft*, 52, 84–101.

Fath, C. (2004). Konfigurationstheoretische Analyse der Business–Angel–Finanzierung in Österreich. Dissertation, Wirtschaftsuniversität Wien.

Freear, J., Sohl, J. & Wetzel, W.E. (1994). Angels and non-angels: Are there differences? *Journal of Business Venturing*, 9, 109–123.

Freear, J., Sohl, J. & Wetzel, W.E. (1995). Angels: personal investors in the venture capital market. *Entrepreneurship and Regional Development*, 7, 85–94.

Gaston, R.J. (1989). *Finding Private Venture Capital for Your Firm: A Complete Guide*. John Wiley & Sons, New York.

Haines, G., Madill, J. & Riding, A. (2002). Value Added by Informal Investors: Findings from a Preliminary Study. Unpublished. Carleton University, Ottawa.

Harrison, R.T. & Mason, C.M. (1991). Informal risk capital in the UK and the USA: a comparison of investor characteristics, investment preference and decision-making. *Frontiers of Entrepreneurship Research*, 469–481.

Harrison, R.T. & Mason, C.M. (1992a). International perspectives on the supply of informal venture capital. *Journal of Business Venturing*, 7, 459–475.

Harrison, R.T. & Mason, C.M. (1992b). The roles of investors in entrepreneurial companies: a comparison of informal investors and venture capitalists. *Frontiers of Entrepreneurship Research*, 388–404.

Hemer, J. (2002). Mehrwert von business angels in der Net Economy. In Kollmann, T. (Ed.), *E-Venture-Management, neue Perspektiven der Unternehmensgründung in der Net Economy*. Gabler Verlag, Wiesbaden, 327–343.

Higashide, H. & Birley, S. (2002). The consequences of conflict between the venture capitalist and the entrepreneurial team in the United Kingdom from the perspective of the venture capitalist. *Journal of Business Venturing*, 17, 59–81.

Homan, D. (2001). Planungsfehler, mangelndes Rechnungswesen, Eigenkapital-Mangel und mangelnde Kenntnis der eigenen Branche sind die häufigsten Konkursursachen, Wirtschaftsblatt, D3, 18.09.2001.

Kelly, S. P. (2000). Private Investors and Entrepreneurs: How Context Shapes their Relationship. Dissertation, London.

Klandt, H. (1984). Aktivität und Erfolg des Unternehmensgründers. *Eine Empirische Analyse unter Einbeziehung des mikrosozialen Umfeldes*. Josef Eul Verlag, Bergisch Gladbach.

Lamnek, S. (1995). *Qualitative Sozialforschung Band 1: Methodologie. Deutscher Studien* Verlag, Weinheim.

Landström, H. (1992). The relationship between private investors and small firms: an agency theory approach. *Entrepreneurship and Regional Development*, 4, 199–223.

Landström, H. (1993). Informal risk capital in Sweden and some international comparisons. *Journal of Business Venturing*, 8, 525–540.

Landström, H. & Olofsson, C. (1996). Informal venture capital in Sweden. In Harrison, R.T. & Mason, C.M. (Eds.), *Informal Venture Capital: Evaluating the Impact of Business Introduction Services*. Simon & Schuster, Hertfordshire, 273–284.

Lindsay, N.J. (2004). Do business angels have an entrepreneurial orientation? *Venture Capital*, 16, 197–210.

Lipper, G. & Sommer, B. (2002). Encouraging angel capital: what the U.S. states are doing. *Venture Capital*, 4, 357–362.

Mason, C.M. (2002). Business angels: critical players in the supply of risk capital to entrepreneurial businesses. In *Belgian Yearbook of Corporate Finance*. Intersentia, Antwerpen.

Mason, C.M. & Harrison, R.T. (1993). Informal risk capital: a review of US and UK evidence. In Atkin, R., Chell, E. & Mason, C.M. (Eds.), *New Directions in Small Business Research*, Avebury Business School Library, Aldershot, 155–176.

Mason, C.M. & Harrison, R.T. (1995). Closing the regional equity gap: the role of informal venture capital. *Small Business Economics*, 7, 153–172.

Mason, C. M. & Harrison, R. T. (1996). Informal Venture capital: a study of the investment process and postinvestment experience. *Entrepreneurship and Regional Development*, 9, 105-126.

Mason, C.M. & Harrison, R.T. (2000). Informal venture capital and the financing of emergent growth businesses. In Sexton, D. & Landström, H. (Eds.). *Blackwell Handbook of Entrepreneurship*. Blackwell, London, 221–239.

Mason, C.M. & Harrison, R.T. (2004). Does investing in technology-based firms involve higher risk? *Venture Capital*, 6, 313–332.

May, J. (2002). Structured angel groups in the USA: the Dinner Club experience. *Venture Capital*, 4, 337–342.

Mayfield, W.M. (2000). The formation of the angel-entrepreneur relationship during due diligence. *Frontiers of Entrepreneurship Research*, 551–574.

Mugler, J. (1998). *Betriebswirtschaftslehre der Klein und Mittelbetriebe. 3. Aufl., Band 1*, Springer, Wien.

Neiswander, D.K. (1985). Informal seed stage investors. *Frontiers of Entrepreneurship Research*, 142–154.

Riding, A., Duxbury, L. & Haines, G. (1995). Financing Company Development: Decision Making by Canadian Angels. Unpublished. Carleton University, Ottawa.

Röpke, J. (1999). Der lernende Unternehmer: Läßt sich Unternehmertum lehren und lernen? Zur Evolution unternehmerischen Bewußtseins, Marburger Foerderzentrum fuer Existenzgruender aus der Universität, Marburg.

Rosenstein, J., Bruno, A.V., Bygrave, W.D. & Taylor, N.T. (1993). The CEO, venture capitalist, and the board. *Journal of Business Venturing*, 8, 243–252.

Sapienza, H.J. (1992). When do venture capitalists add value? *Journal of Business Venturing*, 7, 9–27.

Sapienza, H.J., Manigart, S. & Vermeir, W. (1996). Venture capitalist governance and value added in four countries. *Journal of Business Venturing*, 11, 439–469.

Sørheim, R. (2003). The pre-investment behavior of business angels: a social capital approach. *Venture Capital*, 5, 337–364.

Stedler, H.R. & Peters, H.H. (2003). Business Angels in Deutschland: Empirische Studie der FH Hannover zur Erforschung des Erfolgsbeitrages bei Unternehmensgründung. Fachhochschule Hannover. Fachbereich Wirtschaft, Hannover.

Sternberg, R. (1999). Entrepreneurship in Deutschland: Das Gründungsgeschehen im internationalen Vergleich. Länderbericht Deutschland zum Global Entrepreneurship Monitor. Edition Sigma Verlag, Berlin.

Stinakovits, K. (2001). Der Beitrag informeller Investoren zur Schließung der Equity und Experience Gap. Diplomarbeit, Wirtschaftsuniversität Wien.

Suomi, M. & Lumme, A. (1994). *Informal Private Investors in Finland*. Sitra, Helsinki.

Van Osnabrugge, M. & Robinson, R.J. (2000). *Angel Investing: Matching Startup Funds with Startup Companies*. Jossey-Bass, San Francisco.

Wetzel, W.E. (1981). Informal risk capital in New England. *Frontiers of Entrepreneurship Research*, 217–245.

Wijbenga, F.H., Postma, T.J., Witteloostuijn, A.V. & Zwart, P.S. (2003). Strategy and performance of new ventures: a contingency model of the role and influence of the Venture capitalist. *Venture Capital*, 5, 231–250.

Legislative and Programming Initiatives to Prevent and Control Financial Crimes in the United States

18

PETER C. KRATCOSKI

Contents

Introduction

Efforts to control corruption and protect the financial interests of U.S. citizens show a pattern of operationalization during times of financial crisis. One of the earliest efforts occurred in 1865 during the Civil War, when President

Lincoln created the Secret Service for the specific purpose of investigating, preventing, and suppressing counterfeit currency. In 1877, the U.S. Congress passed an Act "prohibiting the counterfeiting of any coin, gold or silver bar." In 1895, it added legislation prohibiting counterfeiting of stamps and dealing in them.

The Secret Service was officially acknowledged as a distinct organization within the Treasury Department in 1883. In 1906, Congress passed the Sundry Civil Expenses Act that provided funds for Secret Service protection of the president (http://www.secretservice.gov/history.shtml, 3/23/11). The service's focus on financial crimes was not lost after the new function of providing security for the president and other dignitaries was added to its mission: "The mission of the United States Secret Service is to safeguard the nation's financial infrastructure and payment systems to preserve the integrity of the economy, and to protect national leaders, visiting heads of state and government, designated sites and National Special Security Events" (http://www.secretservice.gov/mission.shtml, 3/23/11).

In 2002, the Congress passed Public Law 107-296 transferring the Secret Service from the Treasury Department to the new Department of Homeland Security (http://www.secretservice.gov/history.shtml, (3/23/11). This change resulted in an expanded role for the service—investigating financial crimes of all types including identity theft, banking practices, and cyber crimes (White, 2009: 397).

U.S. Securities and Exchange Commission

When the U.S. was in the throes of the Great Depression, Congress enacted the Glass-Steagall Act (1930) that prohibited commercial banks from involvement in investment banking. After this provision of the act was abolished in 1990, large conglomerates of commercial and investment banks emerged and deregulation was the norm.

The U.S. financial crisis began in 2007, spurred by the collapse of such enormous investment enterprises as Bear Stearns, Enron, and WorldCom. The U.S. Securities and Exchange Commission (SEC) reacted by beginning to exercise authority it already possessed to investigate and regulate the complex financial structures that developed.

In 2010, Congress passed the Dodd-Frank Wall Street Reform and Consumer Protection Act to "promote the financial stability of the United States by improving accountability and transparency in the financial system, to end 'too big to fail,' to protect the American taxpayer by ending bailouts, to protect consumers from abusive financial services practices, and for other purposes" (H.R.4173, http//: www.sec.gov/). The major focus of this act as noted in the statement of purpose was to regulate the financial system. Title

IX pertains to investor protection and improvements to the regulation of security (H.R.4173-6), and Title X created the Bureau of Consumer Financial Protection (H.R.4173-8).

Aftermath of 9/11 Attacks

Soon after the terrorist attacks on the World Trade Center in 2001, various security-related agencies of the U.S. government engaged in extensive policy changes and reorganization. Heyman and Ackleson, (2010: 49) note that in the period immediately following the attack, it became clear that the initial border policy response to terrorist threats was largely a disjointed and somewhat confused effort. Recognition of policy inadequacies resulted in the subsequent consolidation, expansion, and reorganization of U.S. homeland security policies and agencies.

One of the major steps undertaken by the U.S. Congress in 2002 was creation of the National Commission on Terrorist Attacks upon the United States (the 9/11 Commission) for the specific purpose of determining what went wrong and what could be done to prevent future attacks. One major conclusion of the commission cited in its report was that long-term success in the "war on terrorism" demanded the use of all elements of national power: diplomacy, intelligence, covert action, law enforcement, economic policy, foreign aid, public diplomacy, and homeland defense (9/11 Commission Report, 2004: 364).

The report emphasizes the connections of criminal activities of terrorist organizations and other forms of crime, including trafficking of drugs, money, and weapons, illegal immigration, human trafficking, forgery of documents and currency, money laundering, and other crimes. One of the commission's many recommendations to prevent terrorism was to target terrorist money. It stated, "Vigorous efforts to track terrorist financing must remain front and center in U.S. counterterrorism efforts." The government recognized that information about terrorist money helps us understand their networks, search them out, and disrupt their operations (9/11 Commission Report, 2004: 382).

Many of the report recommendations, including the establishment of a Department of Homeland Security, led to drastic changes in the U.S. strategies to prevent terrorism. While these strategies and implementations of programs were directed to terrorism, they had the indirect effect of preventing and curtailing other forms of criminal activity and criminal organizations connected directly or indirectly with terrorist groups. For example, Sedgwick (2008: 5–6) lists the types of crimes in which international organized criminal groups are involved: money laundering, manipulation of energy and strategic markets, fraud, cyber crime, smuggling, trafficking of weapons and other goods and people, terrorist operations, and foreign intelligence.

The focus of this chapter is explaining the laws and law enforcement mechanisms used to prevent financial crimes, in particular those that constitute major threats to the security and welfare of society. However, to convey a thorough understanding of the importance of financial crimes, it is necessary to discuss the relationships of various forms of financial crimes with other types of crimes that pose major threats to society.

USA Patriot Act

Another piece of legislation titled The Uniting and Strengthening America by Providing Appropriate Tools Required to Intercept and Obstruct Terrorists Acts (H.R.3162 USA Patriot Act) resulted from the 9/11 terrorist attack on the World Trade Center, and the Pentagon. The U.S. Congress enacted this act in 2001 to expand or revise the provisions of the existing regulations used by law enforcement and investigative agencies to deal with terrorist activities and gave these agencies new powers.

The ten titles (sections) of the act pertain to domestic security, the collection of electronic evidence, regulation of and restriction on banking activities suspected of financing terrorist activities, increased security of U.S. borders, detention of suspected terrorists, sharing of intelligence by federal law enforcement agencies, adding new laws for curtailing terrorist activities, standard definitions of domestic terrorism, criminalization of cyber-terrorism, and authorization of searches of suspected terrorist email. Title X (miscellaneous provisions) clarifies definitions of electronic surveillance, authorizes funding for training, and grants temporary authority to the federal government to contract with local and state governments to provide security at military installations.

International Money Laundering Abatement and Anti-Terrorism Financing Act

Title III, known as the International Money Laundering Abatement and Anti-Terrorism Financing Act of 2001, addresses the need to reduce opportunities for terrorists and other criminals to use illegally obtained funds to finance their activities. Title III includes measures to:

> Provide means for the U.S. to prevent, detect, and prosecute those involved in international money laundering and the financing of terrorism.

Increase the capacity of investigative and law enforcement agencies to enforce the provisions of the law.

Strengthen and expand the provisions of the Money Laundering Control Act of 1986 (18 USC 981).

Provide guidance for domestic financial institutions and financial institutions operating outside the U.S. on what constitute appropriate transactions and possible penalties for violations of the law.

Develop procedures for the forfeiture of assets of those suspected of criminal activity connected with the laundering of money and/or the financing of terrorist activities.

Ensure that the forfeiture of assets in connection with anti-terrorism efforts permits adequate challenge consistent with due process rights.

Ensure that financial institutions can maintain the integrity of their employees and will be provided safe harbors from civil liability in cases of filing suspicious activity reports.

Prevent U.S. financial institutions from receiving personal gain through the actions of corrupt foreign officials or sales of stolen assets.

Detailed knowledge of banking and financial transactions is needed to understand and interpret the specific provisions of Title III. If illegal activities are suspected, representatives of the Secretary of the Treasury consult with officials from the offices of the Secretary of State and the Attorney General.

Section 312 of Title III requires that each financial institution that establishes, maintains, administers, or manages a private banking account or a correspondent account in the U.S. for persons who are not U.S. citizens, including foreign individuals visiting the U.S. or representatives of persons who are not U.S. citizens, must establish appropriate due diligence policies, procedures, and controls designed to detect and report instances of money laundering through such accounts. In cases of correspondent accounts created with offshore banking licenses or under licenses issued by foreign countries, financial institutions must take reasonable steps to ensure the identities of the owners of accounts for which the shares are not publicly traded and the nature and extent of the interests of all owners. The institutions must also scrutinize these accounts to guard against money laundering, report suspicious transactions, and ascertain whether the foreign banks involved provide correspondent accounts through other foreign banks.

Section 317 of Title III sets forth the penalties for money laundering violations. For enforcement purposes, the U.S. District Courts have jurisdiction over actions against foreign persons and financial institutions. The service of process is made under the Federal Rules of Civil Procedure or the laws of the country where the defendant resides, provided that the defendant committed an offense involving a financial transaction conducted in whole or in part in the U.S., converts to his or its own use property in which the U.S. has an ownership interest by virtue of an order issued by a U.S. court, or maintains a bank account at a financial institution in the U.S.

Section 330 of Title III (International Cooperation in Investigations of Money Laundering, Financial Crimes, and the Finances of Terrorist Groups) authorizes the President to direct officials attached to the Secretary of State, the Attorney General, or the Secretary of the Treasury to cooperate with officials of other countries through voluntary information exchanges, mutual assistance treaties, and international agreements. The goal is to ensure that foreign banks and other financial institutions maintain adequate records of transactions and account information related to any alleged terrorist organization, any person who is a member or representative of such an organization, and any person engaged in money laundering or other financial crimes. The legislation provides that a mechanism be established to make such records available to U.S. law enforcement and domestic financial supervisors when appropriate.

Section 356 of Title III sets forth the requirements and procedures for reporting suspicious activities by securities brokers and dealers and investment companies. Section 358 describes the types of depositor records that insured and uninsured banks and depository institutions in the U.S. States should maintain. It lists the amendments to the Right to Financial Privacy Act of 1978 that now allow the government to conduct investigations on matters pertaining to national terrorism when certain conditions exist.

Financial Crimes Enforcement Network

Section 361 delineates the duties, powers, and organizational structure of the network established in 1990 by the U.S. Department of the Treasury. The director of this network is appointed by the Secretary of the Treasury and is responsible for making recommendations to the Undersecretary of the Treasury for Enforcement on matters relating to financial intelligence, financial crimes, and other financial activities. The network maintains a government-wide data access service. When applicable legal requirements are met, the network can provide:

Information collected by the Department of the Treasury
Information about national and international currency flow
Other records and data maintained by federal, state, local, and foreign agencies
Other privately and publicly available information

In accordance with legal requirements, policies, and guidelines, the network can analyze and disseminate available data that may:

1. Identify possible criminal activity to appropriate federal, state, and local agencies
2. Support ongoing criminal financial investigations and prosecutions including civil and tax forfeiture proceedings
3. Identify instances of non-compliance of financial institutions with the law
4. Determine emerging trends and methods in money laundering and other financial crimes
5. Support intelligence and counter-intelligence activities
6. Support government initiatives against money laundering

To allow the network to accomplish its mission, Title III, Section 361, authorizes it to establish a financial crimes communication center to provide research, analytical, and informational services to financial institutions, assist federal, state, local, and foreign law enforcement and regulatory agencies to combat informal non-bank network and barter systems, and provide computer and data support to track foreign assets. The network is also authorized to coordinate its efforts with those of financial intelligence and anti-terrorism and anti-money-laundering units in other countries.

In 1994, the responsibilities of the secretary of the network were expanded to include administration of the Bank Secrecy Act. Enacted in 1970, the legislation set reporting and record-keeping requirements for banks, credit unions, brokers, insurance companies, companies engaged in money services (issuing money orders, cashier's checks), currency exchanges, casinos, and dealers in precious metals and jewels (Title II of the Bank Secrecy Act [31 USC 5311–5332 with implementing regulations at 31 CFR 103]). The Patriot Act broadened the scope of the Bank Secrecy Act to include terrorism financing and money laundering (H.R.3162, USA Patriot Act of 2001, Title III, Subtitle A).

Section 372 of Title III establishes the requirements for maintaining the security of information gathered by the Financial Crimes Enforcement Network. Section 363 details the civil and criminal penalties for international money laundering operations. Section 371 (bulk cash smuggled into or out of the United States) addresses the smuggling of large sums of cash by drug traffickers, terrorists, and racketeers to avoid payments of taxes on the money or for other criminal motives. Smuggling in bulk is a common way to engage in money laundering. The penalties available before the current legislation were considered deterrents but did not allow the confiscation of smuggled currency. Section 371 addresses this problem by making smuggling of bulk cash a criminal offense. It authorizes the forfeiture of the cash or instruments related to the offense and provides criminal penalties for those convicted of the offense.

Section 373 of Title III pertains to sanctions for money-transmitting businesses. Offenders may be fined or imprisoned not longer than five years or both if they knowingly conduct, control, manage, supervise, direct, or own all or part of an unlicensed money transmitting business.

Title III also includes several amendments to the Right to Financial Privacy Act of 1978. They cover the obligations of financial institutions to provide information contained in client files to governmental agencies authorized to conduct investigations of possible terrorist activity.

In Section 374, existing legislation relating to the counterfeiting of domestic currency and possession or selling of impressions of tools used for counterfeiting currency or securities is amended to increase the penalties for those convicted of such activities. Section 375 amends existing law relating to the counterfeiting of foreign currency or securities to increase the penalties for these crimes.

Section 376 sets penalties for laundering the proceeds of terrorism. Section 377 pertains to the prosecution of offenders outside the territorial limits of the U.S. An individual or institution outside the territorial jurisdiction of the U.S. that engages in any behavior that would constitute an offense defined in this act is subject to the fines, forfeitures, and imprisonment penalties provided in the act under certain conditions. The offenses include unlawful use of an access device issued, owned, managed, or controlled by a financial institution, account or credit card user or other entity within U.S. jurisdiction. An individual using such an access device is subject to these sanctions if he or she transports, delivers, conveys, transfers or holds within the U.S. jurisdiction a device used in the commission of the offense or the proceeds or property derived from the unlawful behavior.

Cooperative Efforts of Federal Law Enforcement Agencies to Prevent Financial Crime

The responsibility for the prevention and control of activity that falls into the category of financial crimes does not rest with any single federal law enforcement agency. The responsibility of all such agencies gradually expanded as the concept of financial crime was broadened to include acts such as cyber crimes that were not even possible in the past. As noted, the Secret Service was the first federal agency specifically responsible for the investigation and suppression of counterfeiting. The FBI is authorized to investigate any act that violates federal laws if the illegal behavior is not specifically within the jurisdiction of another federal agency. The next section describes the federal agencies most involved in enforcing laws regulating financial crimes and their specific jurisdictions.

Department of Justice Criminal Division, Computer Crime, and Intelligence Property Section

Nasheri (2005) notes that this section was created in 1995 in response to the inadequacies of existing laws pertaining to violations of trademarks and copyrights. The huge losses suffered by U.S. industries resulting from counterfeit goods and thefts of trade secrets resulted in the creation by Congress of the Computer Crime and Intelligence Property Section of the Department of Justice Criminal Division. The section is responsible for coordinating federal law enforcement activities and prosecuting those charged with committing property-related crimes (illegal email commerce, computer hacking, theft of trade secrets, and fraud).

Federal Bureau Of Investigation (FBI)

The FBI within the Department of Justice is charged with the investigation of federal crimes that fall within its jurisdiction, including civil rights crimes, certain violent crimes, terrorism, organized crimes, and financial crimes. It has 56 field offices and more than 400 satellite offices throughout the U.S. and more than 50 legal attaché offices in U.S. embassies and consulates around the world. The attaché offices were established to prevent criminals from entering the U.S. and to assist the FBI in solving international crimes (FBI, 2007: 1).

The FBI is structured to address national security and criminal priorities. Included within the National Security Division are units focusing on terrorism, counterintelligence, and cyber crime. Units of the Criminal Priorities Division focus on public corruption, civil rights violations, organized crime, white collar crime, violent crime, and major thefts (http://www.fbi.gov/about-us/investigate, 3/23/11).

In addition to basic training, FBI agents generally undergo specialized training before assignment to specific units. The agents attached to the units interact and share information with agents from other units and agents of other U.S. and international agencies. The White Collar Crime Unit is charged with investigating frauds committed by business and government officials, specifically frauds involving

- Asset forfeitures and money laundering
- Bankruptcy
- Illegal corporate activities
- Healthcare
- Hedge funds

- Insurance
- Mass marketing
- Mortgages
- Securities and commodities

The White Collar Crime Unit also investigates other frauds and scans such as identity theft, Internet and computer fraud, public corruption, government fraud, antitrust violations, price fixing, pump-and-dump stock scams, and other crimes related to business and government(http:www.fbi.gov/about-us/investigate/white_collar, 3/23/11).

The Public Corruption Unit (http:www.fbi./gov/about-us/investigate/corruption, 3/23/11) is committed to investigating various types of corrupt practices committed by government officials in the areas of:

Border control
Disasters
Offshore corruption
Economic stimulus
Election crimes
International contracts

Two other FBI units with specific responsibilities for investigating financially related crimes are the Cyber Crime Unit and the Organized Crime Unit. The Cyber Crime Unit has key priorities relating to:

Computer intrusions
Online predators
Piracy and violations of intellectual property rights
Internet fraud

The Cyber Crime Unit shares initiatives and partnerships with cyber crime teams and computer crime tasks forces, identity theft task forces, the National Cyber Investigative Joint Task Force, and the National Cyber Forensics and Training Alliance. (http://www.fbi./gov/about-us/investigate/cyber, 3/23/11).

Along with organized crime investigations, the Organized Crime Unit, in conjunction with other Department of Justice Agencies, now focuses on international organized crime. The recognition of this threat to the national security of the U.S. is summarized in the following statement:

In recent years, international organized crime has expanded considerably in presence, sophistication and significance, and it now threatens many aspects of how Americans live, work and do business. International organized crime promotes corruption, violence and other illegal activities, jeopardizes our border security, and causes human misery. It undermines the integrity of our banking and financial systems, commodities and securities markets and our cyberspace (U.S. Department of Justice, 2008: 1).

The four priorities established by the U.S. Department of Justice (2008: 1) are:

- **Marshall information and intelligence**—Collect information and intelligence from many sources about international criminal organizations and disseminate it to law enforcement agencies, intelligence agencies, foreign partners, and the private sector.
- **Prioritize and target most significant international organized crime threats**—Coordinate the investigations and prosecutions of criminal organizations considered to present the greatest threats to U.S. security.
- **Attack from all angles**—Employ all available tools and national and international law enforcement agencies in a concerted effort to disrupt international organized criminal activity; use every sanction available to bring the criminals to justice.
- **Enterprise theory**—Develop aggressive strategies using proactive techniques to dismantle criminal organizations.

Secret Service

The Secret Service missions are safeguarding the U.S. financial infrastructure, preserving the integrity of the economy, and protecting the nation's leaders by employing a highly trained diverse, dedicated, partner-oriented workforce that utilizes the latest technologies and promotes professionalism (U.S. Secret Service, 2011: 2). Its strategic plan includes the following points:

- Because millions of people and numerous businesses and industries lose billions of dollars each year through identity and product theft, the service in conjunction with other law enforcement agencies will "continue to play a critical role in preventing, detecting, investigating, and mitigating the effects of electronic and financial crimes."
- Because the amount of counterfeit currency in circulation at home and abroad has nearly doubled in the past decade and the resources and technology are available for criminals to produce counterfeit currency, the service will continue to expand and improve its domestic and international relationships to combat criminal operations relating to the counterfeiting of currency and personal identification and other types of documents.

- Drastic increases of crime-related activities due to the expansion of the global communication network and the use of unconventional weapons by organized criminal and terrorist organizations occurred after the 9/11 attacks. The service is committed to using advanced technology, research, and intelligence to counteract these risks by "employing the appropriate operational security plans, measures, equipment, and intelligence to reduce risk and defend protected persons, sites, and events."

The Financial Crime Division has the responsibility of identifying and investigating frauds against financial institutions. A second major responsibility is the investigation of access device fraud—fraudulent use of credit card numbers, personal identification numbers, and computer passwords. A third area of responsibility is computer fraud and fraud relating to computer systems "of federal interest" (Taylor et al., 2006: 265).

One of the provisions of the USA Patriot Act was the development of federal agency task forces to bring about cooperation and the sharing of intelligence on criminal activities and organizations that are considered major threats to the security of the U.S. The incorporation of the Secret Service into the Department of Homeland Security gave the service the responsibility of organizing task forces of federal, state, and local law enforcement personnel to address international and domestic computer fraud. This was done by "providing educational briefings and seminars on financial and electronic crimes to state, federal, local, and foreign law enforcement partners to expand investigative skills and capabilities" (U.S. Secret Service, 2011: 9).

Postal Inspection Service

The Postal Service is one of the oldest federal agencies. The Postal Inspection Service was created to "exercise investigative jurisdiction over more than 200 postal-related statutes pertaining to assaults" against the service or its employees and misuse of the national postal system (Ackerman, 1999: 45). Postal inspectors investigate crimes such as mail theft, fraud, possession of stolen mail, mailed bombs and narcotics, counterfeiting of stamps, embezzlement, child pornography, and money laundering. Postal inspectors share jurisdiction with other federal agencies on criminal activities involving mail services, particularly those related to fraud, identity theft, credit card offenses, mailed explosives and other hazardous materials, and child pornography.

Department of Homeland Security (DHS) and Other Agencies

The U.S. Congress authorized the creation of the Department of Homeland Security in 2003. Twenty-two existing federal agencies were integrated into the DHS structure. Several agencies were renamed and their missions were redefined (Edelbacher & Kratcoski, 2010: 108). The overall mission of the department is to have federal, state, and local law enforcement and investigative agencies coordinate their activities by cooperating in investigations of all matters pertaining to U.S. security including:

Transportation
Domestic terrorism
Infrastructure protection
Defending against catastrophic threats
Responding to natural and human-made emergencies
Developing intelligence and warning systems
Improving border and transportation security and training

The incorporation of existing agencies into the DHS with its more focused goal of protection, broadened the jurisdictions of several agencies. For example, the Customs Service created the Customs Cyber Smuggling Center that is now involved in the enforcement of a variety of financial crimes including international money laundering, intellectual property right violations, and Internet child pornography (Taylor et al., 2006: 270).

International Agreements and Cooperation

The U.S. engaged in numerous treaties and agreements to protect its interests throughout the world. Its agreements pertaining to law enforcement matters involve exchanges of information, providing mutual assistance, and cooperating on international task forces. Some agreements cover cooperation in investigations, providing assistance in training, and supplying equipment to developing countries. The Drug Enforcement Agency (DEA) has liaison offices in many countries and provides training and support to law enforcement agencies. The FBI has a solid network of support in Europe to assist EU nations to detect and prosecute criminals engaged in international crimes.

Some of the most experienced FBI special agents are assigned to the Legal Attaché Program. These agents coordinate international investigations with their colleagues and uncover international leads to aid domestic investigations. This program links U.S. and international resources in critical criminal and terrorist areas and will increase the safety of the American public at home and abroad. The details of joint activities and information sharing are generally explained in agreements between the U.S. and host countries. Another mission is coordinating FBI training in their geographic areas. The training covers topics of vital interest to the U.S. such as counterterrorism, investigating drug and human trafficking, cyber crime, and forensic evidence (FBI, 2007: 1).

The training component of the international law enforcement cooperative programs in which the FBI has become involved has been successful. While the training does not always pertain directly to financial crimes, most of the topics such as drug trafficking, organized crime, cyber crime, corruption and money laundering apply directly or indirectly to financial crimes. The FBI has trained thousands of law enforcement personnel from other countries. It conducts one- and two-week programs in various countries around the world. FBI agents serve as instructors. The focus is on practical training in which foreign officers and FBI agents work together on cases of mutual interest (Edelbacher & Kratcoski, 2010: 16).

Interpol

The collection of valid intelligence and its distribution to interested parties who are authorized to receive the information is vital to the success of any investigation of criminal organizations or individuals. Interpol serves as a clearing house for the collection and distribution of intelligence about crime-related activities and locations of wanted criminals. With nearly 200 member nations, Interpol is in a sense the largest police agency in the world. Interpol is based in Lyon, France, but agents of other nations reside in their native countries. Most Interpol operations related to the collection and distribution of information are conducted electronically. It has modernized its operations and working strategies to keep abreast of changes in police methods and changes in the types of crimes that are of the most importance to the security and welfare of its member countries.

One Interpol goal is to provide accurate information to those who request it as quickly as possible. Another function is training the police of developing countries to use relevant technology. In this regard, it works closely with the United Nations Police (UNPOL) and Europol (Edelbacher & Kratcoski, 2010).

Conclusion

The U.S. government was concerned about threats to its security arising from organized crime, white collar crime, and terrorism. The U.S. Congress enacted legislation and provided funds to implement programs that hopefully would increase the security of the country after the 9/11 attack on the World Trade Center. The final report of the National Commission on Terrorist Attacks upon the United States (9/11 Commission Report, 2004) emphasized the importance for federal law enforcement agencies to understand how closely financial crimes were connected with other types including violent crimes, organized crimes, and white collar crimes.

The 9/11 Commission recommended that strong action be taken to determine the origins of money used to finance terrorist activities and strengthen the mechanisms used to curtail such behavior. Title III of the U.S.A. Patriot Act addresses this recommendation. It is now easier for investigative agencies to trace funds used by terrorist groups to finance their activities. Title II also provides civil and criminal penalties for persons or organizations that benefit financially from terrorist activities.

Another conclusion of the 9/11 Commission Report was that the methods used by the U.S. to assure the safety and security of its people were piecemeal and were usually developed as new security risks arose (9/11 Commission Report: 35). The Department of Homeland Security was created by Congress to address the need for an integrated strategy and operational plan that included federal, state, and local law enforcement agencies that would work together to provide security for the country.

The shock and panic experienced in the U.S. after the 9/11 attacks and the call for immediate counteraction often resulted in the haphazard implementation of programs of questionable value. However, in the years after the 9/11 attacks, significant progress based on research and planning has been made. Legislation geared toward the implementation of programs aimed at eradicating specific types of crimes was enacted. Many of these measures proved successful based on positive outcomes.

The criticisms of the USA Patriot Act and other legislation passed after 9/11 center on provisions that some critics contend infringe on citizens' civil rights because of the expansive powers given to investigative and intelligence agencies. Most of the controversy concerns Title II sections that improve and extend intelligence gathering by federal agencies, particularly in the areas of electronic surveillance and examination of computer data. This concern could also apply to sections of Title III.

References

9/11 Commission Report. (2004). *The 9/11 Commission Report.* New York: Norton.

Ackerman, T. (1999). *Guide to Careers in Federal Law Enforcement.* Traverse City, MI: Sage.

Edelbacher, M. & Kratcoski, P. (2010a). Protecting the borders in a global society: an Austrian and American perspective. In Winterdyk, J. & Sundberg, K. (Eds.), *Border Security in the Al Qaeda Era.* Boca Raton, FL: CRC Press, 77–120.

Edelbacher, M. & Kratcoski, P. (2010b). Providing National and Human Security at Home and Abroad. 17th Annual Meeting of International Police Executive Symposium, Malta.

FBI. (2007). Legal Attaché Offices. http://www.fbi.gov/contact/Legat/legat.htm (accessed April,15, 2007).

Heyman, J. & Ackleson, J. (2010). United States border security after 9/11. In Winterdyk, J.A. & Sundberg, K. (Eds.), *Border Security in the Al Qaeda Era.* Boca Raton, FL: CRC Press, 37–74.

H.R. 3162, USA Patriot Act of 2001. 107th Congress.

H.R.4173. Dodd-Frank Wall Street Reform & Consumer Protection Act. http://www.sec.gov/

H.R.4173-6, http://www.sec.gov/

H.R.4173-8, http://www.sec.gov/

http:www.fbi.gov/about-us/investigate/corruption (accessed March 23, 2011).

http:www.fbi.gov/about-us/investigate/organized crime (accessed March, 23, 2011).

http:www.fbi.gov/about-us/investigate/whitecollar crime (accessed March,23, 2011).

http://www.secretservice.gov/history.shtml (accessed March 23, 2011).

http://www.secretservice.gov/mission.shtml (accessed March 23, 2011).

Money Laundering Control Act of 1986 (18 USC 981).

Nasheri, H., (2005). *Economic Espionage and Industrial Spying.* Cambridge: Cambridge University Press.

National Cyber Forensics and Training Alliance. http:www.fbi/gov/about-us/Investigate/cyber (accessed March 22, 2011).

National Cyber Investigative Joint Task Force. http:www.fbi/gov/about-us/investigate/cyber9 (accessed March 22, 2011).

Right to Financial Privacy Act of 1978.

Sedgwick, J. (2008). International Challenges to Law Enforcement: Policing in the Global Age. 15th Annual International Police Executive Symposium, Cincinnati.

Taylor, R., Caeti, T., Loper, D. & Tritsch, E. (2006). *Digital Crime and Digital Terrorism.* Upper Saddle River: Prentice Hall.

Title II Bank Secrecy Act (31 USC 5311–5332 implementing 31 CFR 103).

U.S. Department of Justice. (2008). Computer Crime and Intelligence Property Section, Criminal Division. http:www.usdoj.gov/criminal/cybercrime/policy (accessed March 20, 2010).

U.S. Department of Justice. (2008). Strategy to Combat International Organized Crime. http://www.justice.gov/criminal/icitap/pr/2008/04-23-08combat-intl-crime.overview.pdf (accessed March 21, 2011).
U.S. Secret Service. (2011). Strategic Plan. Washington: Department of Homeland Security. www.secretservice.gov
White, J., 2009. *Terrorism and Homeland Security*, 6th ed. Wadsworth Cengage.

Financial Crime
Past, Present, and Future

19

MAXIMILLIAN EDELBACHER
MICHAEL THEIL
PETER C. KRATCOSKI

Contents

Introduction

A recent report (Interpol, 2011: 1), *Financial and High-Tech Crimes*, states that "Financial and high-tech crimes [such as] currency counterfeiting, money laundering, intellectual property crime, payment card fraud, computer virus attacks, and cyber terrorism … can affect all levels of society." The report continues. "Currency counterfeiting and money laundering have the potential to destabilize national economies and threaten global security, as these activities are sometimes used by terrorists and other dangerous criminals to finance their activities or conceal their profits."

The chapters in this book illustrate the connections of various forms of financial crimes and their negative effects on the security of the nations of the world. A bulletin titled *New Security Challenges* published by the Academic Council of the United Nations (2010: 1) states that:

> Citizens, governments and international organizations are confronted with an array of security challenges, including new forms of terrorism and international criminal activity; security implications of environmental degradation; instability in the financial system; militarization of space; unregulated flows of small arms, nuclear technologies and illicit goods; and fragile and failing states.

A random perusal of media reports of the combined effects of various types of organized, white collar, and financial crimes illustrates the threats of financial criminal activity to the security and general welfare of nations. For example, due to the violence and terrorism of the drug lord wars in Mexico, the number of U.S. tourist arrivals for January through March declined from a high of almost 6 million in 2007 to fewer than 2 million in 2011 (Castillo & Mendoza, 2011: A3). Crimes such as piracy have emerged as significant threats to physical and financial security for some countries.

The reports of banking fraud and insider trading on the stock exchanges are widespread. *U.K. Says Banks Fail to Combat Laundering* (Enrich & Ball, 2011: C1) notes that, "The U.K.'s financial regulator accused major banks of not doing enough to prevent corrupt politicians and criminals from stashing stolen funds in British bank accounts, as part of a global crackdown on money laundering." Understanding the extent of financial-related crime around the globe and how such crimes affect the lives of people who are victimized by them is the first step in solving this complex problem. Throughout this book, the authors focused on the methods various countries used to control criminal activities directly related to their economic security—organized crime, white collar and corporate crime, corruption, and terrorism.

Some methods failed; others created new complications. For example, the U.S. joined the Mexican government in several agreements designed to bring to justice the leaders of the powerful drug trafficking cartels in Mexico. U.S. and Mexican police cooperation has become so extensive that, "unprecedented numbers of U.S. agents work in Mexico, and high profile arrests occur monthly. U.S. drones spy on cartel hideouts, while U.S. tracking beacons pinpoint suspects' cars and phones" (Castillo & Mendoza, 2011: A3). The U.S. role in Mexico's drug war raises nationalist anger over sovereignty. Castillo and Mendoza noted that, "The bilateral cooperation is touching off Mexican sensitivities about sovereignty, while stoking U.S. debate about the wisdom of having American operatives so deep into the fight."

In *Challenges in Chasing Fraud*, Eaglesham (2011: C1) reported that, although the U.S. Securities & Exchange Commission filed civil fraud suits against officials of securities and banking firms blamed for worsening the financial crisis, "even the agency's most determined enforcement lawyers are struggling to pin the blame on high- ranking executives who were involved in some of the most controversial mortgage-bond deals."

The financial crisis caused by a number of factors, including greed, failure to control the questionable practices of bankers and other financial executives, political corruption, and the influence of criminal organizations, can be recognized as a threat to global financial stability. From 2007 to 2009, the global economy experienced the most severe financial crisis since the Great Depression of 1929.

In Section I of this book, the authors discussed whether the new security philosophy approaches can help prevent a future financial crisis. Section II focuses on explaining the nature of white collar crime and what methods can be used to combat it. Section III deals with an acceptable model for preventing another financial crisis and whether fresh ideas of prevention strategies can be used.

History of Crisis and New Security Philosophy

In Chapter 2, Schöpfer discusses the long history of speculation over the past two centuries. The first worldwide economic crisis occurred in the nineteenth century. The Panic of 1857 in the U.S. was caused by speculation involving railway construction. The Ohio Life Insurance Company became bankrupt, and the ensuing financial panic spread over the world. A similar global economic crisis erupted in 1873 with the crash of the Vienna Stock Exchange. This crisis was also caused by speculation. It spread throughout Europe and North America and was followed by the *Gründerkrise* or long depression that ended about 1896. Schöpfer also noted that security was unachievable in the ancient world. The most severe economic crisis started with the stock market crash in New York on Black Tuesday, October 29, 1929 and traveled around the world. The current global financial and economic crisis that started in 2007 was triggered in the U.S. by a subprime mortgage collapse arising from a liquidity shortfall in the U.S. banking system. Large financial institutions imploded, and banks had to be bailed out by national governments.

Schöpfer observes that the formal structures of religions and government were fundamental steps toward improving life because they created a more peaceful society and provided security. One can assume that even in prehistoric times humans sought protection against physical violence, extreme weather conditions, and famine. The entrepreneur and the bookkeeper became very important to the development of a modern economy.

Schöpfer notes that progress and speculation provoke radical changes and uncertainties.

A special problem of the modern world economy is that all markets are connected, but the disconnectedness of financial and commodity markets presents new risks. In recent years, international trade volume has exceeded the volume of global production. The combination of natural risks, technical risks, environmental risks, and white collar crime broadens the growing gap between quests for security of the rich and the poor. Many boards of directors and credit assessment institutions failed in their functions as controlling bodies.

New Approach to Security

In the twenty-first century, many changes in the field of security can be recognized. This development started in the United States after 9/11. In Europe, especially in Austria, after the tragedy in Galtür, and in Asia, after the Tsunami Experience in 2004, the idea arose to find ways of implementing early warning systems to protect people against catastrophes, crime and other imponderable events.

In Chapter 1, Stummvoll noted that the decline of international threats exerted more pressure on governments to develop new security concepts and deal with security in terms of individual and public safety. The conventional defense design (building walls) has become obsolete and lost its international scope. A new concept of crime prevention to promote public safety and protection of individuals must be established. The shift to protect individuals is a consequence of a change of focus from national security to human security. Public safety has become a multidisciplinary issue involving many entities in the public and private sectors.

Human Security

Because security threats reach far beyond national or military capabilities, economic, societal, environmental, and health problems represent significant security concerns. The United Nations originally motivated researchers of the University in Bonn to create a philosophy of human security and conduct studies after the UNDCP was launched in 1994 and addressed human security via political, social, environmental, economic, and cultural programs designed to improve lives. The starting point of this development was the need for security ideas to be influenced by people, not by states. The research focused on factors that influence the quality of life and conditions necessary to foster human dignity.

Comprehensive Security

The European approach was primarily influenced by studies of military strategic centers. Because the military is very much engaged in solving catastrophes and supporting people against floods, fire, and other dangers, strategies were researched as to which targets had high priorities for society and should be protected first. This approach is called comprehensive security. The idea is to find strategies and methods of recognizing danger as soon as possible and install early warning systems. Comprehensive security now serves as the official model for the European Union.

Today, the new security of the European Union is built on the Lisbon Treaty and the Stockholm Programme. The aim of the Lisbon Treaty is to "promote peace, its values, and the well-being of people." The EU's concepts of security is based on a comprehensive approach. The goal of the Stockholm Programme is to create "an open and secure Europe serving and protecting citizens." The program responds to common threats and challenges, including terrorism, organized crime, cyber crime, cross-border crime, violence, and natural and man-made disasters. Financial risks are not explicitly addressed.

Financial Sector: A Critical Infrastructure?

After the world experienced the dramatic financial crisis that started in the U.S. in 2007 and eventually affected all countries during 2008 and 2009, the question arose whether the changes in government and personal security can influence our thinking about security in the financial sector and help avoid future financial crises. If the financial sector is recognized as a critical infrastructure that should be protected by special measures and regulations, the rules of the global market existing before the latest financial crisis must change or history will repeat itself. After the stock market crash of 1929, the U.S. Congress imposed strict financial regulations and President Roosevelt endorsed them. The regulations were abolished in 1992. The failure to strictly regulate financial markets in the U.S. led to the outbreak of the global financial crisis in 2007 and 2008.

Interest in and Support for Changing Financial System

In 2010, a research study of the financial sector in Austria was proposed. Researchers wanted to determine where the financial sector is especially vulnerable and what to do to guard it. Testing the weaknesses of the financial sector would need support and openness of the financial system. Reactions showed immediately that the financial sector would not develop any sympathy for such security ideas. In 2010, a group of experts wanted to start a study of Austrian banks and quickly realized that no Austrian financial institution wanted to cooperate.

In Chapter 4 addressing security in the EU, Siedschlag tries to find answers to the question of whether the financial sector can be identified as a critical infrastructure. He notes that the Stockholm Programme lists common threats and challenges but does not explicitly address financial risks. Several of the components of the European security model advocated by the strategy appear to be directly relevant for the financial sector and for tackling the security risks posed by the financial crisis. These include addressing the causes of insecurity (not just the effects), prioritizing prevention and anticipation, and assigning all sectors (political, economical, and social) roles to play in public protection.

The financial crisis and the concern about financial crime as a political and societal security issue may be seen as examples of the so-called Titanic effect found by risk researchers. Financial instruments have been placed in the context of providing (or, if improperly used or even misused, hampering) security for society and the country as a whole. These instruments are now seen as instruments for the production of security and factors in the legitimacy of the political system, not just as instruments for the production of wealth.

Comparing how often security research programs explicitly relate to the financial sector in different European countries, Siedschlag's conclusion is that there are indicators in some countries that should be studied in this regard, but they are not strong enough to be of value in understanding the financial sector as a critical infrastructure.

It is disappointing that most countries do not view the financial sector as a critical infrastructure, especially after the events of 2007 and 2008. This financial crisis should have been a clear signal for governments to consider the sector as critical and protect it just as they would protect transportation, communication, and energy systems. This underestimation of risks is typical for our era. If a catastrophe happens, everyone wants change. When the worst seems over, no one worries about finding permanent solutions. Good examples are the aftermaths of Chernobyl, Fukoshima, and the 2007 global financial crisis.

Frame Conditions

On the one side, people are confronted with many forms of insecurity including exploding population growth, wastes from industrial production, global warming, the gap between poor and rich, and the tendency to react violently to events. On the other side is the human desire to be safe and secure. In Chapter 3, Development toward a Security Society: The Case of Austria," Edelbacher and Norden explain that the situation in Austria is symptomatic for the whole western world, the so-called democratic countries. The activities in the financial sector in Austria are difficult to understand because the neo-liberal tendencies in the banking system split into traditional banking and gaming banking based on the wishes and hopes of many people able to participate in this game that promised easy winnings by investing in dubious securities and other offers. As a result, on the one side exists a strong wish to be safe, but people on the other side want to increase their wealth.

UN and New Prevention Model

In Chapter 5, "Human Security and the United Nations Security Council," Lichem presents a global perspective on the development of security. International cooperation in peace building and assuring gender equality are vital. The model of the United Nations, especially the Security Council, is fascinating and opens hope for a peaceful future for next generations. But the structure and the system of the organization of the UN must be modified to enhance efficiency and effectiveness.

What Can Be Learned from White Collar Crime?

In Section II, the authors apply their experiences of combating white collar crime to other financial crimes. They use knowledge gathered by fighting organized crime and white collar crimes to develop proposals to reduce the potential of a new financial crisis. The patterns of criminal white collar crime behavior are similar to those of financial gaming crimes. A free market offers many opportunities to managers and directors in business and industry to make profits. International companies and enterprises producing goods to be sold in foreign countries are very fond of moving in free markets without borders. This concept strengthened the U.S. and the European Union. But this practice also gives opportunity for criminal activities. Freedom of movement, capital, people, and services are very often misused by criminals.

White Collar and Corporate Crime

The definition of white collar crime was created by Sutherland (1949) to define crimes committed by persons of high social status in the course of their occupations. We now are confronted with the fact that top managers of corporations and financial firms frequently commit financial crimes. We have also learned to understand white collar crime in a much broader concept, that is, that persons of high social status and persons of lower socio-economic strata commit such crimes as fraud, embezzlement, and financial theft. Sutherland's definition is applicable today, but it is encompasses a wider range of criminal activity than he originally conceived.

Fundamentals of White Collar Crime

The basic principles of our economic life and performing businesses are *pacta sunt servanda* and *uberimae fidei* which allow us to trust each other because of the functioning of the rule of law in democratic societies. These principles apply even to dictatorships or other political systems.

A criminal-minded person who wants to cheat has to hide his real motives behind a trusted identity, even if he or she has high social status. Bernard Madoff could not openly reveal his pyramid scheme; he had to hide his wrongdoing under the guise of a successful businessman. In financial crime, money is the dictating factor and the criminal activity is motivated by greed.

Another basic element of fraud is cheating. In Austria, the most famous white collar criminal was Udo Proksch. He was a fascinating personality. He had many friends in the Austrian government, and many prominent people of his time celebrated Proksch and his ideas at his "Club 45." He cheated an Austrian insurance company of €2 million by organizing an explosion of a ship and its cargo including an atomic device in the Indian Ocean. The ship was scheduled to deliver the device to Hong Kong. A twenty-year investigation revealed that the ship was transporting industrial parts from a plant in Lower Austria, not a costly atomic device. Six seamen died in the explosion and two ministers had to resign. Proksch was arrested and sentenced to life imprisonment. The case is similar to Madoff's. Some of Madoff's business partners were suspicious about him and his actions, but the general opinion of his character was so high and positive that those who questioned his honesty were unable to present the true facts. Both criminals hid their true personalities, were greed-driven, and cheated—the three elements recognized as the backbones of criminal activities.

Edelbacher, a retired police investigator of major crimes such as financial fraud, money laundering, counterfeiting, and corruption, gives the following advice to those who may be potential victims of white collar type crimes:

1. Know your customers and business partners.
2. Avoid risky businesses.
3. Implement control mechanisms and make your partners and customers aware of them; this will hinder the chances of white collar crime.
4. Utilize transparency for prevention.

After analyzing the recent financial crisis, Hetzer (Chapter 12) writes: "The world crisis has become a keyword in economic and financial policy. Its inflationary use also indicates an intellectual crisis. Behind the concept of crisis, individual and collective self-deception, economic interests and political calculations can be found." He also notes that criminal laws are biased; they apply to "losers" and are not applicable to the rich. The recent financial crisis has shown that the directors and leaders of corporations and financial firms do not always put the common good above their own personal interests and that some of these leaders are motivated by greed and are open to corruption. Hetzer states his belief that, "The financial crisis was not the outcome of a natural catastrophe. The financial crisis was not a tsunami which could not be stopped." It started with Lehman's 2008 policy that offered so-called cheap loans for buying houses. The offer led the company directly into a loan crisis that dramatically ended "the American dream." Many young people lost their jobs, their houses, and their hopes for a better life.

In Chapter 7, Seger makes us aware of the potential danger of the Internet to the global society and cited an estimate that "Internet use grew by some 445% between the years 2000 and 2010 with some 2 billion people using it" (www.Internetworldstats.com/stats.htm). He also noted that cyber crime and the money flows associated with it constitute the most transnational of all types of crime. Cyber crime and information security are the new challenges of the twenty-first century. Successful hacking attacks are reported daily and no individuals, companies, or governments are safe. The Stuxnet attack on the computer systems of the Iran atomic program shows that use of the Internet for a cyberwar has become a reality. Cyber crime, white collar crime, and economic crime are closely connected. Only international cooperation and an international law system can offer a chance to fight them effectively. The Budapest Convention points to the direction that should be followed.

Antinori's Chapter 8 covers the mafia systems. The Cosa Nostra in Sicily, Ndrangheta in Calabria, Commora in Campania, and Sacra Corona Unita in Apulia deal with criminal organizations from Russia, Ukraine, Albania, Moldavia, China, and Nigeria. The 2008 Eurispes report assesses native Italian mafia wealth around €130 billion.

In the GRECO* report of 2009, the increasing unsuccessful percentage of legal proceedings regarding corruption in Italy is seen as "a serious fault" of the Italian justice system. The use of violence is no longer the main tool of mafia organizations. Instead, they attempt to buy off the complicity of needed partners to turn them into co-operative business cohorts. The Italian mafia gradually gained entry into the high finance world by penetrating highly profitable enterprises such as construction, waste disposal, commercial trade, real estate, healthcare, food processing, and other business sectors.

---

* See Group of States against Corruption (GRECO) www.coe.int/t/dghl/monitoring/greco/default_en.asp

The mafia organization transformed from a violent crime organization into a form of invisible power that uses coercive force to assume state functions.

Antinori also describes the rise of the Eco Mafia (ecological Mafia) that focuses on the concrete industry and illicit waste disposal. The modern organization may be called the White Collar Mafia although the code of silence is one factor that links both past and present. Antinori concludes that the mafia became a conflicts negotiator and a problem-solver. Violence is used only when necessary and is no longer obvious. The mafia focuses on business and politics, using intimidation and violence.

Chapter 11 provides a global view of organized crime, white collar crime, and corruption. Mill explains the role of journalism in fighting corruption. Journalists across the world face risks of death, assault, torture, intimidation, harassment, and wrongful imprisonment for lengthy terms simply because their mission is to acquire and deliver information in the public interest. They investigate and unveil corruption. One can find examples of such cases in Africa, the Americas, Asia, and Europe. According to the International Press Institute's *Death Watch* statistics, almost one in five journalists killed in 2010 was covering corruption, making it one of the most dangerous subjects in the world to report. The connection of organized crime, white collar crime, and corruption is one reason investigative reporting is so dangerous.

In Chapter 10, "The Financial Crisis and the Haphazard Pursuit of Financial Crime," Tomasic recognizes "the failure of light-handed regulation and risk assessment by both industry and regulators which made the operation of financial regulatory agencies almost untenable, often leading to calls for their replacement by more effective agencies." He explores factors behind this situation and recommends more effective internal controls and monitoring measures within modern financial corporations. The global financial crisis revealed massive financial frauds and misconduct that have long been present in our markets but were submerged by the euphoria that dominated the markets. He analyzed the huge differences between the United Kingdom and the United States in dealing with the financial crisis.

Prosecutors and courts dealing with the internal affairs of corporations in the UK have generally been reluctant to bring civil, let alone criminal cases against corporations and their controllers (Tomasic, 2009). By contrast, in the U.S., the collapse of the Bear Stearns investment bank shortly after the collapse of Northern Rock plc in the UK immediately led to filing of charges against former officers of Bear Stearns (Goldstein, 2008: 22–23). Viewing the current crisis, Turner (2009: 88) saw the massive corporate governance failures experienced in the crisis as indications of an enormous need for stricter regulations and more intrusive and systemic supervision of financial systems. He states that greater standards of accountability and integrity in markets, more effective internal governance mechanisms and values of modern financial institutions, and the abolishing of illegal and fraudulent practices that flourished undisturbed in normal times can be achieved.

In Chapter 9, "Rule of Law versus Financial Crime," Dobovšek notes that the role and meaning of the rule of law in facing threats of security and risks in a modern society are too passive, and the government should take a more active role in curbing financial crimes that threaten global security. According to Dobovšek, powerful oligarchs have taken over the state (state capture) in some societies and created parallel laws and structures. These structures have been weakened by organized crime and corruption. Capture denotes a state where someone abuses laws and regulations for personal benefit instead of the interests of the public, for example, buying voices in parliament, bribes to influence regulation, and bribes related to judicial decisions. Organized crime participates in all these activities.

In summary, evidence indicates that fraudulent practices in the financial sector were at least partly to blame for the financial crisis. By investigating the operational methods of white collar and corporate crime, early warning checklists can be developed to reveal such behavior and devise methods to stop it. We need more efficient civil and criminal laws. The current laws are too weak to fight financial fraud.

Preventing Another Financial Crisis: Control Mechanisms

Section I of this book focuses on the changes in security philosophy that evolved as nations developed and systems of communications, technology, and transportation advanced. The authors in Section II demonstrated how white collar, organized, and cyber crime contribute to financial crises. Section III covers the appropriate strategies and measures to prevent another financial crisis.

Theil, in Chapter 13, explores why U.S. insurance companies have much greater difficulties than European ones. He describes and reflects on the working methods and instruments used by insurance companies. He notes that taking risks is one of the principal characteristics of enterprises. The situation is more pronounced in the case of insurance companies whose main purpose is to assume risks that other economic entities do not wish to bear themselves. The principal factor of production of an insurance company is equalization of risks by forming a suitable portfolio of insured risks over time. The insurer (company) concludes contracts (risk transfer) with many parties (the insureds) and operates on the basis of the mathematical law of large numbers.

Theil notes that pure risks are different from speculative risks and moral risks. Full insurance means the complete transfer of risk to the insurer. To guarantee that insurance companies are able to deliver their services consistently over very long periods and protect their customers, insurance markets are highly regulated. Theil analyzes five areas: chance, independence, estimation, concreteness, and size. He cautions against taking risks you are unable to analyze thoroughly and for which you lack necessary legal instruments. Insurance companies by law utilize unique measures. No other area of business can use risk pooling and balancing and build reserves. Choosing safety means sacrificing profit in the short run.

In Chapter 15, Felsenreich discusses human factor analysis and building resilience to financial crime. He notes that corruption of values is common in the finance industries and those who should have guaranteed stability became gamblers and dealers of shady products. The ensuing huge loss of accountability, values, and social interactions should have been recognized. The financial world had to face the fact that external control mechanisms were not (and still are not) sufficiently proactive. The financial sector must be considered a high-risk environment and it must become resilient. How can the financial sector be made resilient? Resilience generally is the ability to recover or resist the effects of a shock, insult, or disturbance generated by an external or internal threat.

Resilience is generally based on a safety culture that depends on depth psychological factors (using motivation to achieve positive energies and effective handling of errors). Errors can cause tremendous damages. The solution is to break the devil's circle of motivation traps and illusion of control. Modern error management does not neglect human errors, but tries to overcome worst case scenarios. One tool is the error pyramid illustrated in the chapter. The financial business must focus on sustainable development using knowledge based, depth psychological, socio-technical, and organizational interactions in general and specifically when dealing with mishaps.

In Chapter 14, Dobovšek and Mastnak discuss the relationship between the roles of the press and the police in investigating financial crime, particularly the corruption of political and financial organization leaders. Both the press and the police have the same goal of uncovering criminal behavior, but they sometimes have difficulties in cooperating. Both institutions are essential in a democratic society governed by rule of law. Police serve the rule of law and the press informs the public. In Chapter 11, Mill elaborated on the role of media in investigating crime and corruption. The police and media must find ways to cooperate. The authors state that research findings suggest that a journalistic investigation of a criminal matter starts when a criminal investigation by the police reaches a dead end. This is rather a speculative statement, because the police, for practical reasons, must keep certain sensitive information secret, particularly in high profile cases. However, investigative reporters feel that this information should be available to the media. In the long run a compromise must be reached because complicated corruption cases are easier to cover up if the media cooperate.

An interesting approach to increasing the effectiveness of financial entrepreneurship while preventing the financial crime and corruption often found when developing countries strive to improve their financial situations is found in Noussi's Chapter 16. Noussi reveals that a number of studies have been presented which verify the fact that the financial crisis was caused by financial crimes. These white collar crimes were only possible because of the political ideology in place, the powerful influence of the banking and financial sectors in politics, and insufficient regulation. After the considerable bailouts of financial institutions, governments have committed to increase regulation, oversight, transparency, and predictability. While stronger regulations and controls are hard to achieve, the most promising concept for reform is to develop organizational proliferation by which elites create rules and institutions to improve and regulate competition in order to prevent political extremism. A solution that is self-improving and self-enforcing is needed; market players must improve transparency, accountability, and regulation.

Fath's Chapter 17 covers "business angels" as aids to entrepreneurship and positive influences on businesses. Fath notes that a principle of the neo-liberal economic world is risk taking by enterprises. Young, inexperienced entrepreneurs tend to take more risks than older, experienced entrepreneurs. The concept of business angels tries to achieve a compromise view. How can the expertise of an experienced manager be used to create a productive and efficient enterprise? This chapter shows how business angels can provide guidance in unstable situations (such as a start-up or crisis) by providing value-added services.

In Chapter 18, "Legislative and Programming Initiatives to Prevent and Control Financial Crimes in the United States," Kratcoski reveals that efforts to control corruption and protect the financial interests in the U.S. have a long history. President Lincoln created the Secret Service in 1865 for the specific purpose of investigating, preventing, and suppressing counterfeit currency. This task of the Secret Service was not lost even after the new functions of providing security for the president and other dignitaries was added. The mission of the U.S. Secret Service at present is to safeguard the nation's financial infrastructure and payment system to preserve the integrity of the economy and protect national leaders, visiting heads of state and government, designated sites and special national events (www.secretservice.gov/mission.shtml).

During the great economic depression of the 1930s, the U.S. Congress, with strong leadership by President Franklin D. Roosevelt, took a very active role in stimulating the economy by providing financial assistance to millions of unemployed workers and enacting legislation to avoid future economic depressions. Congress enacted the Glass-Steagall Act (1930) prohibiting commercial banks from participation in investment banking. After this restriction was abolished in 1999, large conglomerates of commercial and investment banks emerged and deregulation became the norm. The collapse of Bear Stearns, Enron, and WorldCom led to new investigations and regulations and most were not effective. In 2010, congress passed the Dodd-Frank Wall Street Reform and Consumer Protection Act for this purpose.

The FBI changed its organizational structure to focus on financial crime as a top priority. Its white collar crime unit is charged with investigations of asset forfeitures, money laundering, and frauds related to bankruptcies, corporation activities, healthcare, hedge funds, insurance, mass marketing, mortgages, and securities and commodities. The Public Corruption Unit is committed to the criminal investigation of various types of corrupt practices by government officials who deal with border violations, disasters, foreign governments, economic stimulus packages, and electronic crimes. The Cyber Crime Unit and Organized Crime Unit specialize in computer intrusions, online predators, piracy, intellectual property rights, and Internet fraud. Wouters (2010: 1) identified the top ten types of Internet crimes. Financial crimes include identity theft, fee fraud, auction fraud, credit card fraud, and illegal computer activities.

In the aftermath of the 9/11 attacks, many legislative and organizational measures were implemented and produced significant progress and positive results. The most important tool for fighting financial crime is Title III of the USA Patriot Act of 2001 (International Money Laundering Abatement and Anti-Terrorism Financing Act). It established many new mechanisms that allow federal investigative agencies to prevent, detect, and prosecute financial crime.

Conclusions

The analysis of financial crime and the efforts to control it presented by the authors reveal that despite differences in the details of financial crimes throughout history, the human factors remain basically the same. Humans are still motivated by greed to commit financial crimes. They also must have opportunities to commit the crimes and believe that the rewards (profits) exceed the costs (possible punishment). In reaction to the worldwide financial crisis, most governments passed legislation and established new regulations to control the questionable and/or illegal practices of financial organizations that many believe caused the crisis. Risky practices continue because the regulations covering investment banking and speculation are too weak to produce the desired effect. In Europe, the problem of stabilizing the euro still has not been solved. The economic powers of the players are changing, and the players fail to act transparently, honestly, and responsibly. The situation in the future is not likely to improve unless stronger, more effective measures are taken. We learned that the times between financial crises are becoming shorter. The next crisis can arise very soon.

References

Academic Council of United Nations. (2010). *New Security Challenges*. New York.

Castillo, E.E. & Mendoza, M. U.S. role in Mexico drug war raises nationalist's anger over sovereignty. *Akron Beacon Journal*, March 20, 2011: A3.

Eaglesham, J. (2011). Challenges in chasing fraud. *Wall Street Journal*, June 23, 2011: C1.

Goldstein, M. (2008). Bear scandal: a widening probe. *Business Week*, July 22, 2008: 3.

Interpol. (2011). Financial and high tech crimes. *http://www.interpol.int/public/financialcrime/default.asp* (accessed February 2, 2011).

Sutherland, E.H. (1949). *White Collar Crime*. New York: Dryden Press.

Tomasic, R. (2009). The financial crisis and the haphazard pursuit of financial crime. *Journal of Financial Crime*, 16: 7–31.

U.S. Secret Service. http://www.secretservice.gov/mission.shtml (accessed June 1, 2011).

Wouters, J. (2011). FBI: 2010, a banner year for online crime. http://www.walletpop.com/2011/02/fbi-2010-a-banner-year-for-online-crime/?icid=mai (accessed February 25, 2011).

Epilogue

Corruption is and has always been one of the biggest challenges societies face. The same applies in the European Union (EU). Although the nature of corruption varies from one member state in the EU to another, it has a negative impact on the economic, political, and social development of the EU. Corrupt activities are, therefore, in no way acceptable and must be properly addressed by political actors. That is why the European Parliament recently called for EU-wide sanctions against corruption and also urged all member states to make a clear political commitment to enforcing rules that prevent corrupt activities from happening.

The EU faces yearly economic costs that amount to more than EUR 100 billion (approximately 1% of the EU's GDP). It not only harms the EU by reducing investments and public finances, but also hinders fair and competitive operation of the internal market. According to a recent Eurobarometer survey, four out of five EU citizens consider corruption a major and immanent problem in their home country that requires a firmer political commitment.

Although we already have several legal instruments in place, both at European and international levels, implementation remains uneven among member states and unsatisfactory overall. In fact, even in cases where anti-corruption legislation exists, its enforcement is generally insufficient. With the adoption of the Stockholm Programme, the European Commission has been given a political mandate that ensures the development of a common and comprehensive anti-corruption approach. In June 2011, the European Commission also adopted a new reporting mechanism, the EU Anti-Corruption Report. This Report will periodically monitor and assess the member states' progress in their fight against corruption. This particular tool certainly helps to foster political will and re-establish mutual trust.

Despite a stronger monitoring and implementation of existing legal instruments, the EU must put a stronger focus on corruption in all relevant EU policies, particularly in the areas of judicial and police cooperation. Anti-corruption considerations should, however, be integrated in both external and internal policies.

I believe that only firmer political commitment by all political actors will help to tackle corruption in a more effective way. At the same time, we should also make use of private–public dialogues at European and international levels on how to prevent corruption within the business sector.

Mag. Othmar Karas, M.R.I., HSG.
Vice-president of the European Parliament
Member of the Conservative Party Fraction

Index

A Call for Authors

Advances in Police Theory and Practice

AIMS AND SCOPE:

This cutting-edge series is designed to promote publication of books on contemporary advances in police theory and practice. We are especially interested in volumes that focus on the nexus between research and practice, with the end goal of disseminating innovations in policing. We will consider collections of expert contributions as well as individually authored works. Books in this series will be marketed internationally to both academic and professional audiences. This series also seeks to —

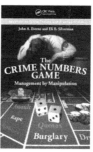

Police Reform in China

- Bridge the gap in knowledge about advances in theory and practice regarding who the police are, what they do, and how they maintain order, administer laws, and serve their communities
- Improve cooperation between those who are active in the field and those who are involved in academic research so as to facilitate the application of innovative advances in theory and practice

Mission-Based Policing

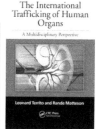

The International Trafficking of Human Organs

The series especially encourages the contribution of works coauthored by police practitioners and researchers. We are also interested in works comparing policing approaches and methods globally, examining such areas as the policing of transitional states, democratic policing, policing and minorities, preventive policing, investigation, patrolling and response, terrorism, organized crime and drug enforcement. In fact, every aspect of policing, public safety, and security, as well as public order is relevant for the series. Manuscripts should be between 300 and 600 printed pages. If you have a proposal for an original work or for a contributed volume, please be in touch.

Series Editor
Dilip Das, Ph.D., Ph: 802-598-3680
E-mail: dilipkd@aol.com

Dr. Das is a professor of criminal justice and Human Rights Consultant to the United Nations. He is a former chief of police and, founding president of the International Police Executive Symposium, IPES, www.ipes.info. He is also founding editor-in-chief of *Police Practice and Research: An International Journal* (PPR), (Routledge/Taylor & Francis), www.tandf.co.uk/journals. In addition to editing the *World Police Encyclopedia* (Taylor & Francis, 2006), Dr. Das has published numerous books and articles during his many years of involve-ment in police practice, research, writing, and education.

Proposals for the series may be submitted to the series editor or directly to —
Carolyn Spence
Senior Editor • CRC Press / Taylor & Francis Group
561-998-2515 • 561-997-7249 (fax)
carolyn.spence@taylorandfrancis.com • www.crcpress.com
6000 Broken Sound Parkway NW, Suite 300, Boca Raton, FL 33487

For Product Safety Concerns and Information please contact our EU
representative GPSR@taylorandfrancis.com
Taylor & Francis Verlag GmbH, Kaufingerstraße 24, 80331 München, Germany

www.ingramcontent.com/pod-product-compliance
Ingram Content Group UK Ltd.
Pitfield, Milton Keynes, MK11 3LW, UK
UKHW021624240425
457818UK00018B/721